梁骏吾

大学时期

大学时期

1955 年与夫人闻瑞梅

1955 年与夫人闻瑞梅

1957 年在莫斯科留学

1957 年在莫斯科留学

1957 年在莫斯科留学

1957 年在莫斯科留学

1957 年在莫斯科留学

1957 年在苏联科学院实验室

1958 年在莫斯科留学

1959 年在莫斯科留学

1959 年国庆十周年苏联科学院冶金研究所的中国留学生合影

20 世纪 60 年代的梁骏吾

1955 年与夫人闻瑞梅

1962 年与家人

1963 年与夫人闻瑞梅

1974 年全家在武汉

1980 年与夫人闻瑞梅

1980 年与林兰英在丹麦海边

1980 年与林兰英在美国前总统华盛顿的故居

1981 年在巴黎机场

1981 年在美国硅谷

1981 年在美国硅谷

1981 年在美国硅谷

1981 年与夫人闻瑞梅在颐和园

1981 年与王守武院士在纽约

1983 年全家

1983 年与夫人闻瑞梅在家中

20 世纪 90 年代在实验室

20 世纪 90 年代在实验室

1998 年观察区熔硅单晶

1998 年观察缺陷

1998 年与学生杨辉在
分子束外延炉前

1998 年给参观人员讲解

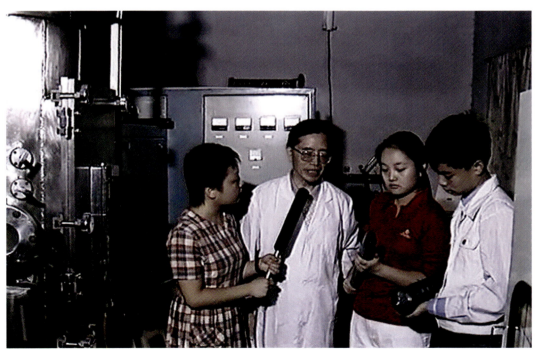

1998 年给参观人员讲解

在办公室工作

与夫人闻瑞梅教授在办公室切磋

与博士生操作设备中

与工作人员在一起

2005 年作报告

2006 年作报告

2011 年作报告

2006 年与国际友人在一起

2006 年与国际友人在一起

2006 年在香港中文大学与其他工程院院士一起

2012 年和夫人闻瑞梅与学生们在一起

2006 年的梁骏吾

2006 年的梁骏吾

2006 年与夫人闻瑞梅金婚纪念

2006 年与家人

2006 年全家

华年日拾

梁骏吾院士 80 华诞记怀

中国科学院半导体研究所 编

科学出版社
北京

内 容 简 介

本书梳理和总结了中国工程院院士、物理学家梁骏吾50多年来从事半导体材料和材料物理学科研活动的历程。主要包括科研成果、学术论文、专利发明、学术报告、获奖情况和生平年表等内容。梁骏吾是我国早期半导体硅材料的奠基人,长期从事半导体硅材料的物理性质、硅单晶的质量、硅单晶中的杂质行为、微缺陷等方面的研究,以及开拓新型半导体硅单晶材料的研究。

本书为中国科学院半导体研究所提供了宝贵的图文资料,可供从事半导体材料和材料物理学等相关专业的科研人员和管理工作者参考。

图书在版编目(CIP)数据

华年日拾:梁骏吾院士80华诞记怀/中国科学院半导体研究所编. —北京:科学出版社,2013.8
ISBN 978-7-03-038444-7

Ⅰ. 华… Ⅱ. 中… Ⅲ. 梁骏吾-生平事迹 Ⅳ. K826.16

中国版本图书馆 CIP 数据核字(2013)第 195086 号

责任编辑:李 敏 / 责任校对:赵桂芬 郑金红
责任印制:徐晓晨 / 封面设计:王 浩

科 学 出 版 社 出版
北京东黄城根北街 16 号
邮政编码:100717
http://www.sciencep.com

北京厦诚则铭印刷科技有限公司 印刷
科学出版社发行 各地新华书店经销

*

2013 年 9 月第 一 版 开本:787×1092 1/16
2017 年 4 月第二次印刷 印张:22 彩插:11
字数:900 000

定价:500.00元
(如有印装质量问题,我社负责调换)

序

值此中国工程院院士梁骏吾先生80华诞之际,中国科学院半导体研究所编辑出版《华年日拾 梁骏吾院士80华诞记怀》一书。我们有幸作序,谨在此先向梁骏吾院士表达崇高的敬意和深切的仰慕之情。

梁骏吾院士是我国半导体材料和材料物理学家,也是我国早期半导体硅材料的奠基人。他长期从事半导体硅材料的物理性质、硅单晶的质量、硅单晶中的杂质行为、微缺陷等方面的研究,以及开拓新型半导体硅单晶材料的研究,对我国半导体材料的发展与人才培养做出了重要贡献。

梁骏吾院士从事科研50多年来,辛勤耕耘,开拓创新,取得了一系列重大的科研成果:20世纪60年代解决了高纯区熔硅的关键技术。1964年制备出室温激光器用GaAs液相外延材料。1979年研制成功为大规模集成电路用的无位错、无旋涡、低微缺陷、低碳、可控氧量的优质硅区熔单晶。80年代首创了掺氮中子嬗变硅单晶,解决了硅片的完整性和均匀性的问题。90年代初成功研制了MOCVD生长超晶格量子阱材料,在晶体完整性、电学性能和超晶格结构控制方面,将中国超晶格量子阱材料推进到实用水平。主持国家"七五"、"八五"重点硅外延攻关,完成了微机控制、光加热、低压硅外延材料生长和设备的研究。2007年完成了国防"973"项目——日盲型铝镓氮紫外材料。目前,仍在太阳电池用多晶硅的研究和产业化等方面发挥着积极作用。

梁骏吾院士先后获得各种科学技术奖励20多次,其中获得国家科学技术委员会科学技术成果二等奖和新产品二等奖各1次,国家科学技术进步三等奖1次、中国科学院重大成果和科学技术进步一等奖3次、二等奖4次,上海市科学技术进步二等奖1次。另外,获得专利15项,出版专著3部,发表论文及国际、国内大会学术报告100余篇。

梁骏吾院士始终关注着半导体科学技术事业的发展,从战略高度向国家提出了一系列重要建议,并多次主持和参加国家重要科学技术项目,积极推动国际间的交流与合作,关注前沿学科的发展与研究。他还为半导体研究所的可持续发展倾注了大量心血和汗水,在研究所战略规划、学科布局建设、承担国家重大科学技术任务等方面建言献策,发挥了不可替代的作用。

梁骏吾院士是我们的良师益友,他积极提携后人,在科学技术领域中树立起典范,是科学技术人员的楷模和学习的榜样。50多年来,他热爱祖国、追求真理的优秀品格,奋力拼搏、不断创新的卓越精神令人钦佩。他光明磊落、谦虚儒雅、平易近人的人生态度给我们留下了深刻的印象。他对学生的研究方向与研究途径的选择、具体难点的攻关都给予潜心的指导,并积极推荐学生到国外深造。如今,他的学生都陆续走上了重要的科学技术岗位和管理岗位,发挥着重要的作用。他还关心当代大学生的成长,热心于教育工作,兼任哈尔滨工业大学、同济大学、武汉大学、华中科技大学、河北工业大学和昆明理工大学等高校的教授。他积极参与我国经济建设,是多个省政府的顾问,特别在我国单晶硅多晶硅材料产业的规划布局、建设等方面凝聚着他的心血。

　　该书编录了梁骏吾院士生活和工作的珍贵照片、有代表性的研究论文以及学术报告。它是一部珍贵的历史资料,记载了梁骏吾院士的业绩、贡献和崇高的精神境界。

　　该书的出版,对弘扬梁骏吾院士热爱祖国、献身科学的精神将起到特殊的不可替代的作用,广大的科学技术工作者尤其是年轻的一代可以从中受到教育和启迪,为发展科学技术,实现中国梦奋勇攀登。

　　最后,敬祝梁骏吾院士健康长寿,科学技术之树常青!

2013年9月

我国新型硅材料的开拓者

记中国科学院半导体研究所研究员梁骏吾

何春藩

梁骏吾,半导体材料和材料物理学家,我国早期半导体硅材料的奠基人,中国工程院院士。长期从事半导体硅材料的物理性质、硅单晶的质量、硅单晶中的杂质行为、微缺陷等方面的研究及开拓新型半导体硅单晶材料的研究。研究成果曾获国家和中国科学院科学技术进步奖及国家重点科技攻关奖多项。对我国半导体材料的发展与人才培养做出了重要贡献。

人们都说,他才思敏捷,精明强干,身上有一股神奇的力量。

1955年,他以"学习成绩优等"毕业于武汉大学,加之"社会关系简单,历史清白",被派往苏联科学院留学。

1960年,他在莫斯科冶金研究所的研究生毕业考试中,哲学、俄文、基础课、专业课等门门满分,论文答辩出众,被授予副博士(相当于现在的博士)学位。

1963年,他研制成功的区熔硅单晶,填补了国内空白,居世界先进水平,获国家科学技术委员会科学技术成果二等奖。

1965年,他用液相外延法生长砷镓材料成功,材料的迁移率指标达国内最好的水平。中国科学院半导体研究所用它在国内首次研制成功室温相干激光器。

1966年至1969年,他研制成功多晶硅反外延材料,用以制作双极型集成电路,胜利完成了"156工程"任务。

1978年至1980年,他负责4K位和16K位DRAM研制中的材料问题,为器件提供高质量的硅材料。4K位和16K位的DRAM大规模集成电路,分别获得1979年和1980年中国科学院科学技术成果一等奖。

1980年,他负责的直拉硅单晶质量的研究,承担的区熔硅单晶中微缺陷及P型(100)硅单晶中微缺陷和夹杂物的研究,均获中国科学院科学技术成果三等奖。

1983年,他从事硅单晶材料中杂质碳的行为研究,获中国科学院科学技术成果二等奖。

1987年,他研制成功中子嬗变掺氮区熔硅单晶,获中国科学院科学技术进步一等奖。

1990年,他研制成功微机控制光加热硅外延炉,填补了国内空白,研究成功CMOS硅外延技术,完成了国家"七五"重点科技攻关任务。外延片的参教,已达到或超过攻关任务指标。

……

创造这些累累硕果者,就是1991年国家有突出贡献的中青年优秀专家,后来获得中国工程院院士称号的中国科学院半导体研究所研究员梁骏吾。

研制成功区熔硅单晶炉和区熔硅单晶

1960年10月,梁骏吾从苏联留学归国时,正值中国科学院半导体研究所刚刚成立。崭新的科学殿堂,给他发挥聪明才智和创造力开拓了广阔的天地。早在学生时代就立志要在科技领域"为建成共产主义添砖加瓦"的梁骏吾,来到了该所的半导体材料研究室,从事国内蓬勃兴起的硅材料的研究工作。室主任林兰英教授,非常器重他的才华,任命他为课题组长,要他从事区熔硅单晶炉和区熔硅单晶的研制。

在新生祖国这块贫瘠的科学园地里,要致力于这类新兴学科的开拓性研究,无可供借鉴的工艺技术,缺必不可少的工艺设备,一切都得从头做起,困难重重。

满怀火热报国心的梁骏吾,在思考中认识到,科学工作者的可贵品质,就是探索者的勇气。爱迪生在火车上仍专心致志地做科学实验,居里夫人在几乎毫无条件可言的情况下仍坚持从成吨的沥青中提取铀……这些卓有名望的科学先行者们的事迹表明,一个科学工作者,只要有对科学事业一往无前的拼搏精神,条件再差也会做出成果来。梁骏吾没有被困难所吓倒,他暗下决心,暗自鼓励,在攻读中实践,在实践中攻读,着手从事区熔炉的设计与区熔硅单晶的研制。

1961年初,梁骏吾和他领导的研制小组开始了工作。那是一个寒冷的冬天,实验室正在翻修,他们挤在一间没有暖气的平房里工作,上班的路上还要拾一些柴火来生炉子。他们住的宿舍是一个大礼堂,上下双层铺,上百人住在一起。那时,粮食定量低,物质生活条件差。可是,这样的一个集体,却充满了为国争光的热情。在工厂加工区熔炉期间，他们深入车间，与工人同吃同劳动。中午下班时，没地方休息，就在车间外的台阶上坐坐。加工好的设备要运回，就靠他们推着人力板车步行十多公里……那是个困难的年代，却也是个充满火热激情的年代。

创造拼搏的火焰，在苏联留学期间研究经验的积累，加上扎扎实实的科学实践，梁骏吾终于闯过来了。在经历了300多个日日夜夜之后，成功地解决了高频感应加热主回路的设计与制作。经过试用和不断改进，效果非常令人满意。他还打破国际惯例，将国外设备沿用的移动感应圈加热，改成了移动硅棒让其受热。感应加热圈的固定，保证了输出功率的稳定；硅棒的上下移动，可保证大直径单晶熔区的稳定。这一关键技术的突破，不仅可以使高频加热圈连续24小时工作不打火，还解决了在对硅材料进行反复多次的区熔（以扫除液硅中杂质，保证硅单晶有高的电阻率）时所必有的长时间加热的稳定性。这一技术上的创新，使加工成的区熔炉，比国外的同类产品还先进，而且还为后来发展起来的外延生长工艺中的感应加热技术，提供了可取的经验，被高熔炉生产厂家一直沿用至今。这一新颖的设计，为我国硅材料工艺和硅材料加工设备的发展，做出了可喜的贡献。

时届1963年5月，国家科学技术委员会下达的重点任务——电阻率高达10^4——欧姆厘米的高纯区熔硅单晶，终于在我国首次研制成功了。因为它的纯度高，含氧量低，可广泛用于制作核探测器及功率器件。这一研制成果，居当时的国际先进水平，并荣获国家科学技术委员会科学技术成果二等奖。研制成功的高频区熔硅单晶炉，填补了国内的空白，并于1964年荣获全国新产品奖。梁骏吾撰写的"高纯硅材料的制备"论文，于1963年在匈牙利的布拉格国际半导体会议上宣读，受到广泛的好评。

探索硅单晶中的微缺陷奥秘成功

1977年10月，描绘我国科学事业远景的"全国自然科学学科规划会议"在北京召开。党中央主要领导邓小平同志在接见与会代表时，特意向半导体科学工作者提出，一定要把大规模集成电路搞上去。党中央的指示，点燃了半导体科学工作者心头为国争光的烈火，激励着早已蕴藏在胸的强烈愿望。

研制大规模集成电路，要在面积不到4厘米×4厘米的硅片上，经过60多道工序,制作 10000 多个形成电路功能的电子元件,电路线宽都是微米、亚微米量级。这么高的集成度,对硅单晶质量提出了越来越高的要求。国外研究工作表明,硅单晶中尺度在微米、亚微米量级的缺陷(简称微缺陷),对集成电路的性能与成品率,有着至关重要的影响。因此,1978 年,国家科学技术委员会向半导体研究下达了"提高硅单晶质量的研究"任务。

为了完成这一重要课题的研究,已任半导体研究所副所长的半导体材料学家林兰英,又想到已于 1969 年从半导体研究所调往宜昌半导体厂的梁骏吾。林兰英说,"这是一项前沿性的探索研究工作,没有扎实的专业基础知识的人不行,只有梁骏吾能胜任这一工作。"林兰英在征得上级主管部门同意后,想尽办法,将梁骏吾调回半导体研究所。

梁骏吾深知任务的艰巨,责任的重大。他一到北京,顾不上安置家庭生活,来不及料理孩子的上学问题,更无心探亲访友,马上到研究所开展工作,潜心于硅单晶中的微缺陷——主要是漩涡缺陷的本质、形成机理及消除办法的研究。

有高度独立钻研能力和灵活思考能力的梁骏吾,率领研究组同志,查阅资料,制备样品,拟定出研究计划与步骤。他们采用化学择优腐蚀显示方法、红外光谱测量分析方法,以及透射电子显微镜观察等现代研究手段,论证了原生态硅单晶中缺陷的本质特征,生成原因及其克服办法。由于在无位错单晶生长中,热点缺陷对单晶完整性起决定性作用,所以控制生长时的热波动、机械稳定性以及氧碳等杂质,是控制漩涡缺陷生成的关键。梁骏吾及其新成立的小组,从单晶缺陷生成机理入手,采取一系列技术措施,反复实践,次次探求,想方设法解决了拉晶炉的热稳定性与机械平稳性,定位了气氛的选择和气流模型。实践证明是可取的。这样一来,就为消除漩涡缺陷指明了正确途径。终于降低了硅单晶中的氧化层错密度,提高了少数载流子的寿命,获得了无位错、无漩涡、低微缺陷和氧含量可控的直拉硅单晶,单晶成品率达 80%。

经梁骏吾等的辛勤操劳,直拉硅单晶质量的突破,为研制大规模集成电路奠定了基础。1979 年至 1980 年,半导体研究所相继研制成功了 4K 位、16K 位的大规模集成电路——硅栅 MOS 随机存储器,两次获得中国科学院重大成果一等奖。梁骏吾直接承担的"提高硅单晶质量的研究",荣获中国科学院"六五"攻关奖。"硅中碳的研究"获中国科学院科学技术成果二等奖。

专业上的进取,是梁骏吾的一贯追求;政治上的进步,也是他孜孜以求的目标。鉴于梁骏吾"入党动机端正,对党忠诚,具有较高的学术理论水平,为我国半导体材料及大规模集成电路的发展做出了可喜的贡献",1980年9月,他光荣地加入了中国共产党。

研制成功中子嬗变掺氮区熔硅单晶

区熔硅单晶质量的改进与提高,经历了一系列变迁和发展过程。20世纪60年代的区熔硅单晶,都是在氢的气氛中生长成的。由于氢极易与硅发生作用,在硅中产生氢致缺陷,单晶质量不好,在制作和发展硅器件方面受到制约,难以制得高成品率的硅器件和发展新型硅器件。到了70年代,生长硅单晶的气氛,由氢气改为氩气。因氩这一惰性气体,不对硅材料本身产生影响,故能得到高电阻率的硅单晶。但是,这种在氩气氛中生成的区熔硅单晶的机械性能,远不如含氧的直拉硅单晶优越。

区熔硅单晶存在的问题,困扰了长期从事区熔工作的梁骏吾,他苦苦地思索:是让其止步不前,自然淘汰,还是探索新路,促其发展,使之在我国电子工业中广开用武之地? 成就事业、勇于开拓科学新领域的梁骏吾,自然地想到了后者。他埋头书案,默默地在学海里寻觅、探求……

区熔硅单晶中氧含量低,好处是电阻率高,便于进行中子嬗变掺杂,即将硅的天然同位素 Si^{30} 吸收中子后嬗变为 P^{31},从而得到均匀掺磷的单晶,这样可以提高材料性能。另外,这种硅单晶中氧含量低,虽有电阻率高的优点,但也有机械性能不好的缺点,位错缺陷容易产生,并能繁殖和移动。这样一来,会降低器件的成品率。因此,为了进一步提高材料性能,除进行中子嬗变技术处理外,还应该在硅中掺入某种杂质,使硅的晶格"强壮"起来,改进硅的机械性能。掺什么杂质呢? 国外有文献记载,掺入氧、氮或者锗,均可能改进硅的机械性能。但是,已被提升为副研究员的梁骏吾考虑到,氧仍有电学活性,而且氧的沉淀会引起缺陷,不是合适的掺杂剂。掺锗均匀性又不好,而且附加成本高,也不适合。氮可以考虑,剩下的问题是在核反应中,氮的加入是否会引来不利的反应? 氮在工艺热处理中是否会引入缺陷? 经过理论推算,梁骏吾认为,这些问题是可以克服的。于是,便产生了将中子嬗变技术和掺氮技术相结合的新思维! 进行新的硅单晶品种的实验开始了。

梁骏吾和他的同事们,经由变温微硬度实验得知,在高温范围内,氮在硅中的存在,增强了硅的临界切应力,增大了屈服强度,其硬变降低率比直拉硅单晶低,因而改进了硅材料的机械性能,验证了前人的结论。梁骏吾想,这一新型硅材料的诞生,必将减少制作器件过程中的崩边率,减少硅片在烧结工艺过程中的弯曲率,提高硅片的利用率,定会受到器件厂家的欢迎。

斗转星移,到了1982年5月,梁骏吾凭他敏捷的思维和坚强的毅力,并集中了组里邓礼生、郭钟光、郑红军等同志的智慧,共同克服了设备上的问题,解决了掺氮所需的气体成分,找到了氮中生长高质量单晶的规律,一步一个脚印地走上了成功之路。

原因找到了,试验也终于成功了。首次在我国研制成功的掺氮区熔硅单晶,还是无位错、无漩涡的硅单晶,质量居国际领先地位。

由于将中子辐照与掺氮区熔工艺相结合,使硅单晶既有良好的机械性能,又能使单晶电阻率得到均匀分布的双重效果。这一大胆的尝试,在当时国际上还别无他例。

掺氮中子嬗变区熔硅单晶终于研制成功了。这种新型硅单晶,能否适宜制造硅器件,能否改进器件的性能、提高器件的成品率,梁骏吾又率领科技人员,对该材料的电学性能,例如浅能级的情况、电子迁移率、少数载流子寿命指标、深能级密度和所处的位置、深能级在热处理过程中的变化和微区杂质均匀性等问题,都一一进行了广泛深入的研究,取得了一系列成果。研究结果表明,硅中所含的氮,在经中子辐照之后,不致引起有害的核反应。只要硅中氮浓度受到定量控制,晶体中的氮原子,就能有效地防止位错的产生与繁殖,对位错起到钉扎的作用。与常规的掺氮区熔硅单晶和不掺氮的中子嬗变区熔硅单晶相比,该材料的电阻率均匀性好,少数载流子寿命高。氮在硅中虽有深能极产生,在经900℃高温处理之后,将会全部消失。因此,掺氮中子嬗变区熔硅单晶,不仅有良好的机械性能,还具有优良的电学性质。

务实的梁骏吾,并不满足于实验依据和理论分析,他要用实践来检验该材料适用结果的好坏,他要努力使科研成果转变为生产力。北京椿树整流器厂的报告称:用该材料制作闸流管,崩边率由33%下降到了12%,因崩边造成的废品率,由3%下降到了2%,在烧结中不再有硅片变形,器件成品率由23%提高到了40%。北京前门器件厂告知:用该材料制作NPN高反压大功率晶体管,成品率提高了1倍,经济效益提高了10%。北京可控硅元件厂更是喜出望外,称道:用该材料制作高压大直径闸流管,工艺流程中造成的崩边损坏率下降 50%~60%,器件合格率提高 20%,成品率增加 10% 左右,年产值增加 20 万元,利润增加 7.5 万元……

经梁骏吾一步一个脚印地实践,朝朝夕夕地奋力拼搏所取得的这一重大科研成果,因具有明显的经济效益和重要学术意义,先后荣获 1983 年中国科学院成果三等奖和 1987 年中国科学院科学技术进步一等奖。他的"掺氮对区熔硅单晶电学性质及位错运动的影响"的科学论文,于 1987 年召开的第四届全国半导体集成电路和硅材料学术会议上宣读后,受到与会同行的一致好评,被会议主席团评为获奖论文。

30 年漫长的科研历程,梁骏吾的贡献与才华,已引起国内外同行学者的注意,享有一定的声望。自 1985 年以来,他曾组织或主持了"全国半导体集成技术和硅材料学术年会"、"全国化合物半导体微波光电器件学术年会"和"全国固体薄膜学术会议"等有影响的学术活动。他还参与组织了第一届和第二届北京"国际半导体与集成技术会议",并担任材料分会主席。1989 年 6 月,他受第三世界科学院的邀请,赴巴基斯坦国立电子研究所、国立硅技术所等单位讲学,向第三世界国家撒播科学、友谊的种子。十几年来,他作为研究生的导师,为国家培养了 7 名硕士研究生和 3 名博士研究生。他已为《中国大百科全书》、《化工大百科全书》撰写有关半导体材料方面的内容。近年来,他在中外学术刊物上发表了 40 多篇科学论文。他是中国电子学会会士、电子材料学会副主任、国家科学技术委员会发明评委会特邀评审员、几所高等学府的兼职教授和一些国家开放实验室学术委员会副主任或委员。他事业心强、刻苦好学、治学严谨、学风正派、有坚实的专业基础和良好的学术造诣。

梁骏吾是我国半导体学术界第二代有影响的半导体材料学家,他的科学生涯,犹如一棵高大的智慧之树,挂满了令人瞩目的科研成果。但是,在梁骏吾的胸怀里,跳动着一颗永不满足、永求创造的心。他虽已年届 80 岁,仍精力旺盛、雄心勃勃地在科学园地里辛勤地耕耘着,决心履行自己入党时的誓言:要为共产主义奋斗不止,为社会主义现代化大业做出更多贡献。我们坚信,凭借他横溢的才智,忘我的进取精神,必将在面向世界、面向未来的科研生涯中,迈着一个又一个的神奇步伐,取得一个又一个更加辉煌的科研成果。

目　录

附　录

学术论文

Investigation of Heterostructure Defects for LPE $Ga_{1-x}Al_xAs/GaAs$

SHEN Houyun*, LIANG Junwu and CHU Jiming

(*Institute of Semiconductors, Academia Sinica, Beijing, People's Rep. of China*)

Received 17 January 1985; manuscript received in final form 2 April; 1985

Abstract: Dislocations in liquid phase epitaxial (LPE) $Ga_{1-x}Al_xAs/GaAs$, grown in a vertical furnace, were studied after etching with molten KOH. The characterization methods used were metallography, cathodoluminescence (CL), and transmission electron microscopy (TEM). The magnitude and distribution of the dislocation density were dependent on the compositional variable x. Dislocation networks of moderate density were observed in a certain composition range at the interface with the GaAs substrate. The dislocations of the GaAs substrate were compensated by the dislocation networks so that the epitaxial layer could be grown free of dislocations. The distance between the interface and the dislocation networks was measured using special techniques.

1   Introduction

The group of Ⅲ-Ⅴ compounds are now widely used in heterostructure photoelectronic devices. Their properties strongly depend on crystal perfection. Dislocation structures have been studied for applications in infrared detectors, photocathodes, and double heterojunction lasers[1-3]. In order to eliminate the dislocations of the substrate which extend into the epitaxial layer various upgrading techniques were used successfully in vapor-phase epitaxial (VPE) and molecular-beam epitaxial (MBE) materials[4,5]. However, these techniques failed for the LPE material for which the substrate dislocations were not completely eliminated by the interface network. Rozgonyi et al.[6] showed that a dislocation network with density $>10^5 cm^{-2}$ in $Ga_{1-x}Al_xAs_{1-y}P_y/GaAs$ (with x =0.34 and y =0.05) could be produced by controlling the concentration of the dopant P. The substrate dislocations were thereby compensated by the interface network and a dislocation-free epitaxial layer was obtained. Kishino et al.[7], however, thought that the substrate dislocations in LPE $Ga_{1-x}Al_xAs/GaAs$ were not eliminated by the interface network.

In this paper, it will be shown that the magnitude and distribution of the dislocations in LPE $Ga_{1-x}Al_xAs/GaAs$ depends on x and that the dislocation networks can be observed metallographically by etching the layers with molten KOH, and by the CL and TEM methods. The substrate dislocations were indeed compensated by the network so that the epitaxial layer could be grown free of dislocations. The distance between the dislocation network and the interface was measured.

原载于: J. Crystal Growth, 1985, 71: 483-490.

* Present address: Department of Physics. Wuhan University. Wuchang HuBei. People's Rep. of China.

2　Characterization methods

$Ga_{1-x}Al_xAs/GaAs$ specimens with $\langle 100 \rangle$ orientation were grown by LPE in a vertical furnace[8]. The substrate dislocation density was in the range 10^3 to $10^5 cm^{-2}$. The epitaxial layers were more than $80 \mu m$ in thickness. The specimens were finished by polishing to remove mechanical damage and then etched with a solution of $3H_2SO_4 : 1H_2O_2 : 1H_2O$ to reduce the thickness of the epitaxial layer. The specimens were then etched with molten KOH at $350\pm3°C$ for 2-8 min.

Using a scanning electron microscope(SEM) of our own construction in the CL mode on an angle-lapped specimen at 30 kV and about $10^{-7}Å$ with a cathode-ray tube (CRT) display, micrographs were obtained with dart.spots or lines to show the region of non-radiative recombination of electrons. For TEM observations a JEM-1000 operating at 1000 kV was used on 90° cross-section and 1° angle-lap specimens which were jet-chemically thinned with chlorine in methanol[9]. X-ray microanalysis(XRMA) was performed on a 90° cross-section polished with bromine in methanol to determine the concentration profiles of Ga and Al near the interface. The diameter of the incident electron beam was about 1. 5μm.

3　Results

3. 1　Characteristics of dislocation distribution in $Ga_{1-x}Al_xAs/GaAs$

The dislocation etch pits of GaAs are generally hexagonal, which is caused by the anisotropy of GaAs in molten KOH. For $Ga_{1-x}Al_x As$, however, this kind of anisotropy effect in molten KOH is less clear than for GaAs. We observed circular and nearly elliptical taper etch pits of dislocations, of which the short and long axes were orientated along $\langle 01\bar{1} \rangle$ and $\langle 011 \rangle$ respectively.

Fig.1 shows a set of micrographs which trace the dislocation etch pits from the substrate to the epitaxial layers in the same field view for specimen 78113I. Figs. 1a-1d correspond to the 56 μm epitaxial layer, the 40μm epitaxial layer, the interface and the substrate, respectively. The etch pits designated A_1-A_4 in fig.1a correspond to the etch pits present in the same levels in figs.1b-1d, although their extension directions were not quite the same. Fig. 1 shows that all the dislocations in the epitaxial layer resulted from the substrate. One can also find that the dislocation extension orientations represented by the etch pits labelled A_2 and A_3 are almost unchanged, whereas those represented by the etch pits A_1 and A_4 are changed apparently.

Figs.2a-2c are micrographs corresponding to the 40μm epitaxial layer, the interface and the back side of specimen 78011, respectively. For the specimen, the back side of the substrate was lapped by c_4 borumdum only, without any chemical treatment before it was etched in molten KOH. It is very interesting to compare these micrographs. First, the dislocation density of the substrate GaAs is about $2\times10^4 cm^{-2}$, as shown in fig.2c. Second, fig.2b shows that the dislocation density increases to about 200 times higher than in fig.2c and a dislocation network is formed there. Finally, in fig.2a, one can see that there is no dislocation at all in the epitaxial layer of $Ga_{1-x}Al_xAs$. Generally, it is difficult to eliminate dislocations in crystals, and therefore the fact that the epitaxial layer in this specimen was dislocation-free might be due to the existence of an interface dislocation network which restrained the dislocations of the substrate from penetrating

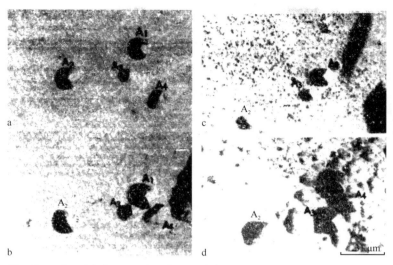

Fig.1   Metallographs of dislocation distribution: (a) 56μm epitaxial layer, (b) 40μm epitaxial
layer, (c) interface and (d) GaAs substrate, for LPE $Ga_{1-x}Al_xAs/GaAs$ (specimen 781131,
$x = 0.15$). Scalemark represents 31μm

into the epitaxial layer. The formation mechanism of the dislocation network will be discussed in
detail in section 4. This kind of dislocation network is found to be asymmetric. The density of dislocations along the longitude is slightly different from that along the lattitude. The asymmetry of
the dislocation network was also observed by TEM and will be discussed in section 4.

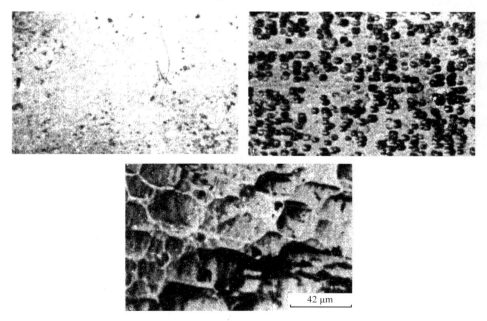

Fig.2   Metallographs of dislocation distribution: (a) dislocation-free in epitaxial layer,
(b) dislocation network at interface, (c) dislocations in GaAs, for LPE $Ga_{1-x}Al_xAs/$
GaAs (specimen 78011, $x = 0.36$). Scalemark represents 42μm

For the specimens which had a dislocation density (N_D) of N_D(GaAs) $> 10^5$ cm^{-2}, dislocation-free epitaxial layers were not found.

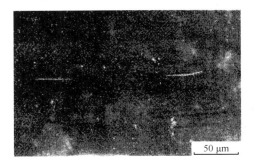

Fig.3   CL micrograph showing a dislocation network at the interface of Ga$_{1-x}$Al$_x$As/GaAs(specimen 78011, x = 0.36). Scalemark represents 50μm

3.2   Cathodoluminescence

Fig.3 is a CL micrograph which was taken on the 1° angle-lap specimen of fig.2. The dark spots and lines indicate the set of dislocation networks [10]. The big spot in the middle of the micrograph resulted from mechanical damage. The CL micrograph shows that the dislocation network existed in specimen 78011.

From the above results, the dislocations in Ga$_{1-x}$Al$_x$As/GaAs can be divided into three classes. These are (1) dislocations that directly pass through the interface from the substrate to the overgrown film, i.e. A$_2$ and A$_3$ in fig.1. (2) dislocations that pass through the interface but are slightly bent there and then extend into the overgrown film, i.e. A$_1$ and A$_4$ in fig.1, and (3) dislocations that pass through the interface but are severely bent so that they move along the interface and eventually out of the crystal(such examples are included in fig.2).

3.3   X-ray micro-analysis

It is obvious that the magnitude and the distribution of the dislocation density for specimen 78113I are different from those of specimen 78011, especially at the interface. In addition, the measurement of the composition x is also different: for specimen 78113I, x = 0.15 and for specimen 78011, x = 0.36. These results may indicate that the composition x at the interface might be an important factor contribution to the magnitude and distribution of the dislocation density. Therefore, we measured the composition x at the interface and the density of dislocations in the epitaxial layer, at the interface and in the substrate for some of the specimens and listed these data in table 1.

In table 1, 78011, 72002, 78116 and 61201 were four specimens which had no dislocations in their epitaxial layers; the dislocation densities in their substrates were ~ 10^4 cm^{-2} which at their interfaces increased by a factor of order of $1-2$ to $(2-46) \times 10^5$ cm^{-2}. The corresponding compositions x at their interfaces ranged from 0.35 to 0.37 atomic fraction. For the other specimens in table 1, dislocations existed in the epitaxial layers; the corresponding compositions were $x < 0.29$, and the dislocation densities at their interfaces did not increase as much as in the four specimens mentioned first.

3.4   Transmission electron microscopy

Fig.4 shows a dislocation network in the TEM micrographs of a typical 90° cross-section specimen viewed in the bright and dark fields in the two-beam condition. The diffraction vector is $g = [400]$. From the principles of TEM diffraction and contrast, a dislocation network appears as a dark line in the bright field and as a bright line in the dark field, which are indicated by

DsB and DsD in figs.4a and 4b, respectively.

Table 1   Data of composition x measured at interface and density of dislocations(N_D), N_{D1} in epitaxial layer, N_{D2} at interface and N_{D3} in substrate for LPE $Ga_{1-x}Al_xAs/GaAs$ ($N_D cm^{-2}$)

Specimen	x	N_{D1}	N_{D2}	N_{D3}
78113I	0.15	2.0×10^4	3.0×10^4	2.0×10^4
78113II	0.28	2.5×10^4	2.5×10^4	2.7×10^4
78102	0.18	2.0×10^4	—	3.0×10^4
76701	0.29	3.5×10^4	4.0×10^4	3.0×10^4
77811	0.22	1.5×10^4	—	2.0×10^4
78011	0.36	0	4.6×10^6	2.0×10^4
72002	0.35	0	2.0×10^5	1.0×10^4
78116	0.37	0	7.0×10^5	4.0×10^4
61201	0.37	0	4.6×10^5	1.0×10^4

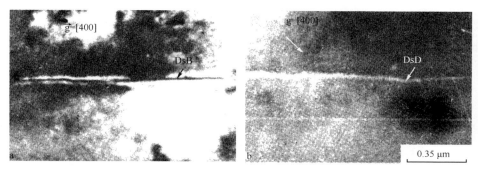

Fig.4   Electron micrographs showing a dislocation network in a cross-section of $Ga_{1-x}Al_xAs/GaAs$ (specimen 78116, $x = 0.37$). $g = [400]$, $s > 0$. (a) In bright field. (b) In dark field. Scalemark represents $0.35 \mu m$

Apart from the instrument's optical errors, in the two-beam case, the resolution of the dislocation images is also limited by factors such as diffraction contrast; the distance between the dislocations and the interface could not be distinguished in fig.4. Therefore, in the bright field mode a high-order reflection was used and weak beam conditions were applied with $(g, 5g)$ in order to reduce the width of the contrast[11]. Figs.5a and 5b show the distance between the dislocation network and the interface in the bright field mode of a high-order reflection and in the dark field mode of a weak beam having $(g, 5g)$ ($g = [220]$) in the same field view, respectively. The demarcations labelled Inf and DL were the interface and dislocation lines respectively. From fig.5a, we can see that there are differences in contrast between the regions above and below the demarcations labelled Inf, which resulted from the differences in lattic constant and in absorption of the incident electron between the GaAs substrate and the $Ga_{1-x}Al_xAs$ epitaxial layer. The DL was determined to be a dislocation line by its contrasts in bright and dark fields; therefore, the distance between Inf and DL corresponded to the distance between the dislocation line and the interface. In addition, it is interesting to note that the dislocation networks in figs. 4 and 5 were not two straight lines, but wavy lines. This is different from the result of Hockly et al.[10]. The largest and the smallest distances between DL and Inf were measured to be about 650 and 360 Å, which shows that the interface dislocation network might be within a region of about 300 Å in thickness.

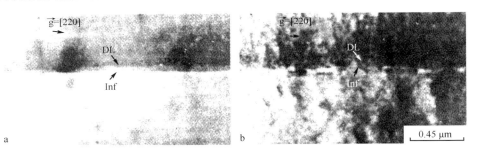

Fig.5 Electron micrographs showing the distance between the dislocation network and the interface in the same field view. (a) Bright field(0,5g). (b) Weak beam(g,5g). g = [220].
Scalemark represents 0. 45μm

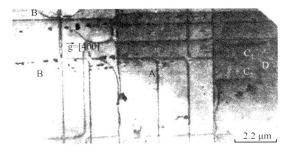

Fig.6 Electron micrograph showing a dislocation network at the interface of $Ga_{1-x}Al_xAs/GaAs$(specimen 78116, x = 0. 37) in plan-view. Bright field, g = [400]. s>0. Scalemark represetns 2. 2μm

The dislocation network near the interface in the plan-view is shown in fig.6. The specimen used is the same as that shown in fig.4, in the two-beam condition and g = [400]. In fig.6, the dark lines indicate dislocation networks in a bright field. The network consisted of some regular arrangements of dislocations lying along the orientations [01$\bar{1}$] and [011]. In group III-V compounds with the zincblende structure, the dislocation slip plane is {111}; the Burgers vertors are mainly $\frac{1}{2}a_0\langle 110 \rangle$ so that the predominant dislocation type is 60°. Moreover, we have found that the dislocation density of along[01$\bar{1}$] is 1. 2-1. 5 times that along[011]. This asymmetrical density distribution of dislocations is identical with the results shown by etching with molten KOH. From the dislocation network shown in fig.6, the lines which form the network may be classified into the following types: the first is type A in the middle of the field, the second is type B with some oscillations at the end of the lines on the left of the photograph, and the third is type D. All of them will be explained in section 4.

4 Discussions

4. 1 The relation between dislocation distribution and composition for LPE $Ga_{1-x}Al_xAs/GaAs$

We have found that the magnitude and distribution of dislocations in LPE $Ga_{1-x}Al_xAs/$ GaAs were dependent on the compositional variable x. Some theoretical models and experimental results have been proposed by Matthews et al.[12,13].Obviously,in contrast with our results, the chracteristics of the dislocation distribution are affected by lattice misfits.The lattice misfit between GaAs and $Ga_{1-x}Al_xAs$ resulted from the different coefficients of thermal expansion between the two materials.Ettenberg and Paff[14] established the relation between the lattice misfit and the temperature for GaAs and $Ga_{1-x}Al_xAs$ by means of X-ray diffraction.Their results showed that GaAs and $Ga_{1-x}Al_xAs$ were almost perfectly lattice matched at the growth temperature of 800℃；the lattice misfit was more evident as the temperature was lowered.The lattice misfit and introduction of misfit stress seemed to take place during the process of crystal cooling.Rozgonyi et al.[15] determined the lattice misfit and misfit stress of $Ga_{1-x}Al_xAs/GaAs$ as a function of AlAs mole fraction.Their results showed that the more the composition x changed, the more that lattice misfit and misfit stress increased.The misfit stress between the two crystals may be resolved into a tangential and a normal component with respect to the interface.In the general case,the thickness of the overgrowth is less than the thickness of the substrate and the lateral displacement,the normal component of the misfit stress can be neglected,and the tangential component plays an important role in the formation of misfit dislocations(MDs).Dislocation networks can be observed in those specimens with $x = 0.35 - 0.37$；this is because of the misfit stress at the interface which is being accommodated by MDs and a network is being formed.The stress misfit is the first cause for the formation of an interface network.In addition to MDs,it should be born in mind that some dislocations which came from the substrate could be bent by the action of the tangential component of the misfit stress at the interface.Fig.7 shows three classes of dislocations which are effected by the tangential component,and which then extend into the epitaxial layers.Figs.7a and 7b show that substrate dislocations extend directly into the epitaxial layer or indirectly after being slightly bent,while the tangential stress was less than the tension of the dislocations owing to the lower lattice misfit；such examples correspond to dislocations A_1-A_4 in fig.1.Fig.7c shows the third class of dislocations which are seriously bent and which slip along the interface and out of the crystal.The bending is caused by the high misfit stress which occurred at higher values of the composition x.Such examples are included in figs. 2 and 6.Thus the third class of dislocations compose a part of the interface network.The third class has been explaincd by a slip mechanism by Matthews and Blakeslee[16].This is also the second mechanism of formation of an interface network.

4.2 The distribution characteristics of the interface dislocalion network

The reason for the asymmetrical density distribution of dislocation lines in fig.6 is that the polarity which exists in Ⅲ-Ⅴ compounds having the zinc-blende structure causes two dislocations to slip disparately on one pair of {111} planes. The fact that $N_D[01\bar{1}] > N_D[011]$ showed that the misfit stress to be relieved along $[01\bar{1}]$ was faster than that along $[011]$ at the interface. The dislocations labelled type A may be MDs,which resulted from misfit

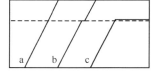

Fig.7　Schematic of the dislocation extension in $Ga_{1-x}Al_xAs/GaAs$

stress to be accommodated. The dislocations labelled type B came from the substrate and bent along the interface by the action of the misfit stress. The dislocation labelled type D may be a complex dislocation which was formed by two $60°$ dislocations C_1 and C_2. The reaction between the two dislocations is probably as follows:

$$C_1 + C_2 \rightarrow D, \boldsymbol{b}_1 + \boldsymbol{b}_2 = \boldsymbol{b}_3.$$

where $\boldsymbol{b}_1, \boldsymbol{b}_2$ and $\boldsymbol{b}_3$ are the Burgers vectors of C_1, C_2 and D respectively. If $\boldsymbol{b}_1 = \dfrac{1}{2} a_0 [101]$ and $\boldsymbol{b}_2 = \dfrac{1}{2} a_0 [\bar{1}10]$, which are called $60°$ dislocations. then $\boldsymbol{b}_1 + \boldsymbol{b}_2 = \dfrac{1}{2} a_0 [101] + \dfrac{1}{2} a_0 [\bar{1}10] = \dfrac{1}{2} a_0 [011] = \boldsymbol{b}_3$. Therefore, $\boldsymbol{b}_3 \perp D$. and D is a Lomer Cottrell dislocation.

From fig.6. we know that the interface network mainly consists of the misfit dislocations.

4.3 Discussion for composiuons of $x = 0.4$ and $N_D(GaAs) - 10^5 cm^{-2}$

Dislocation-free epitaxial layers were not obtained in specimens wich a dislocation density of $N_D(GaAs) > 10^5 cm^{-2}$. This means that the interface network has a limited possibility to compensate for the substrate dislocations, but is not unlimited in doing so. For specimens with compositions of $x > 0.4$, like most VPE materials, the misfit stress will increase as the composition x increases, so that the misfit stress can not be completely accommodated by the interface network. Dislocations can be formed in the nucleation process and then extend into epitaxial layer, lowering the perfection of the crystal[17].

5 Conclusions

(a) Three classes of dislocations in LPE $Ga_{1-x}Al_xAs/GaAs$ were observed.

(b) The magnitude and distribution of the dislocation density depended on the compositional variable x. For the specimens with $x \leqslant 0.29$ no dislocation network was observed at the interface. For $x = 0.35 - 0.37$. there were asymmetrical dislocation networks with a density of $2 \times 10^5 - 4.6 \times 10^6 \ cm^{-2}$ at the interface, but the epitaxial layers were dislocation-free.

(c) The distance between the interface and the dislocation network was measured: the dislocation network was found to exist in a region about $300Å$ in thickness at the position of $350Å$ above the interface.

Acknowledgements

The authors wish to thank Professor L. Y. Lin for her enthusiastic encouragement. Mr. X. Tu for supplying specimens .Mrs. S. B. Lu for XRMA. Mr. Z. P. Zheng for CL and Mr. Y. H. Li for use of a 100 kV TEM.

References

[1] P.M.Petroff and R.L. Hartman. Appl.Phys.Letters 23(1973)436.

[2] G.R.Woolhouse.IEEE J.Quantum Electron.QE-11(1975)556.

[3] S. Kishino.H Nakishrma.N.Chinonl and R.Ito.Appl.Phys Letters 28(1976)98.

[4] M.Dupuy and D.Lafeuille,J.Crystal Growth 31(1975)244.

[5] C.A.Chang and C.M.Serrano,L.L.Chang and L.Esaki,Appl.Phys.Letters 37(1980)538.

[6] G.A. Rozgonyi, P.M.Petroff and M.B.Panish, Appl.Phys.Letters 24 (1974) 251.

[7] S.Kishino, M.Ogirima, T.Kajimura and K.Kurata, J.Crystal Growth 24/25 (1974) 266.

[8] X.Z.Tu and Y.Y.Ge, in: Proc.2nd Natl.Conf.on Compound Materials and Microwave Devices, Kuming, People's Rep. of China, 1982, p.98.

[9] M.S.Abrahams, L.R.Weisberg, C.J.Buiocchi and J.Blanc, J.Mater.Sci.4 (1969) 223.

[10] M.Hockly, M.Al-Jassim, G.R.Booker and R.Nicklin, J.Microscopy 118 (1980) 117.

[11] G. Thomas and M. J. Goringe, Transmission Electron Microscopy of Materials (Wiley-Interscience, New York, 1979) p.39.

[12] J.W.Matthews, S.Mader and T.B.Light, J.Appl.Phys.41 (1970) 3800.

[13] J.W.Matthews and A.E.Blakeslee, J.Crystal Growth 27 (1974) 118.

[14] M.Ettenberg and R.J.Paff, J.Appl.Phys.41 (1970) 3926.

[15] G.A.Rozgonye, P.M.Petroff and M.B.Panish, J.Crystal Growth 27 (1974) 106.

[16] J.W.Matthews and A.E.Blakeslee, J.Crystal Growth 32 (1976) 265.

[17] C. H. L. Goodman.Ed., Crystal Growth; Theory and Techniques, Vol.2 (Plenum, New York.1978), p.24.

Investigation of N-doped FZ Si Crystals

LIANG Junwu, DENG Lisheng, LUAN Hongfa, and ZHENG Hongjun

(*Institute of Semiconductors, Academia Sinica Beijing, China*)

The doping of N into Si crystals has attracted much interest because of its role in improving mechanical properties of the crystals. We have studied the optical, electrical and mechanical properties of the N-doped FZ Si. In view of the importance of the NTD Si, we also investigated the optical and electrical properties of the N-doped NTD FZ Si.

The samples used in our experiments were dislocation-free FZ Si grown in the mixed ambient of N_2 and Ar. The nitrogen content in the samples was measured by means of IR absorption coefficient at $963 cm^{-1}$. The concentration of nitrogen in samples was in the range of $1.3-2.8 \times 10^{15} cm^{-3}$. The Si crystals before doping are n type with resistivity larger than 1000om-cm. p-doping was achieved by both direct doping and NTD(neutron transmutation doping).

IR measurements have shown that two peaks($963 cm^{-1}$ and $767 cm^{-1}$) appear in the spectrum of unirradiated N-doped samples. In the spectrum of NTD N-doped samples, besides these two peaks, some additional peaks(887, 824 and $785 cm^{-1}$) also appear, but at the same time the absorption coefficient at $963 cm^{-1}$ decreases. A model that nitrogen interacts with defects forming complex has been proposed and discussed.

Only one shallow donor level(Ec-0.045eV) have been found in both the N-doped irradiated and unirradiated Si samples by means of low temperature Hall measurements. This level is the same as that of substitutional phosphorus. The results of the donor concentration measurement have shown that for carrier concentration $<1.0 \times 10^{14} cm^{-3}$ no detectable effect of nitrogen on the resistance of NTD crystals have been found.

The results of spreading resistance and mobility measurements have shown that the resistance homogeneity and mobility of N-doped si are at least the same as that of non-N-doped samples, especially the mobility at low temperature is higher in N-doped Si.

Four deep levels have been detected in phosphorus and nitrogen doped Si by means of DLTS(see Fig.1). They are located at Ec-0.14, Ec-0.22, Ec-0.27 and Ec-0.52 eV. The densities corresponding to above four levels are 1.3×10^{13}, 1.3×10^{13}, 1.1×10^{14} and $1.5 \times 10^{14} cm^{-3}$ respectively. However, no deep electron traps have been found in the non-N-doped samples. It can be deduced that the four levels mentioned above are related to nitrogen. Only one deep level (Ec-0.20 eV) has been observed after high temperature annealing. In N-doped NTD Si, only 0.20 eV level can be measured after high temperature annealing. This shows that the majority of the deep levels related to nitrogen is unstable. A comparison has been made between our results

原载于：World Scientific, 1986, 771-773.

and literature data.

Results of lifetime measurements have shown that the lifetime of minority carrier in N-doped samples, whether irradiated or not, is higher than that in the non-N-doped samples.

We have also carried out the measurements of hardness in the range of 600 − 1100℃. Fig. 2 gives the curve of hardness vs. temperature. We found that the hardness order is in sequence of CZ Si>N-doped FZ Si>FZ Si at low temperature, but at high temperature the hardness order appears as N-doped FZ Si>CZ Si>FZ Si. The reason of rapid hardness decreasing in CZ Si at high temperature is due to the precipitation of oxygen during annealing.

The results of indentation rosette experments have shown that the distance of dislocation moving

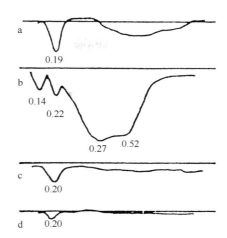

Fig.1   The DLTS spectra for nitrogen doped Si

a. NTD Si

b. Conventional P-doped Si

c. NTD Si after annealing

d. Conventional P-doped Si after annealing

in conventional FZ Si was much larger than that in N-doped FZ Si. Calculation has shown that the critical shear stress of N-doped FZ Si is three times larger than that of the conventional FZ Si.

We have also investigated the motion of dislocation by means of four-point bending method. Fig.3 gives the curve of velocity of dislocation moving vs. temperature in the range of 665-884℃. The velocity of dislocation moving of N-doped FZ Si is found to be

$$V = 4.87 \times 10^{10} \exp(-1.94/KT) \ (\mu m/min)$$

The obtained activation energy of dislocation motion is 1. 94 eV.

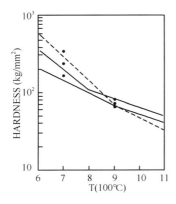

Fig.2   Temperature dependence of

·   CZ Si

X   N-doped FZ Si

O   Fz Si grown in Ar

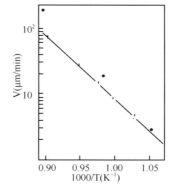

Fig.3   Velocity of dislocation as a temperature

X   N-doped FZ Si

O   Fz Si grown in Ar

From the results of mechanical experiments, it is confirmed that nitrogen in silicon increases critical shear stress and enhances yield strength hence improves mechanical properties.

From the results of optical and electrical experiments, we conclude that doping of N has no harmful effect on properties of silicon crystals. Most of the deep levels related to nitrogen are vanished by high temperature annealing.

The Interaction Between Impurities and Defects in Semiconductors

LIANG Junwu

(*Institute of Semiconductors , Academia Sinica , Beijing , P.R. China*)

Abstract: The extrinsic properties of semiconductors depend on impurities and their states in the semiconductors as well as defects. In addition, the interactions between impurities and defects make the semiconductors present some distinct properties. In this paper, we will discuss the interactions between impurities and between impurities and defects in Si and GaAs.

1. The energy levels in Si and GaAs induced by interaction between impurities and defects

The impurities energy levels are depended on their existing states in materiais. About 1% of nitrogen is ionized at room temperature. Three energy levels: Ec-0. 20eV, Ec-0. 28eV and Ec-0. 57eV have been observed by DLTS which have been shown to be related to nitrogen. The Ec-0. 20eV level possibly consists of nitrogen and Si vacancy. After treatment of 0. 5hr at temperature 300 ℃ the densities of the three deep levels decrease and Ec-0. 20eV level is too low to be detected. After the annealing for 0. 5hr at 400 ℃ , none of them can be detected, but, simultaneously, three new energy levels are produced which located at 0. 17eV, 0. 37eV and 0. 50eV below the conduction band, respectively. The densities of the new levels increase with temperature ranging from 400℃ to 600℃ and reach their maximum at about 600℃ [1,2].

The impurity complex formation is often observed in semiconductor matrixes. The new donor may be the complex containing oxygen and carbon. Combinations of C and III-A elements produce acceptors, i. e. X-centers. E-centers are the complexes of group Ⅴ impurities and single vacancy.

The group Ⅳ elements become N-type impurities if they combine with Ga vacancy but they become P-type impurities if they combine with As vacancy.

There are more kinds of thermal point defects in GaAs than in Si. The kinds of the complexes of impurities and point defects are also much more in GaAs than in Si.

Si-GaAs with resistivity of 10E8 ohm-cm can be obtained by compensating the residual shallow donors (Si) or residual shallow acceptors (C) in GaAs.

Undoped Si-GaAs was obtained by LEC method without Cr doping using PBN crucible. It has been shown that the main residual impurity is C with concentration ranging from 10E15 to 10E16 cm^{-3} and the deep donor EL-2 (Ec-0. 825±0. 01eV , $\sigma = 1. 5±0. 5E-13cm^2$) compensate C acceptor.

原载于: International Academic Publisher, 1989, 23-25.

Experiments have shown that the concentration of EL-2 is higher than [O]. So EL-2 could not be related to oxygen. EL-2 exists in HB, LEC, VPE, MBE and MOCVD-GaAs but dose not appear in LPE-GaAs which is abundant of Ga. It is necessary that [As] is great than 0.475 for obtaining SI-GaAs. The concentration of EL-2 decreases with [As]. Several models have been proposed including As_{Ga}, $As_{Ga}V_{As}$, $(As_{Ga})n$, $(As_1)4$, $V_{Ga}V_{As}$ and $As_{Ga}V_{As}V_{Ga}$.

2. The segregation of amphoteric impurities in GaAs

The group IV elements of C, Si, Ge and Sn in GaAs present as acceptors when they combine with V_{As} and as donors when combine with V_{Ga}. The concentration of the acceptors and the donors are [Na] and [Nd]. For Ge doping there are two segregation coefficients: Ka = Na/[Gel] and Kd = Nd[Gel]. The total segregation coefficient of Ge incorporate into GaAs is K = Ka+Kd.

We have studied the segregation coefficient of the amphoteric impurity Ge exper imentally and theoretically[3].

$$Gal+Gel \xrightleftharpoons{k1} GaGe^S$$

$$Gel+Asl \xrightleftharpoons{k2} GeAs^S$$

$$Gal+Asl \xrightleftharpoons{k3} GaAs^S$$

$$\text{Then } Ka = k_1 r_{Ga}^l [Ga^l] r_{Ge}^l \left\{ 1 + \frac{1}{g_a} \exp[(E_F - E_A)/KT] \right\} / 2r_{GaGe}^S$$

$$Kd = k_2 r_{As}^l [As^l] r_{Ge}^l \left\{ 1 + \frac{1}{g_d} \exp[(E_D - E_F)/KT] \right\} / 2r_{GeAs}^S$$

where the impurities ionization have been taken into account. In order to calculate Ka and Kd the activity coefficients ri must be known. We suppose that the Ge-Ga-As ternary solution is a regular solution and the solld phase is GaAs-GaGe-GeAs ternary regular solution, than we can obtain

$$RT\ln r_i = \sum_{\substack{i=1 \\ i \neq j}}^{m} \alpha_{ij} x_j^2 + \sum_{\substack{k=1 \\ k=j, j \neq i, i \neq k}}^{m} \sum_{j=1}^{m} x_k x_j (\alpha_{ij} + \alpha_{ik} - \alpha_{jk})$$

in which α_{ij} is the interaction parameters of component i and j. α is, generally, a linear function of the temperature. However, we found that the interaction parameters in the GaAs-GaGe-GeAs system are non-linear. Using simulation methods we have obtained the following expressions of the interaction parameters in the GaAs-GaGe-GeAs system:

$$\alpha_{GaAs-GaGe}^S = 21860 - 80.7T + 0.0378T^2 \quad cal/mole$$

$$\alpha_{GaAs-GeAs}^S = 8942 - 41.3T + 0.0211T^2 \quad cal/mole$$

We also obtained the ratio of Gega/Geas as a function of the temperature. As the temperature increases, the As vacancy concentration decreases, and the Ga vacancy concentration increases so that the concentration of Ge on Ga site increases. The critical temperature for transform from P-type to N-type is calculated to be 1235℃. At melting point (1513K) N-type materials can be obtained with Nd/Na = 1.59 and the segregation coefficient of Ge is 0.0483. On the other hand, the GaAs crystals grown by LPE is always P-type.

3. Impurities and the perfection of crystals

3.1 The stress caused by mismatch of the impurity atoms

The difference between the radii of impurity atoms and those of atoms of matrix may cause a stress. When the stress is large enough it can produce the mismatch dislocations. High concentration of B and P in Si will cause mismatch dislocation net-work during diffusion. Heavily Sb doped Si crystals have the tendency of produce dislocation when grown from melt.

The oxygen content in Si can reach $2.0 \times 10E18 cm^{-3}$, which is greater than the other electrically active impurities. The oxygen in Si may become supersaturated and precipitated after heat treatment. The volume will be doubled when silicon is oxidized into SiO_2, and the SiO_2 precipitates may punch out prismatic dislocation loops, or emit self-interstitial during oxidation, However, we can use these defects for the heavy metal impurities gettering so that the yield of the devices may rise.

3.2 The impurities and the dislocation density of GaAs crystals

It has been found experimentally that the dislocations are reduced apparently by the doping of impurities. The doping of In in concentration of 10E-2 may reduce the dislocation density down to $10E2/cm^{-2}$. This has been explained and calculated with the model of the hardening of the impurities by many authors. According to the data of the EXAFS, it was found that the lattice of the GaAs is distorted by in doping.

The distance of Ga-As is shorter than that of In-As. Bond expansion is 7% so that expansion of GaAs materials is 21% which is high than the expansion of metals caused by substitutional impurities. The elastic energy of the mismatched atoms and edge disiocations is

$$E(r,\theta) = (\frac{\mu+(1+\nu)}{3\pi(1-\nu)}\delta V)\frac{\sin\theta}{r} = \beta\frac{b}{r}\sin\theta$$

The doping of 3% In can increase the critical stress by a factor of 4.

The impurities of oxygen and nitrogen in Si also have the function of pinning dislocation. It is worth to mention that only a small concentration of nitrogen about $10E15 cm^{-3}$ is sufficient to reduce the dislocation moving.

4. Effect of the point defects on impurity diffusion

The thermal point defects have an obvious effect on the diffusivities of III and V impurities in Si. Let's examine the boron diffusion under Si_3N_4 covered region and under emitter region as well.

The thickness of SiO_2 in P diffusion region is the biggest, and, simultaneously, the B diffusivity in base region under the P diffusion region is the biggest and the B diffusivity under Si_3N_4 region is smallest. These can be explained by the mechanisms of vacancy-assisted diffusion and self-interstitial-assisted diffusion.

During formation of silicon dioxide the Si is emitted. Under high P diffusion region in addition to high [Si] there are high concentration of electrons. These cause iacrease in diffusivity.

These effects must be taken into account during fabrication of submicron devices.

5. The passivation of Si surface by hydrogen

These are many examples on the interaction between impurities and defects. The electrically active impurities or defects in Si can be passivated after H^+ plasma treatment and the leakage of the P-N junction is reduced.

The a-Si and a-SiC films containing hydrogen also can be used as passivation layers, which can reduce the interface state density and the recombination current.

References

[1] Liang Junwu, Deng Lisheng, Luan Hongfa and Zheng Hongjun. The Proceedings of Int. Conf. on Semiconductor and I.C. Tecnology, world scientific, p.771(1986).

[2] Luan Hongfa, Liang Junwu, Deng Lisheng, Zheng Hongjun and Huang Dading. Chinese Journal of Semiconductors, 9, No. 3, 312(1988).

[3] Yang Hui and Liang Junwu. Chinese Journal of Semiconductors, 9, No.4, 429(1988).

Behaviors of Dislocations During Sl's Growth and Crystal Quality Assessment

LIANG Junwu, YANG Hui, DENG Lisheng, ZHENG Lianxi and ZHANG Xia

(*National Research Center for Opto-Electronic Technology Institue of Semiconductors Chinese Academy of Science*)

Abstract: Suppression of dislocation propagation is investigated by using $Al_xGa_{1-x}As/GaAs$ Superlattice and $Al_xGa_{1-x}As/GaAs$ simple heterostructure grown by low pressure MOVPE. The efficiency of bending dislocation is compared. Dislocation-free GaAs epilayer can be grown by using undoped $Al_xGa_{1-x}As/GaAs$ superlattice with X = 0.5. High purity GaAs epilayers were grown by LP MOVPE. A layer with μ_{77} of $122,700 cm^2v^{-1}s^{-1}$ at an electron concentration of $2.6 \times 10^{14} cm^{-3}$ was grown. Double-crystal X-ray diffraction and PL measurements were used for crystal quality assessment. 11K PL spectrum of a 20 period MQW $Al_{0.35}Ga_{0.65}As/GaAs$ with FWHM of 3.3meV was observed. It corresponds an interface roughness of a monolayer.

Introduction

The MOVPE growth of III-V semiconductor superlattices have attracted more and more attentions. Their properties depend on dislocation density, impurity concentration, interfaces uniformity and chemical composition variation.

It is well known that dislocation threading can be effectively suppressed by using strained-layer superlattice buffer layers such as GaAs-GaAsP [1] or GaAsP-InGaAs [2]. M. Shinohara[3] reported that by using a modulation-doped AlAs(Si)-GaAs superlattice grown by MBE, dislocation threading can be almost suppressed. The AlAs-GaAs superlattice is not mismatched as a typical strained-layer superlattice. The results showed that the undoped AlAs-GaAs, modulation-doped AlAs-GaAs(Si) and equally doped AlAs(Si)-GaAs(Si) superlattices could partly suppress dislocation threading. M. Shinohara thought that dislocation bending at the AlAs/GaAs interface is due to the interaction between dislocations and electric charges.

In our previous paper[4], it was reported that dislocation density in liquid phase epitaxial $Al_xGa_{1-x}As/GaAs$ depended on the compositional variable X. It was found, that for X = 0.35 ~ 0.37 the epitaxial layers were dislocation-free. However, there is lack of literatures about the influence of compositional variable X on efficiency in suppressing dislocation threading for MOVPE growth.

In this paper, with the use of an undoped MOVPE $Al_xGa_{1-x}As/GaAs$ superlattice which is

原载于: Warrendale, PA,. 1992, 527-530.

The First Pacific Rim International Conference on Advanced Materials and Processing(PRICM-1)

Edited by Changxu Shi, Hengde Li and Alexander Scott The Minerals, Metals & Materials Society © 1992

a nearly matched system, the GaAs epilayer could be grown free of dislocation, The dependence of dislocation density in epilayers on X value were shown. Using Hall measurement, double-crystal X-ray diffraction and photoluminescence spectroscopy, the MOVPE $Al_xGa_{1-x}As/GaAs$ quality were characterized.

Growth and Characterization

The samples studied here were grown by low-pressure MOVPE using triethylgallium, trimethylaluminium and arsine. The (100) oriented GaAs substrates were semi-insulating with dislocation density of $6 \times 10^4 cm^{-2}$. Growth was carried out at $610 ℃ - 650 ℃$ under 0.1 bar pressure. Growth rate ranged from $3 \sim 10 Å/sec$.

The experiments were divided into two groups. In the first group, initially an $Al_xGa_{1-x}As/GaAs$ superlattice was grown and then a GaAs top layer with thickness from $2.1 \mu m$ to $5.3 \mu m$ was grown on the substrate. In the second group, only simple $Al_xGa_{1-x}As/GaAs$ heterostructure was grown without using superlattice to suppress dislocation propagation. In order to investigate the influence of X value on dislocation bending effect, X value used here varied from 0.1 to 0.54.

Dislocation in the epilayer were detected by molten KOH etching at $350 \pm 3 ℃$ for $1 \sim 6 min$ or AB etching. In order to verify that after etching the epilayer remained on the substrate the etched sample was cleavaged, chemically decorated and finally examined by microscope.

Carrier concentrations and mobilities were measured by the conventional Van der Pauw technique. Double-crystal X-ray diffraction was used to assess crystal quality at interface and reproducibility of superlattice growth. The structural interface disorder and variations of chemical composition of $Al_xGa_{1-x}As/GaAs$ SL's was studied by photoluminescence at 11K, with excitation power ranging from $0.2 mW/cm^2 \sim 20 mW/cm^2$.

Result

Propagation of dislocation in $Al_xGa_{1-x}As/$ GaAs epilayers

In fig. 1, typical etch pit images of the substrate was shown. The dislocation etch pits were traced from the epitaxial layer to substrate.

For all cases the dislocation density is much lower than that in the substrate. This means that both simple heterojunction and superlattices have efficiency in suppressing dislocation threading. However, there exist distinct differences in their efficiencies.

The efficiency in preventing dislocation threading for two groups of experiments is summarized in Table 1.

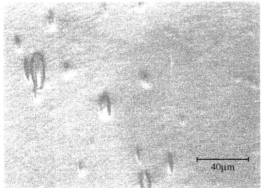

40μm

Fig.1　Etch pit images of the substrate

Table 1 Propagation of dislocation in MOVPE grown $Al_xGa_{1-x}As/GaAS$ [*]

Specimen	X	Structure	R [**]	D [***]
911115	0. 20	$Al_xGa_{1-x}As/GaAs$	0. 11	3. 7
2216	0. 52	$Al_xGa_{1-x}As/GaAs$	0. 032	2. 0
222	0. 54	$Al_xGa_{1-x}As/GaAs$	0. 012	3. 3
11109	0. 20	single well[1]	0. 011	2. 1
2105	0. 10	10-period SL[2]	0. 050	5. 3
2220	0. 50	40-period SL[3]	≈ 0	2. 8
11221	0. 50	2-period SL[4]	≈ 0	2. 3

* For all specimens the dislocation density of substrate is $6 \times 10^4 \, cm^{-2}$

* * Ratio of dislocation density in the epilayer to that in substrate

* * * Top layer thickness(μm)

1. well thickness $= 50 Å$

2. well thickness $= 100 Å$, barrier thickness $= 350 Å$

3. well thickness $= 300 Å$, barrier thickness $= 350 Å$

4. well thickness $= 100 Å$, barrier thickness $= 350 Å$

It is obvious that the magnitude of the dislocation density for specimens with X value equal or greater than 0. 5 is less than those of specimens with X value less than 0. 2.

In table 1, one can see that the dislocation propagation is almost completely prevented for the specimens 2220 and 11221, which have a $Al_xGa_{1-x}As/GaAs$ superlattice with X = 0. 5. For specimen 222 grown with simple $Al_xGa_{1-x}As/GaAs$ structure and X = 0. 54 dislocations still remain with lowered density.

Carrier concentration, mobility and double crystal X-ray diffration

Under optimum conditions, high purity MOVPE GaAs material can be grown repeatly. The mobility of GaAs can reaches $7000—7580 cm^2 V^{-1} s^{-1}$ at 300K and $105,000—122,700 cm^2 V^{-1} s^{-1}$ at 77K, while the electron concentration is $1. 0 \times 10^{14} - 2. 6 \times 10^{14} cm^{-3}$. Based on Brook-Heering Formula, $N^d + N^a$ were calculated to be $1. 6 \times 10^{15} cm^{-3}$. Double-crystal X-ray diffraction spectra showed that the full width at half-maxium(FWHM) of epilayer and substrate is 22. 4″ and 19. 3″, respectively, which means the material is perfect.

Photoluminescence spectra for high purity GaAs

The high purity GaAs grown by LP MOVPE was studied by photoluminescence spectroscopy at 10K. Figure 2 shows a typical photoluminescence spectrum for high purity GaAs.

From the peak position one can finds a free exciton PL peak($\lambda = 8179 Å$), and two bound exciton peaks: B ($D^\circ X$) ($\lambda = 8187 Å$) and C ($A^\circ X$) ($\lambda = 8191 Å$). The total FWHM of two exciton peaks is only 1. 7meV. From figure 2 it can be seen, that the main residual acceptor impurities in our high purity sample are carbon (E = 1. 491eV) and silicon(E = 1. 480eV). No other acceptor impurities could be detected.

Due to the use of alkyls during MOVPE growth, contamination of carbon is unavoidable, but the intensity of carbon peak in figure 2 is very weak. It means that under the condition of

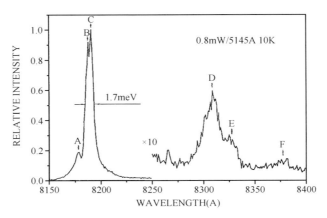

Fig. 2　PL spectrum for high purity GaAs grown by LP MOVPE

A-X(Free Exciton)

B-D°X(Exciton bound to donor)

C-A°X(Exciton bound to acceptor)

D-C_{AS}

F-Si_{AS}

MOVPE growth the carbon incorporation was suppressed. In addition, figure 2 shows that in the region from E = 1. 511eV to E = 1. 503eV there are no detectable exciton peaks related to defects, which exist usually for MBE material. Thus, the LP MOVPE samples have been grown with high crystal perfection and purity.

Photoluminescence spectra for MQW

A 20 period $Al_X Ga_{1-X}$As/GaAs MQW'S with period of 28nm has been grown. The well thickness was 8nm. Double-crystal X-ray diffraction spectrum showed satellite peaks of first and second order. Figure 3 shows photoluminescence spectrum of the $Al_X Ga_{1-x}$As/GaAs MQW at 11K.

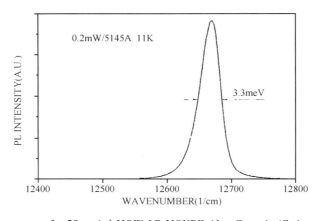

Fig. 3　PL spectrum of a 20 period MQW LP-MOVPE $Al_{0.35} Ga_{0.65}$As/GaAs sample at 11K

One can observe high intensity and small width of the peak. The small FWHM means that the experimental result approximately equal theoretical FWHM with monolayer fluctuation. It means, that the interface roughness is small and the fluctuation of well width nearly reaches the magnitude of a monolayer. In addition, the reproducibility of well growth in chemical composition and width is very well.

Figure 4 shows a typical PL spectrum at 11K for a four-well structure of $Al_{0.35}Ga_{0.65}As/$ GaAs. The narrowest well has a thickness of six monolayers.

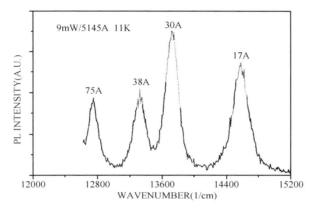

Fig. 4　Photoluminescence spectrum for a four-well structure of $Al_{0.35}Ga_{0.65}As/GaAs$

Figure 5 shows the PL spectrum of a 20 period $Al_{0.35}Ga_{0.65}As/GaAs$ quantum well with well width of 8nm. The PL spectrum exhibits three peaks, which can be attributed to light hole-electron transition A, heavy hole-electron transition B and exciton C. The 11K PL spectrum shows clear light hole peak, evidencing a good quality of QW.

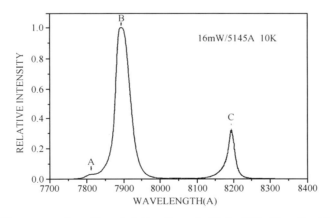

Fig. 5　PL spectrum for a 20 period $Al_{0.35}Ga_{0.65}As/GaAs$ QW with well width of 8nm

　　　　A: light hole-electron

　　　　B: heavy hole-electron

　　　　C: exciton

Discussion

We have found that the density of dislocations in LP MOCVD GaAs was suppressed by using undoped $Al_xGa_{1-x}As/GaAs$ superlattice. The efficiency in suppressing dislocation threading were depend on the aluminium composition value X. The difference of lattice constants between AlGaAs and GaAs at MOVPE growth temperature of $\sim 630℃$ is very small. It is the different coefficients of thermal expansion between the two materials resulting in lattice misfit. During the process of furnace cooling the lattice misfit and misfit stress take place. The greater the aluminium composition value X is, the more misfit stress occurs. Dislocation which propagating from the substrate are forced to bend at heterointerface by the action of misfit stress. This means that the great values of composition $X(X \approx 0.5)$ cause effective bending of dislocations. This result is qualitatively coincident with that obtained for LPE growth[4]. Shen Houyun and coworkers[4] have reported that in their dislocation-free $Al_xGa_{1-x}As/GaAs$ sample dislocation network was found to exist in a region 300Å in thickness at the position of 350Å above the interface. M. Shinohara [5] have found that dislocation bending occurred at the AlAs(Si)/GaAs(Si) interface when the thickness of each layer is in the order of $100 \sim 300$Å. However, critical thickness at which dislocation bending takes place is calculated to be about 300Å from Matthew's equation for AlAs/GaAs system[6]. The experimental value is lower than theoretical value by one order of magnitude. Based on above facts, the reason why AlGaAs/GaAs superlattice has greater efficiency in suppressing dislocation propagation than the simple AlGaAs/GaAs heterostructure could be explained by assuming that dislocation bending occurs at each heterointerface of the superlattice.

Conclusions

[1] High purity GaAs epilayers were grown by LP MOVPE. A layer with electron mobility at 77K of $122,700cm^2v^{-1}s^{-1}$ at an electron concentration of $2.6 \times 10^{14}cm^{-3}$ was obtained.

[2] $Al_xGa_{1-x}As/GaAs$ multi-quantum wells were grown by LP MOVPE. Double-crystal X-ray diffraction and PL measurements were used for crystal quality assessment. 11K PL spectrum of a 20 period MQW's A $l_{0.35}Ga_{0.65}As/GaAs$ sample with FWHM of 3.3meV was observed. It corresponds an interface roughness of a monolayer.

[3] Dislocation-free MOVPE GaAs epilayers can be grown by using undoped $Al_xGa_{1-x}As/GaAs$ SL with X approximately equal to 0.5.

Reference

[1] J.W.Matthews and A.E.Blakeslee,J.Cryst. Growth 32(1976),265.

[2] M.A.Tisher,T.Katsuyama,N.A.El-masry and M.Bedair,Appl.Phys.Lett.46(1985),294.

[3] M.Shinohara,Appl.Phys.Lett.52(1988),543.

[4] Shen Houyun,Liang Junwu and Chu Jiming,J.Cryst.Growth 71(1985),483.

[5] M.Shinohara,T.Ito and Y.Imamura,J.Appl. Phys.58(1985),3449.

[6] J.W.Matthews,A.E.Blakeslee and S.Mader,Thin Solid Films 33(1976),253.

Thermodynamic and Fluid Dynamic Analyses of
GaAs Movpe Process

YANG Hui, LIANG Junwu, DENG Lisheng, ZHENG Lianxi and ZHANG Xia National
Research Center for Opto-Electronic Technology

(*Institue of Semiconductors, Chinese Academy of Science*)

Abstract: A new theoretical model has been proposed in a laminar flow III - V MOVPE system.
The fluid dynamic partial differential equations describing the mass, momentum and energy conservation are coupled with the thermodynamic calculations. The spatial distributions of various species
are given in the TMG-Arsine-Hydrogen MOVPE system. The dominant Ga containing species is
GaH_2 near the substrate and the most abundant arsine related species is As at substrate temperature
of 650℃. The influence of reactor geometry on the growth rate profiles are calculated, which shows
the importance of the reactor height for balancing the growth efficiency and uniformity. Theoretical
results are compared with experiments.

Introduction

The MOVPE technique becomes more and more important in the semiconductor technology
nowadays. Various kinds of high speed electronic devices and opto-electronic devices have been
fabricated using MOVPE methods, such as high electron mobility transistors, quantum well
lasers and detectors. All these enforce the studies on the fundamental understanding of the growth
mechanism. Many attentions have been attracted to the theoretical analysis of the MOVPE
process. Two or three dimensional fluid dynamic models of the MOVPE process have been
extensively studied by many authors[1-5]. The studies on the pyrolysis of various sources were
reported [6-8, 12, 13]. Recently, some authors have attempted to incorporate the chemical
reaction mechanism into the fluid dynamic models[9-10]. But, only few papers have been reported on this kind of theoretical models due to the complexity of the chemical kinetics involving
organometallic species and the insufficiency of the data used for calculating reaction rates.
Another approach to the understanding of the growth mechanism has been made in this paper.
Homogeneous equilibrium calculations are combined with the fluid dynamic equations to give out
the spatial distributions of various intermediate species. The influences of reactor geometry on the
growth rate profiles are also considered which are very useful to optimising growth conditions and
the reactor design to achieve satisfactory uniformity with the lowest sources consumption.

原载于: Warrendale, PA. 1992, 541−545.

The First Pacific Rim International Conference on Advanced Materials and Processing (PRICM-1)

Edited by Changxu Shi, Hengde Li and Alexander Scott, The Minerals, Metals & Materials Society ©1992

Theoretical analysis

Many papers have been published on the studies of the pyrolysis of source materials. Stringfellow[11] has shown that equilibriums are established near the surface of the substrate. Leys and Veenvliet [12] and Nishizawa and Kurabayashi[13] used IR spectroscopy to identify the gas molecules present in the boundary layer at temperature above 550℃. They found only CH_4, indicating that the TMGa is completely decomposed by homogeneous reaction in the vapor phase before reaching the interface. We assume that the concentrations of the intermediate species in the gas phase are determined by homogeneous equilibriums and mass transport process. The standard equilibrium calculations are adopted here by relating the partial pressures p_i through equilibrium constants. Ten different intermediate species are included here and the thermochemical data needed to estimate the magnitudes of the equilibrium constants are taken from reference [14] . The various species are in equilibrium and their concentrations are not depent on reaction mechanism. Therefore, any set of independent mass reaction equations will give the same result and we do not need to list a particular set of reactions.

Apart from the set of reaction equations four additional equations are required for obtaining the concentrations of various species because there are four different types of constituent atoms in the system. The first equation is that the total pressure of the system remains constant and equals to the summation of various species pressures. The second equation is related to the conservation of carbon atoms. It is assumed that there are no carbon consumption in the system and the distribution of carbon atoms is uniform in the reactor. Therefore, it is no necessary to include the transport equations for carbon atoms. The third one is the conservation equation of As atoms. Because of the high V / III ratio used in the MOVPE system the consumption of As atoms is very low. We also assume that the distribution of As atoms is uniform. The last equation which is the most important one is the conservation equation of Ga atoms. A new parameter, Ga/H ratio is introduced is this equation. This ratio is varied in the reactor because of the exhaust of Ga-containing species at the surface of the substrate. Therefore, fluid dynamic transport equations are required to determine the distribution profile of the Ga/H ratio. The calculations of the temperature dependent equilibrium constants also require incorporating the transport equations to determine the temperature profiles in the reactor.

The horizontal rectangular reactor considered here is depicted in figure 1. We assume that the gas flow is laminar flow and is fully developed before reaching the susceptor. Steady-state transport in the horizontal reactor is governed by the following two dimensional coupled conservation equations for mass, momentum, energy, and species

$$\frac{\partial \rho u}{\partial x} + \frac{\partial \rho v}{\partial y} = 0 \tag{1}$$

$$\rho u \frac{\partial u}{\partial x} + \rho v \frac{\partial u}{\partial y} = \frac{\partial}{\partial y} (\mu \frac{\partial u}{\partial y}) - \frac{\partial P}{\partial x} \tag{2}$$

$$\rho u C_p \frac{\partial T}{\partial x} + \rho v C_P \frac{\partial T}{\partial y} = \frac{\partial}{\partial y} (k_T \frac{\partial T}{\partial y}) \tag{3}$$

$$\rho u \frac{\partial W_i}{\partial x} + \rho v \frac{\partial W_i}{\partial y} + \rho F_i(W_i) = \frac{\partial}{\partial y}(\rho D_i \frac{\partial W_i}{\partial y}) + \frac{\partial}{\partial y}(\frac{\rho D_i \alpha_i W_i}{T} \frac{\partial T}{\partial y}) \tag{4}$$

$$\rho = \frac{PM}{RT} \tag{5}$$

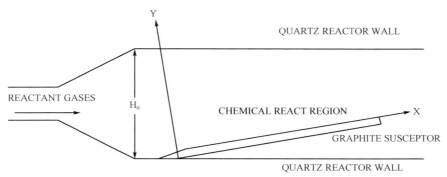

Fig. 1   Schematic diagram of a horizontal rectangular MOVPE reactor

Where ρ is the density of mixture, u and v are the velocity components in the x and y directions respectively, μ is viscosity of the mixture, P is total pressure, C_p is heat capacity of the mixture at constant pressure, k_i is thermal conductivity of the mixture, W_i is mole fraction of species i, D_i is diffusion coefficient of species i in carrier gas, M is mean molecular weight of the mixture, and $F_i(W_i)$ is the yield of the species i. Equation (4) is the mass transport equation of species i.

We assume that the nucleation of the solid particles does not occur in the MOVPE systems, then the total yield of Ga atoms in each species is zero at every point of the reactor,

$$\sum M_i F_i(W_i) = 0 \tag{6}$$

where M_i implies the number of Ga atoms in the molecular of species i. For species GaH_2 and CH_4, M_i equal 1 and 0, respectively. Using Equation (6) the mass transport equation (4) can be simplified and takes the follow form:

$$u \frac{\partial X}{\partial x} + v \frac{\partial X}{\partial y} = T \frac{\partial}{\partial y}\left(\frac{1}{T} \sum N_i D_i \frac{\partial W_i}{\partial y}\right) + T \frac{\partial}{\partial y}\left(\frac{1}{T^2} \frac{\partial T}{\partial y} \sum M_i D_i \alpha_i W_i\right) \tag{7}$$

where X is the total concentration of Ga atoms and equation (7) describes the distribution of Ga atoms in the MOVPE system. By the use of equations (1)−(7) together with the chemical equilibrium equations of the mass reaction law, the partial pressures of various species are determined.

The partial pressures of various species at the interface of the solid and gas phases is determined by heterogeneous equilibrium calculations [17, 18]. It has been shown that the equilibrium concentrations of Ga-containing species are several orders of magnitudes lower than the input concentration of TMGa. Therefore, we assume that the concentrations of Ga-containing species are zero at the surface of the substrate. The boundary conditions at the upper quartz wall are species diffusion flux equal to zero.

The dynamic parameters such as viscosity μ, thermal conductivity k_i, diffusion coefficient D_i, and thermal diffusion factor α_i are calculated using standard methods of molecular theory of gases[16]. The Lennard-Jones Fore Constants used in the calculation are determined through Svehla's methods and data[15].

Results and discussion

In the MOVPE systems where the reactants are diluted in a carrier gas, the continuity equation(1), the momentum equation(2) and the energy equation (3) are generally decoupled from the species equation(4) and could be resolved prior to the resolving of the species equations(4). The discrete differential equations are calculated numerically at a AST386 PREMIUM personal computer.

Iterative methods were adopted here in resolving the coupled mass transport equation (7) and chemical equilibrium equations. The species partial pressures were obtained.

Figure 2 and Figure 3 show the calculated spatial distributions of various species in a MOVPE system using TMGa and AsH_2, as sources at different pressure. It could be seen that arsine is mainly decomposed into As_4. The partial pressure of As_2 is lower than that of As_4 for the

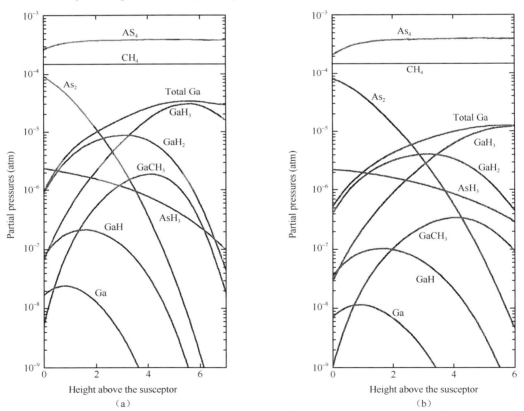

Fig. 2　Partial pressures of species via position in the reactor. Total system pressure is 1 atm, TMG concentration at inlet is 5E-3 mole%, V/III ratio is 30. Substrate temperature is 650℃. (a): x=2.5cm, (b): x=5.0cm

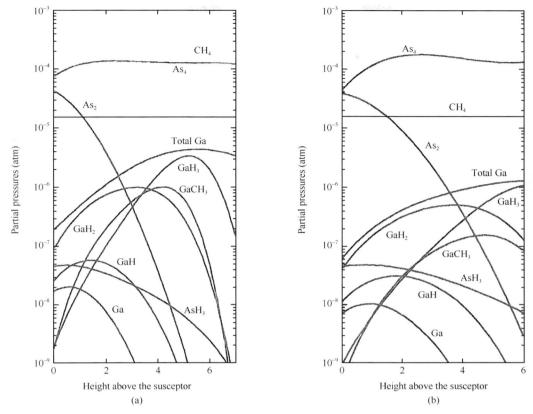

Fig. 3　Partial pressures of species via position in the reactor. Total system pressure is 0. 1 atm, TMG concentration at inlet is 5E-3 mole% , V/Ⅲ ratio is 100. Substrate temperature is 650℃. (a) ; x = 2. 5cm

(b) ; x = 5. 0cm

substrate temperature used here. At substrate temperature higher than 750℃ the partial pressure of As_2 might become dominant at the region close to the substrate. The most abundant Ga-containing species is GaH_2 in the lower half part of the reactor whereas in the upper half part of the reactor GaH_3 becomes dominant. The simple homogeneous equilibrium calculations have predicted that the partial pressure of $GaCH_3$ is higher than that of GaH_3 at atmospheric pressure and reduced pressure[14,17]. From the calculations here we might conclude that the partial pressure of $GaCH_3$ is at least one order of magnitude lower than the total pressure of Ga-containing species. The by-product of the growth is hydrogen and its diffusion away from the substrate is not a rate limiting step. The growth rate is determined chiefly by the diffusion of GaH_2 species towards the substrate.

It is clear from the calculations that the Ga-containing species are exhausted at the interface of the solid and gas phase while the As-containing species is nearly uniform in the reactor due to the large V/Ⅲ ratio used in the MOVPE system. The V/Ⅲ ratio near the surface of the substrate is much larger than the V/Ⅲ ratio at the inlet.

Figure 4 shows the calculated growth rate profile alone the susceptor. It have been shown that thermo-diffusions have large influence on the growth rate profiles. The growth rates at the entrance region are decreased quickly due to the thermo-diffusion. Therefore, the large temperature gradient in the entrance region of the reactor is good for the growth rate uniformity. After the rapid decrease the growth rate profile becomes flat and then decreases quickly again due to the exhaustion of the group Ⅲ elements. The length of the flat region of the growth rate profiles is greatly influenced by the height of the reactors. When the reactor height is bigger, longer flat region could be obtained even with the same total gas flow. The increase in the reactor height would improve the uniformity of the epilayer, but will decrease the efficiency of the growth. Low growth efficiency implies larger consumptions of the sources which are not economic and higher concentrations of unreacted sources at the outlet of the reactor which requires more efficient scrubbing system.

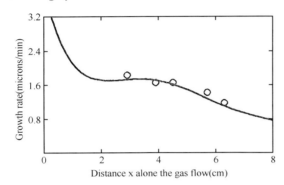

Fig. 4　Growth rate profile along the susceptor. The solid line is calculated from our model. The circles are experimental results of growing from TEG

The results obtained here are analogous to the MOVPE system using TEG and arsine as sources because the equilibrium gas phase compositions for TEG-AsH$_3$-H$_2$ system are essentially the same as those of TEG-AsH$_3$-H$_2$ system, except that the partial pressure of CH$_4$ is doubled. The experimental results of growth rates from TEG are also shown in figure 4. The growth conditions are: growth temperature 650℃; total pressure 0.1 atm; TEG molar fraction 5E-5 mole%; Ⅴ／Ⅲ ratio 100; Hydrogen flow 7 liters/min. Good agreement between theory and experiments were obtained.

Conclusion

A new theoretical model has been proposed in a laminar flow Ⅲ-Ⅴ MOVPE system. The fluid dynamic partial differential equations describing the mass, momentum and energy conservation are coupled with the thermodynamic calculations. It is reasonable to set the concentrations of Ga-containing species to zero at the surface of the substrate. The spatial distributions of various species are given in the TMG-Arsine-Hydrogen MOVPE system. The dominant Ga containing species is GaH$_2$ near the substrate and the nost abundant arsine related species is As$_i$ at the substrate temperature of 650℃. The influence of reactor geometry on the growth rate profiles is calculated. The design of reactor height is very important for obtain satisfactory uniformity with the lowest sources consumption. Theoretical results were compared with experiments and good agreement were obtained.

References

[1] K.F.Jensen, Journal of Crystal Growth, 98(1989), 148.

[2] E.P.Viser, C.R.Kleijn, C.A.M.Govers, C. J. Hoogendoorn and L.J.Giling, Journal of Crystal Growth, 94(1989) ,929.

[3] H.K.Moffat and K.F. Jensen, J.Electrochem.Soc, 135(1988) ,459.

[4] S.Patnaik, R.A.Brown and C.A. Wang, Journal of Crystal Growth, 96(1989) ,153.

[5] J. Ouazzani and F.Rosenberger, Journal of Crystal Growth, 100(1990) ,545.

[6] G.B.Stringfellow, Journal of Grystal Growth, 115(1991) ,1.

[7] N.I.Buchan, C.A.Laesen, and G.B.Stringfellow, Appl.Phys.Letters, 51(1987) ,1024.

[8] G.B.Stringfellow, Organometallic Vapor Phase Epitaxy:Theory and Practice(Academic Press, Boston, MA, 1989).

[9] M.E.Coltrin and R.J.Kee, Proc.Mater.Res.Soc. , 145(1989) ,119.

[10] K.F.Jensen, Journal of Crystal Growth, 107(1991) ,1.

[11] G.B.Stringfellow, Journal of Crystal Growth, 70(1984) ,133.

[12] M.R.Leys, and H.Veenvliet, Journal of Crystal Growth, 55(1981) ,145.

[13] J.Nishizawa, and T.Kurabayashi, J.Electrochem.Soc. , 130(1983) ,413.

[14] M.Tirtowidjojo and R.Pollard, Journal of Crystal Growth, 77(1986) ,200.

[15] R.A.Svehla, NASA Technical Report R-132(1962).

[16] J.O.Hirschfelder, C.F.Curtiss, and R.B.Bird, Molecular Theory of Gases and Liquids (John Wiley and Sons, New York, 1954).

[17] Jindrich Leitner, Jan Mikulec, Journal of Crystal Growth, 112(1991) ,437.

[18] A.Koukitu, T.Suzuki and H.Seki, Journat of Crystal Growth, 74(1986) ,181.

Photoluminescence Spectrum Study of the GaAs/Si Epilayer Grown by using a Thin Amorphous Si Film as Buffer Layer

Mao-Sen HAO, Jun-Wu LIANC, Lian-Xi ZHENG, Li-Seng DENG,
Zi-Bao XIAO and Xiong-Wei Hu

(*National Research Center for Optoelectronic Technology, Institute of Semiconductors,*
Chinese Academy of Sciences, P.O.Box 912, *Beijing* 100083, *China*)

(Received March 14, 1995; revised manuscript received April 28, 1995; accepted for publication June 12, 1995)

Abstract: Recently, we reported successful growth of high-quality GaAs/Si epilayers by using a very thin amorphous Si film as buffer layer. In this paper, the impurity properties of this kind of GaAs/Si epilayers have been studied by using PL spectrum, SIMS and Hall measurement. Compared to a typical PL spectrum of the GaAs/Si epilayers grown by conventional two-step method, a new peak was observed in our PL spectrum at the energy of 1.462 eV, which is assigned to the band-to-silicon acceptor recombination. The SIMS analysis indicates that the silicon concentration in this kind of GaAs/Si epilayers is about 10^{18} cm^{-3}. But its carrier concentration (about 4×10^{17} cm^{-3}) is lower than the silicon concentration. The lower carrier concentration in this kind of GaAs/Si epilayer can be interpreted both as the result of higher compensation and as the result of the formation of the donor-defect complex. We also found that the high-quality and low-Si-concentration GaAs/Si epilayers can be regrown by using this kind of GaAs/Si epilayer as substrate. The FWHM of the X-ray (004) rocking curve from this regrowth GaAs epilayer is 118″, it is much less than that of the first growth GaAs epilayer (160″) and other reports for the GaAs/Si epilayer grown by using conventional two-step method (~200″).

Keywords: GaAs/Si, photoluminescence, amorphous Si, SIMS, Hall measurement, double crystal X-ray

The integration of Si- and GaAs-Based circuits on the same Si wafer requires high-quality GaAs epitaxial layers on Si substrates. But due to the large difference in lattice constants (4%) and in the polar/nonpolar character of the two semiconductors, to get the highquality GaAs epitaxial layers on Si substrates is very difficulty. A large number of studies have concentrated on these problem. These works include the two-step growth technique,[1] the use of a strained layer superlattice,[2] and thermal annealing.[3] The crystal quality of the GaAs/Si epilayer was truely improved by these techniques, but it still have not arrived the level of the bulk GaAs wafers. Recently, we have found[4] that using a very thin amorphous Si(a-Si) film (~15Å) as buffer layer fellowed by the conventional two-step growth can greatly improve the quality of the GaAs epitaxial layer on Si substrates. Photoluminescense spectroscopy has been widely used to study impurity properties of the GaAs/Si epilayers.[5] In the near-band-gap region five charac-

teristic luminescence peaks are observed, which are labeled A-E in the literature. The peaks A
(1.50 eV) and B (1.48 eV), respectively, are identified as the heavy hole ($m_j = 3/2$) and
light hole ($m_j = 1/2$) bound exciton features. The difference in the thermal expansion coefficient
between GaAs and Si cause biaxial tension in the GaAs/Si epilayer and result in heavy and
light hole bands splitting. The peak C at 1.47 eV is attributed to band-to-carbon acceptor recombination, and the peak D at 1.45 eV may be a donor-related (perhaps Si) bound excitonic
transition. The peak E at 1.411 eV is assigned to a defect-to-carbon acceptor recombination.

In this letter, we present photoluminescense spectrum study of the GaAs/Si epilayer grown
by using a thin amorphous Si film as buffer layer. The band-to-silicon acceptor transition, which
corresponds to the peak at 1.46 eV, was observed in this kind of GaAs/Si epilayers.

Our sample was grown by using a low-pressure (76 Torr) metalogranic chemical vapor
deposition (MOCVD) equipment. P-type Si(001) substrates were cleaned *ex situ* in concentrated HF for 2 min at room temperature prior to loading into growth chamber. In the chamber, the
substrate was outgassed at 400℃ for 30 min, cleanned at 900℃ for 10 min. Then the substrate
temperature was reduced to 600℃ and 15 Å amorphous Si film was deposited by using SiH_4 as
source reactant at a growth rate of about 0.05Å/s. After depositing 180Å GaAs initial layer at
400℃, the final 2.2 μm-thick GaAs layer was grown at 700℃. Arsine and trimethyl-gallium
were used as source reactants for GaAs growth.

Our PL spectrums were obtained at low temperature (10 K) using an Ar^+ laser at 488 nm.
Figure 1 shows PL spectrums of the same sample measured with different excitation densities.
Because of the higher quality of this kind of GaAs/Si epilayers, the linewidth (FWHM) of 2.1
meV is observed for peak B, which is, to our knowledge, the narrowest reported so far.[6~8]
Compared to a typical PL spectrum of the GaAs/Si epilayers grown by conventional two-step
method, a new peak was observed in our PL spectrums at the energy of 1.462 eV, which is
labeled F and assigned to the band-to-silicon acceptor recombination. And the peak F is higher
than the peak C. This result shows that the concentration of the Si acceptor centers may be higher than that of the C acceptor centers in this case.

The biaxial tensile strain in GaAs epilayers on Si caused by the thermal expansion mismath
between GaAs and Si leads to a reduction of the band gap and the valence-band degeneracy. The
energy difference between conduction band to heavy-hole (ΔE_{hh}) and to light-hole valence band
(ΔE_{lh}) at the Γ point with respect to the unstrained value is given to the first order in ε by[9]

$$\Delta E_{hh} = [-2a(C_{11} - C_{12})/C_{11} - b(C_{11} + 2C_{12})/C_{11}]\varepsilon \qquad (1)$$
$$\Delta E_{lh} = [-2a(C_{11} - C_{12})/C_{11} + b(C_{11} + 2C_{12})/C_{11}]\varepsilon \qquad (2)$$

where C_{ij} are the elastic stiffness coefficients, a is the hydrostatic and b is the shear deformation
potential. The numerical value[10] for GaAs are $C_{11} = 11.8 \times 10^{11}$Pa, $C_{12} = 5.36 \times 10^{11}$Pa, $a = -9.8$
eV, and $b = -2.0$ eV.

W. Stolz, Guimaraes and Ploog[5] have used PLE spectroscopy measured at 4.5 K to
deduce a band gap of 1.494 eV associated with the heavy-hole valence band. The respective
band gap associated with the light-hole is determined to be 1.507 eV. So, the valence-band

splitting amounts to 13 meV. They also found that up to temperatures of 80 K the strain splitting of the valence band remains constant. Therefore we can use these values to analyze our PL spectrum measured at 10 K. According to eqs. (1) and (2), we can deduce a strain of $\varepsilon = 1.7 \times 10^{-3}$ in the GaAs/Si epilayer. A strain splitting of the acceptor level and the energy difference between the acceptor level and the conduction band with respect to unstrained value can also be calculated from eqs. (1) and (2), which is 21.137 meV for the acceptor level related to heavy-hole and 15.232 meV for the acceptor level related to light-hole (following from an acceptor deformation potential of $b' = -0.91$ eV[10]). Therefore the band-to-silicon acceptor recombination is expected at transition energies of 1.4626 eV and 1.4698 eV on the basis of the silicon acceptor binding energy of 35 meV. The calculated transition energy compares favourably with peak F at 1.462 eV. The recombination at slightly lower energies (1.459 eV) observed with lower excitation density can be assigned to the donor-to-acceptor recombination, which is saturated with increasing excitation density (Fig.1).

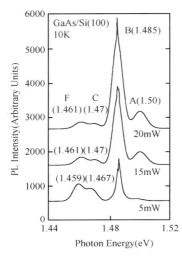

Fig.1 PL spectrums of the GaAs/Si epilayer grown by using a thin a-Si film as buffer layer

The above results show that in the GaAs/Si epilayer grown by using a thin a-Si film as buffer layer, there are some incorporated Si atoms occupying the As sites, and acting as acceptor. The SIMS analysis indicates that the two main residual impurities in GaAs/Si epilayers grown by using a thin a-Si film as buffer layer are also silicon and carbon. But the average concentration of silicon in this kind of GaAs layers is 1×10^{18} cm^{-3}. It is about one order of magnitude larger than that in the GaAs/Si epilayer grown by conventional two-step method.[11] In our sample the carbon concentration is about 10^{17} cm^{-3}, lower than the silicon concentration. Carbon, on the other hand, is incorporated both as a donor and as an acceptor in the MOCVD-grown GaAs layer.[12] The Hall measurement shows that the GaAs/Si epilayer grown by using a thin a-Si film as buffer layer is still n-type under our growth condition, and its carrier concentration is about 4×10^{17} cm^{-3}. This value is lower than the silicon concentration incorprated in the GaAs/Si epilayer. The lower carrier concentration in this kind of GaAs/Si epilayer can be interpreted both as the result of higher compensation and as the result of the formation of the donor-defect complex.[13]

A group of Nagoya Institute of Technology[14-16] have studied the mechanism of the Si-incorporation in the GaAs/Si epilayers carefully. They proposed that Si is in-corporated into the GaAs/Si epilayers mainly through a gas phase reaction and transport of Si to the growing GaAs layers. First, Si is incorporated into the gas phase by chemical reaction. Then Si is transportrated to the growing surface by diffusion within the boundary at the substrate surfaces. In our case, when the thin a Si film is deposited at 600℃ at the beginning of the growth, silicon atoms are also deposited on the graphite susceptor and on the chamber wall. Si "etching" in the following growth steps can take place not only at the back and the side of the Si substrate but also at the graphite susceptor and the chamber wall. The Si incorporation in the gas phase and growing GaAs layers will be greatly enhanced. So, our results provide evidence of the mechanis of the Si incorporation in the GaAs/Si epilayers proposed by the group of Nagoya Institute of Technology.

This problem greatly restricts the applicability of such structure. To overcome this problem, we used this kind of GaAs/Si epilayer as substrate to regrow GaAs epilayer in another growth run (still using MOCVD) and obtained the high-quality and low-Si-con-centration GaAs epilayer. The SIMS analysis indicates that the Si concentration in this GaAs layer is about 10^{17} cm^{-3}, much lower than that in the first growth GaAs layer. In PL spectrum from this GaAs layer, the peak of the band-to-silicon acceptor transition becomes very low showing the concentration of the Si acceptor centers in this GaAs layer is very low (Fig.2). The PL intensity of this GaAs layer is about two order of magnitude larger than that of the first growth GaAs layer. The X-ray rocking curve for this GaAs epilayer was also measured by using Rigaku SLX-1AL double X-ray diffractometer. The full width at half maximum (FWHM) of the X-ray (004) rocking curve (Fig.3) for this GaAs epilayer is 118″, lower than that of the first growth GaAs epilayer (160″) and other reports for the GaAs/Si epilayer grown by using conventional two-step method (~200″).[17-20] These results show that the crystal quality of this GaAs layer is much higher than that of the first growth GaAs layer. This improvement can be ascribed to thermal cyclic annealing because the sample was cooled down to the room temperature after first growth.

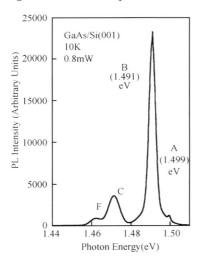

Fig.2   PL spectrum of the regrown
GaAs epilayer

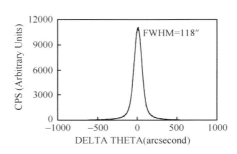

Fig.3   The X-ray (004) rocking curve
of the regrown GaAs epilayer

In summary, we have studied the impurity properties of the GaAs/Si epilayers grown by using a thin amorphous Si film as buffer layer. The band-to-silicon acceptor transition was observed in this kind of GaAs/Si epilayers. Because of the higher compensation and the formation of the donor-defect complex, the carrier concentration $(4 \times 10^{17}\ cm^{-3})$ in this kind of GaAs/Si epilayer is lower than its silicon concentration $(10^{18}\ cm^{-3})$. With such higher Si concentration, this kind of GaAs/Si epilayer is infavourable to fabricate optical device. But it can be used as substrate to regrow the high-quality and low-Si-concentration GaAs epilayer.

References

[1] M.Akiyama, Y.Kawarada and K.Kaminishi: Jpn.J.Appl.Phys.23 (1984) L843.

[2] T.Soga, S.Hattori, S.Sakai, M.Takeyasu and M.Umeno: Electron.Lett.20 (1984) 916.

[3] N.Chand, R.People, F.A.Baiochi, K.W.Wedcht and A.Y.Cho: Appl.Phys.Lett.48 (1986) 1815.

[4] M.S.Mao, J.W.Liang, X.J.Jing, L.S.Deng, Z.B.Xiao, L.X.Zheng and X.W.Hu: to be published in Chinese Phys.Lett.

[5] W.Stolz, F.E.G.Guimaraes and K.Ploog: J.Appl.Phys.63(1988) 492.

[6] Y.R.Xing, Z.Jamal, T.B.Joyce, T.J.Bullough, C.J.Kiely and P.J.Goodhew: Appl.Phys.Lett.62 (1993) 1653.

[7] V.Alberts, J.H.Necthling and A.W.Leitch: J.Appl.Phys.75(1994) 7258.

[8] G.W.Turner: *Semiconductor-based Heterostructure: Interfacial Structure and Stability* (1986) p.235.

[9] C.P.Kuo, S.K.Vong, R.M.Cohen and G.B.Stringfellow: J.Appl.Phys.57 (1985) 5428.

[10] O.Madelung, M.Schulz and H.Weiss: *Semiconductors*, eds.Landolt-Bornstein Bd. (Springer, Berlin, Heidelberg, New York, 1982) Vol.17a.

[11] S.Nozaki, N.Moto, T.Egawa, A.T.Wu, T.Soga, T.Jimbo and M.Umeno: Jpn.J.Appl.Phys.29 (1990) 138.

[12] P.D.Dapkus, H.M.Manasevit, K.L.Hess, T.S.Low and E.Stillman: J.Cryst.Growth 55 (1981) 10.

[13] T.N.Theis, P.M.Mooney and S.L.Wright: Phys.Rev.Lett.60 (1988) 361.

[14] S.Nozaki, J.J.Murray, A.T.Wu, T.George, E.R.Weber and M.Umeno: Appl.Phys.Lett.55 (1989) 1674.

[15] T.George, E.R.Weber, S.Nozaki, J.J.Murray, A.T.Wu and M.Umeno: Appl.Phys.Lett.55 (1989) 2090.

[16] T.Egawa, H.Tada, Y.Kobayashi, T.Soga, T.Jimbo and M.Umeno: Appl.Phys.Lett.57 (1990) 1179.

[17] C.C.Phua, T.C.Chong and W.S.Lau: Jpn.J.Appl.Phys.33(1994) L405.

[18] N.Chand, F.Ren, A.T.Macrander, J.P.Van der Ziel, A.M.Sergent, R.Hull, S.N.G.Chu, Y.K.Chen and D.V.Lang: J.Appl.Phys.67 (1990) 2343.

[19] A.Georgakilas, P.Panayotatos, J.Stoemenos, J.L.Mourrain and A.Christou: J.Appl.Phys.71 (1992) 2679.

[20] T.Yodo, M.Tamura and T.Saitoh: J.Cryst.Growth 141(1994) 331.

Dissociated Screw Dislocation Which Can Relieve Strain Energy in the Epitaxial Layer of GeSi on Si(001)

Xue-Yuan Wan and Jun-Wu Liang

(*Institute of Semiconductors, Chinese Academy of Sciences, P.O. Box 912, Beijing 100083, People's Republic of China*)

Ming-Liang Liu

(*Institute of Computer Science and Technology, Peking University, Beijing 100080, People's Republic of China*)

Xiao-Jun Jin

(*Institute of Semiconductors, Chinese Academy of Sciences, P.O. Box 912, Beijing 100083, People's Republic of China*)

(*Received 3 October* 1996)

Abstract: A dissociated screw dislocation parallel to the interface was found in the epitaxial layer of the $Ge_{0.17}Si_{0.83}$ Si(001) system. It is shown that this dissociated screw dislocation which consists of two 30° partials can relieve misfit strain energy, and the relieved misfit energy is proportional to the width of the stacking fault between the two partials. [S0163-1829(97)08815-2]

Lattice-mismatched semiconductor heterostructures have been researched extensively in the last two decades. In lattice-mismatched semiconductor heterostructures, there are misfit dislocations introduced in the interface to relieve the misfit strain energy between the growing layer and the substrate when the thickness of the growing layer reaches a critical thickness.[1] It is generally believed that a dislocation which can relieve misfit strain must have an edge component, so a single screw dislocation cannot relieve misfit strain, although in some circumstances arrays of screw dislocations can relieve misfit energy.[2] If a screw dislocation in the interface dissociates into two 30° dislocations, can it relieve misfit strain? Dissociated 60° misfit dislocations have been observed often in strained interfaces or epilayers, such as in $In_xGa_{1-x}As/GaAs$ (Refs. 3 and 4) by high-resolution transmission electron microscopy (HRTEM), in $Si_{1-x}Ge_x/Si$ (Refs. 5 and 6) by plan-view TEM or weak beam TEM, but few dissociated screw dislocations have been observed in strained interfaces and epilayers. We observed a dissociated screw dislocation consisting of two 30° partials in a $Ge_{0.17}Si_{0.83}/Si$ epilayer by HRTEM, and we will discuss whether it can relieve misfit strain in this paper.

The epitaxial $Ge_{0.17}Si_{0.83}/Si$ layers with thickness of 4000 Å were grown at 870℃ on a Si(001) substrate by low-pressure chemical vapor deposition. The material structures were examined by cross sectional HRTEM performed in a H9000NAR microscope operated at 300 kV.

原载于:Phys.Rev.B,1997,55(15):9259-9262.

Figure 1(a) shows a HRTEM image of the epitaxial layer of the sample looking along $[\bar{1}10]$ zone axis. Figure 1(b) is the magnified image. There is a dissociated dislocation with an intrinsic stacking fault (SF) between its two partials. It is well established that HRTEM can directly characterize dislocations through Burgers circuit analysis. When an end-on straight dislocation is imaged by HRTEM, it has only the edge component of its Burger vector projected.[7] So in a lattice image, a Burgers circuit around a dislocation results in a vector which is the edge component of the Burgers vector of the dislocation. A screw dislocation has a zero edge component, so a Burgers circuit around a screw dislocation in a lattice image results in a null vector. A 30° Shockley partial and a 90° Shockley partial has an edge component of <112>/12 and an edge component of <112>/6, respectively,[7] so a Burgers circuit around a 30° partial results in a vector of <112>/12, whose magnitude is $\frac{1}{3}$ the distance between projected lattice points along the <112> direction in this lattice image (which is <112>/4); a Burgers circuit around a 90° partial results in a vector of <112>/6, whose magnitude is $\frac{2}{3}$ the distance between projected lattice points along the <112> direction in the lattice image.[8] Based on the above discussion, we can draw Burgers circuits around dislocations to characterize them. Figure 2 is a schematic diagram of a partial whose line direction is $[\bar{1}10]$, the same as the dislocation in Fig. 1. Some crystalline directions are indicated. By the method which is also used by Hwang et al.,[8] we can draw a Burgers circuit around the partial and get a vector (which is represented by an arrow), if its magnitude is $\frac{1}{3}$ the distance between projected lattice points along $[\overline{112}]$ direction, then it is a 30° partial; if its magnitude is $\frac{2}{3}$ the distance between lattice points along $[\overline{112}]$, then it is a 90° partial.

In Fig. 1 (b) a Burgers circuit around the whole dissociated dislocation results in a null vector, so the dissociated dislocation might be a screw dislocation. A careful Burgers circuit around the lower partial yields a vector whose magnitude is $\frac{1}{3}$ the distance between lattice points in this $(\bar{1}10)$ projected plane. So it is a 30° partial. Similar analysis of the upper partial shows that it is also a 30° partial. So, we think that this is a screw dislocation which dissociated into two 30° partials, e.g., $\frac{1}{2}[\overline{110}]-\frac{1}{6}[\overline{211}]+\frac{1}{6}[\overline{121}]$.

In a compressive film system where the lattice constant of the film is larger than that of the substrate, for total dislocations which are parallel to the interface, not all of them can relieve the misfit strain energy. If the inserted half atomic plane (extra half plane) of such a dislocation lies on the side of the substrate, it can relieve the misfit strain; if the inserted half atomic plane lies on the side of the film, it cannot relieve, but rather increases the misfit strain.

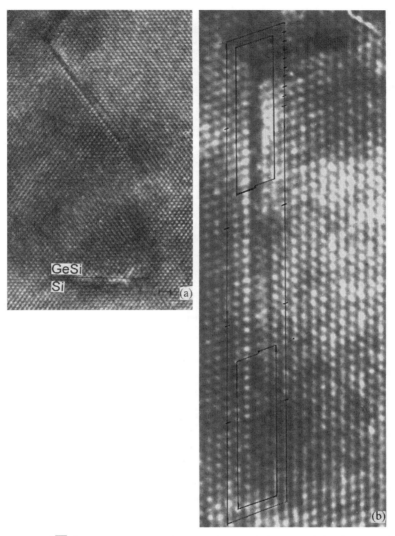

Fig. 1　High-resolution $[\overline{1}10]$ lattice image of a dissociated screw dislocation. (a) The original image with the interface. (b) The magnified image. The Burgers circuits around the partial dislocations results in Burgers vectors whose projected magnitude is $\dfrac{1}{3}$ the distance between lattice points in this $(\overline{1}10)$ projected plane. Note that for the lower partial (which is nearer to the interface than another partial), the distance between the atomic planes below the SF is smaller than that above the SF, so it can relieve misfit strain energy; for the upper partial, the circumstance is reversed. The marker represents 10 Å

For a partial dislocation, the distance between the atomic planes on one side of the SF is smaller than that on another side of the SF, we can use the conception of the "inserted plane" for 30° partials used by Gerthsen *et al*.[9] For the lower partial, the distance between the atomic planes below the SF is smaller than that above the SF, so we can say the inserted plane of the lower partial lies on the side of the substrate and terminates at the SF, while the inserted half plane of the upper partial lies on the side of the film and terminates at the SF. So the upper partial increases the misfit strain, while the lower partial relieves the misfit strain. Reference 3 shows a dissociated 60° dislocation consisting of a 90° and a 30°partial which can relieve the misfit strain in compressive films, we can see that the distance between the atomic planes below the SF is indeed smaller than the one above the SF,[3] and this kind of 30° partial can relieve the misfit strain. Also, the misfit strain relieved or increased by such a dislocation is proportional to the distance from it to the free film surface [Eq. (3) in Ref. 4].

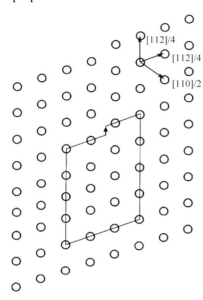

Fig. 2　The schematic diagram for the analysis of Shockley partial dislocations. We can draw a Burgers circuit from the stacking fault, around the partial, and end at the stacking fault, then we can get a vector (represented by an arrow). If the magnitude of the vector is $\frac{1}{3}$ the distance between lattice points along $[\overline{1}12]$, then it is a 30° partial; if the magnitude of the vector is $\frac{2}{3}$ the distance between lattice points along $[\overline{1}12]$, then it is a 90° partial

It must be indicated that it is the edge component of the 30° partials that relieves misfit strain, not the 30° partials themselves. The strain energy relieved per unit length of the lower partial is given by[4]

$$E_{\varepsilon1} = \frac{2\mu b_p(1+\upsilon)}{1-\upsilon}\varepsilon h_1 \cos\theta_1 \tag{1}$$

and the strain energy relieved per unit length of the upper partial is given by

$$E_{\varepsilon2} = \frac{2\mu b_p(1+\upsilon)}{1-\upsilon}\varepsilon h_2 \cos\theta_1 \tag{2}$$

so the net strain energy relieved per unit length of the two partials is given by

$$\begin{aligned} E_{\varepsilon} &= \frac{2\mu b_p(1+\upsilon)}{1-\upsilon}\varepsilon(h_1-h_2)\cos\theta_1 \\ &= \frac{2\mu b_p(1+\upsilon)}{1-\upsilon}\varepsilon(\Gamma\cos\phi)\cos\theta_1, \end{aligned} \tag{3}$$

where b_p, υ, ε, and μ are the magnitude of the Burgers vectors of the partials, Poisson's ratio, the residual misfit strain, and the shear modulus, respectively, h_1 and h_2 are the distances of the lower and upper partial from the free epitaxial surface, respectively, $h_1 \approx h$, the film thickness, because the lower partial is near the interface. Γ is the SF width, θ_1 is the angle between the Burgers vector and the direction in the interface which is perpendicular to the intersection line of the glide plane and the interface. For the 30° partial, $\theta_1 = 73.2°$. ϕ is the angle between the normal to the surface and the direction in the glide plane that is perpendicular to the intersection of the glide plane and the interface. So in this circumstance, a dissociated screw dislocation parallel to the interface can relieve misfit strain energy, and the relieved strain energy is proportional to the SF width. The calculated SF width Γ by the formulation of SF width[10] in bulk materials is about 30 Å. Here we use the following values: $\mu = 6 \times 10^{10}$ Nm^{-2}, $v = 0.28$ and $b_p = 2.22$ Å. The SF energy[11] is 50–80 mJ/m^2, here we use the value of 65 mJ/m^2. The actual SF width obtained from Fig. 1 is about 120 Å, which is larger by a factor of 4 than the calculated value of the formulation for bulk material. However, the force exerted on the edge components of the two partials from the stress in the film contributes to the SF width (the forces exerted on the screw components of the two partials from the stress in the film have no contribution to the SF width because they are in the line direction of the partials), also the forces from the stress in the film make the two partials glide in opposite directions, because their edge components are in opposite directions. This is different from the case of a dissociated 60° dislocation where the edge components of the two partials are in the same direction. In the compressive film case, for a dissociated 60° dislocation, the force acted on the trailing 90° partial from the stress in the film is two times as large as the one acted on the leading 30° partial,[12] so the SF is narrowed by the stress in the film.

Zou and Cockayne[4] have presented formulations of dissociation width for dissociated 60° misfit dislocations by the method of energy minimization. This formulation can be extended to the case of a screw dislocation with "$E_{\varepsilon r(A)}$" in Eq. (3) in Ref. 4 substituted by "$E_{\varepsilon 2}$" here, thus we can get an equation similar to Eq. (13) in Ref. 4, which is

$$\Gamma = \frac{\mu b^2 (2 - v)}{24\pi (1 - v)(\gamma - \sigma_d - \sigma_{ss})} \left(1 - \frac{2v\cos 2\theta}{2 - v} \right) \tag{4}$$

with

$$\sigma_d = \frac{\mu b^2 (1 - v\cos^2\theta_p)\cos\theta_1}{12\pi (1 - v)(h_1 - \cos\theta_1 \Gamma)} \tag{5}$$

and

$$\sigma_{ss} = \frac{2\mu b (1 + v)}{\sqrt{3}(1 - v)}\cos\theta_p \cos\theta_1 \varepsilon, \tag{6}$$

where $\theta = 0$ (which is the angle between the Burgers vector of the screw dislocation and its line direction), $\theta_p = 30°$ (which is the angle between the Burgers vector of the partial dislocations and their line directions), ε is the residual strain which cannot be substituted by the misfit strain f, it can be calculated according to Hu.[12]

In Eq. (4), the sign in front of "σ_{ss}" is "$-$," this is different from Eq. (13) in Ref. 4 where the one is "$+$," this indicates that the residual strain in the epilayer will widen the dissociate screw dislocation described here, and narrow the dissociated 60° dislocations as indicated by Marée *et al.*[13] Equation (4) might be one explanation for the SF width observed here being so large.

However, there are other factors that affect the SF width, such as the Peierls frictional forces and the structure of the partials. The surface relaxation effect[14,15] in the strained thin foil sample of HRTEM might also affect the width of the SF.

In conclusion, in the epitaxial $Ge_{0.17}Si_{0.83}$ layer on $Si(001)$, we observed a dissociated screw dislocation parallel to the surface dissociated into two partials with the inserted plane of the lower partial in the side of the substrate and the inserted plane of the upper partial lying in the side of the film. This dissociated screw dislocation can relieve misfit strain; the relieved misfit energy is proportional to the width of the SF between the two partials.

The author is indebted to L. P. You and X. P. Zhang for technical assistance. The work has been partly supported by the Beijing Zhongguancun Collaborated Measurement and Testing Foundation.

References

[1] F. C. Frank and J. H. Van der Merwe, Proc. R. Soc. London Ser. A 198, 205 (1949).

[2] J. W. Matthews, in *Dislocations in Solids*, Dislocations in Crystal, edited by F. R. N. Nabarro (North-Holland, Amsterdam, 1979), Vol. 2, p. 492.

[3] Y. Chen, N. D. Zakharov, P. Werner, Z. Liliental-Weber, and J. Washburn, Appl. Phys. Lett. 63, 1536 (1993).

[4] J. Zou and D. J. H. Cockayne, J. Appl. Phys. 77, 2448 (1995).

[5] R. Hull, J. C. Bean, D. Bahnck, J. M. Bonar, L. J. Peticolas, D. Gerthsen, F. A. Ponce, and G. B. Anderson, Inst. Phys. Conf. Ser. 117, 497 (1991).

[6] K. Rajan, Appl. Phys. Lett. 57, 1135 (1990); 59, 2564 (1991).

[7] Schwartzman and Sinclair, J. Electron. Mater. 20, 805 (1991).

[8] D. M. Hwang, R. Bhat, S. A. Schwarz, and C. Y. Chen, Mater. Res. Soc. Proc. 263, 421 (1992).

[9] D. Gerthsen, F. A. Ponce, and G. B. Anderson, Inst. Phys. Conf. Ser. 100, 23 (1989).

[10] J. p. Hirth and J. Lothe, *Theory of Dislocations* (Wiley, New York, 1982).

[11] A. Geoge and J. Rabier, Rev. Phys. Appl. 22, 941 (1987).

[12] S. M. Hu, J. Appl. Phys. 70, R53 (1991).

[13] P. M. J. Marée, J. C. Barbour, J. F. van der Veen, K. L. Kavanagh, C. W. T. Bulle-Lieuwma, and M. P. A. Viegers, J. Appl. Phys. 62, 4413 (1987).

[14] M. M. J. Treacy and J. M. Gibson, J. Vac. Sci. Technol. B 4, 1458 (1986).

[15] R. E. Mallard, G. Feuillet, and P.-H. Jouneau, Inst. Phys. Conf. Ser. 117, 17 (1991).

Hrtem Study of Dislocations in GeSi/Si Heterostructures Grown by VPE

JUNWU LIANG, XUEYUAN WAN

(*Institute of Semiconductors, Chinese Academy of Sciences, P. O. Box* 912, *Beijing* 100083, *China*)

Abstract: GeSi/Si heterostructures grown by atmospheric chemical vapor epitaxy have been studied by cross sectional high resolution transmission electron microscopy (HRTEM). For the first time we have observed an interstitial-type dislocation loop which is located near to a 60° misfit dislocation in the initially prepared GeSi/Si sample. After 30 minutes observation, the interstitial-type dislocation loop disappeared and the 60° dislocation climbed. Moreover, we have observed dissociated 60° dislocations with about 9 nm width of stacking fault existing in silicon substrate.

Introduction

In lattice-mismatched semiconductor heterostructures, there are misfit dislocations introduced in the interface to relieve the misfit strain energy between the growing layer and the substrate when the thickness of the growing layer reaches a critical thickness[1].

High resolution transmission electron microscope (HRTEM) is a powerful tool for the study of dislocations in crystals. HRTEM has been also widely used in the research of dislocations in lattice-mismatched semiconductor heterostructures. By cross sectional HRTEM, the core of a dislocation can be researched conveniently.

The climb phenomenon of a $1/3<111>$ Frank dislocation in CdTe material has been observed by Yamashita and Sinclair [2] using HRTEM. However, the existence of interstitial-type dislocation loop and its interaction with a 60° dislocation have never been reported for GeSi/Si heterostructures. In this paper we present the observation of the climb of a 60° dislocation induced by a nearby interstitial-type dislocation loop. As far as we know, this is observed for the first time.

Dissociated 60° misfit dislocations have been observed often in strained heterostructures, such as in $In_xGa_{1-x}As/GaAs$[3, 4] in $Si_{1-x}Ge_x/Si$[5, 6, 7] by HRTEM, plan-view TEM or weak beam TEM. Y. Xin et al.[7] reported that the leading 90° partial is at the SiGe/Si interface while the 30° partial located in the Si substrate and the dissociation width of the dissociated dislocation is 6 nm. In the present work, the dissociation of 60° dislocations in GeSi/Si heterostructures is examined by HRTEM.

Experiment

The epitaxial Ge_xSi_{1-x} layers with x = 0.15−0.17 and thickness of 4000Å were grown at

---

原载于：Mat. Res. Soc. Symp. Proc. 1997, 442: 349-352.

870℃ on Si(001) substrate by atmospheric chemical vapor phase epitaxy. The resource gases are dichlorosilane and germane. Before deposition, the Si wafers are chemically polished by HC1.

The material structures were examined by HRTEM performed using a H9000NAR microscope operated at 300kV. The cross sectional samples are prepared by mechanic polishing and argon ion beam thinning procedure.

Results and discussion

Climb of a 60° misfit dislocation

Fig. 1 (a) is a [110] lattice image of a $Si_{0.85}Ge_{0.15}/Si$ sample in which the misfit is about 0.6%. There is a Lomer dislocation which consists of two 60° misfit dislocations. In the upper right side of the Lomer dislocation, we can see another high contrast area (indicated by dots). Here is an interstitial-type dislocation loop which squeezes in between two atomic planes. This loop is only about one lattice spacing apart from the right-sided 60° misfit dislocation which forms the Lomer dislocation with another 60° misfit dislocation. It is obvious that the lower part of the loop nearly touches the right-sided 60° dislocation. In Fig.1(b) the schematic lattice fringe corresponding to the HRTEM image in Fig. 1 (a) is shown.

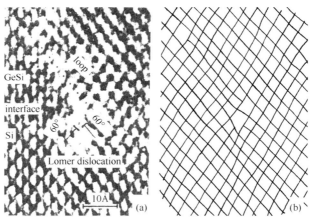

Fig. 1　HREM image taken initially showing a Lomer dislocation consisting of two 60° dislocations and an interstitial type dislocation loop and the schematic lattice fringe corresponding to it. (a) the HRTEM image. (b) the schematic lattice fringe

Fig. 2(a) is the lattice image of the same area of the same sample taken after thirty minutes. It is evident that the interstitial loop has been attracted to the right-sided 60° dislocation and disappeared, and this right-sided 60° dislocation has climbed by about 30Å. Fig.2(b) represents the schematic lattice fringe corresponding to Fig. 2(a).

It is well known that ion radiation during preparation of TEM specimens by ion milling and electron radiation during TEM observation of specimens might generate defects, such as interstitial-type loops [8], and can affect the configuration of defects in the specimens.

The interstitial-type loop in Fig. 1(a) might be generated during the preparation of TEM

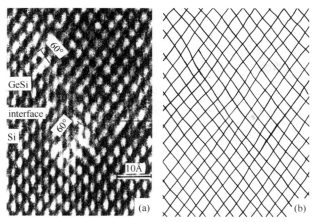

Fig. 2　HREM image taken after 30 min. showing the disappearance of the interstitial type loop and the climbing of the right-sided 60° dislocation and the schematic lattice fringe corresponding to it. (a) the HR-TEM image. (b) the schematic lattice fringe

sample or during the TEM observation. When observed by TEM the second time, the electronic beam increased locally the temperature of the sample and the loop moved to the nearby 60° dislocation, so the loop disappeared, the 60° dislocation climbed.

The Dissociated 60° Dislocation

We have observed some 60° and a few screw dislocations. Some of them dissociated. Fig. 3 shows a HRTEM image of a $Si_{0.83}Ge_{0.17}$ sample. There is a dissociated dislocation located near the interface in the epilayer. Using the Burgers vector analysis method of dislocations, a Burgers circuit around this dissociated dislocation shows it is a dissociated 60° dislocation. A Burgers circuit around the upper partial yields a vector whose magnitude is 2/3 the distance

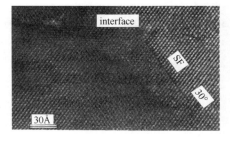

Fig. 3　A dissociated 60° dislocation. The 90° partial is located near the interface, and the 30° partial is located in the substrate

between lattice points in this ($\bar{1}10$) projected plane, this is the nature of 90° partials. The stacking fault between the two partials is an intrinsic one.

The 90° partial is located at the $Si_{0.17}Ge_{0.83}/Si$ interface whereas the 30° partial is toward the inside of silicon substrate. This is consistent with the result reported by Y. Xin et al. [7] Nevertheless, the tails associated with the 90° and 30° partials reported by them are not observed in our samples.

In close vicinity to the dissociated 60° dislocation also exist some defect configurations whose nature and the reason remain unclear.

The dissociation width of the stacking fault is about 9 nm which is greater than the reported width value of 6 nm. This might be caused by the inhomogeneous strain existing in the GeSi/Si heterostructures.

CONCLUSIONS

In conclusion, by means of HRTEM, for the first time we observed climb process of a 60° misfit dislocation by a nearby interstitial-type dislocation loop in the GeSi epilayer near the interface of SiGe/Si. Also we observed a dissociated 60° misfit dislocation with 90° partial lying near the interface and the 30° partial lying in the inside of the silicon substrate. The dissociation width of the stacking fault reaches about 90Å.

References

[1] F. C. Frank and J. H. Van der Merwe, Proc. R. Soc. London Ser. A 198, p. 205 (1949).

[2] T. Yamashita, and R. Sinclair, 1983, in Defects in Semiconductors, edited by J. Narayan and T. Y. Tan (Mat. Res. Soc. Sym. Proc. 14, North-Holland, New York:), p. 295.

[3] Y. Chen, N. D. Zakharov, P. Werner, Z. Liliental-Weber, and J. Washburn, Appl. Phys. Lett. 63, p. 1536 (1993).

[4] J. Zou and D. J. H. Cockayne, J. Appl. Phys. 77, p. 2448 (1995).

[5] R. Hull, J. C. Bean, D. Bahnck, J. M. Bonar, and L. J. Peticolas, D. Gerthsen, F. A. Ponce, and G. B. Anderson, in Microscopy of Semiconducting Materials 1991, edited by A. G. Cullis and N. J. Long (Inst. of Phys. Conf. Ser. No. 117, Bristol, 1991), p. 497.

[6] K.Rajan, Appl. Phys. Lett. 57, p. 1135 (1990), 59, 2564 (1991).

[7] Y. Xin, P. D. Brown, R. E. Schaublin and C. J. Humphreys, in Microscopy of Semiconducting Materials 1995, edited by A. G. Cullis and A. E. Staton-Bevan (Inst. of Phys. Conf. Ser. No. 146, Bristol, 1995), p. 183.

[8] G. Lu and F. Phillipp, in Microscopy of Semiconducting Materials 1991, edited by A. G. Cullis and N. J. Long (Inst. of Phys. Conf. Ser. No. 117, Bristol, 1991), p. 367.

Kinetics and Transport Model for the Chemical Vapor Epitaxy of Ge$_x$Si$_{1-x}$

Xiaojun Jin*, Junwu Liang

(*Institute of Semiconductors, Chinese Academy of Sciences, P.O. Box 912,*

Beijing 100083, People's Republic of China Received 8 September 1995; accepted 20 August 1996)

Abstract: A numerical model that combines mass transport and surface kinetics was applied, for the first time, to the chemical vapor epitaxy of Ge$_x$Si$_{1-x}$. The temperature, velocity and concentration fields were calculated from the conservation equations for energy, momentum and species coupled with the boundary conditions on the growth surface which were determined by surface kinetics. The deposition rates of Si and Ge were assumed to be limited, respectively, by surface kinetics and mass transport. A theoretical relation between the initial conditions and the Ge composition in the solid was established. The calculated growth rate as well as the Ge composition in the solid and its dependence on growth temperature agree well with experimental data.

1. Introduction

The epitaxial growth of Ge$_x$Si$_{1-x}$ strained layers on Si substrates has been attracting increasing interest in recent years due to the potential application in the field of high speed devices and infrared detectors. Ge$_x$Si$_{1-x}$ epilayers have been grown either by molecular beam epitaxy (MBE) or by chemical vapor deposition (CVD)[1-3]. Deposition temperatures used range from 500℃ to 1000℃, and total pressures from 0.001 to 1×10^6 Pa. Recently, various investigations of the Si-Ge-H-Cl system have been based on the successful hydrogen reduction of chloride and chlorosilane in Si technologies. For the SiH$_2$Cl$_2$+GeH$_4$+H$_2$ source, both atmospheric and low pressure processes at lower temperatures have been reported [4-6].

Theoretical models for the growth of Si$_{1-x}$Ge$_x$ epilayers have been proposed by numerous authors[6-10]. In these works, it was assumed that the surface kinetics of Ge$_x$Si$_{1-x}$ growth in the temperature range 550-1000℃, the range in which the growth was usually carried out, is limited by the rate of chemical surface reactions. These reactions were denoted as MH$_4$ = (H-MH$_3$)* →H(a)+MH$_3$, where M=Si or Ge, and (H-MH$_3$)* represents an activated complex generated on collision with the surface. Since the desorption of H from the substrate surface has a great influence on the growth, the difference between the H desorption from a Ge$_x$Si$_{1-x}$ surface and from a Si surface was used to explain the growth rate enhancement experienced with Ge$_x$Si$_{1-x}$ epilayers. In the above works, the partial pressures of reactants near the surface of the substrate were simply assumed to be equal to their initial partial pressures. The Ge composition

原载于:J. Cryst. Growth,1997,172:381-388.

* Corresponding author. Fax: +86 10 6256 1250.

(mole fraction x) of the solid film was estimated from the initial ratio of Si source to Ge source prior to the calculation of the growth rate. A theoretical relation between the initial conditions (including the flow rate of the Ge and Si source and carrier gas, and deposition temperature, etc.) and the Ge composition in the solid film was not established. In addition, the fact that in Ge_xSi_{1-x}, epitaxy the deposition of Ge below 650℃ is limited by surface diffusion/reactions while above 650℃ it is limited by the mass transport [4, 10] was not taken into account.

In the following, we present a combined kinetics and transport model for the chemical vapor epitaxy of Ge_xSi_{1-x} in which the above findings are appropriately accounted for. In particular, we incorporate the modification of the vapor species concentration by thermal expansion, i.e. the by the temperature distribution in the reactor. We apply the model to the Ge_xSi_{1-x}. chemical vapor epitaxy under atmospheric and low pressure conditions and compare the resulting flow, temperature and concentration fields. The resulting Ge composition is investigated as a function of growth temperature and compared with experimental results.

2. Model description

The velocity, temperature and concentration fields can be described by the following well-known equations

$$\nabla \cdot (\rho u) = 0, \tag{1}$$

$$(u \cdot \nabla) u = \nabla \cdot (\mu \nabla u) - \nabla p, \tag{2}$$

$$\nabla \cdot (\rho c_p \nabla T) = \nabla \cdot (k_T \nabla T), \tag{3}$$

$$\nabla \cdot (u w_i) = \nabla \cdot \{D_i [\nabla w_i - \alpha_i w_i \nabla \ln(T)]\}, \tag{4}$$

$$\rho = \sum_i \frac{p_i}{RT} m_i \tag{5}$$

where ρ is the gas density, u is the velocity vector, μ the absolute viscosity, p the total pressure, c_p is the heat capacity at constant pressure, k_T is the thermal conductivity, T is the temperature, w the weight fraction, i denotes the species of reactant, p is the partial pressure and m is the molecular weight. D_i and α_i represent the binary molecular diffusion coefficient and thermal diffusion coefficient, respectively.

Ouazzani and Rosenberger [11] compared the result of the two-dimensional and three-dimensional fluid-dynamic model with the experimental data. They showed that for a high aspect ratio the side-wall of the reactor has little influence on the velocity, temperature and concentration fields in the reactor. The aspect ratio of our reactor is about 3.5. Thus, to reduce the CPU time and simplify the calculation, we restrict our model to two dimensions, with coordinate x along the substrate, with $x = 0$ at the substrate's leading edge. The coordinate y characterizes the height above the substrate. The upper reactor wall is positioned at $y = H$. In addition, our model is based on the following assumptions:

1. The flow of the reaction mixture is steadily laminar, with fully developed velocity before arriving at the substrate.

2. Forced flow dominates over buoyancy-driven flow, such that the gravity force can be ignored.

3. The diffusion of mass and heat along the direction of flow is negligible.

4. Chemical reactions take only place on the surface of the substrate. There are no chemical reactions in the gas mixture.

For the $SiH_2Cl_2 + GeH_4 + H_2$ source, the dominant transport species are $SiH_2Cl_2 + GeH_4$ under the assumption that there are no chemical reactions in the gas mixture. The surface reactions for Si incorporation from SiH_2Cl_2 are [12]

$$2H \longleftrightarrow H_2(g), \tag{6}$$

$$SiH_2Cl_2(g) \longrightarrow \mathbf{SiH_2Cl_2}, \tag{7}$$

$$\mathbf{SiH_2Cl_2} \longrightarrow \mathbf{Si} + 2HCl(g), \tag{8}$$

$$\mathbf{SiH_2Cl_2} \longrightarrow SiH_2Cl_2(g), \tag{9}$$

where (g) denotes molecules in the gas, and the bold symbols denote molecules on the growth surface. The deposition rate of Ge is assumed to be limited by mass transport.

Considering the assumptions made above, Eqs.(1)—(5) can be simplified to

$$\rho \frac{\partial u_x}{\partial x} + \rho \frac{\partial u_y}{\partial y} = 0, \tag{10}$$

$$\rho u_x \frac{\partial u_x}{\partial x} + \rho u_y \frac{\partial u_y}{\partial y} = \frac{\partial}{\partial y}\left(\mu \frac{\partial u_x}{\partial y}\right) - \frac{\partial P}{\partial x}, \tag{11}$$

$$\rho u_x c_p \frac{\partial T}{\partial x} + \rho u_y c_p \frac{\partial T}{\partial y} = \frac{\partial}{\partial x}\left(k_T \frac{\partial T}{\partial x}\right) + \frac{\partial}{\partial y}\left(k_T \frac{\partial T}{\partial y}\right), \tag{12}$$

$$u_x \frac{\partial w_{SiH_2Cl_2}}{\partial x} + u_y \frac{\partial w_{SiH_2Cl_2}}{\partial y} = \frac{\partial}{\partial y}\left(D_{SiH_2Cl_2} \frac{\partial w_{SiH_2Cl_2}}{\partial y}\right) + \frac{\partial}{\partial y}\left(D_{SiH_2Cl_2} \alpha_{SiH_2Cl_2} \frac{1}{T} \frac{\partial T}{\partial y}\right), \tag{13}$$

$$u_x \frac{\partial w_{GeH_4}}{\partial x} + u_y \frac{\partial w_{GeH_4}}{\partial y} = \frac{\partial}{\partial y}\left(D_{GeH_4} \frac{\partial w_{GeH_4}}{\partial y}\right) + \frac{\partial}{\partial y}\left(D_{GeH_4} \alpha_{GeH_4} \frac{1}{T} \frac{\partial T}{\partial y}\right), \tag{14}$$

where u_x and u_y are the velocity in of x and y direction, respectively.

The numerical solutions of Eqs. (10)—(12) give the temperature and velocity fields. For our simulations, the initial flow of SiH_2Cl_2 and germanium is about 1% of the carrier gas H_2. Hence, their effects on the flow and temperature distributions in the reactor were assumed to be negligible, and the difference between the coupled solution and uncoupled solution is insignificant [12]. Thus the concentration fields of SiH_2Cl_2 and germanium are obtained from the uncoupled Eqs. (13) and (14).

The boundary conditions for SiH_2Cl_2, under the assumption that the growth rate is limited by surface kinetics, are as follows:

$$D_{SiH_2Cl_2} \frac{\partial w_{SiH_2Cl_2}}{\partial y} + D_{SiH_2Cl_2} \alpha_{SiH_2Cl_2} w_{SiH_2Cl_2} \frac{1}{T} \frac{\partial T}{\partial y}\bigg|_{y=0} = R_{Si}, \tag{15}$$

$$\frac{\partial w_{SiH_2Cl_2}}{\partial y} + \alpha_{SiH_2Cl_2} w_{SiH_2Cl_2} \frac{1}{T} \frac{\partial T}{\partial y}\bigg|_{y=H} = 0. \tag{16}$$

Eq. (15) couples the deposition rate of Si, R_{Si}, to the SiH_2Cl_2 concentration field in the reactor. On the other hand, as discussed in the introduction, the Ge incorporation rate is limited by diffusion. Hence, we assume that the concentration of germanium on the surface is zero. This results in the boundary conditions

$$P_{GeH_4}\big|_{y=0}, \tag{17}$$

$$\frac{\partial w_{GeH_4}}{\partial y} + \alpha_{GeH_4} w_{GeH_4} \frac{1}{T} \frac{\partial T}{\partial y}\bigg|_{y=H(x)} = 0. \tag{18}$$

Since H_2 is in excess in the gas mixture, we can obtain the surface coverage, $\theta(x)$, from the reaction of Eq. (6) under the assumption that $\theta(x)$ equals the hydrogen surface coverage $\theta_H(x)$ where x denotes the composition (mole fraction) of Ge in the solid film [8]. The adsorption rate of H is

$$R_a = Z_H [1 - \theta(x)]^2 \exp\left(\frac{E_{aH}}{RT}\right), \tag{19}$$

where E_{aH}, the activation energy of hydrogen adsorption on the surface, is taken as 19 kcal/mol, the same as for hydrogen adsorption on the Si(100) surface [12]. Z_H denotes the gas-surface collision rate of hydrogen:

$$Z_i = \frac{p_i}{(2\pi m_i kT)^{1/2}} (\text{mol m}^{-2}\text{s}^{-1}), \tag{20}$$

where p_i and m_i are the partial pressure near the substrate and molecular weight of species i, respectively. The desorption rate of H for $Ge_x Si_{1-x}$ deposition is quite different from that for Si deposition[6]. The presence of Ge in the solid enhances the desorption of H from the substrate, since the desorption energy of H from Ge atoms in the $Ge_x Si_{1-x}$ is much lower than that from Si atoms. The desorption rate of H from $Ge_x Si_{1-x}$ was suggested by Garone et al. [6] to follow

$$R_d = N_s [\theta(x)]^2 v \left[x\exp\left(-\frac{E_{dG}}{RT}\right) + (1-x)\exp\left(-\frac{E_{dS}}{RT}\right) \right], \tag{21}$$

where N_s is the atom density, $v = 8\times10^{11}\text{s}^{-1}$ is the frequency factor, and E_{dS} and E_{dG} are the activation energies of hydrogen desorption from Si and Ge, respectively. In our model, the values of E_{dS} and E_{dG} are taken as 47 and 37 kcal/mol, respectively [7]. The surface coverage for the dissociative adsorption can be solved by letting the adsorption rate equal the desorption rate [13]

$$\frac{[1-\theta(x)]^2}{[\theta(x)]^2} = \frac{N_s v \left[x\exp\left(-\frac{E_{dG}}{RT}\right) + (1-x)\exp\left(-\frac{E_{dS}}{RT}\right) \right]}{Z_H(\text{molecules/m}^2\text{s})\exp\left(-\frac{E_{aH}}{RT}\right)} \tag{22}$$

The growth rate of Si from the SiH_2Cl_2 is given by

$$R_{Si} = GZ_{SiH_2Cl_2} [1-\theta(x)]^2 S_0, \tag{23}$$

where G is the ratio of interplanar distance in growth direction to atom density. S_0 is a sticking coefficient as provided by Coon et al. [14] for deposition from SiH_2Cl_2 neglecting any gas phase reaction

$$S_0 = 0.36 \left[1 + 600\exp\left(-\frac{E_d - E_r}{Rt}\right) \right]^{-1}. \tag{24}$$

where $E_d - E_r$ represents the difference between the activation energies for desorption and reaction of gaseous SiH_2Cl_2 with the substrate surface. This quantity is about -5.0 kcal/mol for $Si(100)$ as discussed by Knutson et al. [12]. For $Ge_xSi_{1-x}(100)$, this value is not known. In our model we chose a value of -4.5 kcal/mol because it provides the best agreement with the experimental data.

After the concentration distribution of germanium is determined, the growth rate of Ge can be calculated from

$$R_{Ge} = GKb \left(D_{GeH_4} \frac{\partial w_{GeH_4}}{\partial y} + D_{GeH_4} \alpha_{GeH_4} \frac{1}{T} \frac{\partial T}{\partial y} \right) \Bigg|_{y=0(x)}, \tag{25}$$

where K is the reaction efficiency, which we assume is a function of the growth temperature, and b is the factor that transforms the mass of GeH_4 to the number of molecules.

The composition of Ge in the solid and the growth rate of Ge_xSi_{1-x} are, respectively, given by

$$X = \frac{R_{Ge}}{R_{Ge} + R_{Si}}, \tag{26}$$

$$R_{total} = R_{Ge} + R_{Si} \tag{27}$$

The viscosity μ, heat capacity c_p, thermal conductivity k_T, diffusion coefficient D and thermal diffusion coefficient α vary with the temperature and concentration distribution; hence, their evaluations are coupled to those of the temperature and concentrations fields. For the parameter evaluations we used relations introduced by Wilke for μ [15], Mason and Saxena for k_T [16], Reid for D [17] and Hirschfelder et al. for α [18], respectively. The c_p, of the gas mixture was calculated using the relation

$$c_{p,mix} = \sum_i x_i c_{p,i}, \tag{28}$$

where x_i is the concentration of species i, and $c_{p,i}$ its heat capacity which was calculated from

$$c_{p,i} = A + BT + CT^{-2} + DT^2, \tag{29}$$

with the materials constants A, B and C taken from Ref. [19].

3. Numerical solution method

For the numerical solutions, a two-dimensional grid was used in the deposition zone with

$$(x_i, y_j) = (ih_x, jh_y), \tag{30}$$

where $h_x = 1.5$ mm, $h_y = 1.0$ mm. Eqs. (6)—(8) and the boundary conditions may be cast in discrete forms by replacing them with first- and second-order finite differences. Implicit difference forms were taken to assure stability and continuity.

In the calculation of temperature and flow distributions, an initial temperature distribution is assumed. Based on this T distribution, the flow field is calculated. Then physical parameters (ρ and μ) and new temperature distribution are calculated based on the flow field. The Newton iteration method is applied until a prescribed precision is satisfied. After the temperature and flow fields have been determined, the concentration fields, growth rate and composition are similarly calculated. Firstly, an initial concentration distribution is given. Secondly, the physical parameters (c_p, k_T, D and α) are calculated. Thirdly, the Si growth rate is obtained from

Eq. (23) coupled with the Ge growth rate obtained from Eq. (25) by the composition (mole fraction) in the solid film. Then, a new concentration distribution is calculated using the growth rate and composition as boundary conditions, etc.

4.Results and discussion

Fig.1a and Fig.1b give the velocity distribution above the substrate at $T = 700\,^{\circ}\!\text{C}$ for various axial positions x at atmospheric pressure and $p = 6.0$ Torr, respectively. The flows of H_2, SiH_2Cl_2 and GeH_4 are 20 slm, 20 sccm and 1.5 for atmospheric pressure CVD (APCVD) and 3 slm, 26 sccm and 1.5 sccm for low pressure CVD (LPCVD) used in earlier Ge_xSi_{1-x} epitaxy experiments[4-6, 20]. One can see that the average velocity increases about 100 times in LPCVD compared to APCVD.

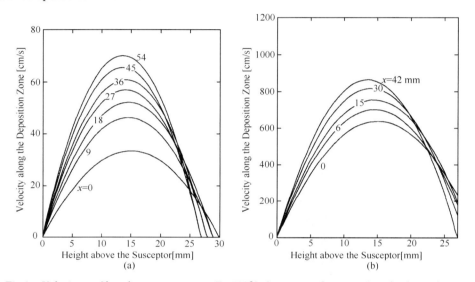

Fig.1   Velocity profiles above susceptor at $T = 700\,^{\circ}\!\text{C}$ for various distances from leading edge, x.
(a) Atmospheric pressure; (b) $p = 6.0$ Torr

Fig. 2 shows the corresponding calculated temperature profiles in the reactor. The dashed curves and the solid curves, respectively, are the temperature distributions in the APCVD and LPCVD system. The substrate temperature is $700\,^{\circ}\!\text{C}$, which is commonly used in Ge_xSi_{1-x}, epitaxy. The temperature of the upper wall, which is mainly heated by radiation, is assumed to be $127\,^{\circ}\!\text{C}$ for both APCVD and LPCVD. As shown in Fig. 2, in the LPCVD system the center of the flow remains essentially at room temperature due to the much higher velocity of the gas mixture; see above. The gradients of temperature along the substrate change less in LPCVD than that in APCVD.

Fig. 3 and Fig. 4 show the spatial distributions of SiH_2Cl_2 and GeH_4 in the reactor under atmospheric pressure. As shown in Fig. 3, the partial pressure of SiH_2Cl_2 near the surface is lower than that in the gas mixture because of the heat diffusion and the consummation of Si from the gas phase during the deposition. The partial pressure of SiH_2Cl_2 near the substrate surface increases along the deposition zone because the temperature gradient decreases (see Fig. 2).

This is a consequence of thermal diffusion. The change in the temperature gradient also causes the decrease in the partial pressure gradient of GeH_4 along the deposition zone. This result indicates that the mass transport has great influence on the growth.

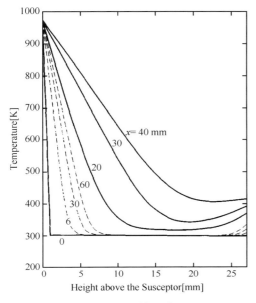

Fig. 2　Temperature profiles above susceptor under atmospheric pressure (solid curves) and $p = 6.0$ Torr (dashed curves)

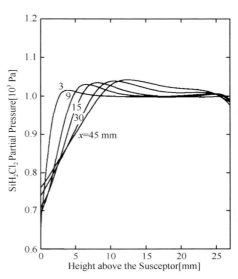

Fig. 3　SiH_2Cl_2 concentration profiles for H_2 (20 slm) with SiH_2Cl_2 (20 sccm) + GeH_4 (3 sccm) at $T = 700 ℃$ under atmospheric pressure

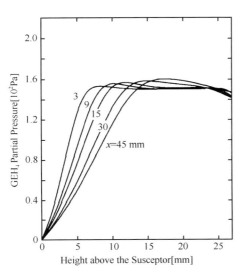

Fig. 4　GeH_4 concentration profiles for H_2 (20 slm) with SiH_2Cl_2 (20 sccm) + GeH_4 (3 sccm) at $T = 700 ℃$ under atmospheric pressure

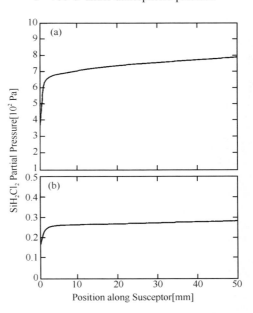

Fig. 5　Distribution of SiH_2Cl_2 1 mm above susceptor under (a) atmospheric pressure and (b) $p_{total} = 6.0$ Torr

Fig. 5 shows the distributions of SiH_2Cl_2 near the susceptor in the APCVD and LPCVD systems. Note that the concentration of SiH_2Cl_2 near the substrate surface changes much less along the substrate in LPCVD than that in the APCVD. This is due to the more uniform temperature gradient along the susceptor in LPCVD system, and results in an improvement of uniformity for the Si growth in LPCVD. The lower concentration at the entrance of the deposition zone is caused by thermal diffusion in the higher temperature gradient.

Fig. 6a shows the growth rate at 625℃ as a function of the initial partial pressure of GeH_4 under atmospheric pressure. The experimental data are from Meyer and Kamins' experiment [20]. In the calculation, the value of K (germanium reaction efficiency) is taken as 80% in order to obtain better agreement with the experiment. Fig. 6b shows the growth rate of Ge_xSi_{1-x}, at 700℃ as a function of the initial GeH_4 flow under $p_{total} = 6.0$ Torr. The experimental data are as reported by Garone et al. [6]. As shown in Fig. 6, the growth rates of Ge_xSi_{1-x}, Si and Ge, which are calculated from our model, are all in good agreement with the experimental data. Both the calculation and experiments show that two factors contribute to an increase in Ge_xSi_{1-x} growth rate. First, the Si growth rate increases due to the desorption of H, which itself is enhanced by the presence of Ge. Second, the Ge growth rate increases linearly with the germanium flow.

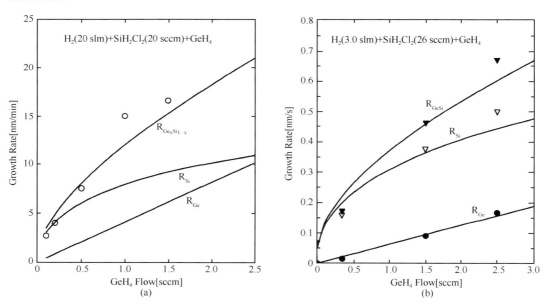

Fig. 6   Growth rate as a function of the initial GeH_4 flow (a) at 625℃ under atmospheric pressure, (○) denotes the experimental data of Meyer and Kamins [20], the solid curves are the calculated results, (b) at 700℃ under p = 6.0 Torr; (▼), (▽) and (○) denote the experimental growth rates for GeSi, Si and Ge, respectively, obtained by Garone et al. [6]

Fig. 7 presents the dependence of the composition x in the solid film on deposition temperature. The experimental data are taken from Meyer et al. [20]. To simplify the calculation, we have fixed the germanium reaction efficiency at 85%. Both experimental and numerical data reflect that x decreases with increase in deposition temperature. The Ge growth rate, being limited by the diffusion process, increases more slowly with temperature than the surface kinetics limited Si growth rate. Therefore, more Si than Ge deposits as the temperature increases, resulting in the decrease in x as the temperature increases. We believe that the difference between our calculated result and the experimental data stems from two aspects. One is that the germani-

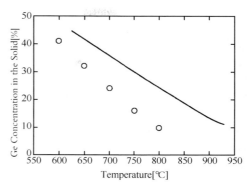

Fig. 7 Relation of the composition x in the solid film to the growth temperature, (○) denote the experimental data of Meyer and Kamins [20]

um reaction efficiency varies with growth temperatures. The other aspect is that there are significant differences between our model system and the experimental system, including the size and shape of reactor, the size and shape of deposition zone, the temperature of reactor wall etc. However, to our knowledge, our simulations are the first ones that reproduced the overall trend in Ge composition dependence on deposition temperature.

5. Conclusions

In summary, a model that combines mass transport and surface kinetics has been applied to the analysis of Ge_xSi_{1-x}, APCVD and LPCVD processes. The calculated growth rate of Ge_xSi_{1-x} as well as the composition x and its temperature dependence are found to be in good agreement with experimental results. The simulations indicate that the deposition uniformity can be improved in LPCVD.

Acknowledgements

We thank Professor Franz Rosenberger and Dr. Hong Lin for their help in writing the manuscript.

References

[1] B.S. Meyerson, K.J. Uram and F.K. LeGoues, Appl. Phys.Lett. 53 (1988) 2555.

[2] W.B. de Boer and D.J. Meyer, Appl. Phys. Lett. 58 (1991) 1286.

[3] J.C. Beam, L.C. Feldman, A.T. Fiory, S. Nakahara and I.K. Robionson, J. Vac. Sci. Technol. A 2 (1984) 436.

[4] T.I. Kamins and D.J. Meyer, Appl. Phys. Lett. 59 (1991) 178.

[5] T.I. Kamins and D.J. Meyer, Appl. Phys. Lett. 61 (1992) 90.

[6] P.M. Garone, J.C. Sturm and P.V. Schwartz, S.A. Schwarz and B.J. Wilkens, Appl. Phys. Lett. 56 (1990) 1275.

[7] D.J. Robbins J.L. Glasper, A.G. Cullis and W.Y. Leong, J. Appl. Phys. 69 (1991) 5129.

[8] S.-M. Jang and R Reif, Appl. Phys, Lett. 59 (1991) 3162.

[9] H. Kuhne, Appl. Phys. Lett. 62 (1993) 1967.

[10] N.M. Russell and W.G. Breiland, J. Appl. Phys. 73 (1993) 3525.

[11] J. Ouazzani and F. Rosenberger, J. Crystal Growth 100 (1990) 545.

[12] K.L. Knutson, R.W. Carr, W.H. Liu and S.A. Campell, J. Crystal Growth 140 (1994) 191.

[13] M.A. Morris, M. Bowker and D.A. King, Kinetics of Adsorption, Desorption and Diffusion at Metal Surface, Comprehensive Chemical Kinetics (Elsevier, Amsterdam, 1984) p. 19.

[14] P.A. Coon, P. Gupta, M.L. Wise and S.M. George, J. Vac. Sci. Technol. A 10 (1992) 324.

[15] C.R. Wilke, J. Chem. Phys. 18 (1950) 517.

[16] E.A. Mason and S.C. Saxena, Phys. Fluid 1 (1958) 361.

[17] R.C. Reid, The Properties of Gases and Liquids (McGraw-Hill, New York, 1966) p. 527.

[18] J.O. Hirschfelder, C.F. Curtiss and R.B. Bird, Molecular Theory of Gases and Liquids (Wiley, New York, 1950) p. 484.

[19] D.R. Stull, Editor JANAF Thermochemical Tables, Natl. Bur. Std., NSRDS-NBS 37 (1971).

[20] D.J. Meyer and T.I. Kamins, Thin Solid Films 222 (1992) 30.

The Dependence of Ge_xSi_{1-x} Epitaxial Growth on GeH_4 Flow Using Chemical Vapour Deposition

JIN XIAOJUN

(*Institute of Microelectronics, Tsinghua University, Beijing* 100084, *China*)

LIANG JUNWU

(*Institute of Semiconductors, Chinese Academy of Sciences, Beijing* 100083, *China*)

Abstract: Ge_xSi_{1-x} epilayers were grown at 700—900℃ by atmospheric pressure chemical vapour deposition. Ge_xSi_{1-x}, Si and Ge growth rates as functions of GeH_4 flow are considered separately to investigate how the growth of the epilayers is enhanced. Arrhenius plots of Si and Ge incorporation in the Ge_xSi_{1-x} growth show the activation energies associated with the growth rates are about 1.2 eV for silicon and 0.4 eV for germanium, indicating that Si growth is limited by surface kinetics and Ge growth is limited by mass transport. A model based on this idea is proposed and used to simulate the growth of Ge_xSi_{1-x}. The calculation and experiment are in good agreement. Growth rate and film composition increase monotonically with growth pressure; both observations are explained by the model.

1. Introduction

Many investigations have been carried out on Ge_xSi_{1-x} heteroepitaxy on Si in recent years. Enhancement of Ge_xSi_{1-x} growth with GeH_4 flow was reported by many authors using various chemical vapour deposition (CVD) techniques, such as ultrahigh vacuum chemical vapour deposition (UHVCVD) [1], low pressure chemical vapour deposition (LPCVD) [2–4] and atmospheric pressure chemical vapour deposition (APCVD) [5,6]. Surface kinetics has been applied to explain the enhancement, but the influence of mass transport in APCVD and LPCVD has been somewhat neglected.

The growth of pure Si and Ge on Si(100) were carried out by Garone *et al.* [4] and Cunningham *et al.* [7], respectively. Arrhenius plots for pure Si and Ge are given in Fig. 1. The curve of pure Si growth, in which SiH_2Cl_2 was used as the Si source and the working pressure was 6.0 torr (800 Pa) shows that Si growth is limited by surface diffusion and reactions below 1000℃. The curve of pure Ge growth, in which GeH_4 was used as the Ge source and the working pressure was 20 mtorr (2.7 Pa), suggests that Ge growth is limited by mass transport above 600℃. Kamins and Meyer used APCVD to investigate the kinetics of Ge_xSi_{1-x} epitaxy using SiH_2Cl_2 and GeH_4 as Si and Ge sources [5]. In their work the growth rate of the Si and Ge component over the temperature range 600—900℃ were normalized by the Ge content in the film. Their results showed that, in Ge_xSi_{1-x} epitaxy, the deposition of Ge below 650℃ is limited by

原载于:Journal of Materials Science: Materials in Electronics,1997,8:405-408.

surface diffusion and reactions whereas above 650℃ the Ge growth is limited by mass transport.

This work investigates the growth of Ge_xSi_{1-x} over the temperature range 700-900℃ using APCVD. Ge_xSi_{1-x}, Si and Ge growth rates as functions of the GeH_4 flow are discussed separately to explain the enhancement of Ge_xSi_{1-x} growth by GeH_4 flow. Arrhenius plots of Si and Ge incorporation in the Ge_xSi_{1-x} growth shows that the Si growth is limited by surface kinetics and the Ge growth is limited by mass transport. A model based on this is proposed and applied to simulate Ge_xSi_{1-x} growth. The growth rates of Ge, Si, and GeSi versus GeH_4 flow are calculated and compared with experimental data. The growth pressure effects on the Ge_xSi_{1-x} growth rate and composition are simulated. The simulated results are compared with the experiment results reported by other authors [6, 8].

2. Experimental procedure

The experiments were carried out in a horizontal quartz reactor with a rectangular cross-section. The deposition zone was heated by halogen lamps. The epilayer was deposited on an Si(100) substrate. The sources were dichlorosilane (DCS) and germane for Si and Ge, respectively. The carrier gas was H_2. The deposition temperature was 700—900℃, and the deposition pressure was $1×10^6$ Pa. The thickness of the film was measured by Rutherford back-scattering spectrometry (RBS) and transmission electron microscopy (TEM). The composition of Ge in the film was measured by double-crystal X-ray and RBS.

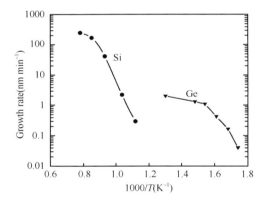

Fig. 1　Arrhenius plots for pure Si and Ge growth on Si(100)

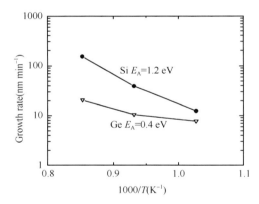

Fig. 2　Arrhenius plots for the growth rate of Si and Ge in Ge_xSi_{1-x} epitaxy over the temperature range 700-900℃, where the flows of H_2, SiH_2Cl_2 and GeH_4 are 3 slm, 20 sccm and 1.35 sccm, respectively

Arrhenius plots of Si and Ge growth are given in Fig. 2, where the flows of SiH_2Cl_2, GeH_4 and H_2 are 20 sccm, 1.35 sccm and 20 slm, respectively. The growth rates of Ge and Si were obtained by multiplying the Ge_xSi_{1-x} growth rate by the Ge composition and the Si composition in the film, respectively. The activation energies associated with the growth rates are about 1.2 eV for silicon and 0.4 eV for germanium. The activation energy for silicon in our GeSi growth is much lower than for pure Si growth, where the activation energy is about 2.0 eV. This result is also lower than the experimental results of Garone *et al.* [4] and Kamins and Meyer [5]. A possible explanation for the lower activation energy during Si growth in our GeSi epitaxy is the presence of Ge, which may enhance the desorption of hydrogen on the surface, increasing the Si growth rate and decreasing the activation energy for Si growth. The activation energy for Ge growth of our experimental data coincides with values reported by other authors [4]. The weak temperature dependence of the Ge growth suggests it is limited by mass transport of the germanium-containing species of the surface over our experimental temperature range (700-900°C). The experimental data of other authors [4, 5, 7] also suggests that Si growth is limited by surface kinetics for $T<1000°C$ and that Ge growth is limited by mass transport for $T>650°C$. A model based on this idea is proposed to explain enhancement of the Ge_xSi_{1-x} growth rate by GeH_4 flow.

3. Theory

Silicon incorporation from DCS for $T<1000°C$ is limited by reaction kinetics and can be expressed as where (g) denotes the species in the gas, an underline denotes the adsorbed molecule on the growth surface, α is the condensation coefficient and k_r, k_d are the reaction and desorption rates of the adsorbed molecule. The growth rate of Si can be calculated by assuming the adsorption rate is equal to the reaction rate plus the desorption rate:

$$SiH_2Cl_2(g) \xrightarrow[k_d]{\alpha} \underline{SiH_2Cl_2} \xrightarrow{k_r} \underline{Si} + 2HCl \tag{1}$$

$$R_{Si} = \frac{\alpha k_r}{k_d + k_r} P_{SiH_2Cl_2}(1 - \theta(x))^2 \tag{2}$$

where $P_{SiH_2Cl_2}$ is the partial pressure of SiH_2Cl_2 near the growth surface, which can be calculated by fluid dynamics; $\theta(x)$ is the surface coverage.

The surface coverage can be calculated by considering adsorption and desorption of H_2 on the growth surface:

$$\underline{H_2} \xleftrightarrow[R_d]{R_{ad}} 2\underline{H} \tag{3}$$

where R_{ad} and R_d represent the adsorption and desorption rates of H_2 on the growth surface:

$$R_{ad} = \frac{P_{H_2}}{(2\pi m_{H_2} kT)^{1/2}} (1 - \theta(x))^2 \exp(-E_{aH}/kT) \tag{4}$$

$$R_d = v N_s \theta^2(x) [(1-x)\exp(-E_{dS}/kT) + x\exp(-E_{dG}/kT)] \tag{5}$$

E_{aH} is the activation energy for H_2 adsorption. The desorption rate of H from the Ge_xSi_{1-x} growth surface is suggested by Garone *et al.* [4], where $v = 8 \times 10^{11} s^{-1}$ is the frequency factor, E_{ds} and E_{dG} are the activation energies of hydrogen desorption from Si and Ge, respectively, and N_s is the number of sites per square centimetre. The surface coverage $\theta(x)$ can be solved by setting the adsorption rate of hydrogen equal to the desorption rate.

The Ge growth rate, which is limited by the mass diffusion, can be calculated as follows:

$$R_{Ge} = K \left(D \frac{\partial w}{\partial y} + D\alpha w \frac{1}{T} \frac{\partial T}{\partial y} \right) \tag{6}$$

K is the reaction efficiency. D and α represent the diffusion coefficient and thermal diffusion coefficient, respectively; w is the fractional concentration of GeH_4 in the gas mixture.

The growth rate and composition x of Ge_xSi_{1-x} are given as follows:

$$R_{Ge_xSi_{1-x}} = R_{Si} + R_{Ge} \qquad (7)$$

$$x = \frac{R_{Ge}}{R_{Si} + R_{Ge}} \qquad (8)$$

4. Results and discussion

Fig. 3 shows the Ge_xSi_{1-x}, Si and Ge growth rates as functions of GeH_4 flow, with flows of SiH_2Cl_2 and H_2 of 20 sccm and 20 slm, respectively. The growth rates simulated by the model are in good agreement with the experimental data; they indicate that two factors contribute to the increase of Ge_xSi_{1-x} growth rate with GeH_4 flow. The Ge growth rate increases linearly due to a linear increase in the GeH_4 concentration with increasing GeH_4 flow. And Si growth is enhanced by GeH_4 due to the desorption of H, itself enhanced by the presence of Ge on the growth surface. The Si growth rate increases rapidly with GeH_4 flow at lower GeH_4 flows (0- 0.5 sccm); the increase in the Si growth rate becomes slower for higher GeH_4 flows. Since the composition x is calculated by Equation 8, Fig. 1 also implies that composition x simulated by the model is in agreement with the experimental data.

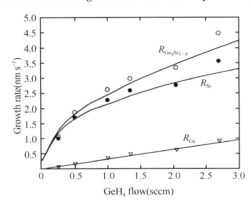

Fig. 3　Growth rates as functions of the initial GeH_4 flow at 900℃ under atmospheric pressure: experimental growth rates for (○) Ge_xSi_{1-x}, (●) Si and (▽) Ge; the solid curves are the calculated results

The model was also used to simulate the growth pressure effects on the Ge_xSi_{1-x} growth rate and composition. The solid curves in Figs.4 and 5 show the calculated result of growth rate and composition as functions of GeH_4 flow under growth pressures of 6, 60 and 220 torr (800 Pa, 8 kPa, and 29 kPa). The flows of H_2 and Si_2Cl_2 are 3 slm and 26 sccm. The growth temperature is 625℃. The other symbols are experimental data evaluated from the report of Matutinovic et al. [8] under the same growth pressures, flow and temperature as the calculation. Both calculation and experiment show the trend that growth rate and film composition increase monotonically with growth pressure. According to the literature [8], the reason for this effect is believed unknown, but we can explain it for our calculation. The concentration gradient of GeH_4 near the growth surface increases due to the increase in growth pressure. Ge growth, which is limited by the mass transport of GeH_4, increases the concentration gradient of GeH_4. The growth rate of Si is enhanced by the greater Ge composition on the growth surface. Consequently, the growth rate of Ge_xSi_{1-x} and the composition x increase monotonically with the growth pressure. There are differences between the calculated result and the experimental data in Figs 4 and 5. Some factors that may cause the difference are (1) the system simulated by the model is different from the system in the experiment; (2) some parameters in the calculation, such as reaction efficiency K, should be revalued for the low pressure growth.

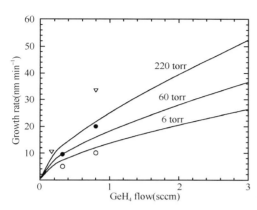

Fig. 4　Growth rate versus GeH_4 under different growth pressures: experimental data at (○) 6 torr, (●) 60 torr and (▽) 220 torr from the report of Matutinovic et al. [8]; H_2 flow = 3 slm, DCS flow = 26 sccm

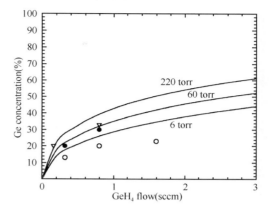

Fig. 5　Ge fraction versus GeH_4 under the same conditions as in Fig. 4; see Fig. 4 caption for key to symbols

5. Conclusion

Ge_xSi_{1-x}, Si and Ge growth as functions of GeH_4 flow were considered separately to investigate the growth of Ge_xSi_{1-x} enhanced by GeH_4 flow. Si growth is enhanced by the GeH_4; the Ge growth rate increases linearly with the GeH_4 flow. Arrhenius plots showed that Si growth is limited by surface kinetics and Ge growth is limited by mass transport. A model based on this was applied to simulate the growth of Ge_xSi_{1-x}. The calculated growth rate and composition appear to be in good agreement with our experimental data. The growth pressure effects on the Ge_xSi_{1-x} growth rate and composition were simulated by the model, which successfully explained monotonic increases of growth rate and film composition with growth pressure.

Acknowledgements

We gratefully acknowledge Ms Yin Chidden and Mr Wan Yutian, Institute of Semiconductors, Chinese Academy of Sciences, for the RBS and X-ray measurements.

References

[1] B.S. MEYERSON, K. J. URAM and F. K. LEGOUES, *Appl. Phys. Lett.* 53 (1988) 2555.

[2] SYUN-MING JANG and R. REIF, *ibid.* 59 (1991) 3162.

[3] D. J. ROBBINS, J. L. GLASPER, A. G. CULLIS and W. Y. LEONG, *J. Appl. Phys.* 69 (1991) 5129.

[4] P. M. GARONE, J. C. STURM, P. V. SCHWARTZ, S. A. SCHWARZ and B. J. WILKENS, *Appl. Phys. Lett.* 56 (1990) 1275.

[5] T.I. KAMINS and D. J. MEYER, *ibid.* 59 (1991) 178.

[6] D.J. MEYER and T. I. KAMINS, *Thin Solid Films* 222 (1992) 30.

[7] B. CUNNINGHAM, J. O. CHU and S. AKBAR, *Appl. Phys. Lett.* 59 (1991) 3574.

[8] Z. MATUTINOVIC-KRSTELIJ, E. CHASON and J. C. STURM, *J. Elec. Mater.* 24 (1995) 725.

Physical Properties and Growth of SiC *

LIANG Junwu and ZHU Jianjun

(Institute of Semiconductors, Chinese Academy of Sciences, Beijing 100083, China)

Abstract: Some properties of SiC crystals have been studied. The main features of five primary SiC polytypes, i.e. 3C-, 2H-, 4H-, 6H- and 15R-SiC are described. Among various polytypes of SiC the 4H- SiC crystals have been successfully used to fabricate excellent microwave and power devices. Although the nearest coordination number in all polytypes of SiC is the same, the next nearest neighbouring numbers of heteroatoms may be different for hexagonal and cubic sites in some polytypes. The existence of different ionization energies for a particular substitutional impurity, for example, the three ionization energies of nitrogen on carbon sites, has been explained by different next nearest neighbouring numbers of heteroatoms in 6H-SiC.

3C-SiC epilayers were grown on silicon(100) and(111) substrates by CVD methods. An optimum condition for 3C-SiC/Si growth was determined by RHEED images and X-ray double crystal diffraction measurements.

The bulk and epitaxial SiC crystal growth have also been reviewed.

Key words: Silicon carbide, Polytypes, Inequivalent sites, Crystal growth.

I. Introduction

Silicon carbide materials have been recently given renewed attention as a third generation of electronic materials. The driving force is the need of high power, high temperature and high speed devices. In addition, the SiC research has been driven by the development of semiconductor technology for devices working in corrosive and high radiation environments.

Althongh the growth of large diameters and low defect density SiC substrates is difficult, the SiC technology has made great progress. For example, at 850 MHz, the power density of 4H-SiC MESFET has reached 3.3W/mm$^{2[1]}$, being approximately three times the output power density typically seen in GaAs FETs. The highest f_{max} of 4H-SiC MESFET has been reported to be 42 GHz, and the highpower 4H-SiC static induction transistors (SITs) with 470W total output power at 600MHz have been fabricated[2]. The SiC SITs have extremely high power density of 26kW/cm^2, which is over two times the power density currently seen in Si devices. SiC materials and devices will have a long term impact on the semiconductor industries.

原载于: Chinese Journal of Electronics,1998,7(1):28-33.

* Manuscript Received Aug. 1997; Accepted Sept. 1997. This work is supported by the National Natural Science Foundation of China (contract No. 67576024)

II. Physical Properties of SiC

1. Inequivalent sites in polytypes of SiC

There are over 175 polytypes of SiC. Polytypism is one of the most unique features of SiC. In all polytypes of SiC, the fundamental unit is tetrahedron of SiC and the nearest neighbour coordination number is four. Let's designate a SiC atom pair in an A-plane of close packing lattice as Aa, in the B-plane as Bb, and in the C-plane as Cc. The 3C-SiC has $AaBbCcAaBbCc...$ stacking sequences. For $AaBbAaBb...$ stacking sequences we obtain the 2H-SiC wurtzite lattice and for $AaBbCcAaCcBbAaBbCcAaCcBb...$ stacking sequences we obtain 6H-SiC.

In Table 1, the stacking sequences of five most important SiC polytypes are shown. If we designate k position which Si-C atom pair occupy as a cubic site and h position as a hexagonal site, then we obtain Wyckoff 's notation of stacking sequences (see Table1). The 3C-SiC is pure cubic structure with hexagonal fraction of 0, whereas 2H-SiC is pure hexagonal structure with hexagonal fraction of 1.

Table 1   Stacking sequences of five Silicon carbide polytypes

Polytype	Stacking sequences	Hexagonal Fraction	Wyckoff's notation
3C	$AaBbCc$	0	kkk
15R	$AaBbCcAaCcBbCcAaBbAaCcAaBbCcBb$	0.4	$hkkhkhkkhkhkkkhkh$
6H	$AaBbCcAaCcBb$	0.33	$hkkhk$
4H	$AaBbAaCc$	0.5	$khkh$
2H	$AaBb$	1.0	hh

Although the nearest neighbouring coordination number in all SiC polytypes is the same and equals four, the next-nearest neighbour numbers of heteroatoms may be different in different SiC polytypes. For example, the next-nearest neighbour number is 12 for 3C-SiC, and 9+1 for 2H-SiC. Furthermore, in more complicated polytypes of SiC there are defferent k or h sites. For example, in 6H-SiC the Bb atomic layer consists of two subatomic layers. One is B-layer, in which the next-nearest neighbouring number of heteroatoms is 9+1. The other is b-layer, in which the next-nearest neighbouring number is 12. In the Cc atom-layer, the next-nearest neighbouring number of heteroatoms is 12 and 9+1 in C and c-subatomic layers, respectively. If we designate the capital A, B and C as carbon layer, then there are two kinds of carbon k-sites, one has 9+1 next-nearest neighbours of hetroatoms and the other has 12. Thus, 6H-SiC has three inequivalent sites, i.e. two k sites and one h site. 4H-and 15R-SiC have two and five inequivalent sites, respectively[3]. In Table 2 the next-nearest neighbouring numbers of heteroatoms in some SiC polytypes are shown. The number of inequivalent sites and other selected physical properties of the five important SiC polytypes are listed in Table 3.

Table 2 Next-nearest neighbouring numbers in some SiC polytypes

Polytype	Atom layer	N.N.N.N.* k	N.N.N.N.* h	Polytype	Atom layer	N.N.N.N. h	Polytype	Atom layer	N.N.N.N. k	Polytype	Atom layer	N.N.N.N. k	N.N.N.N. h
4H	A	10		2H	A	10	3C	A	12	6H	B	10	
	a	10			a	10		a	12		b	12	
	B		12		B	10		B	12		C	12	
	b		12		b	10		b	12		c	10	
	A	10						C	12		A		12
	a	10						c	12		a		12
	C		12								C	10	
	c		12								c	12	
											B	12	
											b	10	
											A		12
											a		12

* N.N.N.N.: next-nearest neighbouring number

Table 3 Inequivalent sites and other physical properties of SiC polytypes

Polytype of SiC	Lattice constant (A) a	Lattice constant (A) c	Space Group	Inequivalent sites h site	Inequivalent sites k site	Excitonic energy gap* (E_g-E_b) eV at 2K
3C	4.349		T_d^2	0	1	2.390
15R	3.073	37.700	C_{3V}^5	2	3	2.986
6H	3.073	15.079	C_{6V}^4	1	2	3.023
4H	3.073	10.050	C_{6V}^4	1	1	3.265
2H	3.076	5.048	C_{6V}^4	1	0	3.330

* E_g represents energy gap, E_b is the binding energy of excition

In Fig.1 and Fig. 2 the 4H-and 3C-SiC lattice is shown and Fig.3 shows the 6H-SiC structure and its cubic (k) sites and h sites.

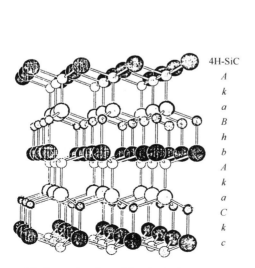

Fig.1 A drawing of the 4H-SiC structure

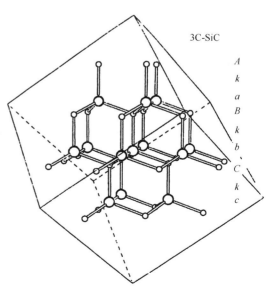

Fig.2 A drawing of the 3C-SiC structure

2. Behavior of dopants in SiC

The existence of inequivalent sites can be used to explain the different donor or acceptor ionization energies for a particular substitutional impurity. For example, nitrogen atoms substitute on carbon-sites in 6H-SiC and act as donors. In the photoluminescence spectrum of nitrogen doped 6H-SiC with electron concentration of 5×10^{16} cm^{-3}, three no-phonon lines P_0, R_0 and S_0 have been observed[4,5]. The three lines correspond to the one h-site and two k-sites, respectively (Fig. 4). The ionization energies of nitrogen donors measured by optical absorption method are $E_c - 83$ meV, $E_c - 137$ meV and $E_c - 142$ meV. The ionization energies of nitrogen donors in a lightly doped 6H-SiC sample are obtained by using Hall measurement and the values are $E_c - 125$ meV and $E_c - 85$ meV.

The value of $E_c - 85$ meV is consistent with that of $E_c - 83$ meV obtained by IR absorption, while the value of $E_c - 125$ meV is due to the fact, that the difference in ionization energies between the two k-sites is too small to resolved by electrical method.

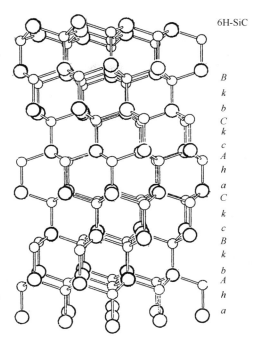

Fig.3   The 6H-SiC structure projected

on its $(1\,1\,\bar{2}\,0)$

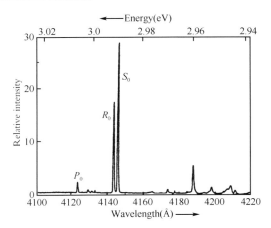

Fig.4   Photoluminescence spectrum taken from a 6H-SiC cpilayer doped with nitrogen ($n_e = 5\times10^{16}$ cm^{-3}), where P_0, R_0 and S_0 are three nophonon peaks

For 4H-SiC, the Hall measurement from an unintentionally doped 4H-SiC CVD layer has shown that the ionization energies for nitrogen are $E_c - 102$ meV and $E_c - 59$ meV, which correspond nitrogen on k site and h site, respectively.

Aluminum atoms in SiC occupy the Si-sites and act as acceptors. The ionization energy of Al is ~ 200 meV and only weakly depends on polytype or hexagonal and cubic sites. In contract to above mentioned impurities, boron atoms reside at Si sites as well as C sites. Boron on Si sites serves as an acceptor and has an ionization energy of ~ 300 meV, which is not dependent on polytype or lattice sites. Boron atoms occupying C sites act as deep center called D-center and have ionization energies between 600—700 meV.

3. Mobility of Sic

Among the primary SiC polytypes, the 3C-and 4H-SiC have higher values of electron mobility. In the 4H-SiC epilayer with donor concentration of $3 \times 10^5 \, cm^{-3}$, μ_e reaches $948 cm^2/Vs$ at 300K[5]. In the 6H-SiC with donor concentration of $10^{16} \, cm^{-3}$, the electron Hall mobility can reach $400 cm^2/Vs$ at room temperature, and the mobility decreases as the donor concentration increases.

At the same electron concentration of $10^{17} \, cm^{-3}$, μ_e in 4H-and 6H-SiC is equal to $500 cm^{-2}/Vs$ and $250 cm^{-2}/Vs$. In addition, the ionization energies in 4H-SiC are lower than those in 6H-SiC. Therefore, 4H-SiC is a better substrate for device fabrication.

The electron mobility in 4H-, 6H-and 15R-SiC is not isotropic but anisotropic[6]. In 4H-SiC the electron mobility parallel to the c-axis with magnetic field perpendicular to the c-axis is greater than the one perpendicular to the c-axis. While in 6H-and 15R-SiC the electron mobility parallel to c-axis is smaller than the one perpendicular to the c-axis. Obviously, the anisotropy of electron mobility can be used to improve device performance.

III. Crystal Growth of SiC

1. Bulk crystal growth

Growth of bulk single crystal of SiC with low defect densities is a very difficult task for many reasons. Firstly, SiC does not melt under any attainable pressure in laboratory, rather it sublimates at temperature above 1800℃. Next, the solubility of carbon in silicon melt is very small at reasonably high temperatures and the melt growth techniques are not applicable for SiC. Thirdly, SiC has over 175 polytypes and more than one polytype can growth under the same pressure and at the same temperature.

Now, the modified Lely process[7] which is based on the sublimation and uses a seed crystal is the main method for bulk crystal growth. The seeded sublimation grown crystals contain micropipe defects with densities of $10 \sim 10^3 \, cm^{-2}$. The micropipe defects are small-diameter(0.1 ~ 5μm) holes that may exten through the entire crystal along the growth axis. These defects are very harmful, especially for high voltage devices. It is believed that a micropipe defect is the hollow core of a screw dislocation which has a large Burgers vector. The mechanism of micropipes formation has been discussed in [8,9]. It is reported[9] that the density of micropipes has been reduced to $0.8 cm^{-2}$ on a 30 mm 4H-SiC wafer.

Dislocation densities of 6H-and 4H-SiC wafers are in the range of $10^4 \sim 10^5 \, cm^{-2}$. It is well known that during the growth of SiC by sublimation method, screw dislocations occur and spiral growth steps are formed. On a growing crystal surface, several growth spirals exist. When two growth spirals meet together, low angle boundaries are formed, which contain series of dislocations.

For n-type SiC, nitrogen is introduced into the growth furnace. Low resistivity crystals are required for many device structures. Nitrogen doped 4H-and 6H-SC crystals with resistivities as low as $10^{-3}\Omega \cdot$ cm can be obtained. For p-type SiC, Al is used as dopant.

On the other hand, semi-insulating substrates are also required for fabrication of microwave devices. By using deep-level dopants and/or intrinsic point defects processes for producing semi-insulating SiC, 4H-SiC substrates have been developed[10]. At 100°C the resistivity of a semiinsulating SiC wafer was $10^{10}\Omega \cdot$ cm and by extrapolating to room temperature a resistivity of $10^{15}\Omega \cdot$ cm was given.

2. Epitaxial growth of SiC

Numerous epitaxial methods have been reported for producing SiC films, including atmosphere pressure chemical vapor deposition (APCVD), low pressure CVD, metalorganic CVD, rapid thermal CVD, molecular beam epitaxy and liquid phase epitaxy. Among them the CVD methods are commonly used, and yield the best SiC epilayers.

The 3C-SiC can be grown on large diameter silicon substrates. We have grown 3C-SiC epilayers on Si(100) and Si(111) substrates[3]. In Fig. 5 the typical X-ray double crystal diffraction of a 3C-SiC/Si(100) epilayer is shown. The 2θ peak at 41.38° characterizes the (200) planes in 3C-SiC. Fig.6 are RHEED patterns taken from a 3C-SiC epilayer. The RHEED patterns show that the surface quality of epilsyer is good.

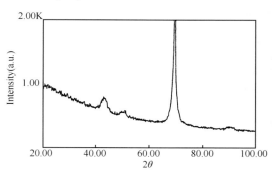

Fig.5   X-ray double crystal diffraction measurement on a 3C-SiC/Si (100) epilayer

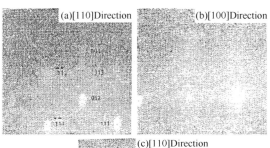

Fig.6   RHEED patterns taken from a 3C-SiC/Si (100) epilayer

The main drawback of heteroepitaxial growth of SiC/Si is the large lattice mismatch. High quality epitaxial films of 6H-and 4H-SiC can be grown on 6H-and 4H-SiC substrates. Electron and hole concentration from 10^{14}cm^{-3} to greater than 10^{19} cm^{-3} can be obtained for both n-type and p-type epilayers.

Recently much epilayer crystal research has focused on 4H-SiC mainly because of higher electron mobility and lower dopant ionization energies. It is reported that the incidence of 3C-SiC inclusions in 4H-SiC epilayers was eliminated by using 8° off-axis 4H substrates[11].

IV. Summary

Polytypism is one of the unique characteristics of SiC. Among various polytypes of SiC the 4H-SiC crystals have been successfully used to fabricate excellent microwave and power devices.

Although the nearest coordination number in all polytypes of SiC is the same, the next nearest neighbouring numbers of heteroatoms may be different for hexagonal and cubic sites in some polytypes. The existence of different ionization energies for a particular substitutional impurity can be explained by different next nearest neighbouring numbers of heteroatoms.

The bulk and epitaxial SiC crystal growth have been reviewed. 3C-SiC epilayers were grown on silicon substrates by CVD method. An optimum condition for epilayer growth was determined by RHEED images and X-ray double crystal diffraction measurements.

References

[1] K. Moore, C. Weitzel, K. Nordquist, L. Pond, III, J. Palmour, S. Allen and C. Carter, *Jr. IEEE Cornell Conf. on Advanced Concepts in High Speed. Semiconductor Devices and Circuits* (The Insistitute of Electrical and Electronics Engeneers, Ithaca, 1955) p. 40.

[2] A. Morse, P. Esker, R. Clarke, C. Brandt, R. Siergiej and A. Agarwal, *IEEE MTT-S Digest* p. 677, 1966.

[3] LIANG Junwu, *Proc. of the 10th National Conf. on IC and Si material*, CIE, p.4,1997 (in Chinese).

[4] G.Pensl and W.J. Choyke, *Physica B*, Vol. 185, P. 264, 1993.

[5] W.J. Choyke and G. Pensl, *MRS Bulletin*, Vol. 22, No. 3,p. 25, 1997.

[6] M. Schadt, G.Pensl, R.P. Devaty, W.J. Choyke, R. Stein and D. Stephani, *Appl. Phys. Lett.*, Vol. 65, p. 3120, 1994.

[7] Yu. M. Tairov and V.F. Tsvetkov, *J. Crystal Growth*, Vol. 43, p. 209, 1978.

[8] R.A. Stein, *Physica B*, Vol. 185, p. 211, 1993.

[9] R.C. Glass, D. Henshall, V.F. Tsvetkon and C.H. Carter, Jr., *MRS Bulletin*, Vol. 22, No. 9, p. 30,1997.

[10] H.M. Hobgood, R.C. Glass, G. Augustine, R.H. Hopkins, J. Jenny, M. Skowronski, W.C. Mitchel and M. Roth, *Appl. Phys. Lett.*, Vol. 66, p. 1364, 1995.

[11] V.F. Tsvetkov, S.T. Allen H.S. Kong and C.H. Carter, Jr., *Proc. 6th Conf. on Silicon Carbide and Related Materials* 1995 (Institute of Physics, Conf. series No. 142, Bristol, 1996),p. 17, 1995.

LIANG Junwu (Fellow, CIE) graduated from Wuhan University in 1955 and received the Ph.D degree from the Baikov Institute of Metallurgy, Moskow, in 1960. His major is in semiconductor materials science. In 1960 he joined the Institute of Semiconductors, Chinese Academy of Sciences, concentrating on silicon and III - V componds crystal growth, including bulk crystals and epitaxial films. He is currently a professor at the Institute of Semiconductors, Director of Chinese Materials Research Society of CIE and Chiarman of the Electronic Materials Society, CIE. His recent interests include the growth and charecterization of silicon-germanium, silicon carbide and gallium nitride materials.

Study on Photoluminescence Spectra of SiC*

Zhu Jianjun, Pang Hai, Liu Suying and Liang Junwu

（朱建军）　（庞　海）　（刘素英）　（梁骏吾）

（ *Institute of Semiconductors Chinese Academy of Sciences, Beijing* 100083, *China*）

Received 4 November 1997

Abstract: 3C-SiC, 4H-SiC and 6H-SiC are the three kinds of silicon carbide（SiC）applied most extensively in semiconductor device fabrications. This work is engaged in analyzing their photoluminescence（PL）spectra and then summarizing the characteristics of the spectra. Special attention was paid to the inequivalent sites existing in SiC and their effects on the PL spectra of SiC.

Key Words: SiC, Inequivalent sites, Photoluminescence, 4A or 4D complex

1. Introduction

SiC, currently the primary widebandgap semiconductors with a bandgap ranges from 2.2eV（3C-SiC）to 3.3eV（4H-SiC）at room temperature, has excellent electrical properties and thermal stability. As a potential candidate for semiconductor device applications involving "extreme" conditions: high temperature, radiation and/or erosion environments, high electrical power applications, high thermal power dissipation *etc.*, SiC is receiving increasing attention in recent years. At the begining, the lack of single-crystal SiC substrates hampered the development of SiC in semiconductor device fabrications. With the improvement of crystal growth techniques, high quality single crystal SiC can be grown now using modified Lely method. Meanwhile, great breakthrough has been achieved in SiC homoor hetero-epitaxy growth. All these achievements promote the development of SiC-based devices. As the defects in SiC have important effects on the performance of SiC-based devices, it is necessary to make clear the behavior of defects. The PL has been proved to be a convenient and nondestructive method for identification and characterization of optically active impurities and defects in semiconductors. In this paper, the properties of 3C-, 4H- and 6H-SiC are studied and the characteristics of their PL spectra are analyzed.

2. Physical Properties of SiC

2.1 *Inequivalent Sites in* SiC

SiC polytypes are classified by the stacking sequence and periodicity of each tetrahedrally bonded Si-C bilayer along the c-axis direction. Each Si-C bilayer, while maintaining the tetrahedral bonding scheme of the crystal, can situate in any one of the three possible positions with

原载于：Rare Metals, 1998, 17:273-280.

* This work was supported by the National Natural Science Foundation of China（contract No.67576024）

respect to the lattice. These positions are arbitrarily assigned the notation A, B or C. The numerous possible sequences of ABC lead to many SiC crystal structures whose symmetries are determined by stacking periodicity. In all SiC polytypes, the first-nearest neighbouring atom configuration of Si or C atom is identical. However, as the second-nearest neighbouring atoms provide a slightly altered atomic environment[1], the inequivalent lattice sites are formed, which are important in the substitutional impurity incorporation and electronic transport properties.

The inequivalent sites are divided into two kinds. One is a cubic-like(k) arrangement of first-and second-nearest neighbouring atoms and the other is a hexagonal-like (h) arrangement. Stacking sequences in the c-axis direction and numbers of cubic-like and hexagonal-like sites are given for 2H-, 3C-, 4H-, 6H- and 15R-SiC in Table 1.

Table 1 SiC polytypes with two common notations and numbers of inequivalent sites[2]

Ramsdell notation	ABC notation	Numbers of inequivalent sites	
		Hexagonal	Cubic
2H(wurzite)	AB	1	0
3C(zinc blende)	ABC	0	1
4H	ABAC	1	1
6H	ABCACB	1	2
15R	ABCACBCABACABCB	2	3

2.2 *Effect of Inequivalent Sites on Energy Levels of Impurities*

Except 3C-SiC, every SiC has various numbers of cubic-like(k) and hexagonal-like (h) sites. Impurity atoms can take any one of the inequivalent sites, hence impurity atoms occupied different sites have altered neigh-bouring atom configuration and show different electrical and optical characteristics.

The polytype 6H-SiC provides three inequivalent silicon/carbon lattice sites: one hexagonal-like(h) site and two different cubic-like (k_1, k_2) ones that can be occupied by nitrogen or aluminum atoms. Nitrogen is the prevailing shallow donor species in SiC who substitutes C atom. Having studied 6H-SiC samples with various N doping concentrations by means of Hall Effect and FTIR absorption, Suttrop *et al*[3] determined the ionization energies and binding energies of excited states of the nitrogen donor, and proposed an energy level scheme based on the effectivemass approximation(EMA) taking into account the anisotropy of the effective electron masses, the valley-orbit splitting of the ground state and the symmetries of the inequivalent sites. Their observed binding energy values of Is (A_1) ground state (ionization energy) are $\Delta E(h) =$ 81.0meV, $\Delta E(k_1) = 137.6$meV, $\Delta E(k_2) = 142.4$meV, corresponding to 667cm^{-1}, 1123cm^{-1} and 1162cm^{-1} lines in Fig. 1, respectively.

Aluminum occupies Si site in 6H-SiC and acts as shallow acceptor. In contrast to N atom residing at C site, there is no big difference among the ionization energies of Al occupying h-, k_1-, k_2-site. The ionization energies of Al at k_1- and k_2-site are almost the same, and the ioniza-

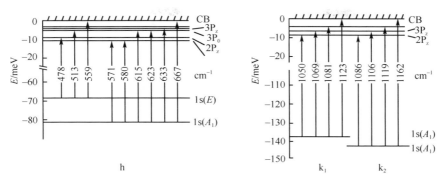

Fig.1　Energy level scheme of nitrogen donors residing at h-, k_1-and k_2-lattice

sites in a 6H-SiC single crystal

tion energies of Al at h-site and k_1-or k_2-site are 239 meV and 248.5meV, respectively.

2. 3　*Phonon Spectra of SiC*

　　The unit cells of SiC polytypes contain a large number of atoms. For instance, the hexagonal unit cell of 4H-SiC contains 8 atoms (4 Si atoms and 4 C atoms), and the numbers for 6H- and 15R-SiC are 12 and 30, respectively. Therefore, the lattice wave consists of many accoustic and optical branches, which make the phonon spectrum of SiC very complicated. Choyke *et al.*[4] performed PL measurements of SiC and obtained the energies of phonons associated with bound excitons (N_x). Ikeda[5] determined energies of phonons associated with free excitons (F_x) also by PL experiments and their values is similar to those of Choyke's. The values are listed in Table 2.

Table 2　Energies of phonons associated with the free excitons(F_x)and those associated

with bound excitons (N_x) for 4H-,6H-,15R- and 3C-SiC (in meV) [5]

	4H		6H		15R		3C	
	F_x	N_x	F_x	N_x	F_x	N_x	F_x	N_x
TA	33.9	33.5		33.5	33.9	34.4		
	38.0	37.2		36.3	35.0	35.0		
	40.8	41.4	39.4	39.2	39.2	39.3		
	43.5	42.4	41.0	40.3		39.7		
	47.7	46.7	43.8	44.0	42.7	43.2		
	51.0	51.4	46.7	46.3	46.0	46.3	46.3	45.8
	55.3	53.4						
LA	63.2		52.0	50.6		51.3		
	68.6	68.7	54.7	53.5	52.4	51.9		
	72.6	69.7	66.8	67.0		69.2		
		76.9		69.0	70.3	70.2		

	4H		6H		15R		3C	
	F_x	N_x	F_x	N_x	F_x	N_x	F_x	N_x
	79.4	78.8	77.3	77.0	75.2			
					78.2	78.2	79.5	79.4
TO	89.7		94.3	94.7	94.2	94.6		
	91.8		95.8	95.6		95.3		
		95.0	97.0	97.8	95.5	95.7	94.4	93.7
		96.1			96.7	97.1		
	99.0	96.7						
LO		104.0		104.2	103.2	103.7	102.8	103.3
	104.6	104.3	105.0	105.5		106.3		
		107.0		107.0	107.2	106.9		
		107.4						

3. PL Spectra of SiC

The PL spectra involving exciton include three kinds of progress: one is recombination radiation spectrum of free excitons (intrinsic spectrum); another is spectrum of excitons bound to neutral nitrogen atoms, which is relative to the donor four particle neutral complex (4D complex) made up of a neutral nitrogen donor and an exciton; and the last one is the spectrum of exciton bound to neutral Al acceptor, which is relative to acceptor four particle neutral complex (4A complex) composed of a neutral Al acceptor and an exciton.

3.1 *PL Spectrum of 6H-SiC*

Fig.2[6] is the PL spectrum of lightly P-doped epitaxial films of 6H-SiC grown on 6H-SiC substrate. The series lines marked I_{44}, I_{46}, I_{77}, I_{95}, I_{104} and I_{107} represent the radiative recombination of the intrinsic exciton in 6H-SiC with the emission of a momentum-conserving phonon whose energy in meV is given as a subscript. At low doping levels the ratio of the I_{77} intrinsic line to the three nitrogen non-phonon lines, or other non-phonon lines due to incorporation of impurities, is an excellent indication of concentration of such impurities. Three non-phonon lines P_0, R_0, S_0 are shown in Fig.2, which are the recombination radiation of an exciton in a 4D complex at the three inequivalent donor sites of the 6H-SiC unit cell. Among the P, R and S series lines, P series is due to 4D complex at h-site and the other two are ascribed to 4D complex at k_1- or k_2-site. The total recombination rate at one of the three sites can be found by integrating over a series of lines. Choyke[4] found experimentally that the recombination rate at the h-site is four or five times larger than that at k_1- or k_2-site, while the rates at k_1- and k_2-site are nearly the same. The recombination rate depends on capture, dissociation and recombination probabilities. At low temperature, such as 6 K, dissociation is negligible, and the recombination is not important in the case of 6H-SiC that the complexes are not approaching saturation. Hence, the greater h-site recombination rate is an indication of a larger h-site exciton capture cross section. This shows that the donor at h-site has a larger radius, i. e. , the h-site donor binds exciton more loosely, because the larger the hydrogen-like donor radius is, the greater Van der Waals attraction is between the donor and another hydrogen-like exciton. And the donor would have larger capture cross section.

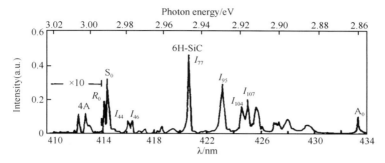

Fig.2　Low-temperature photoluminescence spectrum of epitaxial film of 6H-SiC

Exciton recombination in 6H-SiC is an indirect one, hence recombination without phonon absorption or emission is forbidden for free excitons. The localization of exciton by binding to a donor makes the P_0, R_0 and S_0 lines possible. At 6K, the R_0 and S_0 lines are considerably stronger than P_0. This is consistent with the stronger binding, hence greater localization, of the exciton at k_1-or k_2-site than that of the exciton at h-site.

Between the P_0 and the R_0, S_0 lines of nitrogen 4D complex, there are some other lines marked 4A. The very sharp lines show splittings as small as 0.1 meV, and the strongest one is as intense as P_0. The 4A lines are indentified with the recombination of an exciton in a 4A complex involving Al on Si site. Clemen et al[7] argued that a large number of closely spaced lines will be given rise to by the recombination radiation of shallow 4A complex in 6H-SiC. The 4A complex consists of neutral acceptor and an exciton. The binding energy arise from the exchange interaction between the indistinguishable holes. Fig. 3 illustates their scheme. The diagrams show how two holes and an electron are combined to obtain a multiplet of closely spaced initial states of the complex. The degeneracies of

6H-SiC silicon site C_{3v} symmetry

2 hole coupling symmetry state Γ_1 only	
1 electron low density at core	Add spin 1/2

$(2)\Gamma_3$ ———⟨ $(2)\Gamma_{56}$ / $(2)\Gamma_4$

$(2)\Gamma_3$ ———⟨ $(2)\Gamma_{56}$ / $(2)\Gamma_4$

$(1)\Gamma_1$ ——————— $(2)\Gamma_4$

$(1)\Gamma_1$ ——————— $(2)\Gamma_4$

2 holes + 1 electron

		Polarization
$\Gamma_1 \times \Gamma_{56} = \Gamma_{56}$	$(2)\Gamma_{56}$	E//C
$\Gamma_1 \times \Gamma_4 = \Gamma_4$	$(2)\Gamma_4$	E⊥C
$\Gamma_1 \times \Gamma_{56} = \Gamma_{56}$	$(2)\Gamma_{56}$	E//C
$\Gamma_1 \times \Gamma_4 = \Gamma_4$	$(2)\Gamma_4$	E⊥C
$\Gamma_1 \times \Gamma_4 = \Gamma_4$	$(2)\Gamma_4$	E⊥C
$\Gamma_1 \times \Gamma_4 = \Gamma_4$	$(2)\Gamma_4$	E⊥C

Fig. 3　Schematic representation of the symmetry for an acceptor four particle complex at a silicon site in 6H-SiC

level are shown in parentheses, and the ordering of the levels is arbitrary. The final states of this system are those of the neutral acceptor in its ground state.

3. 2　PL Spectrum of 4H-SiC

PL spectra of 4H-SiC are given in Fig. 4[5]. 4H-SiC possesses one half k-site and another half h-site in its unit cell. So its PL spectra at low temperature should consist of two series

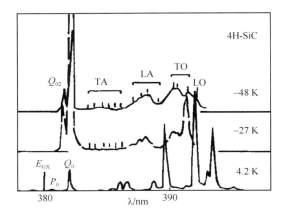

Fig. 4   Exciton luminescence of 4H-SiC

lines: P and Q series. But from Fig. 4 we can not observe P series lines except a very weak P_0 line. P_0 and Q_0 lines are non-phonon lines of the recombination radiation of excitons in 4D complex at the two inequivalent h- and k-sites of 4H-SiC. The weak P_0 line states that the energy of donor on h-site binding exciton is very small. When the temperature rises up to 27 K, P_0 line has disappeared at all, while Q_0 line is still very strong. This is because that the donor at h-site can not bind exciton at the temperature of 27 K, and the 4D complex at h-site dissociated and recombination without phonon absorption or emission becomes forbidden. The behavior of P_0 and Q_0 lines at various temperatures suggests the stronger binding, hence greater localizaton, of the exciton at k-site, which is similar to the cases of 6H-SiC.

3. 3   PL Spectrum of 3C-SiC

3C-SiC takes a relatively simpler crystal structure with higher symmetry compared with other SiC polytypes. There is only one cubic-like site in 3C-SiC, and its PL spectrum consists of one series line corresponding to the excitons bound to donors at k-site.

By using of RTCVD system, we have epitaxially grown 3C-SiC films on Si substrates. The thickness of epilayer ranges from 50 nm to 250 nm. Results of double crystal X-ray diffraction and RHEED show that the epilayers are exellent single crystal layer. Fig. 5 is a PL spectrum of 3C-SiC epilayer grown on Si (100) substrate. As shown in Fig. 5, the P_0 line locates at the position of 522 nm with photon energy of 2.38 eV. The value is the same as Choyke's[8]. On the basis of phonon spectrum of 3C-SiC given by Ikeda, we positioned the phonon replica of P_0 lines and marked them in Fig. 5. In addition to the one or two phonon replicas, the other lines

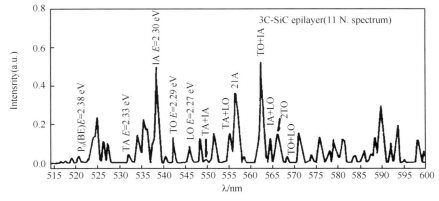

Fig.5   Low-temperature photoluminescence spectrum of 3C-SiC epilayer grown on Si(100) substrate

may be due to the transition process in which N donor jumps onto excited states while phonons are emitted. Choyke *et al.*[8] determined the exciton gap E_{GX} as 2.39eV through absorption spectrum, hence the value of energy of N donor binding exciton is found to be 10meV. The small binding energy suggests that the donor to which excitons are bound should be neutral. Therefore, we can conclude that there exists neutral N impurity in our 3C-SiC epilayer, which is unintentionally incorporated.

The PL spectrum results also prove that our single crystal 3C-SiC epilayer has high quality.

4. Conclusions

Summarizing the studies on PL spectra of SiC and referring to the FTIR results, we can draw the following conclusions:

1. Energy levels of acceptors residing at h-or k-site of SiC are not quite different.

2. In SiC, energy levels of donors strongly depend on the inequivalence of h-or k-site where the donors situate and differ from each other obviously.

3. The energy level of impurity occupied k-site is deeper than that of the impurity occupied h-site.

4. The larger number of atoms contained in unit cell of SiC lead to the complicated phonon spectra of SiC.

References

[1] Liang Junwu and Zhu Jianjun. *Chinese Journal of Electronics*, 1998, 7(1): 28.

[2] Ikeda M, Matsunami H and Tanaka T. *Phys.Rev.B*, 1980, **22**(6): 2842.

[3] Yang C Y and Rahman M M ed. Amorphous and Crystalline Silicon Carbide (Springer-Verleg, Berlin, 1992). 129.

[4] Choyke W J and Patrick L. *Phys.Rev.*, 1962. **127**(6): 1868.

[5] Ikeda M and Matsunami H. *Physica.Status.Solid(a)i*, 1980. **58**: 657.

[6] Pensl G and Choyde W J. *Physica B*, 1993, **185**: 264.

[7] Yang C Y and Rahman M M ed. Amorphous and Crystalline Silicon Carbide (Springer-Verleg, Berlin, 1992). 105.

[8] Choyke W J, Hamilton P R and Patric L. *Phys.Rev.*, 1964, **133**(4a): 1163.

Raman Study on Residual Strains in Thin 3C-SiC Epitaxial Layers Grown on Si(001)

Jianjun Zhu*, Suying Liu, Junwu Liang

(*Institute of Semiconductors, Chinese Academy of Sciences, Beijing 100083, People's Republic of China*)

Abstract: Raman scattering measurement has been used to study the residual strains in the thin 3C-SiC/Si(001) epilayers with a variation of film thickness from 0.1 to 1.2μm, which were prepared by chemical vapor deposition (CVD) growth. Two methods have been exploited to figure out the residual strains and the exact LO bands. The final analyzing results show that residual strains exist in the 3C-SiC epilayers. The average stress is 1.3010GPa, and the relative change of the lattice constant is 1.36‰. Our measurements also show that 3C-SiC phonons are detectable even for the samples with film thickness in the range of 0.1 to 0.2μm. © 2000 Published by Elsevier Science S.A. All rights reserved.

Keywords: Raman spectrum; Thin film; Chemical vapor deposition

1 Introduction

SiC is a potential material for high temperature and high-power applications. Among all the SiC polytypes, 3C-SiC has the most excellent electrical properties, which makes it a candidate for developing high frequency and high-speed devices. Recently, an increasing number of people are using 3C-SiC as substrates for GaN growth by MOCVD or molecular beam epitaxy (MBE). The crystal quality of 3C-SiC layers is very important for growing high quality GaN films on the 3C-SiC substrates. Therefore, it is neces-sary to investigate the properties, such as strains and stres-ses, of 3C-SiC epilayers in order to improve the crystal quality of 3C-SiC epilayers grown on Si substrates.

Growing 3C-SiC epilayers on Si substrates by the CVD method is an important way to get large area 3C-SiC films and has been studied extensively by many groups in the last few dozen of years. Due to the lattice misfit between 3C-SiC and Si being as large as 20%, the poor completeness of 3C-SiC/Si interface has been the main obstacle to grow high quality 3C-SiC film on Si. The large misfit produces a high density of dislocations and these interfacial misfit dislocations greatly release the interfacial strains. However, there must be residual strains in the 3C-SiC epilayers, especially in our very thin films. Raman scattering measurement is a powerful technique for the study on strains in SiC because the Raman efficiency of this material is high with the strong covalency of the bonding. In this work, we prepared 3C-SiC/Si samples and

---

原载于:Thin Solid Films, 2000, 368:307-311.

* Corresponding author.

worked out the residual strains and stresses in the 3C-SiC epilayers through Raman scattering measurement of the materials.

2 Experimental details

We have grown 3C-SiC/Si (001) epilayers by CVD method, using SiH_4 and C_3H_8 as source gases and H_2 as carrier gas. The growth temperature was 1330℃ and nitrogen has been used as doping gas. Resistance of the 3C-SiC epilayers has been measured by expanding resistance measurement. Raman scattering spectra of 3C-SiC/Si epilayers were conducted at room temperature using 488 nm Arion laser as incident light. The spectra were attained in back scattering geometry. Table 1 gives some parameters of the 3C-SIC samples.

3 Results and analysis

Fig. 1a-e are the Raman spectra corresponding to 3C-SiC samples listed in Table 1. We can see from the figures that TO modes of all the samples were observed and the LO modes overlapped with the second order Raman spectrum of silicon. For back scattering geometry, TO mode of 3C-SIC, which has a zinc-blend-type crystal structure, is not Raman active. The appearance of TO mode in the Raman spectrum of 3C-SiC shows that the actual scattering geome-try was no longer an exact back scattering one, in which the TO mode scattering turned to be Raman active. This can be ascribed to the following two causes: (a) there exist stacking faults and interfacial dislocations and offset between the crystal orientation of epilayer and substrate; (b) multireflection of the 488nm incident light occurs in the 3C-SiC layers, which makes the forward and back scattering observable at the same time.

Table 1   Paramters of 3C-SiC/Si samples

Samples	3C-SiC epilayers			SiSubstrates	
	Thickness(μm)	$\rho(\Omega\ cm)$	Conducting type	Conducting type	$\rho(\Omega\ cm)$
A	1.2	0.02-1.5	n	p(001)	30
B	0.11	0.3-0.5	n	n⁻n⁺(001)	8/0.06
C	0.16	0.01-0.1		n⁻/n⁺(001)	8/0.06
D	0.13	7.0-10.0	n	p(001)	8
E	0.6	2.7-9.0	n	n⁻/n⁺(001)	8/0.06

The lineshapes of TO mode in the figures has a shoulder instead of being symmetric. This type of lineshape can be attributed to the existence of biaxial tensile strains in 3C-SIC layers in the plane paralleling the surface of Si substrate. The intensity of TO band peak in Fig. 1a is much stronger than those in the other four figures. This difference arises from that the thickness of sample A is times of that of the other samples, and that Raman intensity of 3C-SiC grows with an increase of 3C-SiC layer thickness. After a systematic study on Raman spectrum of CVD grown 3C-SIC with a variation of SiC film thickness (d_{SiC}) from 600 Å to 17μm, Feng et al. [1] pointed out that no SiC phonon can be detected for samples with $d_{SiC}<0.4\mu m$, and only when d_{SiC} increases to 0.6μm is the SiC LO (Γ) recognizable above the background. In our measurements, 3C-SIC phonons are all detected even for the samples with d_{SiC} in the range of 0.1-0.2μm, although the peaks of LO bands are not sharp and clear.

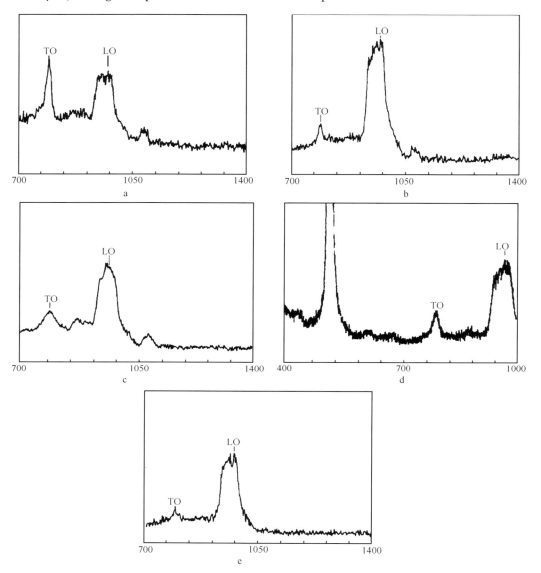

Fig.1   Raman spectra of 3C-SiC/Si(001) samples

4   Discussion

Oleo and Cardona [2] had studied the effects of pressure on the phonons of zinc-blend-type semiconductors and reported the dependence on pressure of the frequencies of the TO (F) and LO (F) modes of 3C-SiC measured for pressures up to 22.5 GPa using fist-order Raman scattering. They found the measured LO (Γ) and TO (Γ) phonon energies can be described within experimental error with the following least-squares fits

$$\omega_{TO} = (796.2\pm0.3) + (3.88\pm0.08)P - (2.2+0.4)\times10^{-2}P^2$$

$$\omega_{LO} = (972.7\pm0.3) + (4.75\pm0.09)P - (2.5\pm0.4)\times10^{-2}P^2$$

$$\omega_{LO} - \omega_{TO} = (176.3\pm0.6) + (8.5\pm0.2)\times10^{-1}P - (2.5\pm1)\times10^{-3}P^2 \qquad (1)$$

with ω_{TO} and ω_{LO} given in cm^{-1} and pressure (P) in GPa. They also related the measured pressure and the corresponding change in the lattice constant

$$\frac{a}{a_0} = \left(\frac{B_0}{B_0}P + 1\right)^{-\frac{1}{3B_0}} \qquad (2)$$

where P represents the pressure, $a_0 = 4.36$Å the lattice constant at room temperature. $B_0 = 321.9$GPa the bulk modulus and $B_0' = 3.43$ the derivative of B_0 with respect to P. From Eqs. (1) and (2) we can obtain

$$\omega_{TO} = (796.5\pm0.3) + (3734\pm30)(-\Delta a/a_0)$$

$$\omega_{LO} = (973\pm0.3) + (4532\pm30)(-\Delta a/a_0)$$

$$\omega_{TO} - \omega_{TO} = (176.5\pm0.6) + (806\pm50)(-\Delta a/a_0) \qquad (3)$$

with ω_{TO} and ω_{LO} also given in cm^{-1}.

Table 2 gives out relative change in the lattice constants of the five 3C-SiC samples, the corresponding LO (Γ) bands and pressure calculated from Raman data using Eqs. (1) and (3).

Table 2 TO bands of 3C-SiC/Si samples and calculated strains, LO bands and pressure of them

Samples	TO bands(cm^{-1})	$\Delta a/a_0$(‰)	LO bands(cm^{-1})	P(GPa)
A	793.0	0.94	968.8	−0.903
B	791.9	1.23	967.4	−1.18
C	792.9	0.96	968.6	−0.922
D	789.6	1.74	965.1	−1.66
E	789.3	1.93	964.3	−1.84

By analyzing the calculated results we can find that the average change in the lattice constant is 1.36‰ and the pressure is averaged to be -1.301GPa. The minus sign of pressure shows that the stresses in the 3C-SiC epilayers are tensile ones, which accords with the actual conditions of 3C-SiC/Si system considering the differences between the lattice constants and thermal-expanding ratio of 3C-SiC and Si.

In order to estimate the stresses in the 3C-SiC layers more exactly and make sure of the LO bands, we figured out the residual strains and stresses in 3C-SiC layers exploiting the method proposed by Cerdeitra et al. [3] and Jusserand et al. [4] when they studied the dependence of optical branch phonon energies on the strains in zinc-blend-type semicon-ductors. In back scattering geometry, TO and LO phonon frequencies in strained 3C-SiC layers can be written as

$$\Omega_{LO} = \omega_0 + 2\Delta\Omega_H - 2/3\Delta\Omega$$

$$\Omega_{TO} = \omega_0 + 2\Delta\Omega_H + 1/3\Delta\Omega$$

$$\Delta\Omega_H = (X/6\omega_0)(p + 2q)(S_{11} + 2S_{12})$$

$$\Delta \Omega = (X/2\omega_0)(p-q)(S_{11}-S_{12}) \text{ for stress in (001) direction}$$
$$\Delta \Omega = (X/2\omega_0) r S_{44} \text{ for stress in (111) direction} \tag{4}$$

where ω_0 is the frequency of TO or LO when the 3C-SiC layers are free of strains; $\Delta \Omega_H$ Raman shift caused by stresses; $\Delta \Omega$ splitting of two degenerate TO mode caused by stresses; p, q, r three constants describing the change in effective spring constants induced by strains; S_{11}, S_{12}, S_{44} the elastic compliance constants; X the strength of the stress. Mukaida [5] and Feng et al. [1] studied the effects of strains on Raman spectra of the TO and LO phonons of 3C-SiC epitaxially grown on Si. According to their study, when 3C-SiC is free from strains, its TO and LO phonon frequencies are 796.1cm and 972.9cm^{-1} respectively, mode-Grüneisen parameter $\gamma = -(p+2q)/6\omega_0^2 = 1.23.$, Young's modulus $E = 7.794 \times 10^{10}$Pa, and Poisson ratio $v = 0.4487$. Using these data and Eq. (4), we can work out values of $\Delta \Omega, \Delta \Omega_H$, and corresponding LO bands with the pressure (P) listed in Table 2 as a starting point. In our calculation, we took P as stress suffered by 3C-SiC epilayer in the plane paralleling the surface of Si substrate because that in 3C-SiC/Si materials the strains in 3C-SiC layers can be considered as strains in a plane. As to the problem of a strain in a plane, we can

$$\varepsilon_{zz} = \varepsilon_\perp$$
$$\varepsilon_{//} = \varepsilon_{xx} = \varepsilon_{yy}$$
$$\sigma = \sigma_{xx} = \sigma_{yy}$$
$$\sigma_{zz} = 0$$
$$E \times \varepsilon_{//} = (1-v)$$
$$E \times \varepsilon_\perp = -2v\sigma$$

In our measurements, there is no pressure in the direction perpendicular to the substrate surface. Therefore, the P in Table 2 should be regarded as a biaxial stress suffered by 3C-SiC layers in the plane paralleling the surface of substrate.

Table 3 is filled out with the values of $\Delta \Omega, \Delta \Omega_H$, and corresponding LO bands figured out from P in Table 2 using Eq. (4). Comparing the LO bands in Table 2 with those in Table 3, we can find that the above two method bring out two very similar LO bands. Basing on these results we supposed that we can single out the LO bands of every Raman spectrum in the neighboring range of our calculated LO bands. To do this we chose two bands nearest to our calculated one for every Raman spectrum of 3C-SiC sample and then obtained the stress strength by calculation. Our calculated results and the two chosen bands (A and B) for every sample are listed in Table 4.

Table 3   Calculated $2\Delta \Omega_H, \Delta \Omega$ and LO Bands using Eqs. (3) and (4)

Samples	P(Gpa)	$2\Delta \Omega_H$(cm^{-1})	$\Delta \Omega$(cm^{-1})	LO bands(cm^{-1})
A	−0.903	−2.86	−0.033	970.1
B	−1.18	−3.74	−0.044	969.2
c	−0.922	−2.92	−0.034	970.0
d	−1.66	−5.26	−0.061	967.7
e	−1.84	−5.83	−0.068	967.1

Table 4　Possible LO bands in Raman spectra of 3C-SiC/Si samples and analyzing results

Samples	TO(cm^{-1})	LO(cm^{-1})		$2s\Delta\Omega_H$(cm^{-1})		$\Delta\Omega$(cm^{-1})		X(GPa)	
		A	B	A	B	A	B	A	B
a	792.1	964.5	973.7	−4.76	−2.09	5.46	−4.34	1.50	0.66
b	791.9	964.7	975.2	−4.82	−1.77	5.07	−6.11	1.53	0.56
c	792.9	962.7	975.0	−4.82	− 1.25	8.07	−5.02	1.53	0.40
d	789.6	967.5	972.9	−5.34	−3.77	0.09	−5.70	1.68	1.20
e	789.3	967.2	971.7	−5.60	−4.30	0.15	−4.65	1.78	1.36

The calculated results of X shows that when LO band of sample D is chosen as 967.5cm^{-1} and the one of sample E as 967.2cm^{-1}, the X in Table 4, accords well with the corresponding P in Table 2. Thus, we granted 967.5cm and 967.2cm^{-1} as LO bands of sample D and E, respectively. As to X values of sample A, B and C in Table 4, that not only X is quite different from the corresponding P but also $|\Delta\Omega|$ is greater than $|2\Delta\Omega|$ is unreasonable. From Table 1 we can find that the resistance of sample A, B, and C are one or two orders smaller than that of sample D and E. This implies that the carrier concentration of sample A, B and C are much greater than that of sample D and E. Since 3C-SiC is a polar semiconductor, its collective excitation of free carriers (plasma exciton) can interacts with the longitudinal optical (LO) phonon via their macroscopic electric fields to form the LO phonon-plasma-coupled mode (LOPC). The LOPC bands are broad and their peaks are shifted to higher frequency with increasing free carrier density. Yugamis et al. [6] also proved that peaks of LO bands of 3C-SiC epilayer shift greatly to high frequency side when the carrier concentration of 3C-SiC epilayer is larger than 5×10^{-7} cm^{-3}. Hence, we prefer to select LO bands of choice B in Table 4 for sample A, B, and C. The subsequent results are that LO bands of sample A, B and C shift greatly to high frequency side, while the strength of stresses in their 3C-SiC layers is smaller than that for sample D and E. This greater shift can be ascribed to the interaction between plasma exci-ton and phonon instead of a value of pressure or stress strength greater than that in sample D and E. Thus, the carrier concentrations of sample, B and C are estimated to be in the range of 5×10^{17} to 1×10^{18} cm^{-3} according to the results of Yugami et. al.

Summarizing the above analyses, we can obtain Table 5 as the final results of our Raman measurements. Since our 3C-SiC layers are all very thin (thousands of Å), the residual strains in our 3C-SiC layers are one to two times larger than the values obtained by Mukaida et. al. whose samples have an average thickness of about 5μm.

Table 5　Raman spectra analyzing results of 3C-SiCISi samples

Samples	TO(cm^{-1})	LO(cm^{-1})	$-P(X)$(GPa)	$\Delta a/a_0$(‰)	$\varepsilon_{//}$(‰)	ε_T(‰)
A	793.0	973.7	0.903	0.94	6.27	−10.20
B	791.9	975.2	1.18	1.23	8.29	−13.33
C	792.9	975.0	0.922	0.96	6.40	−10.42
D	789.6	967.5	1.66	1.74	11.52	−18.75
E	789.3	967.2	1.84	1.93	12.77	−20.79

5   Conclusions

We have conducted Raman scattering measurements of 3C-SiC epilayers grown on Si substrates by CVD method. The final analyzing results shows that there exist residual strains in the epilayers. The average stress is 1.301GPa, and the relative change of the lattice constant is 1.36‰. The strains in the directions paralleling and perpendicular to the surface of substrate are 9.05 and −14.7‰, respectively, which accords well with our double crystal X-ray diffraction results.

References

[1] Z.C.Feng, A.J.Mascarenhas, W.J.Choyke, J.A.Powell, J.Appl.Phys.64(6)(1988)3176.

[2] Diego Olego, M.Cardona, Phys.Rev.B 25(6)(1982)3878.

[3] F.Derdeira, C.J.Buchenauer, F.H.Pollak, M.Cardona, Phys.Rev.B5 (1972)580.

[4] B.Jusserand, P.Voisin, M.Voos, L.L.Chang, E.E.Mendez, L.Esaki, Appl.Phys.Lett.46(1985)678.

[5] H.Mukaida, H.Okumura, J.H.Lee, et al., J.Appl.Phys.62(1)(1987)254.

[6] H.Yugami, S.Nakasima, A.Mitsuishi, J.Appl.Phys.61(1)(1987)354.

Investigation of {1 1 1} A and {1 1 1} B Planes of c-GaN Epilayers Grown on GaAs(0 0 1) by MOCVD

X.H.Zheng[a,*], B.Qu[a], Y.T.Wang[a], Z.H.Feng[a], J.Y.Han[b], Hui Yang[a], J.W.Liang[a]

([a]Institute of Semiconductors, Chinese Academy of Sciences, R&D Center for Optoelec.Technology P.O.Box 912, Beijing 100083, People's Republic of China)

([b]Institute of Minerals and Resources, Chinese Academy of Geological Sciences, Beijing 100037, People's Republic of China

Received 22 May 2001; accepted 23 May 2001)

Communicated by M.Schieber

Abstract: A determination of {1 1 1} A and {1 1 1} B in cubic GaN (c-GaN) was investigated by X-ray diffraction technique in detail. The c-GaN films are grown on GaAs(0 0 1) substrates by metalorganic chemical vapor deposition (MOCVD). The difference of integrated intensities measured by ω scan for the different order diffractions from {1 1 1} A and {1 1 1} B planes in the four-circle diffractometer gives convincing evidence as to which is the {1 1 1} A and which is the {1 1 1} B planes. The lesser deviation between the ratios of $|F_{hkl}|^2/|F_{\bar{h}\bar{k}\bar{l}}|^2$ and the calculated values after dispersion correction for atomic scattering factor shows that the content of parasitic hexagonal GaN(h-GaN) grown on c-GaN {1 1 1} A planes is higher than that on {1 1 1} B planes. The reciprocal space mappings provide additional proof that the h-GaN inclusions in c-GaN films appear as lamellar structure.© 2001 Published by Elsevier Science B.V.

PACS: 61.10.Dp; 81.05.Ea; 68.60.Wm; 78.66.Fb

Keywords: Al. X-ray diffraction; A3. Metalorganic chemical vapor deposition; Bl. Gallium compounds

1 Introduction

GaN-based materials, due to their superior intrinsic properties such as wide range of direct transition-type energy band gaps, high thermal conductivity and high electron saturation velocity, are promising candidates of choice for applications in short wavelength LEDs, LDs, and photodiodes in visible and ultraviolet regions, as well as high-power electronic devices[1-3]. GaN may crystalize in either stable hexagonal(wurtzite) or metastable cubic (zincblende) polytypes. Up to date, considerable efforts have been concentrated on h-GaN. However. C-GaN films on GaAs substrates for LD application have potential superiorities including easy cleavage planes that align with GaN, easier doping, loW resistivity (higher carrier mobility), use of well developed GaAs substrates for GaN technology and monolithic integration of GaN and GaAs devices,

---

原载于: Journal of Crystal Growth 2001, 233: 52-56.

* Corresponding author.

E-mail address: xhzheng@ red.semi.ac.cn(X.H.zheng).

etc. Therefore, interest in c-GaN has grown astronomically [4-7]. Recently, c-GaN LEDs have been successfully realized [8-9].

It is well known that there are four similar {1 1 1} planes in the cubic noncentrosymmetric structure; two {1 1 1} B planes are along the [1 $\bar{1}$ 0] axis and two {1 1 1} A planes are along the [1 1 0] axis. Generally speaking, the {1 1 1} A and {1 1 1} B planes are both composed of identical closepacked double layers. An equivalent definition is based on the generally accepted assumption [10] that one face will be a Ga-terminated plane [symbolically (1 1 1)A] and the other a N-terminted plane [symbolically (1 1 1)B]. In semiconductor physics the electrical and chemical properties of opposite {1 1 1} faces may be very different, and in the actual growth of the epilayers the distinct velocity may be of great importance. Usually, the {1 1 1} A and {1 1 1} B determination may be performed by the utilization of the anomalous X-ray dispersion effect with its resulting differences in the integrated intensities [11-13]. In all these cases, this technique was most applied in the bulk single crystal. However, to the best of our knowledge, the use of such a method in the epilayers has not yet been reported. Therefore, we have determined the {1 1 1} A and {1 1 1} B planes of c-GaN films grown on GaAs (0 0 1) by observing the effects of {1 1 1} A and {1 1 1} B planes on the intensity of scattered X-ray for the first time. Moreover, different contents of parasitic h-GaN inclusions were found by this method. We also employed the reciprocal space mappings to obtain the shape of h-GaN inclusions.

2 Experimental procedure

The c-GaN layers were grown by MOCVD on (0 0 1) GaAs substrates by two-step growth which consists of a 20−30-nm-thick buffer layer grown at 500℃ and a main GaN layer grown at 850℃. Ammonia (NH$_3$) and triethylgallium (TEGa) are used as the precursors of N and Ga, respectively. H$_2$ is used as the carrier gas. X-ray diffraction measurements were performed with a Rigaku four-circle X-ray diffractometer equipped with a rotating anode Cu target. In order to generate Cu K$_{\alpha 1}$ radiation ($\lambda = 1.5405$Å), a very narrow slit was used. In addition, the X-ray beam was collimated by a 0.15×2mm aperture to maintain a beam size which was small compared to the total surface area being studied. A soller slit was placed in front of the detector. The X-ray diffraction pattern of ω scan mode was obtained using a step of 0.001°.

3 Results and discussion

Based on the extinction rule of X-ray diffraction, as far as {1 1 1} planes are concerned, the first, second, etc. order diffractions should appear. The c-GaN {1 1 1} planes are tilted from the GaAs (0 0 1) face by about 54.74°. The diffracted intensities by ω scan mode were recorded and after each measurement the c-GaN epilayers were rotated around the axis perpendicular to the surface of GaAs (0 0 1) substrate. The first and second order diffractions from the {1 1 1} A and {1 1 1} B are shown in Fig. 1. The results show that the integrated intensities of {1 1 1} diffractions and {2 2 2} ones change to a lesser extent, respectively. According to the formula of integrated intensity [14],

$$I = I_0 |F_{h k l}|^2 V L N^2 e^{-2M}$$

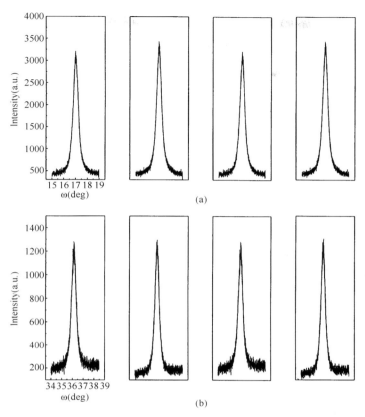

Fig.1 XRD intensity measurements with Cu $K_{\alpha 1}$ radiation showing a series of $\{1\,1\,1\}$ A planes and $\{1\,1\,1\}$ B planes.(a) The first-order diffractions from $\{1\,1\,1\}$ A and $\{1\,1\,1\}$ B faces,respectively.The diffracted intensities from $\{1\,1\,1\}$ A are higher than those from $\{1\,1\,1\}$ B.(b) The second-order diffractions from $\{1\,1\,1\}$ A and $\{1\,1\,1\}$ B faces,respectively.The diffracted intensities from $\{1\,1\,1\}$ A are almost equal to those from $\{1\,1\,1\}$ B planes

where I_0, F_{hkl}, V, L, N and e^{-2M} are the incident X-ray intensity, structure amplitude, volume fac-tor, Lorentz polarization factor, the number of unit cells per unit volume and the temperature factor, respectively. It can be speculated from this formula that the ratio of $I_{(hhh)}/I_{(\bar{h}\bar{h}\bar{h})}$ is only related to the structure amplitude F_{hkl}. According to the definition of F_{hkl}, we may safely obtain the ratios of the structure amplitude of $(h\,h\,h)$ to that of $(\bar{h}\,\bar{h}\,\bar{h})$. The expression is as follows :

$$\frac{F_{(1\,1\,1)}}{F_{(\bar{1}\,\bar{1}\,\bar{1})}} = \frac{|f_{Ga}-if_N|}{|f_{Ga}+if_N|},\ \frac{|F_{(2\,2\,2)}|}{|F_{(\bar{2}\,\bar{2}\,\bar{2})}|} = 1,$$

where f_{Ga} and f_N are atomic scattering factors for Ga and N atoms, respectively. For compound c-GaN, its unit cell contains more than one kind of atom then addition change of phase angle will be introduced by these different atoms. In order to conveniently account for the change of phase angle, the components of the complex structure factors can be expressed in the following form : $f = f_0 + \Delta f' + i\Delta f''$, where f_0 is the normal scattering factor usually tabulated as a real function of

$\sin \theta / \lambda$, and $\Delta f'$ and $\Delta f''$ are called the real and imaginary dispersion corrections. f_0, $\Delta f'$ and $\Delta f''$ can be obtained from the related literature [15]. The values for Ga and N atoms are tabulated in Table 1.

Table 1   Atomic scattering factors and the dispersion corrections f_0, $\Delta f'$ and $\Delta f''$ for Cu $K_{\alpha 1}$ radiation

Atom species	(1 1 1) diffraction			(2 2 2) diffraction		
	f_0	$\Delta f'$	$\Delta f''$	f_0	$\Delta f'$	$\Delta f''$
Ga	24.94	−1.5	0.9	18.28	−1.5	0.8
N	4.62	0	0	2.4	0	0

Considering that the diffracted intensity is proportional to $|F_{hkl}|^2$, we put the calculated values of $|F_{(hhh)}|^2 / |F_{(\bar{h}\bar{h}\bar{h})}|^2$ and the measured ratios of integrated intensities from $\{h\,h\,h\}$ diffractions to $\{\bar{h}\,\bar{h}\,\bar{h}\}$ diffractions in Table 2.

Table 2   Calculated ratios of the scattering factors of $\{h\,h\,h\}$ planes to the opposite $\{\bar{h}\,\bar{h}\,\bar{h}\}$ planes in comparison with the experimental values

	$|F_{(hhh)}|^2 / |F_{(\bar{h}\bar{h}\bar{h})}|^2$ meas.	$|F_{(hhh)}|^2 / |F_{(\bar{h}\bar{h}\bar{h})}|^2$ calc.
1 1 1	0.9	0.97
2 2 2	0.96	1

It should be noted from the above table that there is a little smaller deviation between the measured $|F_{(hhh)}|^2 / |F_{(\bar{h}\bar{h}\bar{h})}|^2$ values and calculated ones. It is well known that the lattice spacings of hexagonal (0 0 0 2) planes and cubic (1 1 1) planes are almost the same, and hence it is possible that the four $\{1 1 1\}$ or $\{2 2 2\}$ diffractions originate from the sum of diffractions from h-GaN(0 0 0 2) and c-GaN(1 1 1) planes. In the previous reports [16-18], XRD, TEM and Raman analysis proved that the hexagonal phase is easily introduced in c-GaN films. In order to distinguish hexagonal (0 0 0 2) diffraction from cubic (1 1 1) diffraction, therefore, we performed the hexagonal diffraction of other planes. A pole figure of h-GaN $\{1\,0\,\bar{1}\,0\}$ planes was generated but is not given here. The X value, which refers to the angle between the GaAs surface [(0 0 1) plane] and the plane under measurement, indicates that the angles between the h-GaN $\{1\,0\,\bar{1}\,0\}$ planes and the c-GaN(0 0 1) plane are 35.26° and 65.9°. This provides a conclusion that the orientation relationship [19] between the parasitic hexagonal GaN and c-GaN films is $(0\,0\,0\,2)_{\text{h-GaN}} \parallel (1\,1\,1)_{\text{c-GaN}}$, $\langle 1\,0\,\bar{1}\,0 \rangle_{\text{h-GaN}} \parallel \langle 1\,1\,2 \rangle_{\text{c-GaN}}$. Moreover, the content of h-GaN inclusions can be estimated by comparing the integrated XRD intensities for h-GaN $\{1\,0\,\bar{1}\,0\}$ and c-GaN (0 0 2) planes. The contents of h-GaN in four $\langle 1\,1\,1 \rangle$ directions are 1.3%, 0.6%, 1.2% and 0.5%, respectively. The content difference can also be verified by the difference of diffracted intensities of h-GaN $\{1\,0\,\bar{1}\,0\}$ on $\{1\,1\,1\}$ A and $\{1\,1\,1\}$ B faces in the Φ scan profile, which is shown in Fig. 2. The data clearly indicate that the content of h-GaN inclusions on $\{1\,1\,1\}$ A planes is a little higher than that on $\{1\,1\,1\}$ B ones. In addition, the expression formula of integrated intensity tells us that the integrated intensities of h-GaN (0 0 0 2) is smaller than those of c-GaN (1 1 1) because of $| F_{111} |^2 / V^2_{cubic} > | F_{0002} |^2 / V^2_{hexagonal}$ when the radiation area ΔV is identical (the letter meaning is the same as ever expressed). The relation of integrated inten-sities from h-GaN (0 0 0 4) and c-GaN (2 2 2) reflec-tions is no exception. As a conse-quence, the increase of h-GaN inclusions on {1 1 1} A planes inversely decreases the intensities of {1 1 1} and {2 2 2} diffractions from {1 1 1} A ones. Here, we

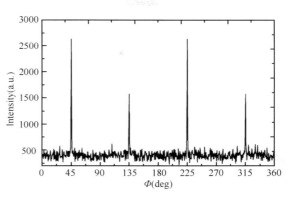

Fig.2 The Φ scan of {1 0 $\bar{1}$ 0} poles of parasitic hexagonal phase.It is obvious that the diffraction intensities of h-GaN {1 0 $\bar{1}$ 0} grown on {1 1 1} A planes are higher than those on {1 1 1} B ones

have identified the {1 1 1} A faces and {1 1 1} B faces of c-GaN films by X-ray method. Hence, it is similarly possible to determine the {1 1 1} A and {1 1 1} B planes of other zincblende modifications presenting stackings of close-packed double layers such as AlN, InN, etc.

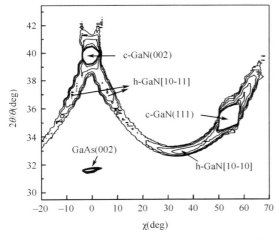

Fig.3 The reciprocal space mappings from reciprocal lattice point 002 to 111.In this figure, the diffractions from c-GaN(0 0 2), c-GaN(1 1 1), h-GaN {1 0 $\bar{1}$ 1} and h-GaN {1 0 $\bar{1}$ 1} can be observed.There is an elongation of diffraction patterns from 002 to 111 points

Further, the shape characteristic of secondary h-GaN can be identified. Fig. 3 displays the X-ray diffraction reciprocal space mappings of the c-GaN films along the $\langle 1\ 1\ 0 \rangle$ direction. The case along the $\langle 1\ \bar{1}\ 0 \rangle$ direction is similar to that along the $\langle 1\ 1\ 0 \rangle$ direction. The related diffractions from different planes are labelled in the figure. It should be noted that the streamlike shape of diffraction patterns from the (0 0 2) reciprocal lattice point to the (1 1 1) point, indicating that the hexagonal phase shows lameller structure both grown on {1 1 1} A planes and {1 1 1} B ones, which is in rather better agreement with the theory of minimum energy when the secondary h-GaN phase has grown on the {1 1 1} planes of c-GaN films based on the former orientation relationship [19]. Moreover, it can be concluded from the calculation and TEM observations that the parasitic hexagonal phase originates from the low-temperature buffer layer. Therefore, in order to decrease or suppress the introduced hexagonal phase, its formation and growth should be controlled in the initial stage of epitaxial growth. Many studies on buffer layer are in progress. In addition, the growth parameters should be changed to suppress the different contents of hexagonal phase grown on c-GaN $\{1\ 1\ 1\}$ A and $\{1\ 1\ 1\}$ B faces.

4　Conclusion

To summarize, we have proposed an X-ray method firstly applied in the determination of the $\{1\ 1\ 1\}$ A and $\{1\ 1\ 1\}$ B planes of c-GaN films. The deviation between the measured $|F_{(h\,h\,h)}|^2 / |F_{(\bar{h}\,\bar{h}\,\bar{h})}|^2$ values and the calculated values is caused by the different contents of parasitic hexagonal phase on $\{1\ 1\ 1\}$ A and $\{1\ 1\ 1\}$ B planes. The reciprocal space mappings provide the additional information that the introduced hexagonal GaN phase appears as lamellate.

References

[1] S. Nakamura, T. Mukai, M. Senoh, Appl. Phys. Lett. 64 (1994) 1687.

[2] S.T. Kim, H. Amano, I. Akasaki, Appl. Phys. Lett. 67 (1995) 267.

[3] Q. Chen, J.W. Yang, R. Gaska, M.A. Khan, M.S. Shur, G.J. Sullivan, A.L. Sailor, J.A. Higgings, A.T. Ping, I. Adesida, IEEE Electron Device Lett. 19 (1998) 54.

[4] O. Brandt, H. Yang, H. Kostial, K.H. Ploog, Appl. Phys.Lett. 69 (1996) 2707.

[5] H. Okumura, S. Misawa, S. Yoshida, Appl. Phys. Lett. 59 (1991) 1058.

[6] H. Tachibana, T. Ishido, M. Ogawa, M. Funato, Sz.Fujita, Sg. Fujita, J. Crystal Growth 196 (1999) 41.

[7] Shikora, M. Hankeln, D.J. As, K. Lishka, T. Litz, A.Wang, T. Buhrou, F. Henneberger, Phys.Rev. B54 (1996) R8381.

[8] H. Yang, L.X. Zheng, J.B. Li, X.J. Wang, D.P. Xu, Y.T.Wang, X.W. Hu, P.D. Han, Appl. Phys. Lett. 74 (1999) 2789.

[9] D.J. As, A. Richer, J. Busch, M. Lubbers, J. Mimkes, K.Lischka, Appl. Phys. Lett. 76 (2000) 13.

[10] W. Srock, V.A. Brophy, Am. Mineralogist 40 (1955) 94.

[11] J.G. White, W.L. Roth, J. Appl. Phys. 30 (7) (1959) 946.

[12] E.P. Warekois, P.H. Metzyer, J. Appl. Phys. 30 (7) (1959) 960.

[13] H. Cole, N.R. Stemple, J. Appl. Phys. 33 (1962) 2227.

[14] B.E. Warren, X-ray Diffraction, Addision-Wesley, Read-ing, 1969.

[15] International tables for X-ray Crystallography, Vol. 3, Birmingham, Eng., Kgnoch Pr. 1974—1983

[16] H. Tsuchiya, K. Sunaba, T. Suemasu, F. Hasegawa, J.Crystal Growth 189/190 (1998) 395.

[17] Z.X. Qin, M. Kobayashi, A. Yoshikawa, J. Mater. Sci 10 (1999) 1999.

[18] X.L. Sun, H. Yang, L.X. Zheng, D.P. Xu, J.B. Li, Y.T.Wang, G.H. Li, Z.G. Wang, Appl. Phys. Lett. 74 (9) (1999) 2827.

[19] B. Qu, X.H. Zheng, Y.T. Wang, S.M. Ling, Hui Yang, J.W. Liang, J. Crystal Growth 227-228 (2001) 399.

Microtwins and Twin Inclusions in the 3C-SiC Epilayers grown on Si(001) by APCVD

ZHENG Xinhe (郑新和), QU Bo (渠波), WANG Yutian (王玉田),

DAI Zizhong (戴自忠), YANG Hui (杨辉) & LIANG Junwu (梁骏吾)

(*Institute of Semiconductors, Chinese Academy of Sciences, Beijing* 100083, *China*)
Correspondence should be addressed to Zheng Xinhe (*email*: *xhzheng@ red. semi. ac. cn*)

Received October 25, 2000

Abstract: Microtwins in the 3C-SiC films grown on Si(001) by APCVD were analyzed in detail using an X-ray four-circle diffractometer. The ∅ scan shows that 3C-SiC films can grow on Si substrates epi-taxially and the epitaxial relationship is revealed as $(001)_{3C-SiC}//(001)_{Si}$, $[111]_{3c-sic}//[111]_{si}$. Other diffractions emerged in the pole figures of the (111) 3C-SiC. We performed the (10 10)h-SiC and the reciprocal space mapping of the (002) plane of twins for the first time, finding that the diffractions at $x = 15.8°$ result from not hexagonal SiC but microtwins of 3C-SiC, and twin inclusions are estimated to be 1%.

Keywords: 3C-SiC, microtwins, X-ray four-circle diffractometer, APCVD.

Silicon carbide (SiC), due to its favourable electronic physical and thermal stability chemical properties, high thermal conductivity, wide-band gap (2.2—3.3 eV), high broken-down voltage, high elctron mobility, high saturation electron drift velocity, radiation hardness and chemical inertness, is a promising candidate material for high power, high frequency, high temperature electronic devices and blue or ultraviolet optoelectronic devices[1-5].

SiC has many crystallographic configurations or polytypes. Among these polytypes of SiC, cubic 3C-SiC is possessed of a unique combination of properties, such as high electron drift velocity, which is suitable for electron devices. However, due to its difficulty in fabricating large-size bulk single crystal, epitaxy of 3C-SiC on silicon is of major technical interest. The heteroepitaxial growth of SiC on Si substrate using conventional CVD reactors has yielded high-quality thin films with the 3C-SiC. This enables the construction of devices which combine the wide bandgap semiconductor properties of SiC with the well-developed technology of Si. Moreover, there is a small difference of lattice constants and thermal-expansion coefficients between SiC and GaN. Therefore, SiC is served as a promising substrate for the GaN epitaxial growth[6-9]. Additionally, SiC is a very convenient intermediate layer for GaN epitaxy[10-14]. However, up to date, the commercial 3C-SiC single crystal is still not available. Therefore, 3C-SiC/Si is still very interesting for subsequent GaN growth. In the 3C-SiC/Si heteroepitaxial system,

原载于:Science in China Series A:Mathematics Physics Astronomy,2001,44:777-782.

3C-SiC films will be introduced to produce a high density of misfit dislocations[15], stacking faults[16], microtwins[17,18] and antiphase boundary[19,20] due to the difference in lattice constants and thermal expansion coefficient between Si and SiC, which has an undesired effect on the performance of the devices. Among these defects, microtwins are often found to form within the epilayers and they have been characterized by X-ray pole figure[15,18] and transmission electron microscopy (TEM)[15,17,18]. There exist over two hundred polytypes[21] such as 3C-SiC, 2H-SiC, 6H-SiC, 8R-SiC, 4H-SiC, etc., among which hexagonal structure is preferential. Therefore, the parasitic hexagonal phase may be easily introduced within the films when 3C-SiC is grown on Si(001) substrate. However, it is difficult to distinguish microtwins from the hexagonal phase owing to almost the same interface spacings between hexagonal (000L) and cubic (111) planes when cubic {111} pole figure or hexagonal (000L) pole figure measurements are performed. In most studies, TEM is used to evaluate the structure and defects, however, a drawback of the preparation of the sample is hard and complicated. Moreover, the sample is destroyed. Additionally, Nagasawa et al.[18] and Long et al.[15] explained the exsitence of microtwins only using cubic [111] pole figures. In our work, however, a four-circle X-ray diffractometer has been used and the other diffraction from hexagonal phase and reciprocal space mapping are utilized to further distinguish microtwins from the hexagonal phase. Moreover, the content of microtwins is also estimated by ω scan method for the first time.

The generation of microtwins lowers the epilayer quality, which influences material properties and the performance of the devices. Therefore, it is worth considering that microtwins or stacking faults should be controlled when the epitaxial growth is carried out. We conclude that the formation of planar defects is related to the size of critical nuclei, and consider that larger size will help to improve the film quality.

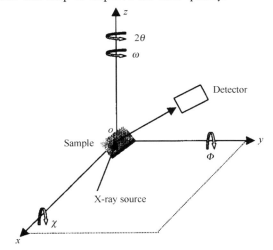

Fig. 1   Schematic description of Φ, χ, ω and 2θ rotations and Descartes coordinate

1   Experimental procedure

3C-SiC films were grown on Si (001) substrates by atmosphere-pressure chemical vapor deposition (APCVD) technique. Silane (SiH_4) and propane (C_3H_8) were used as the precursors of Si and C, respectively. Prior to the deposition of the film a "carbon buffer layer" is formed by exposing the silicon surface to propane, typically at 1300℃. The thick-ness of the 3C-SiC film is approximately 4.5 μm measured by SEM. X-ray four-circle diffraction technique was used to identify structure and defects. The structure was characterized by X-ray diffraction measurement using a 4-circle diffractometer, connected to a Rigaku X-ray generator with a microfocus and the CuKα$_1$ radiation. The first crystal was a Si (111). XRD measurements by rotating samples along the ω-axis, Φ-axis and χ-axis, which are shown in fig. 1, should be carried out. Twodimensional scan composed of Φ and χ scans at a fixed ω-2θ position gives pole figure.

2 Results and discussion

In order to characterize more precisely the epitaxial layer, Φ scan measurements were performed. The (111) poles of the 3C-SiC and the (111) poles of the substrate were measured. Fig. 2 shows the comparison of the Φ scans from 0—360° at the tilt angles of $\chi = 54.7°$. It is seen that the {111} peaks of the 3C-SiC repeat itself every 90°, consistent with the cubic symmetry of epilayers and located at almost the same positions as the {lll} peaks of the Si substrate, although their intensity is sharply different. The results show that the orientation of the major portion of the 3C-SiC is in strong coincidence with the substrate. The epitaxial rela-tionship is revealed as (001)$_{3c\text{-}sic}$//(001)$_{Si}$ and [111]$_{3c\text{-}sic}$//[111]$_{si}$.

There is a noticeable advantage of phase identification and plane orientation for the pole figure measurement. Fig. 3 shows an XRD pole figure of the 3C-SiC film on Si(001) substrate. The {111} pole figures were measured by fixing the detector at 2θ positions of 35.64°. The pole figures were obtained by scanning the tilt angle, i. e. χ from 0°—70°, and the azimuth rotation angle Φ from 0°—360°. The results show that four strong peaks crossing the 3C-SiC(001) pole at approximately 54.7℃ in χ were observed. These four peaks corresponded to the diffraction from the 3C-SiC {111} planes. Four other peaks crossing the 3C-SiC(001) pole at about 15.8℃ in χ were also observed. It is known that the lattice spacings of hexagonal (0006) planes and cubic (111) planes are almost the same, and hence these four weak peaks probably originate from hexagonal (0006) planes. That is to say, the first possibility is that the hexagonal phase can grow on this twinned (111) plane[22]. The second possible origin of the hexagonal phase is directly introduced on 3C-SiC {115} facets because there is a fairly good lattice match between the (0006) hexagonal planes and the cubic {115} facets of 3C-SiC. In order to further confirm the origin of these four weak peaks, we performed the hexagonal {10$\bar{1}$0} pole figure (not shown here). If the hexagonal phase grows on the twinned { 111 } planes or the cubic {115} facets, corresponding {10$\bar{1}$0} peaks should appear and be observed at the θ value around 35.3° 65.9° or 74.2°. However, in our experiment, the intensity of the hexagonal (10$\bar{1}$0) peaks were found to be negligible or nil as shown by the pole figure, proving that a hexagonal SiC phase did not grow on the twinned {111} planes or the cubic {115} facets. Therefore we may safely conclude that from the above these four weak peaks result from the twinned (111) planes, suggesting the existence of a symmetrical twin band around the <111> axis. As we know, related reciprocal lattice has twin relationship due to twin relation of normal crystal lattice. It is supposed that hkl stands for reciprocal lattice point of 3C-SiC films, HKL is the point of microtwins and $h'k'l'$ stands for reciprocal lattice point in the positive reciprocal lattice. Their relations can be expressed in the formula:

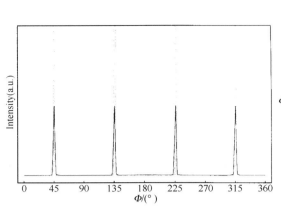

Fig. 2　The Φ scans of {111} planes from the 3C-SiC films (solid line) and the Si substrate (dotted line)

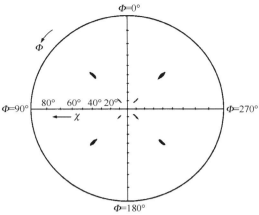

Fig. 3　{111} pole figure of the 3C-SiC film. Detector angle 2θ was set for 35. 64°. Angles χ and Φ were scanned

$$h^t = -h + \frac{2H}{H^2+K^2+L^2}(Hh+Kk+Ll),$$

$$k^t = -k + \frac{2K}{H^2+K^2+L^2}(Hh+Kk+Ll),$$

$$l^t = -l + \frac{2L}{H^2+K^2+L^2}(Hh+Kk+Ll),$$

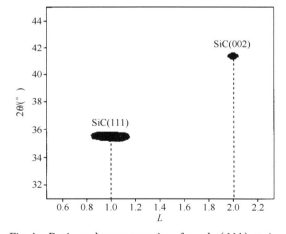

Fig. 4　Reciprocal space mappings from the (111) reciprocal lattice points of base 3C-SiC and the (002) point of twin 3C-SiC

For the win {111} plane, twin (002) plane is parallel to the base (221) plane. Therefore, the interangle between twin (002) plane and base (221) plane is 70.5°. In this case, the diffraction of twin (002) plane will appear at 70.5° in χ when the pole figure or reciprocal space mapping is performed. Fig. 4 shows the reciprocal space mapping from the (111) reciprocal lattice point of base SiC to the (002) point of twin SiC. Considering that the letters h and k among Miller indices of twin 002 point and base 111

point is identical, we used L coordinate rather than χ coordinate. Fig. 5 displays the diagram of twins structure. The relationship between the twins and base SiC is in great coincidence.

　　Fig. 6 shows the ω scans at the tilt angles of $\chi=54. 7°(1)$ and 15. 8°(2) from one of the four directions. In order to estimate the content of microtwins, we performed the ω scans of {111} planes at 45°,135°,225°,315°in Φ, respectively. Dus to similar structure and material characterization, we can directly estimate the content of the twinned 3C-SiC in the 3C-SiC films: their content in four directions is calculated to be about 0. 9%, 1. 05%, 1. 0%, 1. 1%, respectively. Hence, the content of twins can be considered to be approximately 1%.

For the 3C-SiC/Si(001) heteroepitaxial system, misfit dislocations are formed in the vicinity of the SiC/Si interface to

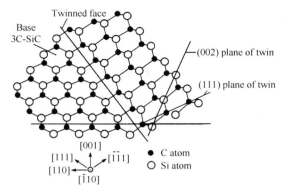

Fig. 5   A schematic diagram of microtwin structure

accommodate the lattice mismatch and relieve the strain. However, planar defects such as stacking faults and twins are still introduced within the 3C-SiC films. The generation of microtwins may be considered to result from inversional stacking of bilayers com-posed of one layer of Si atoms and one layer of C atoms. That is, the bilayer is not stacked in normal structure in a primitive unit cell, but it is arrayed by mistake along some plane or around some axis. If the close-packed arrangement of atoms is maintained in... ABCACBA... (A, B, C standing for the stacking types of bilayers), the microtwins will be generated.

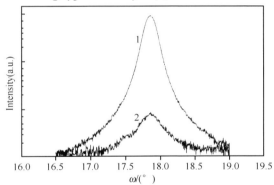

Fig. 6   The rocking curves of the {111} planes at about 54. 7°(1) and 15. 8°(2) in χ, respectively

In a consequence, stacking faults will result in the formation of microtwins. As far as SiC modifications are concerned, the generation chance of stacking faults is very high due to lower fault energy caused by over 200 polytypes. In addition, the formation of stacking faults is related to the coalescence of three-dimensional islands during the growth. The atomic arrangements of neighboring nuclei are not in coincidence due to their different nucleation sites. Hence,

the periodicity of the lattice will be broken upon their agglomeration. It becomes energetically favorable for the small misfit to be accommodated by stacking faults due to low energy of stacking fault. Booker et al. [23] demonstrated that the density of stacking faults is inversely proportional to the size of the coalesced islands. That is to say, the lower the density of stacking faults, the larger the island nuclei, which is favorable for the epitaxial growth. This mechanism was also utilized to explain the formation of stacking faults in the GaAs epilayers grown on Si (001) substrates[24]. Therefore, the larger size of critical nuclei will help to obtain high quality films.

3   Conclusions

The microtwins in the 3C-SiC/Si (001) films have been analyzed by a four-circle X-ray diffractometer. The Φ scans confirm that 3C-SiC can grow on Si substrates epitaxially and the epitaxial relationship is revealed as $(001)_{3C\text{-}SiC}//(001)_{Si}$, $[111]_{3C\text{-}SiC}//[111]_{Si}$. The {111} pole figures of

3C-SiC, $\{10\bar{1}0\}$ pole figures of hexagonal SiC phase and reciprocal lattice mapping of the (002) point of twins give convincing evidence that the diffractions at $\chi = 15.8°$ result from not hexagonal SiC but microtwins of 3C-SiC, and the content of twins is estimated to be 1% by ω scans.

References

[1] Nishino, S., Powell, J., Will, H., Production of large-area single-crystal wafers of cubic SiC for semiconductor devices, Appl. Phys. Lett., 1983, 42: 460-462.

[2] Palmour, J., Kong, H. F., Davis, R., High-temperature depletion-mode metal-oxide-semiconductor field-effect-transistors in beta-SiC thin films, Appl. Phys. Lett., 1987, 51: 2028-2030.

[3] Natus, L., Powell, J., Salupo, C., High-voltage 6H-SiC p-n junction diodes, Appl. Phys. Lett., 1991,59: 1770-1772.

[4] Tong, L., Mehregany, M., Matus, C., Mechanical properties of 3C silicon carbide, Appl. Phys. Lett., 1992, 60: 2992-2994.

[5] Morkoc, H., Strite, S., Gao, G. B. et al., Large-band-gap SiC, III-V nitride, and II-VI ZnSe-based semiconductor device technologies, J. Appl. Phys., 1994, 76: 1363-1398.

[6] Cree Research, Inc. 2810 Meridian Parkway, Durham, NC27713.

[7] Walterit, P., Brandt, O., Trampert, A. et al., Influence of AlN nucleation layers on growth mode and strain relief of GaN grown on 6H-SiC(0001), Appl. Phys. Lett., 1999, 74: 366-368.

[8] Sasaki, T., Matsuoka, T., Substrate-polarity dependence of metal-organic vapor-phase epitaxy-grown GaN on SiC, J. Appl. Phys., 1988, 64: 4531-4535.

[9] Chien, R., Ning, X. J., Stemmer, S. et al., Growth defects on GaN films on 6H-SiC substrates, Appl. Phys. Lett., 1996, 68: 2678-2680.

[10] Takeuchi, T., Amano, H., Hiramatsu, K. et al., Growth of single crystalline GaN film on Si substrate using 3C-SiC as an intermediate layer, J. Cryst. Growth., 1991, 115: 634-638.

[11] Steckl, A., Devrajan, J., Tran, C. et al., SiC rapid thermal carbonization of the (111)Si semiconductors on-insulator struc-ture and subsequent metalorganic chemical vapor deposition of GaN, Appl. Phys. Lett., 1996, 69: 2264-2266.

[12] Paisley, M., Sitar, Z., Posthill, J. et al., Growth of cubic phase gallium nitride by modified molecular-beam epitaxy, J. Vac. Sci. Technol. A, 1989, 7: 701-705.

[13] Moustakas, T., Lei, T., Molnar, R., Growth of GaN by ECR-assisted MBE, Physica B, 1993, 185: 36-49.

[14] Yaguchi, H., Wu, J., Zhang, B. et al., Micro Raman and micro photoluminescenes study of cubic GaN grown on 3C-SiC(001) substrates by metalorganic vapor phase epitaxy, J. Cryst. Growth, 1998, 195: 323-327.

[15] Long, C., Ustin, S., Ho, W., Structural defects in 3C-SiC grown on Si by supersonic jet epitaxy, j. Appl. Phys., 1999,86: 2509-2515.

[16] Nutt, S., Smith, D., Jim, H. et al., Interface structures in beta-silicon carbide thin films, Appl. Phys. Lett., 1987, 50: 203-205.

[17] Zekentes, Z., Papaioannou, V., Pecz, B. et al., Early stages of growth of beta-SiC on Si by MBE, J. Cryst. Growth, 1995, 157: 392-399.

[18] Nagasawa, H., Yagi, K., 3C-SiC single-crystal films grown on 6-inch Si substrates, Phys. Status Solidi B, 1997, 202:335-358.

[19] Pirouz, P., Chorey, C., Powell, J. Antiphase boundaries in epitaxially grown beta-SiC, Appl. Phys. Lett., 1987, 50:221-223.

[20] Shibahara, K., Nishino, S., Matsunami, H., Surface morphology of 3C-SiC(100) grown on Si(100) by chemical vapor de-position, J. Cryst. Growth., 1986, 78: 538-544.

[21] Fisher, G., Barnes, P., Towards a unified view of polytypism in silicon carbide, Phil. Mag. B., 1990, 61: 217-236.

[22] Weimin, S., Michael, D., Kong, H. et al., Investigations of 3C-SiC inclusions in 4H-SiC epilayers on 4H-SiC single crystal substrates, J. Electro. Mater., 1997, 26: 151-159.

[23] Booker, G., Titchmarsh, J., Fletcher, J. et al., Nature, orgin and defect of dislocations in epitaxial semiconductor layers, J. Cryst. Growth., 1978, 45:407-425.

[24] Cho, K., Cho, W., Lee, Y. et al., Defects formation in the solid phase epitaxial growth of GaAs films on Si(001) sub-strate, J. Appl. Phys., 1991, 69: 237-242.

Determination of Structure and Polarity of SiC Single Crystal by X-Ray Diffraction Technique

ZHENG Xin-he, QU Bo, WANG Yu-tian, YANG Hui and LIANG Jun-wu

(*Institute of Semiconductors, The Chinese Academy of Sciences, Beijing* 100083, *China*)

Abstract: Structure and polarity of the SiC single cry st al have been an alyzed with the four-circle X-ray diffraction method by a double-crystal diffractometer. The haxagonal $\{10\bar{1}5\}$ pole figure shows that this SiC sample has a 6H modification. The difference between the integrated intensities measured by ω scan in the triple-axis diffraction set-up finds some Convincing evidence that the surface is either a Si-terminated face or C-terminated face. The experiment al ratios of $F(000L)^2/F(000\bar{L})^2$ are in good agreement with the calculated ones after the dispersion corrections to the atomic scattering factors ($L = 6, 12$ and 18, respectively). Thus, this measurement technique is convenient for the application of the materials with remarkable surface polarity.

Key words: SiC single crystal; polarity; hexagonal 6H; scattering factor

PACC: 6100F; 7870C; 6855; 7360; 7865

CLC number: O766$^+$.4 **Document code:** A **Article ID:** 0253-4177(2001) 01-0035-05

1 Introduction

Silicon carbide (SiC) is a promising candidate for the high-temperature, high-speed, high-frequency and high-power electronic devices owing to its excellent thermal and electrical properties[1-2]. Additionally, SiC is a potential excellent substrate for the GaN epitaxy due to its small lattice constant and the thermal expansion coefficient mismatched the later[3].

It is well-known that SiC can form numerous modifications[4] (the so-called polytypes), including the common polytypes of hexagonal 4H, 6H and 8H, rhombohedral 15R, and cubic 3C. How ever, all 6H, 4H and 3C-SiC are as sumed to be SiC bulk single crystals, so it is very crucial to identify the SiC polytype when the SiC bulk single crystal growth is performed.

In previous papers, a four-circle X-ray diffractometer has been applied to determine the SiC structure. The result shows that SiC has a 6H modification, which is noncentrosymmetric and cont ains a polar axis. Because of this axis, the bonding configuration of the surface atoms depends upon

原载于:Chinese Journal of Semiconductors, 2001, 22:35-39.

ZHENG Xin-he is working for his Ph. D degree and his res earch interest includes physical properties of GaN and SiC materials and related devices.

YANG Hui is en gaged in research on GaN materials and its optoelectronic devices.

LIANG Jun-wu is and academician of Chinese Academy of Engeering. He is concentrating on such research interest as SiC, GaN materials and its related devices.

· 95 ·

the various cryatallo graphic planes are composed of the identical close-packed double layers. Based on a generally accepted assumption[5] ,and equivalent definition is obtained that for two opposite faces of a crystal, which are both perpendicular to the polar axis, one is Si-terminated [sym-bolically (0001)] and the other is C-terminated[symbolically(000-1)]. The [0001] vector points from the C face to the Si face. There might be many diffences between the physical and chemical properties of the (0001) surface and the opposite (000$\bar{1}$) surface.

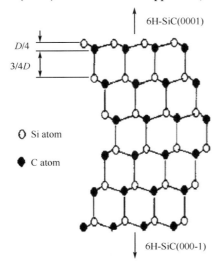

6H-SiC(0001)

$D/4$

$3/4D$

O Si atom

● C atom

6H-SiC(000-1)

Fig. 1   Schematic View of SiC Single Crystallographic Atom Arrangement of (11$\bar{2}$0)
Plane Perpendicular to {0001} Surfaces

6H-SiC cry st allographic structure consists of the stacking of Si-C bilay er in ABCACBA sequence along the c (or z) axis (0001) directions of the hexagonal structure, where each letter (A, B and C) corresponds to a Si-C bilayer. A bulk truncated atomic distribution of this structure in (11$\bar{2}$0) high-symmetry planes is shown in Fig. 1.

From the close-packed structure, it is observed there exist two kinds of different interplanar distances between the neighbor (0001) planes. One is $D/4$, the other is $3/4D$. Here, D stands for the distance between two double layers. The effects of the polarity on the bond structure can be observed on the typical etched surfaces of an opposite face[6-7], by infrared attenuated total reflection spectroscopy[8], the piezoelectric effect[9] and X-ray photoelectron diffraction character-ization[10]. In addition, such identifications can be made by observing the effects of the intensity of scattered X-ray[11-12]. It has been noted in previous papers, that the intensity measurements of the scattered X-ray were taken by a rocking curve on a double crystal X-ray spectrometer.Moreo-ver, no more factors influencing the integrated intensity have been discussed. Besides, in order to reflect this rule better,the diffracted intensity was related to the structure factor for a mosaic crystal. A triple-axis X-ray setup was used in the intensity measurement. When the measurement of the diffracted intensity was carried out, a crystal analyzer had to be placed in front of the de-tector and some other factors taken into consideration. In this paper, the application of the X-ray dispersion effect in the determination of the polarity of SiC single crystal has been presented, using the triple-axis diffraction method with the purpose of our distinguishing between the Si-ter-minated face and C-terminated one prior to the subsequent treatment or deposit.

2   Experimental Procedure

The SiC single crystals were grown by Chemical Vapor Deposition (CVD), with the grow-th details being introduced elsewhere. SiC sample was analyzed by X-ray diffraction with a Rigaku diffractometer equipped with a Cu anode at 40kV and 100mA. Using a four-circle diffractometer, the pole figures are measured, whose geometry in real space is shown in Fig. 2 to identify the structure. The intensity measurement of scattered X-ray was taken according to the triple-axis diffraction method. The X-ray diffraction patterns of ω scan were obtained using a step of 0.002°. CuKα, nmonochromatic radiation was selected by a single crystal Ge(004). Si (220) was used as an analyzer crystal.

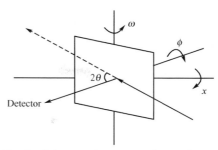

Fig. 2   Schematic Description for Configuration of Four-Circle Geometry

3   Results and Discussion

According to crystallographic theory, it is easy for the close-packed or low Miller-index plane to appear on the surface of single crystal. As long as the hexagonal structure and the cubic structure are concerned, the distances between the crystallographic planes of cubic(111) and some hexagonal (000L) are almost identical. Therefore, X-ray diffraction information from crystal surface may result from either cubic 3C(111) plane or hexagonal (000L)plane (L is a positive integer). To distinguish these information, the diffraction of other plane is performed according to the interangle between two different plane in 3C unit cell and hexagonal unit cell (2H, 4H and 6H). The $\{10\bar{1}5\}$ pole figure shown in Fig. 3 was measured by fixing the detector at 2θ position of 45.28° and scanning the tilt angle X from 0° to 60°, and the azimuth rotation angle Φ from 0° to 360°. Fig.3 shows that peks appear when $X = 45.57°$, which is equal to the interplanar angle between (0006) and ($10\bar{1}5$) planes. It can be seen that the diffraction geometry of the plane is in excellent agreement with that of a 6H structure. Additionally, the $\{10\bar{1}5\}$ diffracted peaks have the exactly symmetrical points of $\{10\bar{1}5\}$ of the hexagonal structure, i. e., the peak repeats itself by every 60°; This is consistent with the hexagonal symmetry of SiC material. therefore, a conclusion is drawn that the SiC single crystal has a 6H structure.

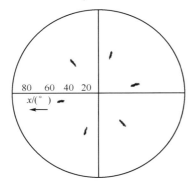

Fig. 3   XRD Pole Diagram Detector angle 2θ was set at 45.28° for ($10\bar{1}5$) H-SiC. Angles X and Φ were scanned

Initial measurements of the intensity of the scattered X-ray from opposite sides of a $\{000L\}$ single crystal were made with a triple-axis setup on a double crystal X-ray spectrometer. The intensity of a diffracted X-ray beam is proportional to F^2 for a mosaic crystal, measurements were taken with triple-axis crystal diffraction. Based on the extinction rule of X-ray diffraction, the (0006) diffraction should be the first order diffraction of the basal plane of a 6H structure. The (00012) and (00018) diffractions are the second and third ones, respectively. The X-ray beam was collimated by a 0.1mm aperture to obtain a beam size, which was small compared with the crystal area being analyzed. The intensities of the reflections by ω scanning mode were recorded and after each measurement, the crystal was displaced laterally with a small distance to obtain the reflection from some locations of each face. The results are shown in Fig. 4.

It is known that the integrated intensity is a function of the structure factor. Brack[11] deduced the ratios of the structure factor of $(000L)$ to that of $(000\bar{L})$ as follow s:

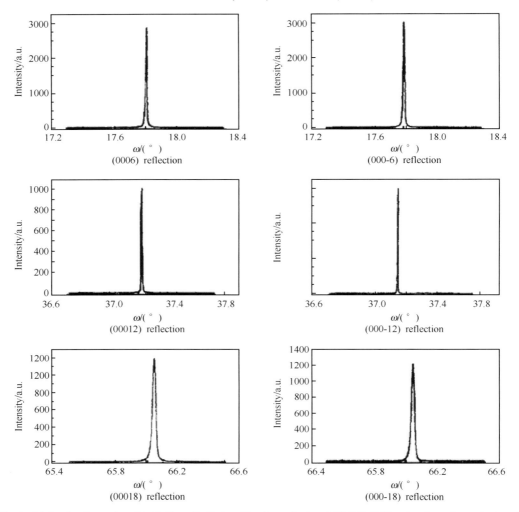

Fig. 4 Reflection Intensity with CuK α_1 Radiation Showing a Series of $(000L)$ Diffraction from Same Surface in Comparison with $(000\bar{L})$ Diffraction of Opposite Surface $(L=6,12,18,\text{Respectively})$

$$\frac{F(0006)}{F(000\bar{6})}=\frac{f_{SI}-if_C}{f_{SI}+if_C}$$

$$\frac{F(00012)}{F(000\ \overline{12})}=1$$

$$\frac{F(00018)}{F(000\ \overline{18})}=\frac{f_{SI}+if_C}{f_{SI}-if_C}$$

where f_{SI} and f_C are atomic scattering factors of dispersion corrections, expressed as $f=f_0+\Delta f'+i\Delta f''$, where f_0 is the normal scattering factor usually tabulated as a real function of $\sin\theta/\lambda$, and Δf and $\Delta f''$ are the real and imaginary parts of a correction factor due to dispersion. f_0, Δf and

$\Delta f''$ can be obtained from the related literature[13]. However, it should be noted that in Brack's work, some factors influencing the integrated intensities are not be mentioned. Based on the expression[14] of integrated intensity, the main factors are L_p, ΔV and F^2, where L_p is Lorentz-polarized factor, which is expressed as $(1+\cos^2 2\theta)/2\sin 2\theta$, ΔV is the crystal volume irradiated by X-ray; and F is the structure factor. Taking these factors into consideration, we obtain the experimental values of the integrated in-tensities among (0006), (00012) and (00018) reflections are in excellent agreement with the theoretical prediction. However, the factors L_p and ΔV are considered to be identical in the $\{000L\}$ and $\{000\bar{L}\}$ reflections. Here, the calculated values of $F(000L)^2/F(000\bar{L})^2$ and the measured ratios of integrated intensities from $\{000L\}$ reflections to those from $\{000\bar{L}\}$ reflections are listed in table 1.

Table 1   Calculated Ratios of Scattering Factors of $\{000L\}$ Planes to Opposite $\{000\bar{L}\}$ Planes in Comparision with Experimental Values

$\{000L\}$	Total Counts		$F(000L)^2/F(000\bar{L})^2$	$F(000L)^2/F(000\bar{L})^2$
	$(000L)$	$(000\bar{L})$	Measure	Calculation
0006	14913	15764	0.946	0.949
00012	3314	3288	1.008	1.000
00018	4519	4135	1.093	1.076

From above, it is evident that the SiC single crystal, as a mosaic crystal, has the intensity rations that are in good agreement with the calculated values. Therefore, according to the above values of $F(000L)^2/F(000\bar{L})$, i. e. 0.946, 1.008 and 1.093, we may conclude that the face, which is arsumed to be the variation of the $F(000L)^2$ values, is Si-terminated face and the opposite is C-terminated face. Hence, it is also possibe to determine the polarity of other SiC polytypes with stackings of Si-C double layers along the Z-axis, such as hexagonal 2H-SiC $\{0001\}$, 4H-SiC$\{0001\}$ and cubic 3C-SiC$\{111\}$.

4   Conclusion

The measurement of hexagonal SiC pole figure proves that the SiC single crystal has a 6H modification. The ratios of the experimental intensities of $\{0001\}$ surface to the opposite $\{000\bar{1}\}$ surface are in excellent agreement with the calculated values of $F(000L)^2/F(000\bar{L})^2$. The result applies to determining which side is the Si-terminated (0001) face and which is the C-terminated (000$\bar{1}$) face.

References

[1] P. A, Ivanov and V. E. Chelnokov, Semiconductor Science and T ethnology, 1992, 7: 863.

[2] LEI T ian-rain, CHEN Zhi-ming, YU M ing-bin et al., X-Ray Photoelectron Spectroscopy Study of 3C-SiC Thin Films Grown on Si Substrates, Chinese Journal of Semiconductors, 2000, 21(2): 303-306.

[3] T. Gerge, W. Pine, M. Dhan, J. Kuznia and P. Chang-Chieu, J. Electron. Mater., 1995, 24: 1241.

[4] G. R. Fisher and P. Barnes, Phil. Mag., 1990, B61: 217.

[5] W. Stroek and V. A. Brophy, Am. Mineralogist., 1955, 40:94.

[6] R. E. Mariuger, J. Appl. Phys. , 1958, 29：1261.

[7] H. A. Sehell, Z, Metallk. 1957, 48, I58.

[8] H. Tsuchida, I. Kamata and K. Izumi, J. Appl. Phys, 1999,85:3569.

[9] J. L. Bischoff, D. Derttel and L. Kubler, Surf. Sci. , 1998, 415:392.

[10] L. M uehlhoff, M. J. Bozack, W. J. Choyke and J. T. Yates, J. Appl, Phys. , 1986, 60: 2558.

[11] D. Coster, K. S. Knol and J. A. Prins, Z. Physik, 1930, 63:345.

[12] K. Brack, J. Appl. Phys. , 1965, 16: 3650.

[13] International Tables for X-Ray Crystallography, V. 3, Birmingham, Eng. , Kgnoch Pr. , 1974-1983.

[14] J, Z, Zhang, C, Z, Yang, Diffraction Foundation of Crystal,Nanjing University Publishing House, 1992.

使用 X 射线衍射技术判定 SiC 单晶体的结构和极性

郑新和　　渠　波　　王玉田　　杨　辉　　梁骏吾

(中国科学院半导体研究所,北京　100083)

摘要:使用四圆衍射仪和双晶衍射技术,分析了 SiC 体单晶的结构和极性. SiC 单晶体由化学气相淀积法获得. 六方 $\{10\bar{1}5\}$ 极图证明了该单晶结构为 6H 型. 三轴晶衍射中的 ω 模式衍射强度的差异判定了该单晶的 Si 终端面和 C 终端面,即极性面。两个面的一、二、三级衍射强度的测量比值与经过散射因子修正后计算的结构振幅平方比值 $|F(000L)|^2/|F(000\bar{L})|^2$ 非常吻合. 因此,利用极性面的衍射强度差异,可以方便、严格地判断具有类似结构如 2H$\{0001\}$、4H$\{0001\}$ 及 3C-SiC$\{111\}$ 的极性。

关键词:SiC 单晶;极性;6H 结构;散射因子

PACC:6100F;7870C;6855;7360;7865

中图分类号:O766$^+$.4　　**文献标识码**:A　　**文章编号**:0253-4177(2001)01-0035-05

郑新和:男,博士生,主要从事 GaN 物理特性和 SiC 及相关器件研究.

杨辉:男,研究员,主要从事 GaN 材料及其光电子器件研究.

梁骏吾:男,中国工程院院上,主要从事 SiC、GaN 材料和相关器件研究.

Is Thin-Film Solar Cell Technology Promising?

LIANG JUNWU

(*Institute of Semiconductors, CAS*)

c-Si solar cells

Suntech's production reached 704MW in 2009.

Suntech planed to produce 1.4GW of PV in 2010 and 2.2GW in 2011

Thin-film cells

First solar produced 1.1GW of PV in 2009 and planed to increase its cell production capacity to 1.4GW in 2010 and 2.0GW in 2011.

Thin-film Technologies

- a-Si (a-Si, μc-Si/a-Si, a-SiGe/a-Si)
- AlGaAs/GaAs, GaInP/ GaAs/Ge, GaInP/GaInAs/Ge
- CdTe/CdS/TCO
- CIGS/CdS/ZnO
- Organic and Dye sensitized solar cells

原载于:2011 年多晶硅及太阳能电池技术发展研讨会,西安.2001.

Techno-logy	Company	
a-Si	United Solar, Sharp, Mitsubishi, Sunfilm, Trony, Kaneka, Bosch, Moser Baer, EPV	9
CIGS	Sunfilm, Wurth Solar, EPV Solar Frontier, Solyndra	5
CdTe	First Solar	1

a-Si:H materials

- a-Si:H deposited by SiH_4 PECVD had a much lower defect density than evaporated or sputtered materials and it is actually an alloy of hydrogen and silicon.
- Due to the absence of long-range order a-Si:H materials have a very high absorption and thus thin film can be used to fabricate PV cells.
- In 1976, Carlson & Wronski reported a-Si:H cells with η of 2%.
- a-Si:H materials can be doped both n-, and p-type and i-layer also can be easily grown.

PIN JUNCTION

- Typical amorphous silicon solar cell structure is based on pin junction, containing an intrinsic layer which separates two heavily doped p and n regions. Generation of holes and electrons occurs within the space charge region. The charge separation can be assisted by the built-in-electric field, thus enhancing the collection efficiency.

PIN JUNCTION

- Due to the low values of τ and μ in a-Si:H associated with the amorphous structure, the diffusion length values are low.

$$Ln=(D_n \ \tau_n)^{0.5}, \quad Lp=(D_p \ \tau_p)^{0.5}$$

- The collection of photogenerated carriers must be assisted by the internal electric field and the photogenerated carriers collected as a drift current, not as a diffusion current.

$$I_n=E\mu_n \ \tau_n, \quad I_p=E\mu_p \ \tau_p$$

Advantages of a-Si PV technology

Reduced costs of semiconductor layers

- An amorphous Si cell uses only about 1/300 the amount of Si in a c-Si cell.
- **Cost percentages for a-Si/a-SiGe tandem modules**.

  Glass-42.3%, SiH_4-1.9%, GeH_4-10.3%, other gases-1.1%, lamination-6.6%, frames and packaging-20.7, connectors-13%, other materials-4.1%.

Advantages

Low production cost

It is predicated that manufacturing costs should be on the order of $1/w when modules are produced at rates greater than $100MW_p$ per year.

Multijunction structures can be grown

- Microcrystalline layers(μc-Si) can be grown with E_g of   1.1eV
- The E_g and α of a-Si:H can be controlled by the concentrations of H, Ge and C. 。
- The phase transition set an upper limit of 1.9eV 。The increase of defects with the incorporation of Ge set the lower limit at 1.3eV for the E_g of a-SiGe:H.
- Amorphous silicon solar cells have been produced in a wide variety of different multijunction structures.

$h\nu \rightarrow$

glass/ textured SnO / $p_1i_1n_1$ / $p_2i_2n_2$ / CVD ZnO / sputtered Al / EVA / glass

	p_1	i_1	n_1	p_2	i_2	n_2
Film	a-SiC:H	a-Si:H	μc-Si	a-SiC:H	graded a-SiGe:H	a-Si:H
Thickness(nm)	10	160	10	10	100	20
Dopant	B, C	_	P	B, C	Ge	P

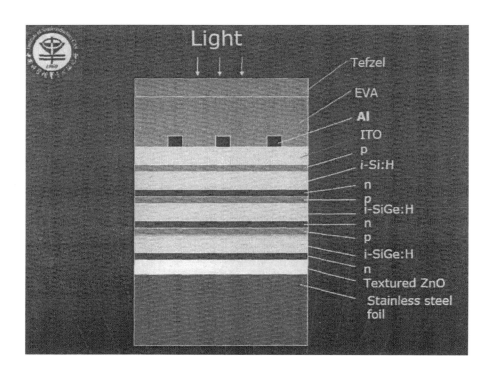

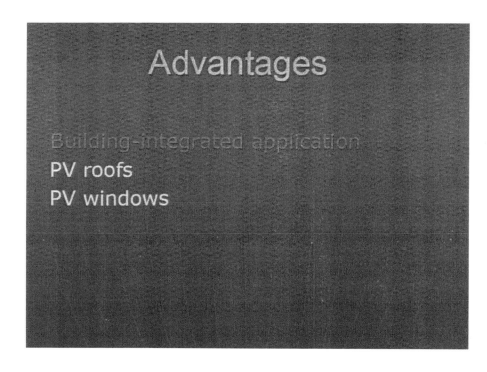

Disadvantages

there are many deep lying states with densities around 10^{16} cm^{-3} in a-Si:H.

    (D^0)-neutral states,

    (D$^-$)- negatively charged defect states

    (D$^+$)-positively charged defect states (D$^+$),

Consequently, the τ_n and τ_p are in the range of 10^{-6}-10^{-8}s

The carrier mobility values for extended states are $\mu_n = 0.5$cm^2/V-s and $\mu_n = 10$cm^2/V-s.

The (μ τ) product are correlated with the conversion coefficients.

Due to the random nature of atomic ordering, a-Si:H solar cells exhibit low conversion efficiencies.

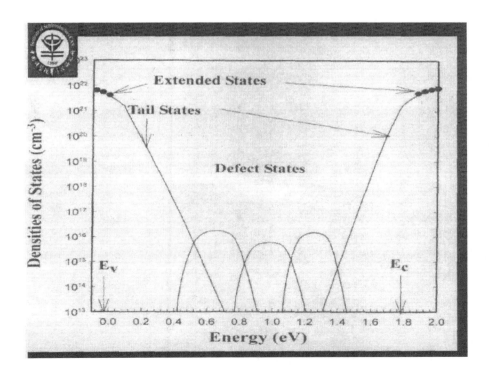

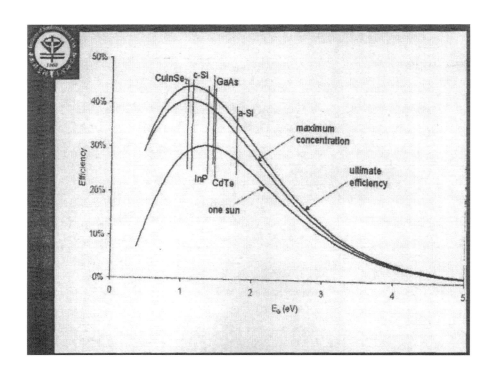

Disadvantages
Light-induced degradation

The Staebler-Wronski effect-

The illumination of a-Si:H with sunlight lower both the photoconductivity and dark conductivity.

Light induced defects adversely affect the carriers transport, which result in a reduction of the performance of the PV cells

Disadvantages

High equipment cost percentages

Although silicon material cost is decreased, the equipment cost percentages are very high which offsets the benefit from the decreased materials cost.

CIGS cells

Structure of CIGS cells

Soda-lime glass—1um Mo back electrode—1-2um CIGS absorber—CBD grown 50nm CdS—sputtered 50-70nm i-ZnO and Al doped ZnO

CIGS materials and cells

- CIGS prepared by co-evaporation at 550°C from Cu, In, Ga, and Se with Ga/(Ga+In)=0.2-0.3 yielded the η of 18.8%.
- During co-evaporation, a feedback based on quadrupole mass spectrometer controls the rate of each source, whereas Se is always in excess. Advanced process includes a Cu-rich stage and an In-rich overall composition.

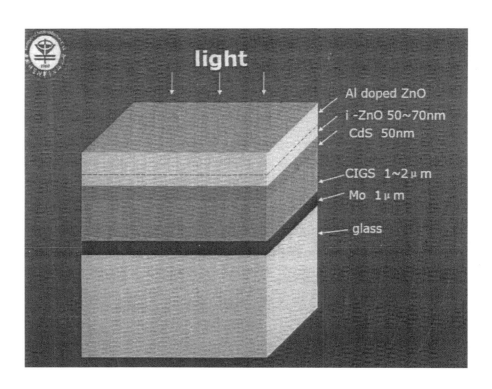

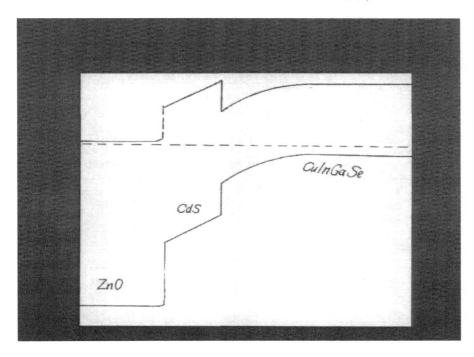

CuInGaSe

CdS

ZnO

Advantages of CIGS technology

Direct band gap

- CIGS have direct band gap, ranging from 1.04eV to 2.4eV. They are suitable for thin film PV absorber layers.

High η

- In 1974 CuInSe$_2$ single crystal solar cell with an η of 12% was fabricated. In 1987 Arco Solar achieved an η of 14.1% for a thin film cell.

- η of 19.9% was reached in 2008

Advantages of CIGS technology

CIGS materials have good tolerance for stoichiometry deviation

- Solar cells with η above 14% are obtained from CIGS with $(In+Ga)/(In+Ga+Cu) = 0.52\text{-}0.64$, if CIGS materials contain Na.

Improvement of film quality by Na incorporation

- The effects of Na incorporation are higher conductivity and better defect distribution of CIGS films.

Advantages of CIGS technology

Air annealing for improved efficiencies

Post deposition air annealing is used for high-efficiency devices.

During annealing, the positively charged V_{Se} at grain boundaries are passivated by O atoms .

Disadvantages of CIGS technology

Large number of intrinsic defects

The PV performance of CIGS is controlled by intrinsic defects. In $CuInSe_2$ materials they are V_{Cu}, V_{In}, V_{Se}, Cu_i, In_i, Se_i. In_{Cu}, Cu_{In}, Se_{Cu}, Cu_{Se}, Se_{In} and In_{Se}.

In PV grade In-rich polycrystalline CIGS with p-type conduction. V_{Cu} is assumed to be the main dopant ($E_v + 30meV$). V_{Se} and In_{Cu} are compensating donors.

Efficiencies of CIGS modules

Process	η (%)	Area(cm²)	Company
Co-evaporation	12.7	800	ZSW
Co-evaporation	12.3	5932	Wurth Solar
Selenisation	12.1	3600	Shell Solar
Selenisation	11.6	864	Showa, Japan

CdTe

- The CdTe are grown by close spaced sublimation or other methods. The CdS are prepared by CBD on SnO_2/glass substrates.
- In spite of the large lattice mismatch (9.7%) between hexagonal CdS and cubic CdTe high performance devices have been obtained.
- During sublimation at 600°C, CdTe liberates Cd and Te in equal amounts. The condensed CdTe on substrates kept at 400°-500°C are stable stoichiometric.
- In CdTe the intrinsic defect V_{cd} is the main p-type dopant.

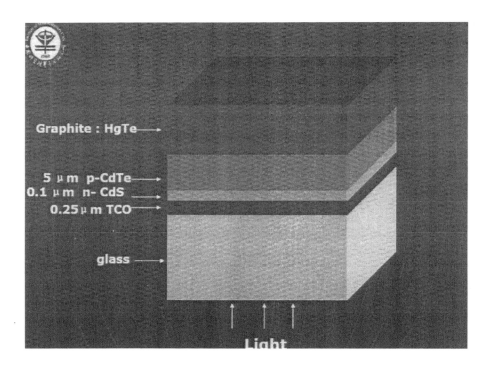

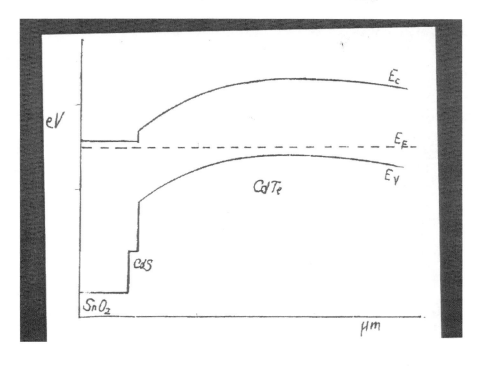

CdTe technology
Advantages

Favorable E_g

- Direct energy gap, E_g=1.45eV,

- The light absorption is about $10^5 cm^{-1}$ for λ less than 800nm.

Stoichiometry

- CdTe has a tendency to grow as stoichiometric materials with p-type conduction. forming p-n junction with n- CdS. CdS has an E_g of 2.4eV.

CdTe technology
Advantages

High stability of CdTe

The bonding energy between Cd and is very strong (5.75eV). The risk of performance degradation is reduced.

CdTe technology
Advantages

Improvement of η by CdCl₂ activation

$CdCl_2$ activation at 400°C after junction formation leads to increase the efficiencies from 2% to 16%.

The reasons for improvement of η

1, CdTe grains grew up.

2, The interdiffusion of CdS and CdTe reduces the effects of lattice mismatch between CdTe and CdS.

3, The carrier lifetime increases . The CdTe films of good devices can show 2000ps lifetime. The lifetime of minority carriers in CdTe (electrons) determines the collection efficiency.

CdTe technology
Advantages

Low manufacturing cost

CdTe films are grown using cheap and simple technology

Production equipments and costs are low.

Production costs of CdTe cells

- In 1Q and 2Q 2010 the gross profits reached 49.7%和48.3% (First Solar)

	2004	2007	4Q 2008	1Q 2009	2Q 2010
Production costs $/W_p$	3	1.23`	0..98 Broke $1/W_p$ barrier	0.87	0.76

CdTe technology disadvantages

Low η levels

Best efficiency was 16.5%(2001 NREL)

η of 12.4% on flexible substrates (2009)

CdTe technology disadvantages

Cd is one of the six most toxic substances.

Te is a rare element

Recycling

Semiconductor films are removed by acid and H$_2$O$_2$ and then precipitated. 90% of semiconductor can be reused for making new cells.

90% of glass are also collected for other usage

Conclusion

Semiconductor materials are essential parts of solar cells. The growth of stable semiconductor films with excellent quality and developing sophisticated processes and equipments are necessary for manufacturing solar cells with high performance.

Thank you!

Optical and Electrical Properties of GaN:Mg Grown by MOCVD*

Wang Lili[†], Zhang Shuming, Yang Hui, and Liang Junwu

(*Institute of Semiconductors, Chinese Academy of Sciences, Beijing* 100083, *China*)

Abstract: Mg-doped GaN layers prepared by metalorganic chemical vapor deposition were annealed at temperatures between 550 and 950℃. Room temperature (RT) Hall and photoluminescence (PL) spectroscopy measurements were performed on the as-grown and annealed samples. After annealing at 850℃, a high hole concentration of $8 \times 10^{17} cm^{-3}$ and a resistivity of 0.8 $\Omega \cdot$ cm are obtained. Two dominant defect-related PL emission bands in GaN:Mg are investigated; the blue band is centered at 2.8 eV (BL) and the ultraviolet emission band is around 3.27eV (UVL). The relative intensity of BL to UVL increases after annealing at 550℃, but decreases when the annealing temperature is raised from 650 to 850℃, and finally increases sharply when the annealing temperature is raised to 950℃. The hole concentration increases with increased Mg doping, and decreases for higher Mg doping concentrations. These results indicate that the difficulties in achieving high hole concentration of $10^{18} cm^{-3}$ appear to be related not only to hydrogen passivation, but also to self-compensation.

Key words: Hall effect; photoluminescence; p-GaN

PACC: 7280; 7850G; 7855

CLC number: TN304.2+3   **Document code:** A   **Article ID:** 0253-4177(2008)01-0029-04

1 Introduction

Well controlled p-type doping is one of the foremost obstacles in the progress of device development of Ⅲ-nitrides for fabricating visible and ultraviolet light-emitting devices. Low energy electron-beam irradiation[1] or thermal annealing in N_2 atmosphere[2] is necessary to obtain significant hole concentrations for GaN grown by metal-organic chemical vapor dep-osition (MOCVD). Although the underlying mechanism for these activation processes is not yet fully understood, it is widely believed that hydrogen impurities created in the growth passivate Mg acceptors by forming Mg-H neutral complexes. Observation of a local vibrational mode (LVM) for the Mg-N-H complex by infrared (IR) absorption[3] and Raman scattering[4] in as-grown samples gives convincing evidence for this hypothesis. Therefore, a postgrowth treatment is required to activate the Mg acceptors through dissociation of Mg-H complexes.

However, there is strong evidence that p-type doping of GaN is a more complex process and Mg-Hcomplexes may not be the only passivating centers[4,5]. Theoretical calculations predict that ni-

原载于:半导体学报,2008,29(1):29-32.

* Project supported by the National Natural Science Foundation of China (Nos. 60506001,60576003,60476021)

† Corresponding author. Email: wangll@ red. semi. ac. cn

Received 31 May 2007, revised manuscript received 16 August 2007

trogen vacancies are the dominant point defects in p-type GaN because of their low formation energy[6,7]. Moreover, due to the high Mg ionization energy, high doping concentrations in the $10^{19} cm^{-3}$ range are required to achieve hole concentrations in the low $10^{17} cm^{-3}$ range. Saarinen $et\ al.$ applied positron annihilation spectroscopy (PAS) to identify Mg_{Ga}-V_N complexes as important compensating centers in Mg-doped GaN layers[5]. Despite that, we still lack an understanding of the defects responsible for determining the electrical and optical properties of Mg-doped GaN layers.

In this work, we perform Hall and photoluminescence (PL) spectroscopy measurements of Mg-doped GaN:Mg layers prepared by MOCVD. Two closely connected effects are observed. First, a RT PL band peaked around 2.8eV dominates the PL spectra. Second, the hole concentration as a function of Mg concentration reaches a maximum value. The stability of defects in heavily Mg-doped GaN layers is also investigated. The role that Fermi level plays on defect stability in p-type GaN:Mg layers is taken into account.

2   Experiment

p-type GaN:Mg layers were grown on sapphire substrate using a horizontal MOCVD reactor. Trimethyl-gallium (TMGa) and ammonia (NH_3) were used as Ga and N precursors, respectively, and bis-cyclopentadienyl magnesium ($Cp_2 Mg$) as the p-type doping source. First, a 4μm semi-insulating GaN ($n < 5 \times 10^{16} cm^{-3}$) layer was grown on sapphire followed by a 1.5μm GaN:Mg layer at 1040℃. The mole ratio of $Cp_2 Mg$ to TMGa ([$Cp_2 Mg$]/[TMGa]) varied between 0.004 and 0.015. To achieve p-type characteristics in the GaN:Mg layer, rapid thermal annealing (RTA) was carried out under various conditions. A one-step RTA process was performed on the samples prepared with a [$Cp_2 Mg$]/[TMGa] ratio of 0.0065 at temperatures of 550,650,750,850, and 950℃ in N_2 atmosphere for 20min. The samples were studied by PL and RT Hall measurements in the as-grown condition and after each annealing step. Photoluminescence was excited with the 325nm line of a He-Cd laser (10mW).

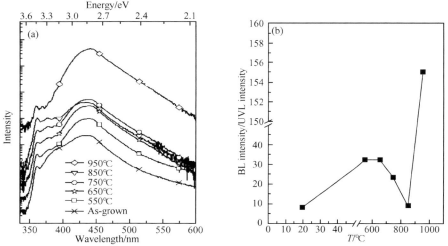

Fig. 1   (a) PL spectra for GaN:Mg layer before and after annealing at different temperatures;
(b) Relative intensity of BL to UVL as a function of annealing temperature

3 Results and discussion

Figure 1 (a) shows the typical PL spectra at 295K of GaN:Mg layers before and after annealing at different temperatures. The peak centered at ~3.5eV corresponds to the band edge emission of the underlying GaN layer. An apparent intensity ultraviolet emission band around 3.2eV (UVL) is observed in the asgrown sample, which was previously attributed to donor-acceptor pair (DAP) emission involving a shallow donor of unknown origin and a Mg acceptor[8]. After annealing, the intensity of this DAP emission band is decreased by one order of magnitude and the peak position gradually shifts to 3.27eV (UVL). The shift in the peak position may be explained by the reduction of potential fluctuations[9] as a result of screening from the carriers. A third band with a peak around 2.8eV (BL) is observed and the intensity of this peak changes significantly after annealing. To clearly demonstrate the change of the intensity of the observed peaks, Figure 1 (b) shows the relative intensity of BL to UVL (BL intensity/UVL intensity) as a function of annealing temperature (T). BL intensity/UVL intensity increases after annealing at 550℃, but decreases when the annealing temperature is elevated from 650 to 850℃, and finally increases sharply when the annealing temperature is raised to 950℃.

The observed change in the PL spectra upon annealing can be attributed to changes in the defect con-centrations. Prior to annealing, shallow donors are present in high concentrations, leading to UVL. Upon annealing at 550℃ in nitrogen, the shallow donors are eliminated and the intensity of UVL decreases sharply. Since the UVL is quenched by annealing at a relatively low temperature of 550℃, it must involve a donor that has a high diffusivity. One possibility is hydrogen, which has a high diffusivity in GaN and has been predicted

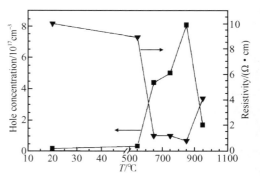

Fig. 2　Hole concentration and resistivity in GaN: Mg layers as determined by Hall measurement versus the annealing temperature

to be a donor[10]. IR absorption[3] and Raman scattering data[4] show clear evidence that H-related complexes are present in as-grown GaN:Mg layers. The BL that becomes dominant upon annealing has been previously attributed to deep donor shallow acceptor (DDAP) emission, where, in this case, the donor is deep and the acceptor is shallow[9].

Figure 2 shows the hole concentration and resistivity in GaN:Mg layers annealed at different temperatures. The layers show poor p-type conductivity before annealing. Thermal annealing from 550 to 950℃ for 20min has no obvious effect on our GaN:Mg layers with high crystal quality, as demonstrated by X-ray diffraction.

After annealing at 550℃, the hole concentration and the resistivity change little. As the annealing temperature increases from 550 to 850℃, the hole concentration continuously increases from 10^{16} cm^{-3} to $8×10^{17}$ cm^{-3} and the resistivity decreases from 9 to 0.8Ω·cm. However, the hole concentration drops dramatically after the annealing temperature is raised to 950℃,

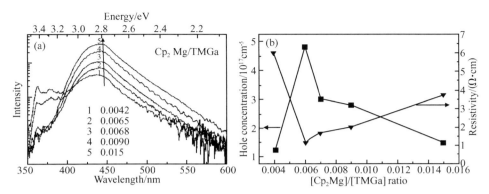

Fig. 3 Dependence of the intensity of the PL bands (a), and the hole concentration of GaN:
Mg layers on [Cp$_2$Mg]/[TMGa] ratio (b)

and the resistivity increases to 4 Ω · cm.

Figure 3(a) shows the dependence of the intensity of the PL bands, and Figure 3 (b) shows the hole concentration of GaN:Mg layers on the [Cp$_2$Mg]/[TMGa] ratio. The p-type GaN:Mg layers under investigation were annealed at 750℃ for 20 min. The increment of the [Cp$_2$Mg]/[TMGa] ratio corresponds to the increase in Mg doping concentration[11].

The data in Fig. 3 (b) show that initially the hole concentration increases as Mg doping increases, but decreases later for higher Mg doping concentrations. The resistivity shows the opposite trend. The difficulties in achieving high hole concentration above 8×10^{17} cm^{-3} and low resistivity below 0. 8 Ω · cm appear to be primarily related to self-compensation of Mg[12]. As indicated in Fig. 3 (a), for moderately Mgdoped p-type GaN, the UVL is seen as a weak peak, compared to the BL. For heavily Mg-doped GaN, however, the UVL quenches, and the BL dominants the spectra. It seems that the intensity of the BL, is not directly related to the p-type conduction mechanism[13], but increases as the Mg doping concentration increases. This band has therefore been assigned to the recombination involving isolated Mg acceptors and deep donors presumably induced by self-compensation. A candidate for the deep donor is Mg$_{Ga}$ associated with a nitrogen vacancy (V$_N$), which is the only native defect with a relevant concentration in p-GaN[7], and has the opposite charge of Mg$_{Ga}$. Thus, neutral Mg$_{Ga}$-V$_N$ complexes are expected to form. At a growth temperature around 1000℃ the constituents are oppositely charged and V$_N$ is mobile.

After thermal annealing at 550~850℃ the Mg$_{Ga}$-V$_N$ complexes dissociate and V$_N$ migrates to the surface. As a result, the hole concentration increases, while the intensity of BL decreases, as shown in Figs. 1 and 2. The Mg$_{Ga}$-V$_N$ complexes are observed in asgrown MOCVD GaN:Mg, but not in the material grown by MBE[5]. The relevant difference is related to the presence of hydrogen in the growth environment. The as-grown MOCVD GaN:Mg commonly shows poor p-type conductivity because Mg acceptors are passivated by hydrogen. A postgrowth thermal anneal is required to activate the Mg acceptors and obtain significant hole concentration, as illustrated in Fig. 2. Hydrogen is absent in the MBE growth and the as-grown material already possesses well p-type con-ductivity. These results suggest that the Mg_{Ga}-V_N complexes are stable at the growth temperature around 1000℃ only if the Fermi level is close to the midgap; otherwise the complexes dissociate. Thereby , as shown in Figs. 1 and 2 , when the annealing temperature is raised from 850 to 950℃ , large amounts of V_N are ex-pected to form. As a consequence, the net hole concentration drops, and the Fermi level moves away from the maximum of the valence band, which results in the formation of Mg_{Ga}-V_N complexes again. Based on the analysis above, the dramatic increase in the intensity of BL in Fig. 1 is understandable.

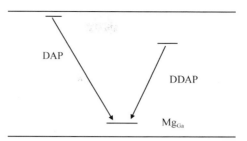

Fig. 4　Schematic energy band diagram to illustrate the peaks observed in Mg-doped GaN D indicates the donor state, and DD indicates the deep donor state

　　In summary, Figure 4 shows a schematic energy band diagram to illustrate the DAP peak (UVL) and DDAP peak (BL) observed in Mg-doped GaN layers. The shallow donor responsible for UVL is attributed to hydrogen, whereas the deep donor defect responsible for BL is attributed to nitrogen vacancy complexes associated with Mg acceptors.

4　Conclusion

　　After annealing at 850℃ , a high hole concentration of 8×10^{17} cm^{-3} of and a resistivity of 0. 8 Ω · cm are obtained. PL and Hall results on Mg-doped GaN layers indicate that the difficulties in achieving higher hole concentration appear to be related to self-compensation and hydrogen passivation. The observed dependence of the relative intensity of BL to UVL on annealing temperatures can be explained in terms of hydrogen donors. Upon annealing, the hydrogen related DAP defects dissociate and the associated luminescence band quenches, whereas Mg acceptors are activated and hole concentration increases. There is evidence that deep donors, which are assigned to Mg_{Ga}-V_N complexes, are formed as the Mg doping concentration increases. The Fermi level position may be a critical factor in the stabilization of Mg_{Ga}-V_N complexes. When the Fermi level position is near the maximum of the valence band, resulting from high hole concentration, Mg_{Ga}-V_N complexes are not stable, and dissociate after annealing between 550 and 850℃ .

References

[1] Amono H, Kito M, Hiramatsu K, et al. P-type conduction in Mgdoped GaN treated with LEEBI. Jpn J Appl Phys Part 2, 1989,28:L2112.

[2] Nakamura S, Iwasa N, Mukai T, et al. Thermal annealing effects on p-type Mg-doped GaN films. Jpn J Appl Phys Part 1, 1992,31:L139.

[3] Götz W,Johnson N,Bour D,et al. Local vibrational modes of the Mg-H acceptor complex in GaN. Appl Phys Lett, 1996, 75:1383.

[4] Reboredo F A, Pantelides S T. Novel defect complexes and their role in the p-type doping of GaN. Appl Phys Lett,1999, 82:1887.

[5] Hautakangas S, Oila J, Alatalo M, et al. Vacancy defects as compensating centers in Mg-doped GaN. Phys Rev Lett,

2003, 90:137402.

[6] Neugebauer J, Van de Walle C G. Theory of point defects and complexes in GaN. Mater Res Soc Symp Proc, 1996,395:645.

[7] Neugebauer J, Van de Walle C G. Atomic geometry and electronic structure of native defects in GaN. Phys Rev B, 1994,50:8067.

[8] Viswanath A K,Shin E, Lee J I, et al. Magnesium acceptor levels in GaN studied by photoluminescence. J Appl Phys, 1998,83:2272.

[9] Reshchikov M,Yi G C, Wessels B W. Behavior of 2.8and 3.2-eV photoluminescence bands in Mg-doped GaN at different temperatures and excitation densities. Phys Rev B, 1999,59:13176.

[10] Van de Walle C G. Interactions of hydrogen with native defects in GaN. Phys Rev B, 1997,56:R10020.

[11] Sugiura L,Suzuki M,Nishio J. P-type conduction in as-grown Mgdoped GaN grown by metalorganic chemical vapor deposition. Appl Phys Lett, 1998,72:1748.

[12] Obloh H, Bachem K H, Kaufmann U, et al. Self-compensation in Mg doped p-type GaN grown by MOCVD. J Cryst Growth, 1998,195:270.

[13] Nakamura S, Iwasa N, Senoh M, et al. Hole compensation mechanism of p-type gan films. Jpn J Appl Phys,1992,31:1258.

MOCVD 生长的 GaN:Mg 外延膜的光电性质[*]

王莉莉[†]   张书明   杨   辉   梁骏吾

(中国科学院半导体研究所,北京   100083)

摘要:用 MOCVD 技术生长 GaN:Mg 外延膜,在 550~950℃温度范围内,对样品进行热退火,并进行室温 Hall、光致发光谱(PL)测试. Hall 测试结果表明,850℃退火后空穴浓度达到 $8 \times 10^{17} \mathrm{cm}^{-3}$ 以上,电阻率降到 $0.8\Omega \cdot \mathrm{cm}$ 以下. 室温 PL 谱有两个缺陷相关发光峰,位于 2.8eV 的蓝光峰(BL)以及 3.27eV 附近的紫外峰(UVL). 蓝光峰对紫外峰的相对强度(BL/UVL) 在 550℃退火后升高,之后随着退火温度的升高(650~850℃)而下降,继续提高退火温度至 950℃,BL/UVL 急剧上升. 空穴浓度先随着 Mg 掺杂浓度的增加而升高;但继续增加 Mg 掺杂浓度,空穴浓度反而下降. 这些结果表明要实现空穴浓度达 $10^{18} \mathrm{cm}^{-3}$,不仅要考虑 H 的钝化作用,还要考虑 Mg 受主的自补偿效应.

关键词:霍尔效应;光致发光;P 型 GaN

PACC:7280;7850G;7855

中图分类号:TN304.2⁺3   文献标识码:A   文章编号:0253-4177(2008)01-0029-04

* 国家自然科学基金资助项目(批准号:60506001,60576003,60476021)

† 通信作者. Email:wangll@ red. semi. ac. cn

2007-05-31 收到,2007-08-16 定稿

Defect Cluster-Induced X-Ray Diffuse Scattering in GaN Films Grown by MOCVD [*]

Ma Zhifang[1], Wang Yutian[1], Jiang Desheng[1], Zhao Degang[1], Zhang Shuming[1], Zhu Jianjun[1], Liu Zongshun[1], Sun Baojuan[2], Duan Ruifei[2], Yang Hui[1,3,†], and Liang Junwu[1]

(1 *State Key Laboratory on Integrated Optoelectronics*, *Institute of Semiconductors*, *Chinese Academy of Sciences*, *Beijing* 100083, *China*)

(2 *Research and Development Center for Semiconductor Lighting*, *Institute of Semiconductors*, *Chinese Academy of Sciences*, *Beijing* 100083, *China*)

(3 *Suzhou Institute of Nano-Tech and Nano-Bionics*, *Chinese Academy of Sciences*, *Suzhou* 215123, *China*)

Abstract: High-resolution X-ray diffraction has been employed to investigate the diffuse scattering in a (0001) oriented GaN epitaxial film grown on sapphire substrate. The analysis reveals that defect clusters are present in GaN films and their concentration increases as the density of threading dislocations increases. Meanwhile, the mean radius of these defect clusters shows a reverse tendency. This result is explained by the effect of clusters preferentially forming around dislocations, which act as effective sinks for the segregation of point defects. The electric mobility is found to decrease as the cluster concentration increases.

Key words: X-ray diffuse scattering; GaN; defect cluster

PACC: 7870; 6855; 7850G

CLC number: TN304   **Document code:** A   **Article ID:** 0253-4177(2008)07-1242-04

1 Introduction

In recent years, group Ⅲ-nitrides have attracted much attention because of their potential for hightemperature and high-power electronic devices. Due to lack of appropriate substrate, high density dislocations ($10^8 \sim 10^{10}$ cm^{-2}) will be generated in group Ⅲ-N epitaxial layers. Various structural investigation methods, such as X-ray diffraction (XRD), transmission electron microscopy (TEM), and Rutherford back-scattering (RBS)/channeling techniques were used to investigate the effect of the threading dislocations on the structural properties of Ⅲ-nitride epitaxial layers. Among these methods, XRD is a well-established technique to analyze crystal lattice perfection. The density of screw and edge dislocations can be characterized by the half widths of diffraction peaks of X-ray Bragg reflection. Although the obtained structural parameters are instructive for the material growth and device design, it is still not enough to de-

原载于:半导体学报,2008,29(1):1242-1245.

* Project supported by the National Natural Science Foundation of China (Nos. 60506001,60476021,60576003) and the State Key Development Program for Basic Research of China (No. 2007CB936700)

† Corresponding author. Email:hyang@ semi. ac. cn

Received 29 February 2008, revised manuscript received 19 March 2008

termine the crystal perfection. In addition to the threading dislocations, the effect of point defects on structural quality can not be neglected. The X-ray diffuse scattering technique, i. e. , Huang diffuse scattering, is applicable for studying point defects, dislocation loops, and small defect clusters in metals[1,2] and semiconductors[3~5]. However, few reports about X-ray diffuse scattering of GaN films are available at present. In this study, we will focus on an investigation of the broad tail of the X-ray rocking curve, which is induced by the diffuse scattering of a large number of defect clusters in GaN film grown on sapphire substrate, as well as the relationship between defect clusters and photoelectric properties. It is found that the carrier mobility decreases as the cluster den-sity increases in GaN films.

2   Theoretic basis of diffuse scattering from point defects

The defect-induced distortions in a crystal lattice gives rise to X-ray diffuse scattering[6]. A review of diffuse scattering of defects has been given by Krivoglaz[7] and Dederichs[8,9]. In addition, experimental results have shown that X-ray diffuse scattering in the vicinity of the Bragg reflection can be used to investigate point defects[1,5,10]. Here we will outline those parts of the theory that are relevant to the understanding of our experimental measurements. If point defects aggregate into a cluster, a statistical distribution of clusters will be formed in the lattice. Under the assumption of a linear superposition of the displacements of the point defects in a cluster of radius R_{cl}, the diffuse scattering is proportional to the density C_{cl} and the square of relaxation volume V_{rel} of defect clusters[8,11]. Depending upon the magnitude of q deviated from the Bragg position, where q is defined as $q = k \pm h$ (where k is the scattering vector and h is the reciprocal-lattice vector), one may distinguish two regions of diffuse scattering. First, at small q, the displacement field is away from the defect centers and scattering function $S(K)$ has q^{-2} dependence. The scattering is Huang diffuse scattering (HDS). Second, at larger q values, diffuse X-ray scattering from strongly distorted regions of the lattice falls off like q^{-4} according to a generalized form of the StokesWilson (SW) approximation[8].

3   Experiment

All the investigated samples were grown by metal-organic chemical vapor deposition (MOCVD) (Thomas Swan Scientific Equipment 3×2 CCSMOCVD with a vertical quartz reactor) on c-axis sapphire substrate. The growth of GaN epitaxial layer takes the conventional two-step method with H_2 carrier gas under low reaction pressure at the temperature of 1040℃. The group-Ⅲ precursor used for the growth of GaN layers was trimethyl-gallium. Diffuse X-ray scattering measurements were performed with a Bede D1 high-resolution X-ray diffractometer (HRXRD), using a conventional sealed X-ray tube and Cu K_{α_1} radiation. The rocking curve (ω scan) was taken to study the X-ray diffuse scattering in GaN films. The full width at half maximum (FWHM) of the ω scan for the symmetric (0002) and skew symmetric (1012) reflections of GaN films was used to characterize the density of screw-type dislocation and edge-type dislocation, respectively. The density of threading dislocation was obtained using the following expression[12,13]: $D \approx \beta^2 / (4.35 \times b^2)$ (where b is the Burgers vector of the threading dislocation; and β is the FWHM of the rocking curve). In addition, the optical and electrical properties of GaN samples were investigated using Hall and photoluminescence (PL) measurements at room temperature.

4 Results and discussion

Figure 1 shows rocking curves (ω scan) around the (0002) reflection in the GaN films. The symmetrical part of the diffuse scattering intensity curves is described by $I = [I(+q) + I(-q)]/2$, where I is the average intensity change measured at equal q on either side of the center of the Bragg peak. Figure 2 shows the symmetric intensity of the diffuse scattering on a double logarithmic plot for (0002) reflection from three GaN samples. These curves indicate that there are two regions of linear behavior with

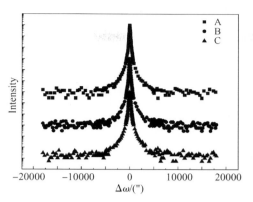

Fig. 1　Rocking curves around the (0002) XRD reflection in three GaN films

different slopes, corresponding to $I \propto q^{-2}$ and $I \propto q^{-4}$, respectively. This suggests that the HDS region (I_H) for smaller q values and the SW scattering (I_{SW}) for larger q values are observed. Therefore, it is possible to determine the average radius R_{cl} of the clusters from the crossing point q_0 of the two straight lines, i. e. , the q^{-2} dependence line of the HDS and the q^{-4} dependence line of the SW scattering, as shown in Fig. 2. Thus, $q_0 \approx 1/R_{cl}$. In fact, this method has been widely used for experimental estimate of defect cluster sizes[3,10,11].

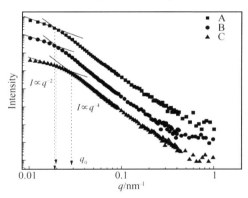

Fig. 2　Log-log (intensity versus q) plots of the symmetric part of the scattered intensity close to (0002) reflection for three samples The data points (squares, circles, triangles) correspond to the ω scan intensity near the (0002) reflection of samples A,B, and C, respectively. The measured curves are fitted by 2 straight lines with 2 different slopes shown by solid lines corresponding to $I \propto q^{-2}$ and $I \propto q^{-4}$, respectively. The intersections of the two solid lines, q_0, are shown by the arrows

Furthermore, for $q > q_0$, the diffuse intensity decreases faster and then follows a relation of $I_{sw}(q) - q^{-4}$. It finally becomes less than the thermal diffuse scattering intensity I_T, which decreases slowly in analogy to I_H.[4] The intensity of the thermal diffuse scattering $I_T(q_T)$ can be used as an internal reference to scale the Huang intensity. Thus, one can obtain an expression for determining cluster concentration C_{cl} from Eq. (1)[3,14].

$$\frac{I_H(q_H)}{I_T(q_T)} = \frac{C_{cl}(\Delta V)^2}{K_B T/E} \times \frac{|q_T|^2}{|q_H|^2} \times \frac{\Pi(m,n)}{\widetilde{K}(m,n)} (1)$$

where K_B is the Boltzmann constant, T is the sample temperature, E is the Young modulus, ΔV is the change in the volume of the crystal produced by a single defect cluster, q_H is the wave vector in the HDS region, q_T is the analogous value in the thermal diffuse scattering region, and $\Pi(m,n)$ and $\widetilde{K}(m,n)$ are dimensionless factors of order 1 that depend on the unit vector m and n, and on the elastic constants of the matrix. Ther ratio of $\Pi(m,n)$ to $\bar{K}(m, n)$ is of order 1. Thus, the corresponding defect cluster concentration C_{cl} can be estimated from the value of I_H/I_T.

Table 1　Results of HRXRD, PL, and Hall measurements

Sample	Screw dislocation density /cm^{-2}	Edge dislocation density /cm^{-2}	Cluster radius /nm	Cluster concentration /cm^{-3}	FWHM of NBE peak /meV	I_0/I_{YL}	Carrier mobility /[cm^2/(V·s)]	Carrier concentration /cm^{-3}
A	7.2×10^7	3.1×10^8	52	9×10^{12}	28	1.6	700	6.8×10^{16}
B	6.8×10^7	2.2×10^8	51	1×10^{13}	31	1.7	600	1.1×10^{17}
C	1.1×10^8	6.3×10^8	35	4×10^{13}	28	0.5	150	1.3×10^{17}

Table 1 presents the density of screw and edge threading dislocations for GaN films, the mean radius R_{cl} and the density of defect clusters C_{cl}, and the resuits of Hall and PL measurements. It is found that the mean defect cluster radius decreases as the dislocation density of the samples increases. Meanwhile, the density of defect clusters seems to have a slight ascending tendency. As shown in Table 1, the cluster size (35nm) is the smallest and the cluster density (4×10^{13} cm^{-3}) is the highest for sample C, which has the highest screw and edge dislocation density in the investigated samples.

The lattice matrix may be distorted by point defects in the crystal. Therefore, in general there will be a long-range interaction between point defect and dislocations. Dislocations provide sites for the segregation of point defects. The accumulation of impurities or native defects at the dislocation lines is usually referred to as a "Cottrell atmosphere"[15]. We think that the same mechanism is valid for wide band gap group Ⅲ-N materials. In view of the presence of a high density of dislocations ($10^8 \sim 10^{10}$ cm^{-2}) in GaN epilayers grown on sapphire, it is reasonable to assume that the dislocation lines are suitable sites for the segregation of point defects like the nitrogen vacancy, oxygen[16] and carbon impurities, and their comple-xes. Therefore, we suggest that the defect clusters observed in GaN samples are related to the threading dislocations, and the density of defect clusters increases as the density of threading dislocations increases. Actually, both edge and screw dislocations may form defect clusters around them. As first reported by Chern et al. , an open core type of nanopipes, 5~25nm in diameter were observed in nominally undoped GaN films grown by MOCVD, which contained threading dislocations with Burgers vectors $\langle 0001 \rangle$ (screw dislocations)[17]. The point defect species such as Ga interstitials and the impurities or its complexes may segregate around dislocations to form clusters. It seems that the stress fields of dislocation represented by the observed HDS are large enough and the point defects thus can be trapped in the vicinity of disloca-tion lines. Table 1 shows that the defect cluster concentration increases as the density of the threading dislocations increases. On the contrary, the cluster radius decreases at the same time. There seems to be a balance of the magnitude between cluster size and concentration. This result can be understood if the total concentration of point defects in these GaN films is assumed to be nearly a constant.

The Hall and PL results measured at room tem-perature are listed in Table 1. The carrier mobility decreases as the defect cluster concentration increases and as the cluster size decreases. However, a reverse dependence is observed for the carrier concentration in the investigated samples. Thus, statistically a lower defect cluster density may be related with a higher carrier mobility and a lower carrier concentration. In other words, the mobility is improved as the cluster size increases. As for the optical property of the measured GaN samples characterized by PL, it seems that there is not a remarkable correlation between the PL properties and the defect clusters in GaN samples. The FWHM of near-band-gap (NBE) luminescence peak is almost the same for all three samples, as shown in Table 1. However, sample C which has a higher defect cluster concentration, displays a lower ratio of I_0/I_{yL}, i. e. , the ratio between the intensity of NBE luminescence peak I_0 and the intensity of yellow luminescence peak I_{YL}.

5 Conclusion

In summary, the defect clusters in GaN films grown by MOCVD are observed by the method of diffuse scattering using HRXRD. A fundamental correlation is found between the density of threading dislocations and the cluster density. The experimental results are explained based on a suggestion that the dislocations act as an ideal sink for the accumulation of the point defects, i. e. , the dislocations play a role of "scavengers" for the point defects in the GaN films. Furthermore, with increasing cluster size and a corresponding decrease of the cluster density, the carrier mobility is improved.

References

[1] Thomas J E, Baldwin T O, Dederichs P H. Diffuse X-ray scattering in fast-neutron-irradiated copper crystals. Phys Rev B, 1971, 3:1167.

[2] Kim C, Feng R, Conrad E H, et al. Nanoclustering of vacancies in thin metal films revealed by X-ray diffuse scattering. Appl Phys Lett, 2007, 91:093131.

[3] Moreno M, Jenichen B, Kaganer V, et al. MnAs nanoclusters embedded in GaAs studied by X-ray and coherent scattering. Phys Rev B, 2003, 67:235206.

[4] Charniy L A, Morozov A N, Bublik V T, et al. Study of microdefects and their distribution in dislocation-free Si-doped HB GaAs by X-ray diffuse scattering on triple-crystal diffractometer. J Cryst Growth, 1992, 118:163.

[5] Patel J R. X-ray diffuse scattering from silicon containing oxygen clusters. J Appl Cryst, 1975, 8:86.

[6] Eckstein H. Disorder scattering of X-rays by local distortions. Phys Rev, 1945, 68:120.

[7] Krivoglaz M A. Theory of X-ray and thermal neutron scattering by real crystals. New York: Plenum, 1969.

[8] Dederichs P H. The theory of diffuse X-ray scattering and its application to the study of point defects and their clusters. J Phys F Metal Phys, 1973, 3:471.

[9] Dederichs P H. Diffuse scattering from defect clusters near Bragg reflections. Phys Rev B, 1971, 4:1041.

[10] Hahn S, Ponce F A, Tiller W A, et al. Effects of heavy boron doping upon oxygen precipitation in Czochralski silicon. J Appl Phys, 1988, 64(9):4454.

[11] Ehrhart P. The configuration of atomic defects as determined from scattering studies. J Nucl Mater, 1978, 69. /70:200.

[12] Gay P, Hirsch P B, Kelly A. The estimation of dislocation densities in metals from X-ray data. Acta Metall, 1953, 1:315.

[13] Dunn C G, Kogh E F. Comparison of dislocation densities of primary and secondary recrystallization grains of Si-Fe. Acta Metall, 1957, 5:548.

[14] Charnyi L A, Sherbachev K D, Bublik V T. Microdefect density determination by X-ray Huang scattering normalized over ther-mal diffuse scattering. Phys Status Solidi A, 1991, 128:303.

[15] Bullough R, Newman R C. The kinetics of migration of point defects to dislocations. Pep Prog Phys, 1970, 33:101.

[16] Hawkridge M E, Cherns D. Oxygen segregation to dislocations in GaN. Appl Phys Lett, 2005, 87:221903.

[17] Cherns D, Young W T, Steeds J W, et al. Observation of coreless dislocations in α-GaN. J Cryst Growth, 1997, 178(1/2):201.

MOCVD 生长的 GaN 薄膜中缺陷团引起的 X 射线漫散射研究[*]

马志芳[1]　王玉田[1]　江德生[1]　赵德刚[1]　张书明[1]　朱建军[1]　刘宗顺[1]
孙宝娟[2]　段瑞飞[2]　杨　辉[1,3,†]　梁骏吾[1]

(1 中国科学院半导体研究所　集成光电子国家重点实验室, 北京　100083)
(2 中国科学院半导体所　半导体照明研发中心, 北京　100083)
(3 中国科学院苏州纳米技术及纳米仿生研究所, 苏州　215123)

摘要: 采用高分辨 X 射线衍射对在蓝宝石(0001)面生长的 GaN 外延膜的漫散射进行了研究. 结果表明, GaN 薄膜中存在缺陷团, 其浓度随着穿透位错密度的增加而增加, 其平均半径呈相反趋势. 基于位错是点缺陷的聚集区, 缺陷团优先在位错附近形成的效应对结果进行了解释. 同时发现电子迁移率随缺陷团浓度的增加而减少.

关键词: X 射线漫散射; GaN; 缺陷团

PACC: 7870; 6855; 7850G

中图分类号: TN304　　**文献标识码:** A　　**文章编号:** 0253-4177(2008)07-1242-04

─────────────

[*] 国家自然科学基金(批准号: 60506001, 60476021, 60576003)和国家重点基础研究发展规划(批准号: 2007CB936700)资助项目

[†] 通信作者. Email: hyang@semi.ac.cn

2008-02-29 收到, 2008-03-19 定稿

Growth of AlGaN Epitaxial Film with High Al Content by Metalorganic Chemical Vapour Deposition[*]

WANG Xiao-Lan(王小兰)[**], ZHAO De-Gang(赵德刚), YANG Hui(杨辉),
LIANG Jun- Wu(梁骏吾)

(*State Key Laboratory on Integrated Optoelectronics, Institute of Semiconductors,*

Chinese Academy of Sciences, PO Box 912, Beijing 100083)

(Received 21 November 2006)

Abstract: A high-Al-content AlGaN epilayer is grown on a low-temperature-deposited AlN buffer on (0001) sapphire by low pressure metalorganic chemical vapour deposition. The dependence of surface roughness, tilted mosaicity, and twisted mosaicity on the conditions of the AlGaN epilayer deposition is evaluated. An AlGaN epilayer with favourable surface morphology and crystal quality is deposited on a 20 nm low-temperature-deposited AlN buffer at a low V/III flow ratio of 783 and at a low reactor pressure of 100 Torr, and the adduct reaction between trimethylaluminium and NH_3 is considered.

PACS: 61.10. Nz, 61.16. Ch, 81.15. Gh

Deep ultraviolet (UV) emitters ($\lambda < 300$nm) have recently become the focus of research due to their many potential applications in biochemical detection, enhanced optical data storage density, and solid-state white lighting by phosphor excitation, etc.[1-4] AlGaN alloys are GaN-based III-nitride materials that have promising applications in the above fields because of their direct energy band gap from 3.4eV to 6.2eV, which lies in the deep ultraviolet range.[5,6]

It is important to obtain thick AlGaN with a high AlN molar fraction to realize a high-efficiency ultraviolet detector. However, it is extremely difficult to grow thick AlGaN with a high Al content directly on GaN since cracks always develop because of the large inplane tensile stress due to the large difference in lattice constant.[7] One solution to this problem was found by Amano et al.,[8] who reported the formation of crackfree AlGaN by inserting low-temperature-deposited AlN (LT-AlN) as an interlayer between AlGaN and the underlying GaN.

Compared with GaN,[9] the growth of AlGaN has proven to be very difficult. The problem is partly because Al adatoms have a much larger sticking coefficient than Ga adatoms. Furthermore, the parasitic reaction between trimethylaluminium (TMA) and NH_3 is unavoidable, especially under a large V/III ratio and at a high pressure in the reactor.[10,11]

原载于: Chinese Physics Letters, 2007, 24: 774-777.

* Supported by the National Natural Science Foundation of China under Grant Nos 60506001, 60476021, and 60576003.

** Email: WXL@ mail.semi.ac.cn

In our work, to avoid the crack problem and to apply to a back-illumination detector, an LT-AlN buffer layer is placed under the AlGaN epilayer to reduce the lattice and thermal mismatches between AlGaN and sapphire. We evaluate the dependence of surface morphology and roughness, tilted mosaicity, and twisted mosaicity under the conditions of the AlGaN deposition on the LT-AlN buffer. We also consider the adduct reaction between TMA and NH_3. The relevant parameters are the LT-AlN buffer thickness, the V/III flow ratio, and the reactor pressure.

The materials were grown in a metalorganic chemical vapour deposition (MOCVD) system (Thomas Swan Scientific Equipment 3×2 CCS-MOCVD) with a vertical quartz reactor. The AlGaN epilayer was grown on a double-polished (0001) sapphire substrate via an LT-AlN nucleation layer. Trimethylgallium(TMG), TMA, and ammonia were used as precursors, with hydrogen as the carrier gas. The AlN buffer layer was grown on a sapphire substrate at 540℃ and annealed in a temperature ramp, and then an AlGaN epilayer in thickness of about 1.5 μm was deposited on the LT-AlN buffer layer at 1100℃. The sapphire substrates for all depositions underwent the same pretreatment, by which the surface of the substrate was cleaned in hydrogen atmosphere and then nitrided with ammonia. The Al content was about 53% in the gas phase, and the solid Al content varied with growth conditions. The variable parameters were the buffer thickness, the V/III ratio, and the reactor pressure. The V/III ratio was changed by the NH_3 flow rate. The conditions of growth and the ranges of these parameters are listed in Table 1.

The surface roughness was evaluated by using a NanoScope III a atomic force microscope (AFM) to de termine the mean surface roughness (RMS) over an area of 20 μm×20 μm. The surface morphology was evaluated with a scanning electron microscope (SEM). The tilted mosaicity along the c-axis was evaluated from the full width at half maximum (FWHM) of xray rocking curves (XRC) for (0002) AlGaN. A significant distortion of the twisted mosaicity around the c-axis was caused by a large number of edge-type dislocations. The twisted mosaicity was evaluated from the FWHM of XRC for (10$\bar{1}$2) AlGaN. The x-ray measurements were performed using a Rigaku SLX-1A x-ray diffractometer equipped with a Si (220) analyser. The Al content was calculated from the optical transmission using a UV-VIS spectrometer.

Table 1　Growth conditions of the AlGaN epilayer.

	Growth temperature (℃)	Thickness (nm)	Pressure in reactor (Torr)	V/III ratio
LT AlN buffer	540	10—45	500	4000
AlGaN epilayer	1100	1500	100—150	783-3133

The dependence of the surface morphology on the LT-AlN buffer thickness was evaluated. Figure 1 shows the surface morphologies of samples with different LT-AlN buffer thicknesses. The main difference between Fig. 1(a) and Figs. 1(b) and 1(c) is readily apparent. In Fig. 1 (a), hexagonal pyramids with diameters larger than 2μm are piled up along the growth direction. This sample is typical of the threedimensional growth mode. Figures 1(b) and 1(c) show several hillocks on the surface. The surface is rather flat compared to the sample with the 10 nm

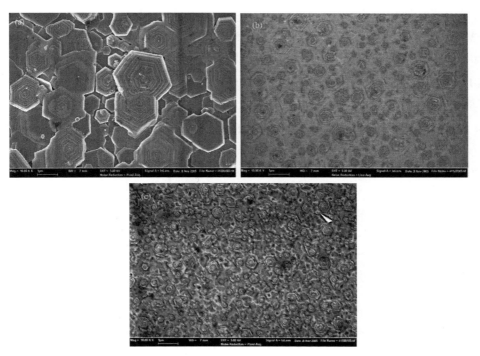

Fig. 1　SEM images of AlGaN surface with LT AlN buffer thicknesses of (a) 10 nm, (b) 20 nm, and (c) 45nm.The other parameters are unchanged (pressure in reactor：100 Torr, V/Ⅲ ratio：783, temperature：1100℃)

LT-AlN buffer, which can be confirmed by *in situ* optical reflectivity, as shown in Fig. 2. For the sample with the 10 nm LT-AlN buffer, the buffer is too thin for twodimensional growth. Thus during the growth of the AlGaN epilayer, the curve gradually decayed to zero after 7 periods. This indicates that the surface of this sample is very coarse.[12] However, according to the *in situ* optical reflectivity curves, the samples with 20 nm and 45 nm LT-AlN buffers exhibit the quasitwo-dimensional growth mode, and there exists only a little attenuation of the intensity of in situ optical reflectivity during the initial period of the growth of the AlGaN epilayer. Thus their surfaces are more flat than that of the sample with the 10 nm LT-AlN buffer, as shown in Fig. 1.

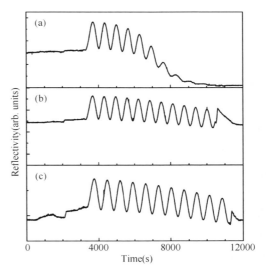

Fig. 2　Traces of *in situ* optical reflectivity measurements for the whole growth process of AlGaN epilayers on the low-temperature AlN buffer layer with different thicknesses of (a) 10 nm, (b) 20 nm, and (c) 45 nm

The FWHM of the XRC as a function of the thickness of the LT-AlN buffer is shown in Fig. 3. We can observe the change in the FWHM for (0002) and (10$\bar{1}$2) at various LT-AlN buffer thicknesses. The FWHM decreases as the buffer thickness increases from 10nm to 20nm. The minimum FWHM for(0002) and (10$\bar{1}$2) AlGaN are 810 arcsec and 1191 arcsec, respectively, when the LT-AlN buffer thickness is 20 nm. At a buffer thickness of more than 20 nm, the FWHM for (0002) and (10$\bar{1}$2) AlGaN increases gradually. Atomic force microscopy images of LT-AlN with different thicknesses can be found in the literature.[12] Because the AlGaN islands in the initial growth stage will coalesce quickly if the LT-AlN buffer layer has small grain size and high nucleus density, many of the formed dislocations will go through the AlGaN epilayers, leading to deteriorated quality. On the other hand, the quality of AlGaN epilayers deposited on the LT-AlN buffer layer with large grain size and low nucleus density will be much better, since the lateral growth and coalescence of AlGaN islands will be promoted, leading to an increasing volume of defect-free columnar domains and thus improving the crystal quality. Of course, when the LT-AlN buffer layer has very large grain sizes and very low nucleus density, the lateral growth of AlGaN islands will take to be very long, and the quality of AlGaN epilayers will also deteriorate.

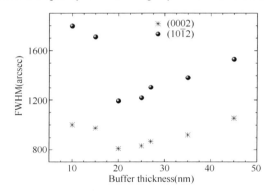

Fig. 3　FWHM values of XRC for (0002) and (10$\bar{1}$2) AlGaN at various LT AlN thickness. The other parameters are unchanged (pressure in reactor: 100Torr, V/Ⅲ ratio:783, temperature:1100℃)

The Al content in the solid phase is calculated by optical transmission, and the results show that the Alcontents of all samples with different thicknesses of LT-AlN buffers are as much as about 44%. This indicates that the LT-AlN buffer thickness has little effect on the incorporation of Al atoms.

AlGaN films were deposited at various V/Ⅲ ratios. Figure 4 (a) shows the rms roughness as a function of the V/Ⅲ ratio. The minimum rms roughness occurs at the smallest V/Ⅲ ratio and increases with the V/Ⅲ ratio. This indicates that a small V/Ⅲ ratio can improve the surface morphology (experiments with smaller NH_3 flow rates are not feasible at present). When the V/Ⅲ ratio is less than 783, the surface morphology cannot be improved because an excessive TMA density results in orientation fluctuation.[13] The FWHM of the XRC as a function of the V/Ⅲ ratio is shown in Fig. 4 (b). It is determined from the FWHM values for (0002) and (10$\bar{1}$2) that the optimum V/Ⅲ ratio is 783. The FWHM values are 770 arcsec and 1129 arcsec for (0002) and (10$\bar{1}$2) Al-GaN, respectively. The above-mentioned result shows that the effect of the V/Ⅲ ratio on the AlGaN epilayer growth is different from that on GaN epilayer growth. When growing a GaN epi-layer, a low V/Ⅲ ratio contributes to the enhanced three-dimensional growth mode, resulting in a rough surface morphology and larger island sizes. A GaN layer was grown at a high V/Ⅲ ratio to enhance the lateral growth, which can lead to wellaligned growth steps, a low dislocation density, and intense band edge emission.[14] The V/Ⅲ ratio has a significant influence on the Al atom incorporation. Figure 4(c) shows the Al content as a function of the V/Ⅲ ratio. It is found that under a higher V/Ⅲ ratio, the adduct reaction is aggravated, and the incorporation of Al atoms is reduced.

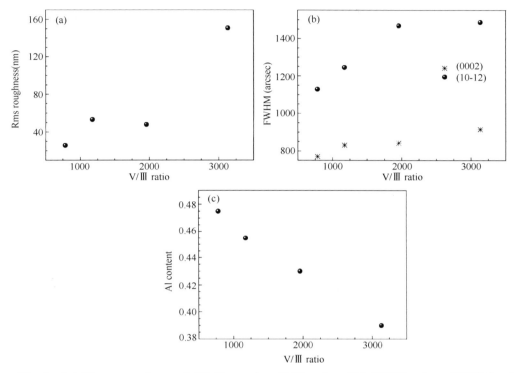

Fig. 4　(a) The rms roughness of AlGaN at various V/Ⅲ ratios, (b) FWHM values of XRC for (0002) and (10$\bar{1}$2)AlGaN at various V/Ⅲ ratios, and (c) Al content in solid phase at various V/Ⅲ ratios. The other parameters are unchanged (LT AlN buffer thickness: 20nm, pressure reactor: 100Torr, temperature: 1100℃)

The surface roughness and crystal quality of AlGaN epilayers at various reactor pressures are investigated. Figure 5(a) shows the rms roughness as a function of pressure in the reactor. In the range of 100-150 Torr, the rms roughness increases with the increasing pressure. The FWHM of the XRC as a function of reactor pressure is shown in Fig. 5(b). The FWHM of the XRC for (0002) and (10$\bar{1}$2) increases with the increasing pressure in the reactor. The FWHMs for (0002) and (10$\bar{1}$2) at 100 Torr are 770 arcsec and 1129 arcsec, respectively. It is believed that the rough surfaces of the AlGaN films at high pressure in the reactor are due to the decrease of gas flow velocity. With the increase of pressure in the reactor, the gas flow velocity decreases and the growth rate decreases. The diffusion length is reduced, thus the lateral velocity is reduced. In addition, the adduct reaction is aggravated when the pressure in the reactor is increased,[15] as shown in Fig. 5(c).

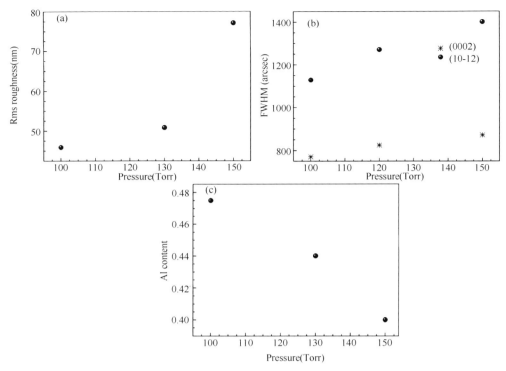

Fig. 5　(a) The rms roughness of AlGaN, (b) FWHM values of XRC for (0002) and (10$\bar{1}$2) AlGaN, and (c) Alcontent in solid phase, versus pressures in the reactor. The other parameters are unchanged (LT AlN buffer thickness:20nm, V/Ⅲ ratio: 783, temperature: 1100℃)

A parasitic reaction is a chemical reaction occurring in the gas state, and impedes the incorporation of Al adatoms. It consumes a large amount of source gas, and deposits white powder-like AlN particles that can fall onto the reaction surface and then act as new unwanted nucleation centres that terminate the epitaxial growth, resulting in surface roughening and defect generation increasing. This is the reason why the crystal quality and surface morphology of a sample can be deteriorated under a severe adduct reaction between TMA and NH_3.

A description of the process related to the parasitic reaction of TMA and NH_3 in the vapour phase can be found in the literature.[16]

It is reasonable to assume that the chance for TMA and NH_3 to come into contact increases at higher reactor pressures, so that the collision frequency increases, and the formation of particles (such as trimers and higher n-mers) is enhanced by the increasing reactor pressure. However, particles that are either deposited on the reactor wall or swept out of the reactor do not contribute to the growth. Since the quantity of particles also influences the growth rate of AlN, this actually results in a decrease in Al incorporation with an increase of reactor pressure. It has been reported that NH_3 can easily reduce the potential energy barrier of particle formation. Therefore, with the increase of the flux of NH_3, the quantities of particles that do not contribute to the growth will increase, thereby affecting the Al incorporation.

In summary, we have deposited a high-Al-content AlGaN epilayer on a (0001) sapphire substrate by metalorganic chemical vapour deposition. The dependences of surface roughness, surface morphology, tilted mosaicity, and twisted mosaicity on parameters of the AlGaN epilayer deposition are evaluated. We find that under a low V/Ⅲ ratio and at low pressure in the reactor, the crystal quality and surface morphology of the AlGaN epilayer deposited on 20nm LT-AlN is optimum. In addition, a higher V/Ⅲ ratio and higher pressure in the reactor aggravate the adduct reaction between TMA and NH$_3$.

References

[1] Zhang J P et al. *Appl. Phys. Lett.* **81** 4910.

[2] Yasan A et al. 2002 *Appl. Phys. Lett.* **81** 801.

[3] Adivarahan V et al. 2002 *Appl. Phys. Left.* **81** 3666.

[4] Zhou S Q, Wu M F and Yao S D 2005 *Chin. Phys. Left.* **22** 3189.

[5] Yoshida S, Misawa S and Gonda S 1982 *J. Appl. Phys.* **53** 6844.

[6] Koide Y et al. 1987 *J. Appl. Phys.* **61** 4540.

[7] Ito K, Hiramatsu K, Amano H and Akasaki I 1990 *J. Crystal Growth* **104** 533.

[8] Amano H et al. 1999 *Phys. Status Solidi B* **216** 683.

[9] Zhou Y G et al. 2000 *Mater. Lett.* **45** 331.

[10] Wang B Z et al. 2006 *Chin. Phys. Lett.* **23** 2187.

[11] Kondratyev A V et al. 2004 *J. Crystal Growth* **272** 420.

[12] Zhao D G et al. 2004 *Appl. Phys. Left.* **85** 1499.

[13] Ohba Y and Sato R 2000 *J. Crystal Growth* **221** 258.

[14] Kim S et al. 2004 *J. Crystal Growth* **262** 7.

[15] Zhao D G et al. 2006 *J. Crystal Growth* **289 72**.

[16] Coltrin M E, Creighton J R and Mitchell C C 2006 *J. Crystal Growth* **287** 566.

Temperature Distribution in Ridge Structure InGaN Laser Diodes and Its Influence on Device Characteristics [*]

Li Deyao[1,†], Huang Yongzhen[1], Zhang Shuming[1], Chong Ming[2], Ye Xiaojun[2],

Zhu Jianjun[1], Zhao Degang[1], Chen Lianghui[2], Yang Hui[1], and Liang Junwu[1]

(1 *State Key Laboratory of Integrated Optoelectronics, Institute of Semiconductors, Chinese Academy of Sciences,*

Beijing 100083, *China*)

(2 *Nano Optoelectronics Laboratory, Institute of Semiconductors, Chinese Academy of Sciences, Beijing* 100083, *China*)

Abstract: Time-dependent thermal simulation of ridge-geometry InGaN laser diodes is carried out with a two-dimensional model. A high temperature in the waveguide layer and a large temperature step between the regions under and outside the ridge are generated due to the poor thermal conductivity of the sapphire substrate and the large threshold current and voltage. The temperature step is thought to have a strong influence on the characteristics of the laser diodes. Time-resolved measurements of light-current curves, spectra, and the far-field pattern of the InGaN laser diodes under pulsed operation are performed. The results show that the thermal lensing effect improves the confinement of the higher order modes and leads to a lower threshold current and a higher slope efficiency of the device while the high temperature in the active layer results in a drastic decrease in the slope efficiency.

Key words: InGaN laser diodes; ridge waveguide; thermal simulation; threshold current; slope efficiency

PACC: 7850G; 7860F

CLC number: TN365   **Document code:** A   **Article ID:** 0253-4177(2006)03-0499-07

1 Introduction

GaN-based violet laser diodes(LDs) are ideal light sources for a wide range of applications such as high density optical storage, laser printing, and spectroscopy. Although several groups have realized room temperature (RT) contlnuous wave(CW) lasing of InGaN multiple quantum well(MQW) LDs[1~3], many fundamental properties require further study and evaluation. A ridge waveguide is frequently used in the GaN-based laser diodes because of it sapparent advantages in selecting the lateral modes, controlling the far-field aspect ratio, and decreasing the lateral current spreading and the threshold current[4,5]. However, an unstable near-field distribution and changes in lateral mode often occur due to the built-in waveguide's weak characteristic in the lateral direction, the poor thermal conductivity of the sapphire substrate, and the large threshold current caused by a high dislocation density and large polarization field in the active layer[6,7]. For the practical application of the LDs, device reliability and stability are indispensable. Improvement in

原载于:半导体学报,2006,27(3):499-505.

* Project supported by the National High Technology Research and Development Program of China(No.2001AA313100)

† Corresponding author. Email: dyli@red.semi.ac.cn

Received 12 September 2005, revised manuscript received 23 November 2005 c2006 Chinese Institute of Electronics

temperature characteristics of InGaN LDs is important for realizing stable device operation at high temperatures. Much study has been conducted on the thermal behavior of LDs under continuous wave operation[8,9], but little on LDs under pulsed operation, which is relevant to the direct modulation. In the work de scribed in this paper, we carried out timedependant numerical analysis of the temperature distribution in the ridge structure of InGaN MQW LDs, and demonstrated that temperature distribution has a strong influence on the characteristics of the LDs. The experimental results coincide well with the theoretical conclusion.

2　Device structure and thermal conductivity model

The laser wafer with a(0001)sapp hire substrate was grown in a closed-space showerhead metalorganic chemical vapor deposition(MOCVD)reactor. The LDs consisted of a 2μm GaN:Si, a 0.9μm cladding layer of $Al_{0.2}Ga_{0.8}N$/GaN:Si superlattices(SLs), a 0.1μm waveguide layer of GaN:Si, an $In_{0.15}Ga_{0.85}N$/GaN MOW structure consisting of five pairs of 3nm undoped $In_{0.15}Ga_{0.85}N$ well layers separated by 5nm undoped GaN barrier layers, a 20nm $Al_{0.2}Ga_{0.8}N$:Mg electron blocking layer. a 0.1μm upper waveguide layer of GaN:Mg, a 0.6μm upper cladding layer of $Al_{0.2}Ga_{0.8}N$/GaN:Mg SLs, and a 0.2μm GaN:Mg layer Aridge structure was formed with reactiveion etching(RIE). The area of the ridge geometry LD was 8μm×800μm. The facets of the laser cavity were formed by cleaving along the($11\bar{2}0$)cleavage plane of the GaN epitaxial layer. A Ni/Au contact was evaporated onto the p-type GaN layer, and a Ti/Al contact was evaporated

onto the n-type GaN layer. The laser structure used in simulation is shown in Fig.1. It is simplified in the active layer with a single InGaN layer instead of the InGaN/GaN MQW, and in the cladding layers with an AlGaN layer instead of $Al_{0.2}Ga_{0.8}N$/GaN SLs. The In concentration in the InGaN layer and Al concentration in the AlGaN layer are obtained according to Vegard's law under the completely elastic approximation. The thick gold and SiO_2 layers on the p-side are taken into account due to their non-negligible heat absorption in the LDs under pulsed operation.

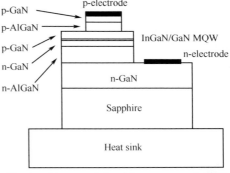

Fig. 1　Diagram of the ridge geometry InGaN MQW LD

The equation governing the temperature distribution throughout the LD chip is

$$C_p\rho\frac{\partial T}{\partial t}=k\Delta^2T+Q_{vol} \tag{1}$$

where C_p is the specific heat, ρ is the density, k is the thermal conductivity, T is the temperature, t is the time, and Q_{vol} is the volumetric rate of internal heat generation. The heat is generated mainly in three layers: a p-type contact layer, a p-type cladding layer, and an active layer. The heat power generated in each layer is determined by the current and voltage, which are obtained from the measured I-V curve and the specific contact resistance to p-GaN. The series resistance at a large current and the contact resistance for the measured LD are 22 and

7.7Ω, respectively.Thus the heat power generated in the P-AlGaN and P-GaN contact layers is 14.3I^2 and 7.7I^2, respectively.The heat power generated in the active layer is 2.1I on the assumption of a 3eV band gap and a 30% external quantum efficiency when the LD lases.

A two-dimensional model is applied in the simulation. Simulation data is obtained from the literature, which is shown in Table 1[10].InGaN and AlGaN data are found by linear interpolation.

Table 1 Parameters of different materials used in simulation

Material	GaN	AlN	InN	Sapphire
Specific heat capacity/($J \cdot kg^{-1} \cdot K^{-1}$)	490	600	320	765
Thermal conductivity/($W \cdot m^{-1} \cdot K^{-1}$)	130	285	45	41.9

For boundary conditions, we assume constant temperature at the bottom of the heatsink (293K) and adiabatic conditions at the other surfaces.The initial temperature at each layer is also assumed to be 293 K.The simulation is carried out in FEMLAB software.

3 Simulation results and discussion

The temperature distribution in the lateral direction of the active layer at 100ns under a current pulse is shown in Fig.2. There is a temprature pulse is shown in Fig.2. There is a temperature gradient in the lateral direction, especially at the edge of ridge. The temperature step between the center point and a point 5μm away from center in the lateral direction is about 10K. The temperature variation with time at the center point of the ridge and a point near the edge is shown in Fig. 3. The temperature at each position increases rapidly within several hundred nanoseconds at first and then increases linearly with time.The temperature step between the center point and a point near the edge under the ridge is shown in Fig.4. It is obvious that the temperature step increases rapidly with time at the outset of the pulse and then remains basically constant though the temperature at each position increases continuously with time.

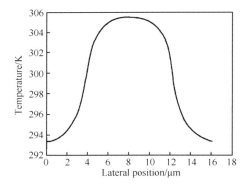

Fig. 2 Temperature distribution in the lateral directionunder ridge at 100ns with a 400mA injection current under 20V The two edge coordinates are 4 and 12μm, respectively

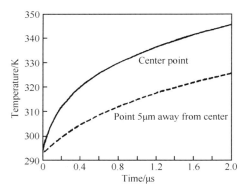

Fig.3 Temperature at different times during a 2μs current pulse with a 400mA injection current under 20V

The distinguishing characteristic of the temperature distribution in the ridge structure LDs under pulsed operation is the occurrence of large temperature steps between regions under and outside the ridge. The temperature step may change the confinement of the guiding mode because the refractive index changes with the temperature. A temperature increase underneath the ridge leads to an increase of refractive index The dn/dT for GaN is about 1.3×10^{-4} K^{-1} [11,12]. When the temperature step exceeds 10K, the refractive index step Δn is about 1.3×10^{-3}, the same order as the effective index step(about 3.7×10^{-3}).

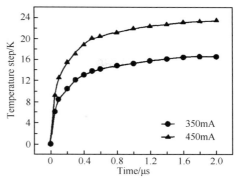

Fig.4 Temperature step between the center and edge of the ridge in the active layer

A simple model can be used to compare the strength of the thermal lens with other wave guiding effects in the ridge waveguide LD. Besides the thermal lens, the lateral change of the effective refractive index due to the ridge structure and the carrier induced index change caused by the current confinement determine the waveguide properties. A simple equation describing the refractive index step between regions under and outside the ridge can be expressed as [13]

$$\Delta n = \Delta n_{\text{eff}} + \frac{\partial n}{\partial T}\Delta T + \frac{\partial n}{\partial T}\Delta N \qquad (2)$$

where Δn_{eff} is the effective refractive index step, ΔN is the difference in carrier concentration, and ΔT is the temperature step between regions under and outside ridge. Δn_{eff} is 3.70×10^{-3} is obtained by waveguide calculation, and the third term on the right-hand side is about 1.0×10^{-3} at a current of 400mA [14]. If there is no thermal lens, the confinement factors of the ridge waveguide with a width of 8μm for the fundamental, first order, and second order TE modes are 0.995, 0.980, and 0.951, respectively. When the temperature step reaches 8K, the anti-guiding effect is exactly compensated by the thermal lensing effect, and the three confinement factors are 0.996, 0.987, and 0.969. respectively. When the temperature step reaches 16K, the three confinement factors are 0.997, 0.991, and 0.978, respectively. Therefore, the anti-guiding and thermal lensing effects have only a slight influence on the fundamental mode confinement, but can clearly improve the confinement of the higher order modes and give rise to a decrease in the threshold current of these modes.

4 Experiment and results

The time-resolved light-current(L-I) curves of the LDs are measured at room temperature with a Tektronix type 109 pulse generator which can provide a current of nearly uniform intensity within a pulse. The pulse width and repetition are 110ns and 300Hz, respectively. After each pulse, the LD has enough time to cool down again due to the very low duty cycle. The output light of the LD is detected by a fast photomultiplier tube with a neutral density filter before the window. Consequently, for a particular current, the light intensity distribution versus time can be observed on an oscilloscope connected to the photomultiplier tube. Scanning the current over a particular range yields a three-dimensional graph with current and time on the x and y axes, respectively, and light intensity on the z axis. From the three-dimensional graph the L-I curves at different times during a pulse can be obtained. The measurement of the time-resolved farfield distribution and spectra can be performed in a similar way.

Figure 5 shows the light output power(LOP)waveforms of the measured LD at different injection currents. It is evident that the LOP is not uniform within a current pulse and that the LOP waveform depends on the current magnitude. When the current is relatively small (about 360mA), the LOP merely increases slowly with time. When the current is 370mA, the LOP increases slowly with time at first and then increases rapidly by a factor of 2 over about 20ns. When the current is larger than 390mA, the LD lases several nanoseconds after the current is turned on, and the LOP increases slowly with time at first and then experiences rapid increase by a factor of 3 over about 10ns. After this rapid increase, the LOP remains steady for a while and then decreases gradually until the end of the pulse.

There are several possible physical mechanisms that may account for this behavior of the LD. First of all, lasing delay can be easily ruled out. From Fig. 5, when the current is larger than 410mA, the LD lases immediately but still experiences a rapid increase in the LOP. Therefore, the rapid increase in the LOP is not caused by lasing delay. Lasing delay can also be ruled out by the uniform LOP in a pulse at currents above the threshold of the LDs, which are fabricated on the same wafer but with a greater etching depth for ridge formation. We think the main reason may be a heating effect. Because of the poor thermal conductivity of the sapphire substrate and the high threshold current and voltage, the temperature of the active layer beneath the ridge increases drastically after the current pulse is turned on. As discussed above, the increasing temperature results in the thermal lensing effect and influences the LD characteristics. The time-resolved spectra and farfield patterns presented later also exclude lasing delay as a possible explanation. Lasing delay only influences the behavior in the initial few nanoseconds of the current pulse, as can be observed in Fig. 5.

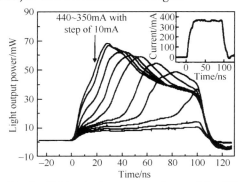

Fig. 5 Light output power waveforms of the LD at different currents. The inset shows a current waveform

The thermal lensing effect can be observed directly from the time-dependent far-field distribution of the LD measured at 380mA, as shown in Fig. 6. At the outset, the confinement to higher order modes is weaker than that for the fundamental mode, so only the fundamental mode lases. However, the temperature step increases, and the confinement of the higher order modes becomes stronger toward the end of the pulse. Therefore, the higher order modes begin to lase. The asymmetric far-field distribution may result from the asymmetric current distribution under the ridge due to the n-electrode fabricated on the same side of the epitaxial layer with the p-electrode.

Figure 7 shows the spectra of the LD at different times in a pulse, where the current is also fixed at 380mA. At 16ns, the full width at half maximum(FWHM) of the spectrum is 0.4nm, and the FWHM of spectrum at other times is 0.3nm. The FWHM of the spectrum of the LD at a current of 250mA is 9.2nm. Therefore, the LD already lases at a current of 380mA before the LOP increases rapidly at about 60ns. Thus the threshold characteristic of the LD under pulsed condition is complicated and requires careful investigation.

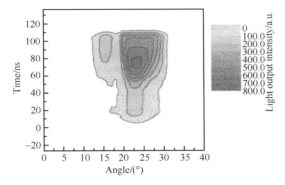

Fig. 6 Far-field pattern versus time in a current pulse of 380mA The angular resolution is 1°

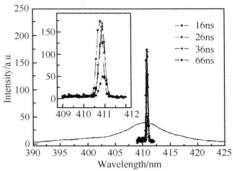

Fig. 7 Spectra of the LD at different times in a pulse at a current of 380mA and the spectrum(the solid line, multiplied by 10) at a current of 250mA The inset shows the spectra at a current of 380mA only

Figure 8 shows the *L-I* curves of the LD at several different times within a pulse. Two threshold currents can be obtained from each *L-I* curve. The first one is about 360mA without evident change to each curve. It is suggested that this threshold current may be related to the fundamental mode because of the slight influence of the thermal lensing effect on this mode. The second threshold current is different for every curve, the later the time is, the lower threshold current the LD has. The second threshold current may be related to higher order modes, especially the first order mode. The difference in the second threshold current at different times in a pulse is attributed to thermal lensing effect. At the out set of a current pulse, there is not thermal lensing effect. The injected carriers lead to the anti-guide effect, and therefore a weaker mode confinement, but the temperature step increases gradually with time, leading to a stronger mode confinement. Accordingly, the mode is confined more tightly, and the absorption and scattering losses at the edge of the ridge decrease with time. The larger confinement factor and the smaller loss coefficient result in a lower threshold current at the end of the pulse.

From Fig. 8, when only the fundamental mode lases, the slope efficiency is much lower

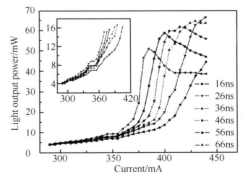

Fig. 8 *L-I* curves of the LD at different times during the current pulse The inset is a magnification of part of the figure

than that when the higher order modes also lase. This is mainly attributed to the poor match of the fundamental mode with the carrier distribution in the lateral direction in the active layer. The light intensity distribution of the fundamental mode in the guiding layer is given by $I = I_0 \cos^2(kx)$, where I_0 is the light intensity at the center of the ridge, x is the distance from the center, and k is the propagation constant of this mode. When the lateral confinement factor of the fundamental mode is almost equal to 1, the light intensity of this mode is close to 0 at the edge. Therefore the carrier injected in the areas near the two edges is far from sufficient to stimulate emission and results in a low slope efficiency, while the a symmetric carrier distribution in the lateral direction under the ridge may aggravate the situation. When a higher order mode lases, its light intensity distribution in the lateral direction under the ridge can compensate the fundamental mode and obtain a much higher slope efficiency. The decreasing internal loss caused by the mode tightening as the thermal lens becomes stronger towards the end of the pulse may also give rise to the increase of the slope efficiency. The elevated temperature in the active layer results in a decrease of internal quantum efficiency. which causes the LOP to decrease gradually and the slope efficiency to decrease drastically when the current is relatively large.

5　Conclusion

Time-dependent thermal simulation for ridge geometry InGaN MQW LDs was carried out with a two-dimensional model. A high temperature in the waveguide layer and large temperature step between regions under and outside ridge are generated due to the poor thermal conductivity of the sapphire substrate and the large threshold current and voltage. The temperature step increases rapidly with time during the initial several hundred nanoseconds and then remains constant. The temperature step is thought to have a strong influence on the dynamic characteristics of the LDs. Time-resolved measurements of L-I curves, far-field pattern, and spectra of the InGaN LDs under pulsed operation were performed. Results show that the temperature step leads to better confinement of high order modes and a lower threshold current and a higher slope efficiency of the device while a high temperature in the active layer results in a drastic decrease in slope efficiency.

References

[1] Nakamura S, Senoh M, Nagahama S, et al. InGaN/GaN/AlGaN-based laser diodes with modulation-doped strained-layer superlattices grown on an epitaxially laterally overgrown GaN substrate. Appl Phys Lett, 1998, 72(2): 211.

[2] Kneissl M, Bour D P, Van de Walle C G, et al. Room-temperature continuous-wave operation of InGaN multiple-quantunr well laser diodes with an asymmetric waveguide structure. Appl Phys Lett, 1999, 75(4): 581.

[3] Goto S, Ohta M, Yabuki Y, et al. Super high-power AlGaInN-based laser diodes with a single broad-area stripe emitter fabricated on a GaN substrate. Phys Status Solidi A, 2003, 200(1): 122.

[4] Kahen K B, Shantharama L G, Shepherd J P, et al. Single depressed-index cladding ridge waveguide laser with a low aspect ratio. Appl Phys Lett, 1993, 62(12): 1317.

[5] Achtenhagen M, Hardy A. Lateral current spreading in ridge waveguide laser diodes. Appl Phys Lett, 1999, 74(10): 1364.

[6] Schwarz U T, Pindl M, Wegscheider W, et al. Near-field and far-field dynamics of (Al, In) GaN laser diodes. Appl Phys Lett, 2005, 86(16): 161112-161111.

[7] Eichler C, Hofstetter D, Chow W W, et al. Microsecond time scale lateral-mode dynamics in a narrow stripe InGaN laser.

Appl Phys Lett,2004,84(14):2473.

[8] Hatakoshi G,Onomuka M,Yamamoto M,et al.Thermal analysis for GaN laser diodes.Jpn J Appl Phys,1999, 38(5A):2764.

[9] Ye Xiaojun,Chong Ming,Chen Lianghui.Thermal simulation of ridge-GaN laser diode.Chinese Journal of Semiconductors, 2004,25(12):1680(in Chinese)[叶晓军,种明,陈良惠.脊形结构蓝光激光器的热模拟分析.半导体学报,2004,25 (12):1680].

[10] Morkoq H.Nitride semiconductors and devices.Berlin:Springer,1999.

[11] Tisch U,Meyler B,Katz O,et al.Dependence of the refractive index of $Al_xGa_{1-x}N$ on temperature and composition at elevated temperatures.J Appl Phys,2001,89(5):2676.

[12] Gan K G,Bowers J E.Measurement of gain,group index,group velocity dispersion,and linewidth enhancement factor of an InGaN multiple quantunr well laser diode.IEEE Photonics Technol Lett,2004,16(5):1256.

[13] Brunner M,Gulden K,Hovel R,et al.Thermal lensing effects in small oxide confined vertical-cavity surface-emitting lasers.Appl Phys Lett,2000,76(1):7.

[14] Schwarz U T,Sturm E,Wegscheider W,et al.Optical gain,carrier-induced phase shift,and linewidth enhancement factor in InGaN quantum well lasers.Appl Phys Lett,2003,83(20):4096.

脊形 InGaN 激光器的温度分布及其对器件特性的影响[*]

李德尧[1,†]　黄永箴[1]　张书明[1]　种　明[2]　叶晓军[2]　朱建军[1]
赵德刚[1]　陈良惠[2]　杨　辉[1]　梁骏吾[1]

(1 中国科学院半导体研究所集成光电子学国家重点联合实验室,北京 100083)
(2 中国科学院半导体研究所纳米光电子学实验室,北京 100083)

摘要:利用含时二维热传导模型分析了蓝宝石衬底上生长、制作的脊形 InGaN 激光器内波导层的温度分布和时间演化规律.由于较大的阈值电流和电压以及较差的衬底导热性能,脊形下波导层内会产生较高温升并在脊形内外形成较大的温度台阶.由于脊形波导的弱自建波导特性,这一温度台阶会对侧向模式的限制产生较大的影响.短脉冲工作下的时间分辨 L-I 测试以及时间分辨远场和光谱测试结果显示,脊形内外的温度台阶会改善波导对高阶模的限制,导致器件的阈值电流下降,斜率效率升高.而有源区的温升又会导致斜率效率的严重下降.

关键词: InGaN 激光器;脊形波导;热模拟;阈值电流;斜率效率

PACC:7850G;7860F

中图分类号:TN365　**文献标识码:**A　**文章编号:**0253-4177(2006)03-0499-07

* 国家高技术研究发展计划资助项目(批注号:2001AA313100)

† 通讯作者.Email:dyli@ red.semi.ac.cn

2005-09-12 收到,2005-11-23 定稿

Abatement of Waste Gases and Water During the Processes of Semiconductor Fabrication

WEN Rui-mei[1], LIANG Jun-wu[2]*

(1. *Tongji University , Shanghai* 200092, *China.* 2. *Institute of Semiconductors , Chinese Academy of Sciences , Beijing* 100083, *China. Email:jwliang@ red. semi. ac. cn*)

Abstract: The purpose of this article is to examine the methods and equipment for abating waste gases and water produced during the manufacture of semiconductor materials and devices. Three separating methods and equipment are used to control three different groups of electronic wastes. The first group includes arsine and phosphine emitted during the processes of semiconductor materials manufacture. The abatement procedure for this group of pollutants consists of adding iodates, cupric and manganese salts to a multiple shower tower (MST) structure. The second group includes pollutants containing arsenic, phosphorus, HF, HCl, NO_2, and SO_3 emitted during the manufacture of semiconductor materials and devices. The abatement procedure involves mixing oxidants and bases in an oval column with a separator in the middle. The third group consists of the ions of As, P and heavy metals contained in the waste water. The abatement procedure includes adding $CaCO_3$ and ferric salts in a flocculation-sedimentation compact device equipment. Test results showed that all waste gases and water after the abatement procedures presented in this article passed the discharge standards set by the State Environmental Protection Administration of China.

Keywords: waste gases ; waste water; abatement; pollutant; semiconductor

Introduction

The rapid development of the electronic industry has brought about new pollution. Numerous laboratories and factories emit increasing amount of untreated wastes to the environment. Typical air-borne pollutants include such as arsine, phosphine, hydrogen chloride, sulfur dioxide, sulfur trioxide, nitric oxide, nitrogen oxide, fluohydric acid, sulfuric acid, nitric acid and other pollutants containing arsenic or phosphorus and so on. Water-borne pollutants include poisonous substances containing arsine, phosphorus and their compounds, ammonia nitrogen, detergents, Cu, Cr, or Cd containing pollutants. These toxic emissions present serious threats to the atmosphere and water resources.

Metallorganic vapor phase epitaxy (MOVPE) is the most important epitaxy production technique. It has been commonly utilized to grow materials for the device fabrication, such as laser diodes, light emitting diodes, heterojunction bipolar transistors (HBT) and heterojunction field effect transistors (HFETs). MOVPE is attractive because it can produce high

---

原载于:Journal of Environmental Sciences-China 2002,14:482-488.

* Corresponding author

quality superlattices and quantum wells, and the technique can be relatively easily put into production. However, poisonous gases, particles, and waste solutions are discharged during the MOVPE process.

1 Abatement of arsine and phosphine during the manufacture of semiconductor materials

1.1 Equipment and procedure

A multiple shower tower(MST) was connected to the exhaust pipe of MOVPE to transform various species of arsenic into AsO_4^{3-}, and phosphorous into PO_4^{3-} through chemical reactions in three stages. The flowchart and MST structure for arsenic and phosphorus abatement are shown in Fig. 1 (a) and (b), respectively.

Tail gas containing AsH_3, PH_3 and their compounds are let into the oil separator (1) to remove oil and increase abatement efficiency. If pressure in 1 exceeds allowable limit for any reason, the gas would go firstly into the pressure protection tank (2), then into the activated carbon absorbing device (3), and trigger the high pressure alarm (4). Under normal pressure, the tail gas will be pumped into the KIO_3, KI and H_2SO_4 solution in the 1st stage treatment tank (5), where the majority of AsH_3 and PH_3 is absorbed. The tail gas, with much of its AsH_3 and PH_3 stripped, moving upward into the 1st stage reverse spray column 5, is showered by the solution drawn from the same tank (5).

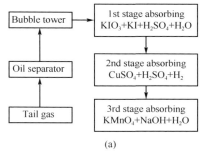

This technology has been used in practice for the treatment of tail gases during MOVPE, MBE, CBE and other processing of GaAs and InP.

(a)

1.2 Results and discussion

1.2.1 Abatement solutions choice

A thermodynamic study (Yang, 1992; Barin, 1991; Dean, 1985) has demonstrated that the main forms for arsenic in MOVPE tail gases are As_4, AsH_3, As_2 and As, and for phosphorus are P_4, PH_3, P_2 and P. According to this study, the most effective chemicals and concentrations were determined to abate As and P in tail gases through a series of tests and simulations. For this purpose gas samples prepared by adding AsH_3 (99.99%) and PH_3(99.99%) into high purity hydrogen, were analyzed by high temperature hydrogen reduction gas chromatography to determine As and P concentrations before and after spray-absorption. The experimental for high temperature hydrogen reduction gas chromatography conditions were as follows: (1) Reduction

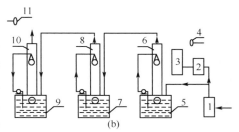

Fig. 1 Multiple shower tower for arsenic and phosphorus abatement: (a) flow chart;

(b) sche matic diagram of equipment

1. oil separator; 2. pressure protection tank; 3. activated carbon absorbing device; 4. high pressure alarm; 5. 1st stage treatment tank; 6. 1st stage counter-current-spray column; 7. 2nd stage treatment tank; 8. 2nd stage counter-current-spray column; 9. 3rd stage treatment tank; 10. 3rd stage counter-current-spray column; 11. monitor/alarm device

system: reducing H_2 flow = 158ml/min, carrying H_2 flow = 4. 0ml/min mixing chamber temperature = 760℃. (2) Gas chromatography system: carrying air flow = 57ml/min, flame H_2 flow = 238ml/min, air flow 1 = 92ml/min, air flow 2 = 182ml/min, detector temperature = 100℃. The results are shown in Table 1.

Table 1 shows that the most effective treatment outcome occurred when iodate, copperate, and manganate were used in various acid and alkaline medium. Major chemical reaction equations for As and P are as follows:

$$5AsH_3 + 8IO_3^- = 5AsO_4^{3-} + 4I_2 + 4H_2O + 7H^+,$$
$$AsH_3 + 8Cu^{2+} + 4H_2O = AsO_4^{3-} + 8Cu^+ + 11H^+,$$
$$5PH_3 + 8IO_3^- = 5PO_4^{3-} + 4I_2 + 4H_2O + 7H^+,$$
$$PH_3 + 8CuSO_4 + 4H_2O = H_3PO_4 + 4H_2SO_4 + 4Cu_2SO_4,$$
$$3AsH_3 + 8MnO_4^- + OH^- = 3AsO_4^{3-} + 8MnO_2 + 5H_2O,$$
$$3PH_3 + 8MnO_4^- + OH^- = 3PO_4^{3-} + 8MnO_2 + 5H_2O.$$

Table 1　Comparison of different solutions for As and P abatement[*]

No.	Solution	As and P concentration, mg/m³				Abatement effectiveness, %	
		Before treatment		After treatment			
		As	P	As	P	As	P
1	Sat. KIO₃ + Sat. KI	0.61	0.052	0.04	0.003	93.4	94.2
2	4% KIO₃ + 0.4% . KI + 1% H₂SO₄	0.91	0.135	0.05	0.005	94.5	96.2
3	5% HIO₃	0.11	0.04	0.01	0.003	90.9	92.5
4	0.5% CuSO₄ + 1% H₂SO₄	0.93	0.08	0.06	0.004	93.5	95.0
5	2 and 4 in series	0.94	0.19	0.04	0.006	95.7	96.8
6	1% KMnO₄ + 1% NaOH	0.69	0.06	0.05	0.004	92.8	93.3

* As and P concentrations were determined by gas chromatography and colorimetry both methods agree well with each other; the experimental conditions for high temperature hydrogen reduction gas chromatography were as follows: (a) reduction system: reducing H_2 flow = 158ml/min, carrying H_2 flow = 4.0 ml/min mixing chamber temperature = 760℃ ; (b) gas chromatography system: carrying air flow = 57ml/min, flame H_2 flow = 238ml/min, air flow 1 = 92ml/min, air flow 2 = 182ml/min, detector temperature = 100℃

As and P concentrations were determined by gas chromatography and colorimetry both methods agree well with each other.

Judging from the effectiveness and cost, we use 4% KIO_3 + 0.4% KI + 1% H_2SO + H_2O, 0.5% $CuSO_4$ + 1% H_2SO_4, and 1% $KMnO_4$ + 1% NaOH + H_2O as the first, the second and the third stage absorbing solution, respectively.

1.2.2　Abatement methods

Various abatement methods for tail gases containing arsenic and phosphorus during MOVPE process were evaluated. The arsenic and phosphorus concentration were determined by high-temperature hydrogen reduction gas chromatograph (Wen, 1997). Table 2 shows the arsenic and phosphorus concentration in tail gases treated by single bubbling, single absorption and bubbling plus spray absorptions. The arsenic and phosphorus abatement effects before and after treatment are listed in Table 3 and 4, respectively.

The results showed that after abatement P and As concentration in tail gas are well below the National Discharge Standard and the abatement efficiency is high. The high efficiency of abatements is due to the multiple shower tower structure and the use of iodate, copperate and manganate in various acid and alkaline medium. Conventional abatement technology for tail gases involves chemical solution to absorb AsH_3 and PH_3(Brookman, 1988). A typical method is simply to pass the gas through the solution. Another method is to pump to the gas upward through a column and spray it into the solution. In our MST, a technology combining the two methods is used to effectively remove AsH_3, PH_3, and other pollutants. Moreover, the oil separator located in fiont of the bubble tower separates gas from oil resulting in more effective abatement during the next step.

Table 2 Comparison of various tail gas absorption methods *

	Untreated	After single bubbling	After single spray absorption	After bubbling plus spray absorptions
As conc. in tail gas, mg/m³	0.91	0.15	0.12	0.05
As abatement effectiveness, %		83.6	86.8	94.5
P conc. in tail gas, mg/m³	0.135	0.05	0.03	0.005
P abatement effectiveness, %		63.0	77.8	96.3

* Determined by gas chromatography as in Table 1

Table 3 Arsenic abatement effectiveness determined by colorimetry and gas chromatography

Sample No.	Before treatment, mg/m³		After treatment, mg/m³		Abatement effectiveness, %	
	A *	B * *	A *	B * *	A *	B * *
1	0.61	0.69	0. 041	0. 040	93.2	94.2
2	0.49	0.51	0. 030	0. 040	93.9	92.2
3	0.91	0.93	0. 046	0. 042	94.9	97.5
4	0.26	0.31	0.033	0.038	87.3	87.7
5	0.32	0.33	0.04	0. 048	87.5	88.1

A * . colorimetry, B * * . gas chromatography

The MST is able to treat tail gas containing AsH_3 and PH_3 of concentration below $1mg/m^3$.

Table 4 Phosphorus abatement effectiveness

Sample No.	1	2	3	4	5
Before treatment, mg/m³	0. 052	0. 091	0.048	0. 047	0. 130
After treatment, mg/m³	<0. 003	0.004	<0.003	0.004	0.004
Abatement effectiveness, %	>94.2	95.6	>93.8	91.5	96.9

2 Abatement of waste gases containing As, P, HF, HCl, NO_2 and SO_3during semiconductor processes

2. 1 Equipment

Waste gases containing As, P, HF, HCl, NO_2 and SO_3 are treated by basic solution containing $KMnO_4$ or H_2O_2. After that, arsenic, phosphorus and other acid radical ions are abated through the oxidoreduction.

An oval spray-absorption tower with a mid-separator was used for above mentioned purpose. This makes a concurrent flow on one side and a counter-current flow on another side for gas and solution. Because of this, the contact area and the time between gas and solution could be aggrandized and prolonged.

The construction of the equipment is shown in Fig.2.

According to the results concerning the selection of absorbers and considering the variety of effluents from laboratories and factors concerning cost and performance, three kinds of absorbers for treating As, P and other kinds of acid gases have been chosen. They are 0.2%—0.5% $KMnO_4$ +0.5 %—1% NaOH, 0.5 %—1% NaOH and 0.2%—0.5% H_2O_2 + 0.5%—1% NaOH. After treatment the quality of the discharged gases have meet National Discharge Standards.

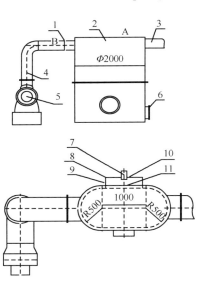

Fig.2　Equipment of oval spray-absorption
plate tower

1. rectangular flange; 2. spray-absorber; 3. vent;
4. inlet; 5. ventilator; 6. water level indicator;
7. pump for chemicals; 8. 90° connector; 9. connector;
10. valve; 11. pipe for chemicals

2. 2　Results and discussion

After treatment the pollutant concentrations were analyzed. The arsenic and phosphorus were determined by gas chromatography and the other anions by ion chromatography (Wen, 1998).

The experimental conditions for ion chromatography are as follows: separation column, IonPac-AS4A; sensitivity of conductometer, $1\mu s$; volume of sample, 100-$480\mu l$; eluent solution flow rate, 3ml/min; regenerating solution flow rate, 2.8ml/min.

The experimental conditions for As and P determination by gas chromatography were the same as in paragraph 1. 2. The analyzed results are shown in Table 5.

The representative chemical reactions are as follows:

$$3As+5MnO_4^-+4OH^-=3AsO_4^{3-}+5MnO_2+2H_2O,$$
$$3P+5MnO_4^-+4OH^-=3P_4^{3+}+5MnO_2+2H_2O,$$
$$2As+5H_2O_2+6OH^-=2AsO_4^{3-}+8H_2O,$$
$$2P+5H_2O_2+6OH^-=2PO_4^{3-}+8H_2O.$$

HF, HCl, H_2SO_4, HNO_3 and H_3PO_4 are neutralized with alkali in spraying liquid to form NaF, NaCl, Na_2SO_4, $NaNO_3$ and Na_3PO_4, respectively.

Table 5 shows that the pollutant concentrations after treatment meet the National Discharge Standards GB16297—96. The oval spray-absorption tower with a mid-separation conjunction with basic solution containing $KMnO_4$ and H_2O_2 proved to be effective for abatement of waste gases during semiconductor processes.

The high efficiency of abatement is partly due to the construction of the oval spray-absorption tower. The construction makes a concurrent flow on one side and a counter-current flow on another side for gas and solution. Because of this, contact area and time between gas and solution could be aggrandized and prolonged. Moreover, within this oval spray-absorption tower gas can flow smoothly beneath the mid-separator. The resistance is very low, only 3.72 Pa, being about 1/5 of the resistance of the linking pipe between two towers in series. Thus, the tower can treat waste gas very well even though the tower is not too high and the lower velocity blast can work well. In the oval spray-absorption tower there are many nozzles spraying water crosswise, so there is no dead corner in this tower. The water velocity is less than 2 m/s in an empty tower. The pressure drop is 400 Pa per meter of fillings. The selected blast has a rotation speed of 2900 r/min, and stands temperature as high as 120℃. Its pressure fits the resistance of the tower well. In contrast with it, the usual motors have a rotation speed of 1450 r/min and stands temperature <50℃, and its pressure does not fit the resistance of the tower. The parameters of selected corrosion-resistant fiberglass pump are as follows: flux of 12.5—18.0m^3/h, lift of 18—14.3(m), 2900 r/min, power of 2.2kW. The pump can transport all kinds of corrosive liquids with temperature of 120℃.

Table 5 Comparison of Pollutant concentration before and after treatment *

Pollutant concentration	Before treatment, mg/m^3	After treatment, mg/m^3
Cl^-	0.23—2.4	0.037
F^-	0.56—0.91	0.010
SO_4^{2-}	0.2—3.1	0.082
NO_3^-	0.88	0.07
Arsenic	0.32	0.04
Phosphorus	0.13	0.09

*. The experimental conditions for Cl^-, F^-, SO_4^{2-} and NO_3^- by ion chromatography are as follows: separation column: Ion-Pac—AS4A, sensitivity of conductometer = 1μs, volume of sample = 100—480μl, eluent solution flow rate = 3ml/min, regenerating solution flow rate = 2.8 ml/min

The experimental conditions for As and P determination by gas chromatography are the same as Table 1

3 Waste water treatment

3.1 Principle

Coprecipitation takes place by the action of neutralization in conjunction with flocculation. According to this principle, $Fe(OH)_3$ precipitates by adjusting pH value to 8—10 and adding Fe^{3+} flocculent. At the same time ions of As, P and heavy metals should be absorbed on the surface of precipitated solid. Small particles in turn agglomerate becoming large precipitates.

The chemical reactions take place according to following equations:

$$3Na_2HAsO_4+3H_2O+2FeCl_3=Fe(OH)_3(s)+Fe(H_2AsO_4)_3(s)+6NaCl,$$
$$3Na_2HPO_4+3H_2O+2FeCl_3=Fe(OH)_3(s)+Fe(H_2PO_4)_3(s)+6NaCl.$$

3.2 Equipment

Specially designed flocculation-sedimentation compact device is made of erosion-resistant steel. In this device there is a slant-pipe settlement device, in which the slant pipes are installed with an angle 60°. Water flows upward with a velocity of 0.5 mm/s while sludge falls down the slant pipes. Its sedimentation efficiency is 5-6 times higher than that of conventional methods.

The flocculation-sedimentation flowchart and the compact device is shown in Fig. 3.

3.3 Results and discussion

The concentrations of heavy metals including Cu, Ba, Cd, Cr, total As and P, chemical oxygen demand (COD) by $K_2Cr_2O_7$ oxidation, biochemical oxygen demand (BOD) by cultivation for five days, suspended solid (SS), linear alkyl benzene sulfonate (LAS), ammonia nitrogen (NH_3-N) and pH values before and after waste water treatment are shown in Table 6. The National Waste Water Discharge Standard GB 8978-96 is also listed for comparison in Table 6, which shows that the pollutant concentrations in waste water after the treatment meet the National Waste Water Discharge Standard.

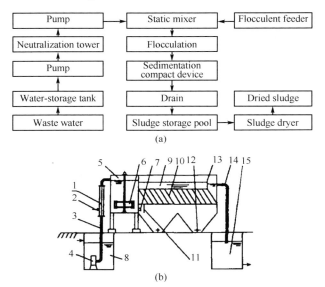

Fig.3　Flocculation-sedimentation compact device

(a) flow chart; (b) schematic diagram of device

1. static mixer; 2. inlet for chemicals; 3. inlet pipe; 4. submerged pump; 5. reaction pool; 6. agitator; 7. inlet port; 8. regulating pool; 9. slant-pipe sedimentation pool; 10. fiber glass slant pipes with hexagonal cross section; 11. water distributor; 12. pipes with holes for removing sludge; 13. triangle weir plate; 14. outlet pipe; 15. water pool

According to our experiment, the method can be applied to waste water containing COD < 500mg/L, BOD<300mg/L, SS<100 mg/L, LAS<20mg/L, As <30mg/L, P<10mg/L, F< 5mg/L, and heavy metal <15mg/L. The enhancement of abatement efficiency by using the flocculation-sedimentation device with a slant settlement pipe is due to the following factors. Firstly, the flocculation-sedimentation device with a slant settlement pipe has a larger surface than that of a conventional one. Secondly, the effective height of sedimentation for this device is higher than that for a conventional one. Calculation results showed that the surface and effective height is increased by a factor of 1.75 and 2.9—3.5, respectively, for waste water rate of $10m^3/h$. The resultant sedimentation efficiency is $1.75 \times (2.9—3.5) = 5—6$ times higher than that of conventional sedimentation device.

Table 6 Comparison of pollutant concentration before and after waste water treatment

No.	Impurity	Concentration, mg/L		National Waste Water Discharge Standard. mg/L First class
		Before abatement	After abatement	
1	Cu	0.0214	0.018	0.5
2	Ba	0.254	0.096	/
3	Cd	0.00050	0.000072	0.1
4	Cr	0.0069	0.0017	1.5
5	Total As	5.42	0.103	0.5
6	Total P	1.2	0.4	/
7	COD_{Cr}	45.7	20.0	60
8	BOD_5	29.7	10.2	20
9	F^-	0.58	0.31	10
10	SS	28.3	9.3	20
11	LAS	0.032	0.023	5
12	NH_3-N	2.84	0.53	15
13	pH	6.8	7.1	6—9

References

[1] Barin I, Knacke O, Kubachewski O, 1991. Thermochemical properties of inorganic substances [M]. Berlin: Springer.

[2] Brookman R P, Flaherty E, Weadock D K, 1988. Semiconductor International[J]. Oct. 88-93.

[3] Dean J A, 1985. Lange's handbook of chemistry.[M]. 13th ed. McGraw-Hill Book Co.

[4] The Chinese National Discharge Standards, 1996. GB 16297-1996[S].

[5] The Chinese National Discharge Standards, 1996, GB 8978-1996[S].

[6] Wen R M, Liang J W, Zhou S J et al., 1997. Measurement of trace phosphorus in dichlorosihane hy high-temperature hydrogen reduction-gas chromatography [J]. J Chromatogr A, 757: 319-323.

[7] Wen R M, 1998. Determination of trace anions in high purity gases in semiconductor process [J]. J Chromatogr Sci[J], 36:579-582.

[8] Yang H, Liang J W, 1992. Thermodynamic and fluid dynamic analysis of GaAs MOVPE process [C]. Proceedings of the 1st Pacific Rim international conference on advanced materials and processing (Shi C D, Scott A, Eds). TMS. 541-545.

Control of Arsenic Pollution from Waste Gases During Fabrication of Semiconductor

Wen Ruimei, Liang Junwu, Deng Lisheng, Peng Yongqing

(*Institute of Semiconductors , Chinese Academy of Sciences , Beijing* 100083 , *China*)

Abstract: The abatement technology of toxic arsenic pollution during fabrication of semiconductor materials and devices has been studied.

Keywords: Semiconductors; arsenic; pollution; abatement.

1 Introduction

The development of high technology has caused in a deteriorating environmental pollution. For example, many kinds of toxic gases are used for fabrication of semiconductor materials and devices. Many of these speciality gases are flammable, explosive, readily hydrolyzable, and with very low value of IDLH (immediately dangerous to life or health), therefore the pollution control of them is difficult. Due to the continued expansion of electronic industry, the chemical pollution becomes severe. We analysed the waste gases from a certain region for last eight years and the data showed that the arsenic concentration in atmosphere from less than 0.001 mg/m^3 in 1984 increased to 0.12 mg/m^3 in 1992. These mean that the toxic arsenic emissions from plants increase rapidly and cause serious pollution.

2 Arsenic pollution during fabrication of semiconductor compounds

Methods used for fabrication of semiconductor compounds are horizontal Bridgman method, liquid encapsulated Czochralski method (LEC), molecular beam epitaxy (MBE), chemical beam epitaxy (CBE), liquid phase epitaxy (LPE), vapor phase epitaxy (VPE) and metalorganic vapor phase epitaxy (MOVPE). During above mentioned processes, the following sources and dopants are used: elements including As, P, Ga, Al and In, chlorides including $AsCl_3$, PCl_3; hydrides including AsH_3, PH_3, H_2Se, H_2S; metalorganics including $Ga(CH_3)_3$, $Ga(C_2H_5)_3$, $Al(CH_3)_3$, $Al(C_2H_5)_3$, $Zn(CH_3)_2$, $In(C_2H_5)_3$ and $Zn(C_2H_5)_2$. In addition to these a wide variety of chemicals and organic solvents are used for semiconductor compounds fabrication. All these hazardous materials may be emitted into atmosphere along vent tubes with tail gases, causing serious environment pollution. We will illustrate the process taking MOVPE as an example.

MOVPE is a kind of newly developed technology for growth of electronic materials including Ⅲ-Ⅴ and Ⅱ-Ⅵ compounds and high temperature superconductor films. MOVPE technology is able to grow high purity materials with abrupt transition region and good uniformi-

原载于：Journal of Environmental Sciences, 1994, 6(1): 123-127.

ty. High quality quantum well and super lattice materials can be grown and high speed electronic devices, lasers and detectors can be fabricated successfully by MOVPE.

During MOVPE process product and unreacted gases are emitted as effluent gases.

The total reaction is

$$Ca(CH_3) + AsH_3 \longrightarrow CaAs + CH_4,$$
$$In(CH)_3 + PH_3 \longrightarrow InP + CH_4.$$

The detail of reaction is (Schlyer, 1977)

$$Ca(CH_3)_3 \xrightarrow{\text{substrate surface}} Ga(CH_3)_3^*,$$
$$AsH_3 \xrightarrow{\text{substrate surface}} AsH_3^*,$$
$$Ca(CH_3)_3^* + AsH_3^* \longrightarrow (CH_3)_2 GaAsH_2 + CH_4,$$
$$(CH_3)_2 GaAsH_2 \longrightarrow (CH_3) GaAsH + CH_4,$$
$$(CH_3) GaAsH \longrightarrow GaAs + CH_4$$

As a rule, the excess quantity of AsH_3 is used, therefore effluent gases contain AsH_3, CH_4, H_2Se (dopant)etc. Arsenic compounds can steady exist in atmosphere as vapor or aerosol. The equipment of MOVPE is shown in Fig. 1.

3 Abatement process design

Generally the abatement technologies used in the world are wet scrubbers including spray tower, packed tower etc, dry adsorption including adsorption and chemisorption, combustion and decomposition.

Twofold abatement for toxic gases released from semiconductor were used in this study.

First step: Thermal decomposition and absorption with $KMnO_4 + NaOH$ or $H_2O_2 + NaOH$ solution.

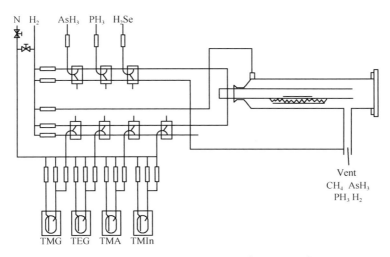

Fig.1 The equipment of MOVPE (sketch map)

---

* Means condensed form on substrate surface.

Second step: Abatement of gases from the first step by using spray-packed tower in which the scrubbing liquid flows in opposite direction to the flow of waste gas. Three kinds of scrubbing liquids were used for various waste gases. The spray-packed tower is effective for controlling of vapors containing acid radicals, such as F^-, Cl^-, SO_4^{2-}, PO_4^{3-} and AsO_4^{3-}. Satisfied results were obtained with these methods.

According to the standard issued by Beijing Environmental Protection Agency, the acceptable level of emission is equal to or less than 0.04 mg/m^3 near a chimney exit being 42 meters high. In the first phase experiment, the effluent gases have been treated by different scrubbing liquid, e.g. $KMnO_4$, KOH, KIO_3, H_2SO_4, H_2O_2 and solid activated charcoal adsorbent. The concentration of AsH_3 were analyzed before and after abatement.

4 Results of AsH₃ abatement by different types of scrubbers

The results of first phase experiment are shown in Table 1.

Considering the high priced HIO_3, difficulty of charcoal activation and low abatement effectiveness of H_2SO_4, in the second phase we have designed an abatement process by using ten spray-packed towers. The scrubbing liquids are $KMnO_4$, H_2O_2, NaOH and their mixing solution.

Table 1 Comparison of AsH₃ abatement with different types of scrubbing materials

Scrubbing materials	AsH₃ concentration mg/m³ Before	After	Abatement percentage, %
1. 5% KMnO₄+1% NaOH	2.54	0.03	98
2. 5% H₂O₂+ 1% NaOH	0.42	0.03	92
3. 2% NaOH	0.49	0.022	95.4
4. 5% HIO₃	0.11	0.01	90.7
5. 1 + 2 in series	6.54	0.038	99.4
6. Activated charcoal and KMnO₄+ NaOH	0.172	0.01	94.7
7. Activated charcoal	0.018	0.01	44
8. 2% H₂SO₄	0.44	0.32	27

The flow chart of abatement by using ten spray towers is shown in Fig.2.

The result of arsenic abatement by using ten spray-packed towers are shown in Table 2.

Table 2 Abatement effectiveness by using ten spray-packed towers

		Tower number				
		W1	W2	W3	W4	W5
Conc. of As.	Before	0.46	0.23	0.01	0.18	0.324
mg/m³	After	0.016	0.04	<0.01	0.025	0.034
Abatement percent, %		96.5	81. 7		86. 1	89.4
		E1	E2	E3	E4	E5
Conc. of As,	Before	<0.01	<0.01	0.31	0.175	0.164
mg/m³	After	<0.01	<0.01	0.021	0.011	0.023
Abatement percent, %				93.2	93.7	85.9

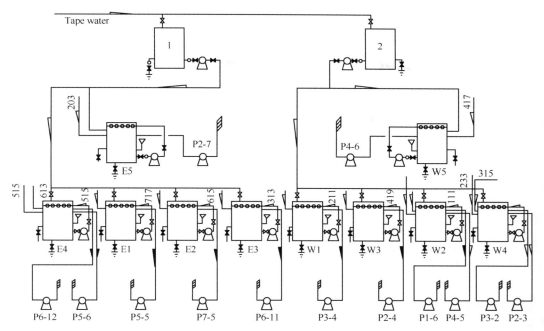

Fig. 2　Flow chart of abatement by using ten spray-packed tower (sketch map)

1.2: solution box

The data showed that after abatement the concentration of arsenic satisfied the standard of acceptable level of emission.

References

[1] Brookman PR, Flaherty E, Weadock DK. Semiconductor International, Oct. 1988; 88.

[2] Schlyer DJ, Ring MA. J Electrochem Soc, 1977; 124; 569.

[3] Wen Ruimei, Peng Yongqing. Science and Technology of Labor Protection, 1993; 13(2); 29.

[4] Wen Ruimei. Low Temperature and Speciality Gases, 1991; 4;1.

(Received July 21, 1993)

О ЛЕТУЧЕСТИ ОКИСИ БОРА В ГЕЛИИ И ВОДОРОДЕ ПРИ НАЛИЧИИ ВОДЯНОГО ПАРА

Н. Х. АБРИКОСОВ, ЛЯН-ЦЗУНЬ-У, Ю. М. ШАШКОВ

(Москва)

Упругость пара B_2O_3 была изучена как методом переноса [1, 2], так и методами эффузии [3-5]. Изучением эмиссионного спектра масс-спектральным анализом [6-8] и определением молекулярного веса [5] было доказано, что окись бора испаряется главным образом в виде B_2O_3. По данным [4], B_2O_3 при 1501° К обладает упругостью паров $3.88 \cdot 10^{-5}$ атм, а при 1566° К — $12.4 \cdot 10^{-5}$ атм. Эти данные, в согласии с нашими опытами, показали, что B_2O_3 очень мало летуча. Однако многие авторы обнаружили, что водяной пар повышает улетучивание ангидрида бора [9-11].

В работе П. Чижевского [9] было найдено, что при пропускании пара воды над B_2O_3, нагретым до 400°, уносилось так много вещества, что пламя бунзеновой горелки окрашивалось в зеленый цвет, а на холодной части получался кристаллический H_3BO_3. Известно также, что присутствие воды усиливает потерю B_2O_3 в процессе стекловарения [11-13] и что для понижения потери B_2O_3 нужно уменьшить влажность шихты. Важное значение имеет введение в шихту борной кислоты в связанном виде — буры. Однако имеющиеся данные [10] по летучести H_3BO_3 и HBO_2 были получены при низких температурах, не превышающих 200°. Для чистой окиси бора, кроме отдельных заметок, систематическое изучение не было проведено.

Для ряда целей представляет интерес исследовать летучесть B_2O_3 при наличии паров воды вплоть до высоких температур. В соответствии с этим нами исследована летучесть B_2O_3 в сухом и во влажном гелии и водороде до температуры 1400.

Из известных методов измерения упругости пара мы выбрали метод переноса, так как он, в отличие от других методов, позволяет проводить измерение в интересующей нас атмосфере и при средних величинах упругости пара обеспечивает достаточную точность результатов.

Схема использованной установки показана на фиг. 1. Установка эта состоит из кварцевой трубки 2 диаметром 24 мм, длиной 1 м, которая за лодочкой 3 на расстоянии 20 мм имеет местное сужение диаметром 5 м для уменьшения обратной диффузии пара.

Трубка помещалась в печь Таммана 1. При помощи двух платиновых проволок 5 можно быстро передвигать лодочку с образцом 3 без доступа воздуха из холодной части печи в горячую зону или наоборот. В печи Таммана устанавливался фигурный графитовый нагреватель, имеющий различное сопротивление по длине. Сопротивление входа и выхода было больше, чем середины. Средняя часть нагревателя, как показали специально проведенные опыты, при 1400° позволяла иметь равномерную температуру на длине 5 см. Длина лодочки составляла 3 см.

Гелий или водород при помощи натекателя 16 или микрокрана после силикагеля 10, активированного угля 9, охлаждаемого жидким азотом, и медного змеевика 8 с определенной скоростью пропускался над

原载于:Металлургия и Топливо,1960,4:156-160.

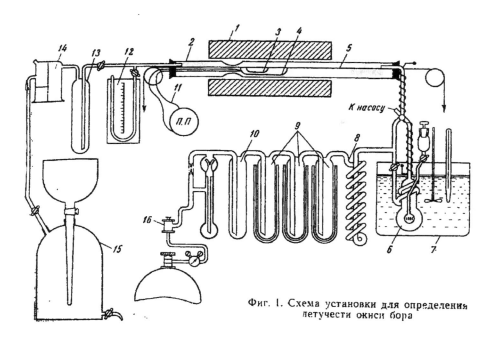

Фиг. 1. Схема установки для определения
летучести окиси бора

образцом. Для измерения объема прошедшего газа применяли газометр *15*, перед которым ставились склянки Тищинко *14* с концентрированной H_2SO_4 и ловушка с силикагелем *13* для устранения диффузии водяного пара.

Объем газа определялся по весу вытесняемой воды с точностью по 0.5 *мл*. В опытах во влажном гелии или водороде газ пропускался дополнительно через насытитель *6*, который находился в термостате *7*. Температура насытителя поддерживалась с точностью до ±0.1°. Общее давление в системе измерялось манометром с диффузионным маслом *12* с точностью до 0.3 *мм* рт. ст. Температура в печи измерялась платино-платинородиевой термопарой с потенциометром ПП *11* с точностью до ±10°.

Перед опытом трубку, нагретую до температуры на 20° выше температуры опыта, продували гелием или водородом в течение 30 *мин* для вытеснения воздуха и удаления сконденсированных на стенке трубки молекул B_2O_3. В опытах в сухом гелии или водороде трубку при откачке форвакуумным насосом тщательно прогревали горелкой и потом

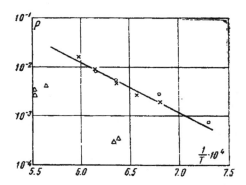

Фиг. 2. Температурная зависимость давления пара B_2O_3, определенная по методу переноса: $\times$ — данные, полученные в работе [1]; $\triangle$ — данные, полученные в работе [2]; $\bigcirc$ — наши данные

продували газ в течение получаса с целью удаления следов влаги, наличие которых приводит к завышенным результатам. При продувке газом платиновая лодочка с веществом *3*, которая помещалась в другую большую лодочку из платины *4*, находилась в холодной части печи. После этого лодочка быстро передвигалась в горячую равномерную зону и температура печи снижалась до нужной. После окончания опыта лодочка быстро передвигалась в холодную часть трубки и эта часть трубки охлаждалась холодной водои Использованныи в опытах борны: ангидрид был предварительно прока?ен в специальнои установке пр: 900° в вакууме в платиновом тигле

На фиг 2 показана температурная зависимость давления пара B_2O: полученная на нашей установке Данные совпадают с результатами полученными таким же методом использованием огнеупорной труб ки [1]

На фиг 3 в логарифмическо? масштабе показана зависимость убыли веса B_2O_3 на единицу пло щади жидкого B_2O_3 от скорости га

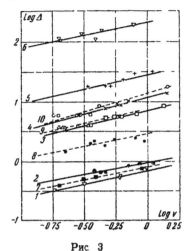

Рис 3

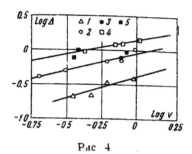

Рис 4

Фиг 3 Зависимость убыли веса B_2O_3 на единицу площади (Δ иг/см²) от скорости влажного или сухого гелия (V, л/час) при разных температурах Сплошные линии — опыты во влажном гелии при $P_{H_2O}=0\,0313$ атм и в кварцевой трубке 1 — при 860° 2 — 920°, 3 — 1100°, 4 — 1200°, 5 — 1300°, 6 — 1400° Пунктирные линии — опыт в сухом гелии в кварцевой трубке 7 — при 1100°, 8 — 1200°, 9 — 1300°, 10 — 1350°

Фиг 4 Зависимость убыли веса B_2O_3 на единицу площади от скорости влажного и сухого водорода, (V, л/час), (Δ, мг/см²) 1 — опыты при 1000° в сухом водороде в квар цевой трубке 2 — 860° во влажном водороде при $P_{H_2O}=0\,0313$ атм в кварцевой трубке, 3 — 860° и при $P_{H_2O}=0\,0313$ атм в фарфоровой трубке, 4 — 960° при $P_{H_2O}=0\,0313$ атм в кварцевой трубке, 5 — 920° при $P_{H_2O}=0\,0313$ атм в фарфоровой трубке

зов при разных температурах Сплошными линиями показаны результаты при пропускании гелия с парами воды Пунктирными линиями показана убыль веса B_2O_3 в сухом гелии Температура насытителя во всех опы тах поддерживалась равной 25°, что соответствует упругости пара воды 0 0313 атм

При всех температурах убыль веса при наличии водяного пара зна чительно увеличивается (до 10 раз) Во всех опытах получается линей ная зависимость $\log \Delta$ (мг/см²) от $\log V$

На фиг 4 в логарифмическом масштабе показана зависимость убы ли веса B_2O_3 в сухом и влажном водороде Опыты в водороде проводи ?ись только до 1000°, так как при температуре выше 1000° кварц уже начинает восстанавливаться

В наших опытах использовалась кварцевая трубка, которая н? была защищена платиновои жестью Для оценки влияния кварца на получен ные результаты были проведены специа?ьные опыты в фарфоровои трубке при пропускании гелия Полученные данные в виде отде?ьных то чек нанесены на фиг 4 Заметного от?ичия в результатах не наблю дается

Из фи? 3 и 4 видно, что летучесть во влажном водороде незначи те?ьно отличается от летучести во влажном гелии

Для вычисления упругости пара из полученных данных необходимо ?нать мо?екулярный вес газового компонента В работе [10] было напдено, что при низких температурах HBO_2 по сравнению с H_3BO_3 имеет значительно меньшую упругость пара Однако экстраполяция температурной зависимости давления пара HBO_2 показывает что HBO_2 при высокой температуре становится также заметно летучей В работах [14—15] изучение эмиссионного спектра B_2O_3 при наличии водяных паров и температуре 1100—1480° C показало присутствие газообразных молекул HBO_2 Поэтому вычисление упругости пара окиси бора при наличии

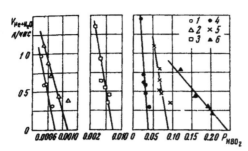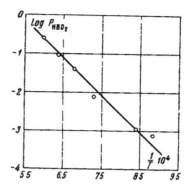

Фиг 5 Степень насыщения влажного гелия паром HBO_2 в зависимости от скорости продувания, $P_{H_2O}=0\,0313$ атм 1 — при 860° 2 — 920°, 3 — 1100°, 4 — 1200°, 5 — 1300° 6 — 1400°

Фиг 6 Температурная зависимость давления пара HBO_2 при $P_{H_2O}=0\,0313$ ати

водяного пара было проведено с предположением наличия в газовой фазе главным образом HBO_2

На фиг 5 показана степень насыщения влажного гелия паром HBO_2 в зависимости от скорости продувания при разных температурах На фиг 6 проведена температурная зависимость давления пара HBO_2, которая имеет вид

$$\log P_{HBO_2} = 5\,043 - \frac{43\,490}{4\,575T} \quad 1133 < T < 1637°K$$

Полученные данные показывают, что в широком интервале температуры от 860° до 1400° летучесть B_2O_3 в гелии или водороде с парами воды значительно выше летучести B_2O_3 в сухом гелии и водороде, что необходимо учитывать при работе с B_2O_3 в атмосфере гелия или водорода

Поступило 22 III 1960

ЛИТЕРАТУРА

1. Cole S S and Taylor N W J Amer Ceram Soc, 1935, 18, 82
2. Soulen J R, Sthapitanonda P and Margrave J L J Phys Chem, 1955 59, 132
3. Speiser R, Naidıtch S and Johnston H L J Amer Chem Soc, 1950 72, 2578
4. Searcy A W and Myers C E J Phys Chem 1957 61, 957
5. Milton D Scheer J Phys Chem, 1957, 61, 1184
6. Bradt P NBS Rep 3016 Jan, 1954
7. Inghram M G, Porter R F and Ckupka W A J Chem Phys, 1956, 25, 498
8. Soulen J R and Margrave J L J Amer Chem Soc, 1956, 78, 2911
9. Tchijewski P Arch Sciences physiques nat Geneve, 1884, 3, 12, 139
10. Von Stackelberg M V, Quatram F und Dressel Jutta Z Elektrochem 1937, 43, 14
11. Weyl W A, Glass Ind 1948 No 3, 131—136, 156—158, No 4, 200—206, 221, No 5—8, 264—265, 284, 328—329, 346, 388—390
12. Варгин В В Оптико-механическая промышленность, 1936 6 № 9, 14—16 № 10, 19—21
13. Kalsıng H Sprechsoal, 1955 88, 267
14. Dows D A and Porter R F J Amer Chem Soc, 1956 78 5165
15. White D Walsh P N and Mann D E J Chem Phys, 1958 28 508

О РАСТВОРИМОСТИ КИСЛОРОДА В ЖИДКОМ КРЕМНИИ

Н. Х. АБРИКОСОВ, ЛЯН ЦЗУНЬ-У, Ю. М. ШАШКОВ

(Москва)

Исследование растворимости кислорода в жидком кремнии проводилось в работе [1] при реакции жидкого кремния со смесью кислорода и гелия. Была найдена линейная зависимость между содержанием кислорода в жидком кремнии и парциальным давлением кислорода в газовой фазе. Максимальная растворимость кислорода в жидком кремнии при температуре, близкой к температуре плавления кремния, достигалась при парциальном давлении кислорода, равном 8 *мм*, и составляла $1.8 \cdot 10^{18}$ *ат/см³*.

Представляет интерес определить растворимость кислорода в жидком кремнии при плавлении в других газовых смесях.

В настоящей работе изучалась растворимость кислорода в жидком кремнии при его плавке в парогелиевой и пароводородной смесях, а также влияние на растворимость кислорода акцепторной примеси.

Методика исследования. Во избежание загрязнений материалом тигля и, в особенности для устранения попадания кислорода из тигля изучение реакции между расплавленным кремнием и пароводородной или парогелиевой смесями были проведено при плавке кремния в установке, вертикальной бестигельной зонной плавки с высокочастотным нагревом. Для опытов использовался кремний *p*-типа с удельным сопротивлением 20 *ом · см*.

Образцы кремния были в виде стержня диаметром около 9 *мм*. Длина расплавленной зоны составляла около 1 *см*. Перед плавкой образцы травились смесью плавиковой и азотной кислот, потом два раза в растворе КОН и окончательно промывались в бидистилляте воды.

Водород (или гелий) очищался, проходя через силикагель и активированный уголь, охлаждаемый жидким азотом, и после прохода насытителя, наполненного бидистиллятом воды, который помещался в термостат, с определенной скоростью пропускался через плавильную камеру. В опытах с пароводородной смесью исходный водород дополнительно очищался при пропускании через никелехромовый катализатор. Трубки, через которые проходил газ, насыщенный парами воды, для устранения конденсации водяных паров подогревались.

Регулировка количества водяных паров в смеси осуществлялась изменением температуры насытителя или соотношения между скоростями очищенного и насыщенного водяным паром газа. Истинные составы смесей гелия и водорода с парами воды были определены градуировкой при улавливании водяных паров пятиокисью фосфора.

Перед опытом установку продували пароводородной или парогелиевой смесями в течение получаса. Скорость подачи газа была постоянной и равной 580 *мл/мин* для пароводородной смеси и 586 *мл/мин* для парогелиевой смеси.

Молибденовые держатели образцов были предварительно прокалены при температуре около 2000° в течение часа в токе очищенного водорода.

Результаты исследования. Специальные опыты по определению времени достижения равновесия для одного и того же значения P_{H_2O}/P_{H_2} при различных длительностях выдержки (от 20 *сек* до 90 *мин*) показали, что уже при выдержке выше 20 *сек* содержание кислорода становится фактически одинаковым (фиг. 1). В наших опытах длительность выдержки была выбрана равной 15 *мин*, заведомо обеспечивающая достижения равновесия.

Для устранения выделения кислорода из кремния при его застывании расплавленная зона закристаллизовывалась в опытах с парогелиевой смесью в течение 30 *сек*. При плавке в парогелиевой смеси не было заметно выделения газов при застывании зоны. В сухом и во влажном водороде при быстром снижении температуры зоны было заметно выделение водорода из жидкого кремния и образование пор в закристаллизовавшейся части слитка. В связи с этим при плавке в пароводородной смеси во избежание образования пор кристаллизация завершалась в течение одной минуты.

5 Металлургия и топливо, № 6

原载于:物理学报,2010,59(12):8903-8909.

Для определения концентрации кислорода в твердом кремнии было применено определение коэффициента поглощения в инфракрасной области спектра при 293° К [2, 3]. Для перехода к содержанию кислорода использовался график, приведенный в работе [3], в которой установлено, что поглощение при волновом числе 1106 $см^{-1}$ пропорционально содержанию кислорода, определенного методом вакуум-плавления.

Оптические измерения проводились на двухлучевом инфракрасном спектрометре типа ИКС-14. При вычислении коэффициента поглощения использовалась формула

$$T = \frac{(1 - R)^2}{l^{ad} - R^2 l^{-ad}}$$

учитывающая многократное отражение, где T — процент пропускания, R — коэффициент отражения, равный 0.3, при волновом числе 1106 $см^{-1}$, α — коэффициент поглощения, d — толщина образца. Точность определения α составляла $\pm 10\%$.

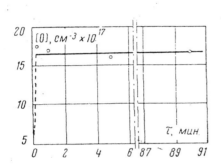

Фиг. 1. Концентрация кислорода в жидком кремнии при значении P_{H_2O}/P_{H_2} равном 0.05 и различных длительностях выдержки

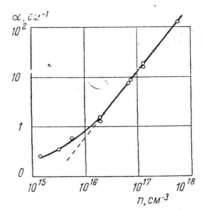

Фиг. 2. Зависимость коэффициента поглощения кремния p-типа от концентрации носителей тока при волновом числе 1106 $см^{-1}$ при 293° К

Как показали специальные опыты, в закристаллизовавшейся зоне кислород распределялся практически равномерно, что совпадает с литературными данными по коэффициенту распределения кислорода в кремнии [4, 5].

В опубликованных работах описано измерение содержания кислорода оптическим методом только в чистом кремнии. Поскольку в общем случае поглощение вызывается также свободными носителями тока, необходимо было учесть этот фактор. Данных по поглощению свободными дырками в чистом от кислорода кремнии в литературе нет. В связи с этим были проведены опыты по определению коэффициента поглощения кремния, легированного акцепторной примесью (бором) в зависимости от длины волны и числа носителей тока.

Для удаления кислорода образцы кремния с различной концентрацией акцепторной примеси были подвергнуты зонной плавке в атмосфере сухого очищенного водорода.

Полученная зависимость коэффициента поглощения от длины волны совпадает (с учетом разницы в концентрации носителей тока) с зависимостью, приведенной в работе [6]. Зависимость коэффициента поглощения от концентрации носителей была снята при волновом числе 1106 $см^{-1}$. Концентрация носителей определялась по эффекту Холла. Полученные данные приведены на фиг. 2.

Как и следует из теоретических соображений, коэффициент поглощения растет с повышением концентрации носителей, причем при концентрации большей 10^{16} $см^{-3}$ коэффициент поглощения становится практически пропорциональным концентрации свободных дырок. В связи с резким возрастанием коэффициента поглощения при концентрации дырок, превышающей 10^{16} $см^{-1}$, что снижает точность определения кислорода, в наших опытах исследовался кремний с концентрацией примеси до 10^{16} $ат/см^3$. Следует отметить, что в этой области концентрации ($>10^{16}$ носителей на $см^3$) определение коэффициента поглощения может быть использовано для определения концентрации бора.

При подсчете коэффициента поглощения, обусловленного кислородом, из общего поглощения вычиталось поглощение, обусловленное свободными дырками.

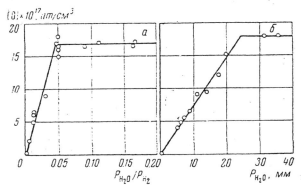

Фиг. 3. Зависимость содержания кислорода в жидком кремнии от P_{H_2O}/P_{H_2} при плавке в пароводородной смеси (а) и от P_{H_2O} при плавке в парогелиевой смеси (б)

На фиг. 3а показана найденная зависимость содержания кислорода в жидком нелегированном кремнии от отношения P_{H_2O}/P_{H_2}. Температура расплавленного кремния была близка к 1410°C. Из графика фиг. 3а видно, что количество кислорода растворенного в кремнии, прямо пропорционально отношению P_{H_2O}/P_{H_2} до точки перегиба, которая соответствует насыщению кислородом. После точки перегиба, которая наступает при значении P_{H_2O}/P_{H_2} равном 0.044, дальнейшее увеличение отношения P_{H_2O}/P_{H_2} не вызывает изменения содержания кислорода, и оно остается постоянным и равным $1.69 \cdot 10^{18}$ $ат/см^3$.

Зависимость концентрации кислорода, растворенного в жидком кремнии, от парциального давления пара воды в парогелиевой смеси приведена на фиг. 3б. Здесь видна линейная зависимость между парциальным давлением водяного пара и содержанием кислорода до точки насыщения, которая наступает при давлении пара воды, равном 23 мм рт. ст. Максимальная растворимость кислорода в жидком кремнии при температуре вблизи температуры плавления кремния равна $1.8 \cdot 10^{18}$ $ат/см^3$, что хорошо совпадает с данными, полученными в работе [1].

Небольшое различие в растворимости кислорода, полученное при реакции кремния с пароводородной смесью и с парогелиевой смесью связано, вероятнее, всего, с выделением водорода при остывании, что вызывает удаление части кислорода, растворенного в кремнии.

Наблюдения в процессе плавки показали, что при P_{H_2O}/P_{H_2} меньше 0.044 в случае пароводородной смеси и при P_{H_2O} меньше 23 мм при плавке в парогелиевой смеси зона не покрыта пленкой из SiO_2. При этом на стенке плавильной камеры и холодной части слитка осаждаются возгоны белого и лимонно-желтого цвета. По данным химического, рентгеновского и минералогического анализов, эти возгоны состоят из SiO_2, SiO и Si. При P_{H_2O}/P_{H_2} или P_{H_2O}, превышающих значения, отвечающие точке насыщения, жидкая зона покрывается пленкой из SiO_2, а количество возгонов становится незначительным.

Для исследования влияния акцепторной примеси на растворимость кислорода в кремнии были проведены опыты по определению содержания кислорода в образцах, легированных бором. В этом случае образцы, легированные бромом, выдерживались в пароводородной смеси 15 мин и после затвердевания в них по эффекту Холла определялась концентрация бора, а по поглощению при волновом числе 1106 $см^{-1}$ — концентрация кислорода. При этом за время опыта в соответствии с литературными данными по плавке кремния в пароводородной смеси [7] происходило интенсивное удаление бора. Полученные результаты показали, что содержание кислорода в кремнии при плавке в пароводородной смеси не зависит от содержания бора и определяется отношением P_{H_2O}/P_{H_2}.

Такой результат может быть обусловлен быстрой диффузией кислорода в жидком кремнии или отсутствием взаимодействия бора с кислородом в объеме кремния или обеими причинами.

Выводы. Подтверждены литературные данные о максимальной растворимости кислорода в расплавленном кремнии при температуре, близкой к 1410°. Показано, что переход от пароводородной смеси к парогелиевой не меняет максимальную растворимость кислорода. Найдено, что акцепторная примесь (бор) не влияет на растворимость кислорода в жидком кремнии.

Поступило 30 V 1960

ЛИТЕРАТУРА

1. Kaiser W. and Breslin J. J. Appl. Phys., 1958, 29, No. 9.
2. Kaiser W., Keck P. H. and Lange C. F. Phys. Rev., 1956, 101, 1264.
3. Kaiser W. and Keck P. J. Appl. Phys., 1957, 28, 882.
4. Trumbore F. A. Bell System. Techn. J., 1960, 39, No 1, 205.
5. Bradshaw S. E. Solid State Phys., 1960, v. 1, 44—60, Land.— N. Y. Acad. Press.
6. Вавилов В. С. Физика твердого тела. 1960, т. II, В. 2, 374.
7. Theuerer H. C. J. Metals, 1956, 8, 1316.

直拉硅单晶碳沾污的研究

梁骏吾　黄大定　汪光川　尹恩华　杨雪珍

（中国科学院半导体研究所）
1982 年 11 月 1 日收到

摘要：本文报道对直拉硅单晶碳沾污机理的研究[1]．用气相色谱法分析了石英与石墨反应生成物 CO 的蒸气压 P_{CO} 以及拉晶条件下石英坩埚和石墨托之间反应的 P_{CO}．在 1512—1600K 温度下测得不同载气 Ar 流速下的 P_{CO}，然后外推至零流速下的 P_{CO}^{0} 数值，由此求得 SiO_2-C 反应产生的 CO 平衡蒸气压值 P_{CO}^{0}．在直拉硅单晶工艺过程中碳沾污的主要来源是石英坩埚与石墨托之间反应产生的 CO．将上面结果与热力学数据比较，可以推出：SiO_2-C 系在上面温度范围内的主要反应是：$C+SiO_2 \longrightarrow SiO+CO$．用钼片隔开石墨托与石英坩埚后，在拉晶过程中 CO 量减少，单晶头部 <50% 处碳含量在红外测量灵敏度以下．此外还研究了晶体中碳含量与层错密度的关系．

一、引　言

大规模集成电路的迅速发展，对无位错直拉硅单晶提出了越来越高的要求．碳是直拉硅单晶中一种重要的残留杂质．碳的主要影响是：它能导致集电区内层错的形成[2]；和硅中的铟形成具有 0.111eV 受主能级的 In-C[3]；此外还和其余的 $Ⅲ_A$ 元素生成 C-$Ⅲ_A$ 对，即所谓 x-中心[4]；碳会降低太阳电池的效率[5]；降低 P-N 结的击穿电压，使结特性变软[6]；直拉单晶在 ~470℃ 热处理时，碳对热施主的形成有抑制作用；而在 ~650℃ 热处理时，碳对新施主的形成有核化作用[7]；还有文献报道，氧碳同时存在时，碳导致氧漩涡的出现[7,8]．我们还发现碳的浓度超过一定值时导致区熔硅晶体中位错的产生[9]．所以，降低硅单晶中碳含量是提高硅单晶质量的重要措施．

1969 年 J.A.Baker[11] 提出：直拉硅单晶中的碳是由于在单晶生长过程中，因单晶炉内的 SiO 气与石墨反应器发生反应：

$$SiO(g)+2C(s) \xrightarrow{1700K} SiC+CO(g) \tag{1}$$

产生的 CO 气被熔硅吸收而引入．如果这个直拉硅单晶碳沾污机理是正确的，那么，只有不使用石英坩埚或不使用处于高温的石墨器具才能解决直拉硅单晶碳沾污问题．然而迄今为止，还未找到能够取代它们的器具．1979 年 Y.Endo 等[12] 用配备气相色谱的气体载带法测量了 1683—1800K 下，SiO_2—SiC—Si 系平衡时的 CO 蒸气压．从而得到平衡常数：

$$K_P = \frac{[CO]}{[C]_{Si}[O]_{Si}} = \begin{cases} 9.6 \times 10^{-8} \text{熔硅} \\ 1.1 \times 10^{-6} \text{固体硅} \end{cases} \tag{2}$$

说明气氛中 CO 的分压强 $[CO]$ 与硅中的碳氧浓度 $[C]_{Si}[O]_{Si}$ 之比为一常数，但如何有效

原载于：半导体学报，1984，5(1)：25-32．

地降低 CO 蒸气压、从而减少硅中的碳含量,文献仍未作报道. F. Schmid 等[13]用热力学数据计算过在硅单晶生长过程中,熔硅、石英坩埚、石墨及周围气体间可能发生的 15 个化学反应,此后梁连科[14]也进行了类似计算,并指出硅单晶碳沾污的几种可能的反应.但迄今为止尚未见到结合直拉硅单晶工艺,进行热力学测量以确定对 CO 气产生及其大小起决定因素是哪一个反应的报道*.

本工作通过对 SiO$_2$-C 系热化学反应平衡时 CO 蒸气压与温度关系的研究,进行了在拉晶工艺条件下石英坩埚与石墨托间热化学反应产生的 CO 蒸气量的测量,提出了直拉硅单晶工艺中碳沾污的主要来源、机制以及降低碳沾污的途径. 并研究了碳含量与直拉硅单晶中体层错密度的关系.

二、实验方法及结果

1. SiO$_2$-C 系反应的测量

测量装置:SiO$_2$-C 系反应设备略图示于图 1. 它是用一台 TDK-36AZ 型直拉单晶炉改装的. 为保证反应时温度均匀,将加热器改为长温区;把反应器做成水平的,以加热器轴线为轴对称的石英圆形环管;除留有石英管及测温热偶的出口外,用石墨和碳毡在加热器的四周、顶部、底部做成热绝缘层.反应器内装有经均匀混合后的 100 目高纯石英粉(99.99%)和纯石墨粉.测量过程中温度波动控制在±3℃以内.

CO 平衡气压的测量方法:在一恒定温度下,以不同流速的载气通过反应器,测量流出气体中的 CO 含量,由 CO 含量

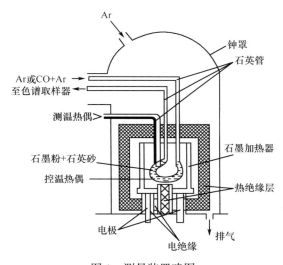

图 1　测量装置略图

与流速的关系曲线外推至零流速,即求得平衡时 CO 蒸气压的数值.

载气用高纯 Ar(纯度>99.999%,CO<0.1ppm,H$_2$O<5.5ppm)或已知 CO 浓度的氩气.反应后产生的气体在出口处用浓缩取样法或直拉取样法取样,用 Perkin-Elmer 公司 Sigma I 型气相色谱仪测量.色谱仪测量误差为±10%—15%.测量结果表明:反应排出气体主要是氩和 CO 气,其它杂质均可忽略不计.

测量结果:用载带法求 CO 平衡蒸气压值的典型例子示于图 2. 这是在温度为 1570K 下测量得到的结果. 图中直线 A 是以高纯氩为载气,流经石英和石墨混合物后,气体中 CO 含量随气流流速的减少而增加.直线 B 是含有 4.5×10^{3}ppm CO 的氩气为载气时,流经

---

* 在付印过程中得知 Ремиэов 等人[19]认为 CO 和 CO$_2$ 二者都是造成炉内碳污染的原因,然而未做这一方面的实验. 其实验是寻找炉内保护气流大小对碳含量的影响. 但其得到的碳含量均大于 1×10^{16}cm^{-3},显然还不够低.

石英和石墨混合物后,气体中 CO 含量随流速的减少而减少. 实验数据用最小二乘方进行处理,将结果外推到零流速,两条直线相交于 2400ppm. 实验证实:测量数据外推到零流速,就可以得到该温度下 CO 气的平衡蒸气压. 1570K 下 SiO_2-C 系反应的 CO 平衡蒸气压值是 2400ppm.

在每一温度下,由流速与 CO 蒸气压的依赖关系求得 CO 平衡蒸气压,从而得到 1512—1660K 下,SiO_2-C 系反应 CO 平衡蒸气压 P_{CO}^0 与温度 T 的关系. 结果示于图 3. 由图可见:$\lg P_{CO}^0$ 与 $\dfrac{1}{T}$ 在此温度范围内呈直线关系:

$$\lg P_{CO}^0(托) = 17.62 - 2.73 \times 10^4/T \quad 1512K < T < 1660K \tag{3}$$

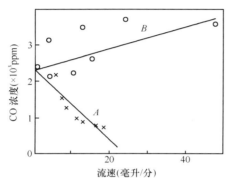 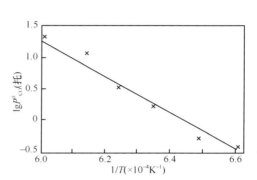

图 2 用载带法求 CO 平衡蒸气压
反应温度:$T = 1576K$
入口载气:A:高纯氩
B:Ar+CO(4500ppm)

图 3 SiO_2-C 系反应 CO 平衡蒸气压
与温度的依赖关系

2. 拉晶工艺条件下 CO 气产生量的测量

直拉硅单晶工艺条件和氧、碳杂质分布:本实验采用的是 TDK-40 型直拉单晶炉拉制的硅单晶. 生长气氛是氩(压力:1.1—1.5kg/cm²;流速:5 升/分);籽晶拉速为 1.5mm/分;籽晶转速为 20 转/分;坩埚转速为 10 转/分. 拉制的无位错晶体为 P 型,掺杂剂为硼;电阻率为 7—10Ω·cm;晶体生长方向[100];直径为 ϕ36—38mm;长度 ~ 15cm.(多晶投料 370g). 晶体中氧、碳含量的轴向分布如图 4 所示. 因为氧、碳杂质在硅中的分凝系数分别为 1.25[15] 和 0.07[16],直拉硅单晶锭条中头部氧浓度比尾部氧浓度高,而碳浓度则相反. 这与其它作者的结果相同[7,17].

测量方法:在拉晶工艺条件下,氩保护气体由顶部通入,底部排出. 用浓缩取样法或直接取样法,对单晶炉排出尾气中的 CO 蒸气量进行了测量. 为检测炉内气体的种类,还用气体质谱计(ZHP-3 型)自炉内排气取样进行了测量.

实验结果:色谱分析结果证明:单晶炉内主要气体产物是 CO. 气体质谱计还检查出 SiO 的存在.

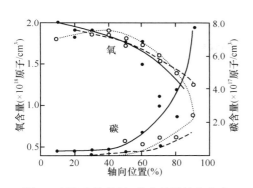

图 4　直拉硅单晶氧、碳含量的轴向分布

轴向位置是按测量处与籽晶间晶体重量占硅投料总量的百分比为标记的.图中圆点、三角点、方点分别代表 110#、135#、129# 晶体的数据.实心点为碳浓度数据,空心点为氧浓度数据

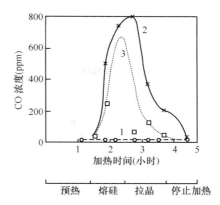

图 5　拉晶工艺条件下单晶炉尾气中 CO 气含量

曲线 1:石墨托内不加石英坩埚;

曲线 2:石墨托内只加石英坩埚不加硅;

曲线 3:石墨托内加石英坩埚和硅

　　拉晶工艺条件下,色谱测量结果示于图 5.图中曲线 1 是未加石英坩埚时测量的结果,最高的 CO 含量~10ppm,使用纯氩(纯度~99.99%)的结果与高纯氩的结果相同.曲线 2 是放入石英坩埚但无硅的情况下测量的结果.此时炉内有大量 CO 气排出.在熔硅温度下 CO 气浓度急剧上升,最高可达~800ppm,拉晶时因温度略有下降,CO 气含量随时间有一滞后之后渐渐减少.曲线 3 是有硅存在时测量的结果,此时尾气中 CO 含量较无硅时的结果略低.曲线 2 和曲线 3 不重合,其间面积的物理意义将在后面讨论.在实际拉晶工艺过程中,因熔硅时间比实验用的时间短很多,所以在实际工艺过程中得到的 CO 含量~30—90ppm.

3. 用钼隔开石英与石墨的实验

　　由前述可知,如果隔绝石英坩埚和石墨托的接触则 CO 不能生成.

　　将钼片剪成坩埚形状,垫在石英坩埚与石墨托之间,在拉晶工艺条件下,测量了石英坩埚内未装硅时单晶炉尾气中 CO 蒸气量.测量结果及其和未隔钼片时测量结果的比较示于表 1.由表可知:用钼隔开石英坩埚和石墨托后,尾气中 CO 气含量降低了约 2—10 倍.在此条件下拉制的单晶与一般工艺拉制的单晶碳浓度的比较示于图 4(129# 为隔钼片拉制的;110# 为一般工艺拉制的)和表 2.为了检查钼是否会引入重金属沾污,表中还列入了寿命值,从表中数据可以看出,用钼将石英坩埚与石墨托隔开后,有效地降低了碳含量,而寿命值不变.

　　此外,我们还在炉内设计了气流导向装置,以阻止石英坩埚与石墨托反应生成的 CO 蒸气流经熔硅表面,这样拉制的晶体头部(10%处)的碳含量由 10^{16} 原子/cm^3 降到红外检测限以下(如图 4 中 135# 晶体).

　　减少炉内 CO 蒸气量及改进气流条件后,多晶材料中原始碳含量对单晶质量的影响就突出了.如果在拉晶过程中,不考虑 CO 气引入的碳,由正常分凝的杂质分布公式可以算出:要使单晶锭 90%处碳的含量控制在 1×10^{17} 原子/cm^3 以下,原始硅中碳含量也必须

控制在 1×10^{17} 原子/cm^3 以下.

表 1　单晶炉尾气中 CO 含量的变化 *

CO 含量（ppm） 加热程序 实验条件	熔硅温度~1970K		拉晶温度~1693K			停止
	开始	20分钟	10~20分	1小时	2小时	30分
未隔钼坩埚	~20	150~750	~800	~360—100	~41	~20
隔钼坩埚	~20	~10	~10	~10	25	~2

* 注:实验时未加硅料

表 2　用钼隔坩埚对降低碳沾污的效果

工艺条件	单晶<50%处碳含量(原子/cm^3)	少数载流子寿命
用钼隔坩埚	小于红外检测限($<1\times10^{16}$)	50—150μs
一般工艺	~1—6$\times10^{16}$	50—150μs

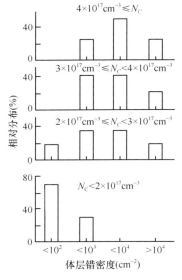

图 6　直拉硅单晶碳含量与
体层错密度的关系

4. 直拉硅中碳含量与体层错密度的关系

我们对生长工艺条件相同的 25 根无位错直拉硅单晶作了统计,结果表明:当氧含量在 1.0—2.0$\times10^{18}$ 原子/cm^3 变化范围内,氧含量与体层错密度没有关系,单晶尾部(90% 位置处)碳含量(8×10^{16}—6×10^{17} 原子/cm^3)与单晶体层错密度的关系如图 6 所示.统计结果说明:直拉硅单晶中 $N_C<2\times10^{17}$ 原子/cm^3 时,体层错密度较小,多数只有 10^2/cm^2,随着 N_C 增大,体层错密度上升,N_C 达到 3×10^{17} 原子/cm^3 以上时,体层错密度增到 10^3—10^4/cm^2.

三、讨　论

1. SiO_2-C 系热化学反应的分析

在 SiO_2-C 系中可能有下列六种化学反应:

$$3C + SiO_2 \longrightarrow SiC + 2CO \qquad (4)$$

$$C + SiO_2 \longrightarrow SiO + CO \qquad (5)$$

$$2C + SiO_2 \longrightarrow SiC + CO_2 \qquad (6)$$

$$3C + 3SiO_2 \longrightarrow SiC + 2CO_2 + 2SiO \qquad (7)$$

$$4C + 2SiO_2 \longrightarrow SiC + 3CO + SiO \qquad (8)$$

$$C + 2SiO_2 \longrightarrow 2SiO + CO_2 \qquad (9)$$

现在,讨论一下哪个反应为主.在实验中,由气相色谱分析得知,反应产生气体由载气 Ar 和 CO 组成,还有 SiO 引起的黄色粉末,质谱还检测到 SiO 的存在.所以可能进行的反应是(4)、(5)和(8),而反应(6),(7)和(9)是生成 CO_2 的,在实验范围内可以忽略.再将反应(4)、(5)和(8)按理论计算所得 P_{CO}^0 和我们实验的结果进行比较,结果示于图7.理论计算引用了文献热力学数据(Manlabs——NPL Data Book)[13],由图可见:在我们测量的温度范围内,实验结果接近于反应(5)的计算结果,而反应(4)和(8)发生的可能性不大.可以认为在6个可能发生的反应中,实际反应是

$$C+SiO_2 \longrightarrow SiO+CO \tag{5}$$

2. 熔融硅对 CO 的吸收

SiO_2-C 反应生成的 CO 为熔硅所吸收,可按下列反应进行:

$$CO \longrightarrow [C]_{Si}+[O]_{Si} \tag{10}$$

$$[O]_{Si}+Si \longrightarrow SiO\uparrow \tag{11}$$

由于 SiO 的挥发性,氧在硅中不易积累,而碳不能挥发,在硅中积存下来.可以认为,被吸收的 CO 中的碳原子全部留在硅单晶中.

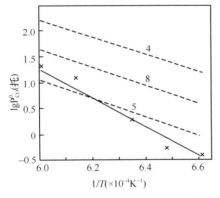

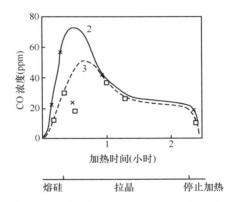

图 7　SiO_2-C 系反应实验结果与理论计算的比较
实线为实验结果.虚线分别为反应:4. $3C+SiO_2 \longrightarrow SiC+$
CO、5. $C+SiO_2 \longrightarrow SiO+CO$、8. $4C+2SiO_2 \longrightarrow SiC+3CO+$
SiO 的理论计算结果

图 8　110# 晶体拉晶工艺过程中,单晶炉尾气中 CO 气含量
曲线 2:无熔硅时
曲线 3:有熔硅时

由拉晶条件下分别测量空石英坩埚及装有熔硅的石英坩埚尾气中 CO 量可知:当有熔硅存在时测得的 CO 量(图5,曲线3)低于空石英坩埚时测得的 CO 量(图5,曲线2),则二曲线中间的面积应对应熔硅中增加的碳应吸收的 CO 体积.另一方面,从硅单晶的碳分布曲线可以得到总碳含量,即包括 CO 中的碳和原料多晶硅中的碳.

以图8和图4中的110#单晶为例.由碳浓度分布曲线(图4),可以求得晶体中总碳含量约为 9.74×10^{-5} 克原子,如果不考虑其它碳来源,相应的 CO 量也为 9.74×10^{-5} 克原子,即消耗的 CO 气体为 2.18 毫升.

另一方面,测量图8中曲线 2 和 3 之间面积,换算为 CO 体积是 2.88 毫升.与图4结果比较,二者十分相近.可以认为我们上述关于 CO 消耗量对应于硅中碳含量增加的机理,基本上是符合实验的.

综上所述,在目前直拉硅单晶工艺条件下,晶体生长过程中,熔融硅和石英坩埚,炉内气体和石墨加热器之间的反应以及因氩气纯度、单晶炉(包括真空系统)本身带来的碳沾污(产生的 CO 气只在 ~10ppm 以内),远不如石英坩埚与石墨托热化学反应(产生的 CO 气严重的可达 ~500ppm 以上)带来的碳沾污严重.因 CO 气与熔硅的反应,碳进入并积存于硅晶体中.

3. 降低碳沾污的途径

上面实验结果说明:直拉硅单晶在生长过程中,碳沾污主要来源于石英坩埚与石墨托在高温下热化学反应产生的 CO 气.所以要降低晶体生长过程中碳沾污可以有两个途径.一是采取措施将石英坩埚与石墨托隔开,阻止它们在高温下热化学反应的发生;另一方面是控制单晶炉内的气体流动,使石英坩埚与石墨托反应产生的 CO 气无法达到熔硅表面.我们用钼隔开石英坩埚与石墨托的实验结果和在炉内设计气流导向装置后的结果都说明,这两个途径都是可行的.当控制了石英坩埚与石墨托反应带来碳沾污后,炉内残留的 CO 气以及多晶中的碳就成了硅单晶中碳的主要来源.

四、结　　论

（1）在 1512—1660K 温度范围内测量了石英与石墨反应,它主要以下列形式进行:
$$C+SiO_2 \longrightarrow SiO+CO$$

（2）在 1512—1660K 温度范围内,SiO_2 与 C 反应生成的 CO 平衡蒸气压和温度的关系可表示为:
$$\lg P_{CO}^0(托) = 17.62 - 2.73 \times 10^4/T$$

（3）在拉制硅单晶过程中,碳沾污主要来源于石英坩埚与石墨托间热化学反应产生的 CO 气.CO 气在熔硅表面与硅反应进入硅内,经分凝即积存在硅晶体中.

（4）将石英坩埚与石墨托隔开或选取适当的气流方式使 CO 气不能达到熔硅表面,都可以减少工艺过程中的碳沾污.

（5）热处理后硅单晶中的体层错密度与碳含量有关,碳含量的增高导致体层错密度增加.

参考文献

[1] 摘要见《第二届硅及集成电路学术会议》文集,p.5(1981).

[2] T. Abe, K. Kikuchi, S. Shirai and S. Muraoka. Semiconductor Silicon, p.54(1981).

[3] R. Baron, J. P. Bankus, S. D. Allen, T. C. McGill, M. H. Young, H. Kimura, H. V. Winston and O. J. Marsh, *Appl. Phys. Lett.*, 34, 257(1979).

[4] C. E. Jones, David Schafer, W. Scott, and K. J. Hager, *J. Appl. Phys.*, 52, 5148(1981).

[5] J. R. Davis, A. Rohatgi. B. H. Hopkins, P. D. Blais, P. Bai-Choudhury, J. R. McCorrnick and H. C. Card, *IEEE Trans.* ED-27, 677(1980).

[6] N. Akiyama, Y. Yatsnrugi, Y. Endo, Z. Imэyoshi and T. Nozaki, *Appl. Phys. Lett.*, 22, 630(1973).

[7] M. Tajima, T. Masui, T. Abe and T. Iizuka, Simiconductor Silicon, 72(1981).

[8] Y. Tarui, *Jpn. J. Appl. Phys.*, 19. Suplement. 19-1. 15(1980).

[9] 岸野正刚,《电子通讯学会志》,别刷 63, 8 号(1980).

[10] 梁骏吾、邓礼生、郭钟光、郑红军、刘凤祥,《第二届硅及集成电路学术会议》文集,p. 10(1981).

[11] J. A. Baker, Semiconductor Silicon, p. 566(1969).

[12] Y. Endo. Y, Yatsurugi, Y. Zerai and J. Nozaki. *J. Electrochem. Soc.* 126,1422(1979).

[13] F. Schmid and C. P. Khattək, *J. Electrochem. Soo.*, 126. 935(1979).

[14] 梁连科,《半导体材料硅论文集》,中国金属学会,p. 83(1980).

[15] Y. Yatgurugi, N. Akiyama and Y. Endo. *J. Electrochem. Soc.*, 120,975(1973).

[16] T. Nozaski, Y. Yatsurugi and N. Akiyama, *J. Electrochem. Soc.*, 117,1566(1970)

[17] F. W. Voltmer and F. A. Padovani, Semiconductor Silicon, p. 75(1973).

[18] N. Inone, K. Wada and J. Osaka, Semiconductor Silicon, 282(1981).

[19] О. А. Ремнэов, М. А. Илвии, Г. П. Боронана, Л. В. Насупкииа, *Цветнble меtаnnbl*, 9, 62(1982).

Studies on Carbon Contamination during Czochraski Growth of Silicon Crystals

Liang Junwu, Huang Dading, Wang Guangchuan,

Yin Enhua and Yang Xuezhen

(*Institute of Semiconductors, Academia Sinica*)

Abstract: Transportation method is used in combination with gas chromatographic technique to measure CO pressure in equilibrium with SiO_2 and C under 1512—1660K. For the above temperature range, the values for equilibrium CO Pressure can be determined. To compare with the thermodyanmical data, it is concluded that the reaction $C + SiO_2 \rightleftharpoons SiO + CO$ is the predominated reaction between SiO_2 and C. The composition of the outgoing gas from the furnace during CZ process is measured. The predominant gaseous product is found to be CO and SiO and the formation of CO only takes place whten there is a quartz crucible in the graphite pedestal, By using a Mo sheet to separate the graphite pedestal from the quartz crucible, the carbon concentration in silicon crystals can be remarkably decreased.

LPE $Ga_{1-x}Al_xAs/GaAs$ 界面缺陷观察

梁骏吾　　褚一鸣　　涂相征　　沈厚运[*]

(中国科学院半导体研究所)

摘要: 本文用 1000kV 高压透射电子显微镜,研究了 LPE $Ga_{1-x}Al_xAs/GaAs$ 界面缺陷,观察到异质结 $Ga_{1-x}Ae_xAs/GaAs$ 界面附近存在的位错网络的平面和剖面分布形貌,分析了位错网络的分布特征,用高阶衍射明场和弱束暗场技术,观察到界面位错网络和 $Ga_{1-x}Al_xAs/GaAs$ 界面的位置关系。

一、引　　言

随着异质结 III-V 族化合物材料在光电器件上的广泛应用,异质结附近结构缺陷的研究引起了人们极大的关注。其中对于气相外延(VPE)的 III-V 族异质结材料做了较深入的工作,人们用化学腐蚀、金相显微镜,X 射线形貌和透射电子显微镜研究了 VPE $GaAs_{1-x}Px/GaAs$, $Ga_{1-x}Ln_xP/GaP$, $Ga_{1-x}Ln_xAs/GaAs$ 等材料中位错延伸,界面层附近由于晶格失配产生的位错网络对外延层晶格完整性的影响。[1]-[3] 对于液相外延(LPE)的 III-V 族化合物异质结材料,虽然取得了一些结果,[4][5] 但总的说来不如 VPE 材料研究得普遍和详细。尤其是对 LPE $Ga_{1-x}Al_xAs/GaAs$ 材料,由于一般器件研制过程中 x 值多取较低范围($x \leqslant 0.28$),晶格失配 $\left(\dfrac{\Delta a}{a_o} \leqslant 10^{-4} \right)$ 对缺陷分布影响较小,不能观察到界面层附近缺陷分布的明显变化。在工作用氯-甲醇化学腐蚀减薄法,制备了 90°角剖面和小角度倾斜平面样品,用 1000kV 的高压透射电镜,研究了位错在 $Ga_{1-x}Al_xAs/GaAs$ 界面分布,在较高 x 值样品中观察到界面附近存在的位错网络的平面和剖面分布的形貌像。结合高阶衍射明场和弱束暗场技术,观察到位错网络和 $Ga_{1-x}Al_xAs/GaAs$ 界面位置关系的新结果。

二、实　　验

$Ga_{1-x}Al_xAs/GaAs$ 样品是在垂直炉中 LPE 法生长的[6]样品表面结晶学方向⟨001⟩, GaAs 衬底位错密度 $N_D = 10^3 - 10^5 cm^{-2}$,外延层厚度 $1 \leqslant 80 \mu m$ 。

90°角剖面样品制备,有利于直接观察界面层附近位错分布。小角度倾斜平面样品制备,基于异质结材料缺陷分布受界面 x 值变化,主要发生在界面层附近约千埃范围内,若采用 0°角平面样品不易找到界面附近缺陷分布位置,在工作采用 1—3°角倾斜平面样品,能使界面区适当扩大,得到界面层附近缺陷分布的平面像。与 90°剖面观察结果结合

原载于:电子显微学报,1984,(2):11-16.

* 现在地址:武汉大学物理系.

得到缺陷分布的三维形貌。以上两种样品制备类似 M. S. Abrahams[7] 使用的方法。制备时使用图 1。所示氯-甲醇化学喷射腐蚀装置。样品一般减薄至 1000—2000Å，能透黄光为宜。

由于Ⅲ-Ⅴ族材料对电子吸收较大，为了提高图像清晰度，TEM 观察使用 JEM-1000 透射电镜，在 1000kv，S≥0 条件下观察。在观察剖面样品中位错网络和界面位置关系时，采用高阶衍射($0.5\vec{g}$)，明场和弱束($\vec{g}$,$5\vec{g}$)暗场技术。($\vec{g}$=[220])。[8]

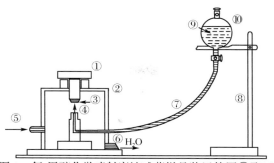

图 1　氯-甲醇化学喷射腐蚀减薄样品装置简图①聚四氟乙烯样品台②有机玻璃盒③样品④喷射液⑤进水口⑥出水口⑦导管⑧铁架台⑨氯甲醇溶液⑩分液漏斗

三、实 验 结 果

1. 90°角剖面样品 TEM 结果

图2〈i〉〈ii〉分别是$Ga_{1-x}Al_xAs/GaAs$(X = 0.37)样品界面附近位错网络在明场和暗场中剖面的 TEM 像[9]（双光束条件、衍射矢量$\vec{g}$ = [400]）另外，从衍射矢量$\vec{g}$ = [400]与 Ds 的相对位置关系，可判定 Ds 的指向是〈011〉。

由图2，我们虽然得到了位错网络的剖面形貌像，但由于位错线周围应力场的存在，在一般双光束条件下，位错线宽度有数百埃，不仅观察所得位错线分辨率不高，而且位错线和界面位置关系不明确。为此，我们采用高阶衍射和弱束暗场技术，观察图2中样品，得到图3，〈i〉〈ii〉高阶衍射明场像和弱束暗场像。图中 DL 指示界面位错网络线，Inf 指示$Ga_{1-x}Al_xAs/GaAs$界面。Inf 线上下衬度差是由于 GaAs 和 $Ga_{1-x}Al_xAs$ 两种材料晶格常数

图 2　$Ga_{1-x}Al_xAs/GaAs$(x = 0.37)样品界面位错网络剖面 TEM 像〈i〉明场〈ii〉暗场$\vec{g}$=[400]Ds 指位错网络线

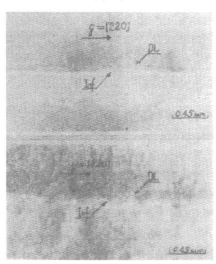

图 3　〈i〉($0.5\vec{g}$)高阶衍射充场位错网络剖面 TEM 像。〈ii〉($\vec{g}$,$5\vec{g}$)弱束暗场位错网络剖面 TEM 像$\vec{g}$ = [220]DL 指位错网络线，Inf 指 $Ga_{1-x}Al_x$-As/GaAs 界面

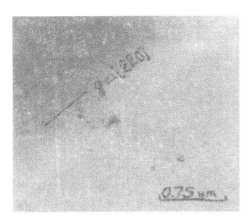

图 4　$Ga_{1-x}Al_xAs/GaAs$ 界面不存在（$X=0.16$）
位错网络剖面 TEM 暗场像。$\vec{g}=[220]$

和对电子吸收不同引起的，因此我们认为 Inf 为 $Ca_{1-x}Al_xAs/GaAs$ 界面，由 DL 线周围在明场和暗场中的衬度变化，可判定为界面位错网络线。DL 线和 Inf 线间的距离，就是其相互位置关系。图中 DL 线并不是一条严格直线，且有明显波动，这种现象和 M. HocRly 等结果不同。[3] 测 DL 和 Inf 间最小距离为 350 埃，最大距离为 650 埃，说明图中界面位错网络分布在 $Ga_{1-x}Al_xAs/GaAs$ 界面 350 埃以上约 300 埃范围内。

另外，在剖面的 TEM 样品中，我们也观察到一些 $Ga_{1-x}Al_xAs/GaAs$ 界面不存在位错网络的现象。图 4 是 $Ga_{1-x}Al_xAs/GaAs$（$x=0.16$）界面不存在位错网络样品的 TEM 暗场形貌像（$\vec{g}=[220]$）。拍摄暗场的目的是为了和图 2.〈ii〉中存在 Ds 进行比较，说明在小失配时由应力产生的衬度变化，不如较高失配时由应力或存在位错线产生的衬度变化明显。[7] 以上观察结果对晶体完整性的影响，我们将在讨论中予以说明。

2. 平面样品 TEM 结果

图 5 是与前图 2 相同样品，~1°角倾斜平面位错网络 TEM 观察结果，双光束条件，衍射矢量 $\vec{g}=[400]$。图中黑线是明场下位错线。其分布持微和其他Ⅲ-Ⅴ族异质结材料中观察结果类似。[3] 图中显示界面位错网络分布在（001）面上，网络由平行于 $[01\bar{1}]$ 和 $[011]$ 方向的位错组成。根据Ⅲ-Ⅴ族化合材料闪锌矿结构，一般说来位错滑移面是 $\{111\}$，伯格斯矢量是 $\frac{1}{2}a_0\langle110\rangle$，属 60°位

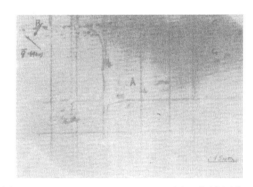

图 5　$Ca_{1-x}Al_xAs/GaAs$（$x=0.37$）界面位错网络平面分布 TEM 像。$\vec{g}=[400]$ A：失配位错；B. 来自衬底在界面变曲位错；D. Lomer-Coffrell 位错

错。从位错密度分布来看，平行于 $[01\bar{1}]$ 和平行于 $[011]$ 方向的位错并不对称。

平行于 $[01\bar{1}]$ 方向的位错密度是平行于 $[011]$ 方向位错密度的 1.2~1.5 倍。说明非中心对称的闪锌矿结构材料中，位错线在一对 $\{111\}$ 面上滑移结果不同，另外，从位错线的分布特征，可将其分为以下类型：视场中央 A 区纵横交错的可能是由于晶格失配在界面附近产生的失配位错；图中左上角标有 B 字样，位错端点有振荡现象的属于来自衬底位错，在向外延层延伸过程中，在界面弯曲的位错[8]；C_1，C_2 可能是两个 60°位错，他们互作用后形成 D 类 Lomer-Cottrell 位错。

在其他平面样品中,我们也观察到如图6所示的位错组态,在界面层中不存在密集位错网络,仅有局布位错排的 TEM 结果。该样品 X=0.29,双光束条件,衍射矢量 $\vec{g}=[220]$,由于该样品中 x 值较低,未能形成如图5中密集网络状分布位错。

图6　$Ga_{1-x}Al_xAs/GaAs(x=0.29)$ 界面局布位错排的平面 TEM 像.$\vec{g}=[220]$

四、讨论和结论

考虑到本实验观察是在 1000KVHVEM 中进行的,Ewald 球半径较大,双光束条件不易满足,加之样品中剩余应力的影响(尤其在较高 X 值样品中),得到图2中象分辨率不高,故采用弱束技术,根据弱束技术要求[8],$|Sg| \geq 2\times10^{-2}$ Å(Sg 为衍射斑点到 Ewald 球距离),几何条件:$Sg=(n-1)g2\lambda/2$,说明在 $\vec{g}$ 一定条件下,衍射阶数 n 和射电子波长 λ 成反比。前面图3中采用的 $(0.5\vec{g})$ 明场和 $(\vec{g},5\vec{g})$($\vec{g}=[220]$)弱束,是按常规的 100KVTEM 使用条件选取的,因此在 1000KVHVEM 中,衍射阶数 n 应予以修正,但从 λ 与 n 的反比例关系,这种修正难以实现。从我们所得结果来看,图3中结果虽然图像衬度要弱一些,但位错线的分辨率比图2中的结果要高,更重要的是获得了 DL 和 Inf 的位置关系的结果。

对于 LPE $Ga_{1-x}Al_xAs/GaAs$ 中界面位错络对外延层晶格完整性的影响,我们已作过一些探讨[9]。观察到在 CaAs 衬底 $N_D \leqslant 10^4 cm^{-2}$ 样品中,在 x=0.35—0.37 的 $Ca_{1-x}Al_xAs/GaAs$ 界面产生适度的位错网络,能阻止衬底位错向外延层延伸,获得无位错的 $Ca_{1-x}Al_xAs$ 外延层,这一结果和 kishino[10] 的观点不同。其主要理由是:在高 x 值样品中,界面晶格失配增加,因而在界面层附近产生 A 类失配位错,使界面应力得以释放,又由于 A 类位错密度一般高于衬底中位错密度 1—2 数量级,因此衬底位错在向外延层延伸过程中和界面失配的 A 类位错互作用,并沿界面滑移的几率大大增加,从而减少了衬底位错向外延层延伸的可能性。界面失配应力除产生失配位错外,失配应力作用于来自衬底位错上,使其弯曲,并沿界面滑移,构成界面网络的一部分,这就是图5中 B 类位错。类似结果在四元系 $Ca_{1-x}Al_xAs_{1-y}P_y/GaAs$ 中也有报导[4]。由图(5)中 G_1,G_2 构成的 D 类 Lomer-Cottrell 位错可表示如下反应:

$$C_1+C_2 \longrightarrow D \qquad \vec{b_1}+\vec{b_2}=\vec{b_3}$$

b_1,b_2 分别是 C_1,C_2 的伯格斯矢量:

$$\vec{b_1}=\frac{1}{2}a_0[101],\vec{b_2}=\frac{1}{2}a_0[\bar{1}10]$$

C_1,C_2 相互平行于 $[01\bar{1}]$,属 60°位错,所以:

$$\vec{b_1}+\vec{b_2}=\frac{1}{2}a_0[101]+\frac{1}{2}a_0[\bar{1}10]=\frac{1}{2}a_0[011]=\vec{b_3}$$

显见,$\vec{D}\perp\vec{b_3}$,这样由 C_1C_2 组成的 Lomer-Cottrell 位错是 90° 刃型位错,由于闪锌矿结构中多数为 60° 位错,这种 90° 刃型位错存在的几率较小,在构成界面网络中占有的比例也少。

有关异质结界面晶格失配,失配应力对产生网络临界厚度 h_c 和失配率 f 的关系,Matthews[11] 提出了详细的理论模型和以下计算公式:

$$f=\frac{b(1-v\cos^2 a)}{8\pi h_c(1+v)\cos\lambda}\left[\ln\left(\frac{h_c}{b}\right)+1\right] \tag{1}$$

式中 b 为柏格斯矢量,v 是泊松比,a 是柏格斯矢量 $\vec{b}$ 和界面层中位错线夹角,λ 是位错滑移方向和垂直于滑移面与样品表面交线的膜平面方向间的夹角,f 是晶格失配率。

根据我们图(3)中的测量结果,取 $h_c=350\text{Å}$,$v=0.3$,$\cos\alpha=\frac{1}{2}$,$\cos\lambda=\frac{\sqrt{2}}{2}$,$b=4.5\text{Å}$ 代入上式计算 $f\doteq2.78\times10^{-3}$,这个结果和 pierron[12] 等人用双晶衍射测量的 GaAs 与 $Ga_{1-x}Al_xAs(x=0.37)$,失配率 $\frac{\Delta a}{a_0}\doteq4.5\times10^{-4}$ 高约 5 倍多,说明理论计算和观察实际数据仍有一定差距。类似有关对 Matthews 理论公式的论证,Kunishige[13] 等人用 $Ga_{1-x}In_xAs_{1-y}P_y/InP$ 材料实验结果进行了对比,和我们的观点有类似之处,由此可见图(3)中的结果,对其他 Ⅲ-Ⅴ 族化合物材料中晶格失配与界面位错网络的理论关系的论证,也是很有意义的。

对于 $Ga_{1-x}Al_xAs/GaAs$ 界面层中位错网络的存在,及其对材料电学性能影响的研究,有待今后进一步完善。

本工作曾得到林兰英先生的热情关怀和鼓励,本所一室107,103组和有色院电镜组给予了大力帮助,在此一并致以谢意。

参考文献

[1] Dupuy, M. & Lafeuille, D., *J. Crystal Growth*. 31, 244(1975).

[2] G. H. Olsen, *J. Crystal Growth*. 31, 223(1975).

[3] M. Hockly, M. AI-Jassim, C. R. Booker and R. Nicklin, *J of Microscopy*, 118, 117(1980).

[4] G. A. Rozgonyi, P. M. Pettroff and M. B. Panish, *Appl. Phys. Lett.*, 24, 251(1974).

[5] K. Ishida and T. Kamejima, *J of Electronic Materials*, 8(1), 57(1979).

[6] 涂相征,砷化镓及其他Ⅲ-Ⅴ族化合物半导体会议文集,333(1977).

[7] M. S. Abrahams, L. R. Weisberg, C. J. Buiocchi, and J. Blance, *J. Mater Sci.*, 4, 223(1969).

[8] Gareth Thomas, *Transmission Electron Microscopy of Materials*, (5th, 1979) Printing in Oxford University, Lodon, 116.

[9] 沈厚运,梁骏吾,褚一鸣.《半导体学报》5.(3),226(1984).

[10] S. Kishino, *Proceedings of 7th Inter Conf on Cystal Growth*, Tokyo, Janpan. 303, (1975).

[11] J. W. Matthews, S. Mader, and T. B. Light, *J. Appl. Phys.*, 41, 3800(1970).

[12] E. D. Pierron, D. L. Pettroff and M. B. Panish, *J. Crystal Growth*, 27, 106(1974).

[13] Kunishige Oe, Yukiuobu shinoda and koichi Sugiyama, *Appl. Phys. Lett.*, 33, 962(1978).

STUDY OF INTERFACE DEFFCT ON LPEGa$_{1-x}$Al$_x$As/GaAs

Liang Jun-Wu, Chu Yi-ming, Tu Xiang-zheng, Shen Hou-yun [*]

(*Institute of Semiconductor, Academia Sinica*)

Abstract: In this paper, the interfacial defect of LPE Ga$_{1-x}$Al$_x$As/GaAs was investigated by 1000KVHVEM. The three dimensional distributions of the dislocation network at the interface of Ga$_{1-x}$Al$_x$As/GaAs were obtained and analyzed.the distance between the dislocation network and the interqace of Ga$_{1-x}$Al$_x$As/GaAs was studied and measured in high order-bright field and weak beam dark sield.

[*] Present address: Department of Physics, Wuhan University.

Si-C 相图的研究及碳对硅单晶质量的影响

梁骏吾　邓礼生　郑红军

(中国科学院半导体研究所)

摘要：本文用气相掺杂法得到低氧区熔硅晶体中熔点附近碳的固溶度为 $8.6 \times 10^{17} \mathrm{cm}^{-3}$。并指出不同的碳含量对晶体结构缺陷产生的影响。当 $1423\mathrm{K} \leqslant \mathrm{T} \leqslant 1573\mathrm{K}$ 时，碳的固溶度表达式为 $[\mathrm{C}] = 3.0 \times 10^{26} \exp(-66\mathrm{kcal/RT}) \mathrm{cm}^{-3}$。求出了 Si-C 相图的硅侧。

一、引　言

高纯硅单晶中一般杂质浓度可以降至 $10^{13} \sim 10^{12} \mathrm{cm}^{-3}$，然而碳、氧元素含量却较高。直拉硅单晶中碳含量一般为 $10^{16} \sim 10^{17} \mathrm{cm}^{-3}$；区熔硅单晶中碳含量达 $10^{16} \sim 10^{15} \mathrm{cm}^{-3}$。碳在硅单晶中是有害杂质。当碳含量为 $5 \sim 10 \times 10^{16} \mathrm{cm}^{-3}$ 时，对功率器件的不利影响很明显，影响中子嬗变掺杂单晶的退火性质[1]。碳的沉淀物降低器件的击穿电压，使 V - I 曲线变软[2]。在掺铟的硅单晶中，代位碳和代位铟结合形成 0.111eV 的受主能级[3]，碳和其余的 III_A 族元素也能形成 C-III_A 对。碳还会降低太阳能电池的效率[4]。文献[5]认为，当氧、碳同时存在时，碳会作为氧沉淀的核心形成氧游涡。我所的工作[6]发现，直拉硅单晶中的体层错密度与碳含量有对应关系，当碳含量增大时，体层错密度增大。直拉硅晶体经 650℃ 热处理时，会产生新施主，报道说碳对新施主的形成有核化作用[7]。

总之，研究碳的有害作用，研究硅单晶热处理中碳的行为，必然要了解碳的溶解度。然而文献中有关碳在硅熔点附近的溶解度数值十分不一致（见表 1）。

R.N.Hall 等[8]和 R.I.Scace 等[9]是将 SiC 浸入液硅后求出 SiC 的失重量，然后求出液硅中碳的溶解度，再乘以碳的分凝系数 0.07[10]，分别得到表 1 所列的 $4.9 \times 10^{17} \mathrm{cm}^{-3}$ 和 $1.75 \times 10^{17} \mathrm{cm}^{-3}$。

T.Nozaki 等[10]是将胶体石墨涂在硅棒表面上，然后进行区熔，当熔区出现 SiC 时，测量硅中碳含量为 $3.5 \times 10^{17} \mathrm{cm}^{-3}$，它被定为硅熔点附近碳的固溶度。此数值经常为人们引用，但是在区熔过程中，局部硅的熔化时间是比较短的，很难保证固体碳颗粒充分溶解，如果溶解不饱和，则测定值偏小。

A.R.Bean 和 Newmaon[11]是将含碳量较多的直拉硅单晶进行热处理，求出 1350℃ 以下的固相线，外推至熔点附近得到 $4.5 \times 10^{17} \mathrm{cm}^{-3}$ 的溶解度值。

F.W.Voltmer 等[12]在直拉炉中气相引入碳或用 $\mathrm{BaCO_3}$ 加入坩埚里，测得溶解度为 $9 \times 10^{17} \mathrm{cm}^{-3}$。直拉硅的含氧量很大，因而要考虑氧的影响，必须在无氧的样品中进行测定。

原载于：稀有金属，1987，336-342.

表1 熔点附近碳在硅中的固溶度

实验者	固溶度,cm^{-3}
R.N.Hall[8]	4.9×10^{17}(按液硅中溶解度标准)
R.I.Scace 等[9]	1.7×10^{17}(同上)
T.Nozakl 等[10]	3.5×10^{17}(区熔硅,固体掺杂剂)
A.R.Bean 等[11]	4.5×10^{17}(外推值)
F.W.Voltmer 等[12]	9×10^{17}(直拉晶体数据)
Endo 等[13]	3×10^{17}(外推值,3.48×10^{17}校正值)

Endo 等[13]求得固溶度的温度关系式为:

$$4.0×10^{24}\exp(-\Delta H/RT)\,cm^{-3}$$

其中 $\Delta H = 55$kcal/mol。由此外推得到熔点时 $3.0×10^{17}$cm^{-3} 的溶解度值。校正换算系数后为 $3.48×10^{17}$cm^{-3},这数值明显的低了。

根据以上所述,碳在硅中固溶度的文献数值十分不一致。此外碳对单晶完整性的影响也是很有意义的问题。本文是用气相方法对区熔硅掺碳,研究了碳含量对硅单晶完整性(即出现位错、游涡缺陷以及多晶)的影响,测定了熔点附近碳在硅中的固溶度,并进行等温热处理,测得碳的固溶度曲线。在此基础上绘出了 Si-C 相图的硅侧液相线、固相线及固溶度线,并对此数值进行了讨论。

二、实 验 方 法

考虑其它杂质对碳在硅中溶解度的影响,尤其直拉单晶中有 ~1×10^{18}cm^{-3} 的氧可能会影响测量,所以我们使用区熔法。考虑固体碳颗粒或 SiC 颗粒溶解速度较慢,我们采用 CH_4+Ar 气相掺杂方法。CH_4(甲烷)在液硅表面热分解,碳进入熔区,这样生长的晶体氧含量均小于红外检测灵敏度(<1×10^{16}cm^{-3})。

为了比较,我们又采用 CO 为掺杂剂,以便同时掺入氧和碳,CO 也用氩气稀释到含 CO 千分之一。

区熔炉是国产 L4575-ZE 型区熔单晶炉,采用单匝感应线圈。CH_4 是北京氧气厂配制,经氩气稀释含量为 10%,通入炉膛进一步稀释,其浓度用本所气相色谱分析测定。

晶体生长方向〈111〉,多晶棒高纯不掺杂,晶体电阻率为 $2×10^2 \sim 2×10^3 \Omega \cdot cm$。P型,采用缩细颈生长无位错硅单晶,熔区移动速度为 2~5mm/min,转速为 20rpm。

用红外分光光度计在室温下测量硅中代位碳含量,样品厚约 2mm,经磨抛清洁处理后测量,由一"无碳"样品作参比,按下式计算碳的浓度

$$N_{[C]} = 1.1×10^{17} \cdot \alpha\,cm^{-3} \tag{1}$$

式中 $N_{[C]}$ 为碳浓度,α 为吸收系数。

样品的完整性用 Wright 或 Sirtl 腐蚀剂显示后,用 Normarski 光学显微镜观察。样品表面用 Φ550 型多用途能谱仪分析。

为了确定碳的固溶度曲线,同时阐明氧在硅中对碳沉淀的影响,我们采用不同含碳量的直拉硅样品以及区熔样品进行等温热处理。样品热处理前和后,均用红外方法测量

氧、碳含量。热处理前,样品经化学清洗后送入扩散炉内进行热处理。用高纯氩气或氮气为保护气体。热处理后将表面重新磨、抛、清洗后再进行测量氧、碳含量。为了形成沉淀核心,使样品先在低温 750℃处理 4h 以上,后高温(1150~1300℃)处理,热处理时间为 50~100h,在某一温度处理,直到碳浓度不再下降为止。

三、实 验 结 果

1. 表面膜的 Auger 谱分析

熔区建立,正常移动以后,通入含 CH_4 的混合气体。炉室里甲烷含量约 700ppm,这时结晶表面虽然发灰,但单晶仍然正常生长。CH_4 含量增加到 1000ppm 以后,熔硅表面出现一层膜,并逐渐布满熔区表面,此时单晶被破坏,生长成多晶。

对表面膜进行 Auger 电子谱分析,结果如图 1 所示。由图 1a、b 可以看出,掺碳和不掺碳单晶表面的 Auger 谱线组基本相同,显示出微弱的碳峰。然而膜表面上碳的 Auger 谱线组与前者不同,呈现典型的 SiC 型谱线组[14]。膜的出现,说明液硅里的碳浓度已饱和,有 SiC 第二相产生。以浮渣呈现的膜是 SiC。

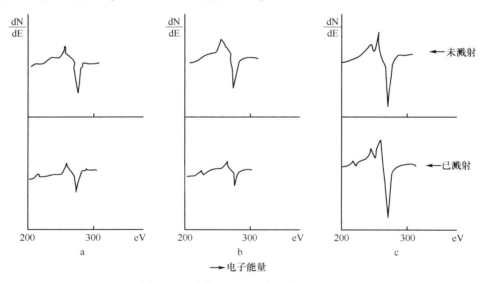

图 1 FZ 硅表面 Auger 峰的位置和形状

a.高纯无位错硅晶体表面的 Auger 峰;b.掺碳无位错硅晶体表面的 Auger 峰;c.掺碳多晶表面膜的 Auger 峰

2. 无位错单晶和有位错单晶与碳含量的关系

含碳的硅晶体在纯 Ar 中缩细颈生长无位错单晶,当无位错晶体稳定后,继续向熔区通入 CH_4 气体,随着熔区移动,晶体中的碳向尾端富集。当生长晶体内含碳量达到一定值时,就导致无位错单晶被破坏,相应晶体中含碳量约为 $5×10^{17} cm^{-3}$。有位错单晶部分,其含碳量由 $5×10^{17}$ 到 $8.6×10^{17} cm^{-3}$ 附近,此时液硅表面出现浮渣,有位错单晶被破坏。多晶部分含碳量最高达到 $8.6×10^{17} cm^{-3}$。所得区熔晶体中含氧量一律小于 $1×10^{16} cm^{-3}$。

在掺 CH_4 过程中要恰当选择 CH_4 的浓度，即不要使 CH_4 浓度太高，以致表面反应生成的碳来不及溶到液硅中去，在液硅表面形成 SiC 膜破坏单晶，这时多晶硅里碳含量一般为 $2 \sim 4 \times 10^{17} cm^{-3}$，显然不能认为这是硅中碳的饱和溶解度。如果使用低的 CH_4 浓度（$500 \sim 700ppm$），多次区熔掺杂（一般三次），一方面使碳充分溶于硅中，另一方面使溶解的碳靠分凝作用在尾部富集。那么所得晶体从无位错部分开始，中间是有位错部分，尾部出现多晶部分。如图 2 所示。这样就求得上述数值。

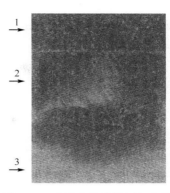

图 2　FZ 硅掺碳晶体纵剖经化学腐蚀显示照片 ×2
1.无位错；2.有位错；3.多晶

3. 区熔单晶用 CO 掺碳和氧与直拉单晶红外分析的结果

为了研究含氧晶体中碳的溶解度，我们使用 CO 掺杂剂区熔。在氧化气氛中生长无位错单晶比在 Ar+ CH_4 气氛中要困难。不过，在 CO 浓度为 500ppm 时，长出了无位错单晶。无位错被破坏时，碳含量达到 1.2×10^{17}，氧含量约为 $1 \times 10^{16} cm^{-3}$。这一数值比 $CH_4 + Ar$ 气氛中得到的 $5 \times 10^{17} cm^{-3}$ 要低，而晶体中的微缺陷密度比 $CH_4 + Ar$ 中区熔单晶高，并出现漩涡花纹。显然，由于气相掺氧时 SiO 生成妨碍单晶生长，所以用此法来观察碳含量对硅晶体结构的影响是不利的。

为了比较，我们分析了直拉硅单晶尾部含碳量，部分典型高碳样品的数据如表 2 所示。

表 2　直拉硅单晶尾部氧、碳含量

样品号	氧含量, cm^{-3}	碳含量, cm^{-3}
0—57 I	1.1×10^{18}	1.3×10^{18}
0—48	1.1×10^{18}	5.18×10^{17}
0—57 II	1.1×10^{18}	1.2×10^{18}
0—62 III	1.9×10^{18}	1×10^{18}

由表 2 可以看出，在直拉硅单晶中，当氧含量高时，碳含量可以高达 $1.3 \times 10^{18} cm^{-3}$ 而不致破坏单晶，这就是氧的影响。产生这种影响的原因似乎可以考虑硅中氧和碳反应产生[C-O]复合物，从而影响碳的溶解度。然而[C-O]复合物在高温时不易形成，所以用这种复合物来解释不太可能。碳的溶解度的提高可以解释为二杂质对晶格畸变的抵消：氧是间隙位会导致晶格膨胀，原子半径小的碳是代位，导致晶格收缩，二者互相补偿，溶解度得到提高。然而，这不是纯硅中碳的固溶度。

4. 碳含量对无位错单晶漩涡缺陷的影响

当碳含量在 $1 \times 10^{16} \sim 5 \times 10^{17} cm^{-3}$ 范围内，无位错单晶中的漩涡缺陷与单晶中碳含量是无关的。只要控制好拉速减少回熔等条件[15]，即使碳含量高也可以得到无漩涡单晶。如果控制不好，即使是低碳晶体也有漩涡缺陷。

5. 碳在硅中的固溶度曲线

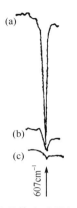

图 3　CZ 硅晶体中碳的红外吸收峰
（a）原生；（b）经 750℃+1150℃热处理；
（c）再经 1200℃100h 热处理

典型的样品退火后,红外吸收谱如图 3 所示。样品经过 750℃ 4h 和 1150℃ 50h 和 100h 退火以后 607cm^{-1} 处的吸收峰大大减少,这说明溶解态的碳浓度下降。(溶解碳浓度下降的同时,出现 12μm 处的碳沉淀峰,图中未包括)同时,样品中的间隙氧含量也下降。实验证明直拉硅单晶中碳容易沉淀。

在 1150~1300℃ 范围内用等温热处理方法测量碳在硅中的固溶度,所得温度关系如图 4 所示。我们得到碳在硅中固溶度的表示式为:

$$[C] = 3.0 \times 10^{26} \exp(-66kCal/RT) \, cm^{-3}$$

式中 1573K≥T≥1423K。由此外推到硅熔点时碳的固溶度是 8.6×10^{17}cm^{-3}.这一数值与前第三节一致,[6] 和 [12] 得到的结果相近,为了对比,图中也绘出 Bean 等[11]以及 Endo 等[13]的数据。前者外推到熔点时的溶解度数值是 4.5×10^{17}cm^{-3},后者是 3.0×10^{17}cm^{-3}。这些数值都太低了。

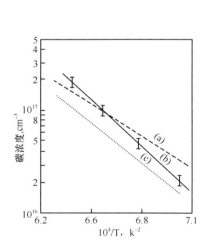

图 4　碳的固溶度曲线
（a）······Bean & Newman 工作；（b）——本工作；
（c）—·—Endo 等人工作

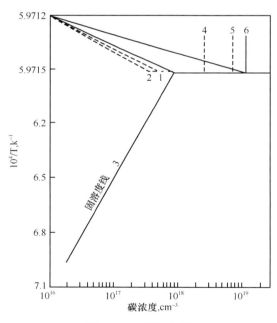

图 5　Si-C 相图硅侧
1.Bean 等人 4.5×10^{17}cm^{-3}；2.Nozaki 等 3.5×10^{17}cm^{-3}；
3.固溶度线；4.Scace 等 2.5×10^{18}cm^{-3}；5.Hall 7×10^{18}cm^{-3}；
6.本工作和 Voltmer

6. Si-C 相图的硅侧(图 5)

由所求熔点附近的固溶度 $8.6×10^{17} cm^{-3}$ 取分凝系数 $K=0.07$,求得液硅在熔点附近的溶解度为 $N_C=1.2×10^{19} cm^{-3}$,按熔点降低公式:$N_C(1-K)=\Delta H/R(1/T-1/T_m)$,求得熔点降低为 0.1K,由此得到 Si-C 相图的液相线和固相线。为了比较,将文献数值也列入图中。图中还有碳在硅中的固溶度曲线,为此,纵坐标取 $1/T(K^{-1})$,横坐标取碳浓度的对数。在熔点以上的 $1/T$ 标度和熔点以下的 $1/T$ 标度是不一样的。(见图 5,纵坐标两种标度)。

四、讨　论

1. 碳在硅中的固溶度

早期 Hall、Scace 及 Slack 的工作是用 SiC 浸入液硅中求 SiC 的失重量而求得碳在硅中的溶解度。由于(i)硅中原有的碳及(ii)加热过程中炉子引入的碳[6]会降低 SiC 的失重,所以这种数据偏低。

T.Nozaki 等的实验是用胶体石墨涂在硅棒表面,经一次区熔,取在表面出现膜时的硅中含碳量作为固溶度,但是从我们的实验得知,在出现膜的多晶硅中,用红外吸收法测碳的浓度有可能低于固溶度。我们也得到多晶硅中含碳为 $2\sim4×10^{17} cm^{-3}$ 的数值,与 T.Nozaki 等的 $3×10^{17} cm^{-3}$ 相一致,但是这数值明显地小于我们得到的固溶度数值。其原因可能是固体碳颗粒来不及溶解于液硅之中。

甲烷高温分解十分完全,(甲烷按下式分解,$CH_4 \longrightarrow C+2H_2\uparrow$,按文献[16],在 1200K 时 $P_{H_2}/(P_{H_2}+P_{CH_4})=0.985$,在 1683K 时则为 0.999。即反应基本完全,甲烷一接触到液硅表面就几乎完全分解)分解出来的原子状态的碳比较容易溶于液硅之中,即使如此也不能用太大的 CH_4 浓度,以免表面上有过多的碳元素来不及溶解而破坏单晶生长。而是经三次左右区熔,把碳富集到尾部以达到碳的真正饱和。

Bean 和 Newman 在讨论它们的固溶度曲线时也认为它们的外推值即 $4.5×10^{17} cm^{-3}$ 是太低了,他们解释说可能是 $[C]=A\exp(-\Delta H/RT)$ 这一关系到接近熔点时就不成立了,从我们的结果看,这一关系一直到熔点仍然是成立的。我们求得的固相线和熔点时碳的固溶度正好衔接。

2. 碳对单晶质量的影响

碳在硅中溶解时是代位形式,仍然为 SP^3 杂化轨道,所以一般扩散很慢,$D_{1300℃}=2.2×10^{-10} cm^2/S$。碳极不容易沉淀。所以,如果一旦用高速成晶,碳和点缺陷都迅速冻结下来,碳由于难沉淀,就不会影响微缺陷的生成。而氧、碳同时存在时,二者能共沉淀下来,微缺陷就容易出现。

Föll 等[17]认为碳与漩涡有关,仔细考察其数据,碳浓度变化是在 $2.5×10^{15}\sim5×10^{16} cm^{-3}$ 之间。我们的实验表明,在此范围内,碳与漩涡没有对应的关系。

然而,用 CO 掺杂的样品比较容易出现漩涡缺陷。似乎氧、碳同时存在就有利于微缺陷的形成。

位错产生的原因：当硅中碳含量为 $5\times10^{17}cm^{-3}$ 时，无位错晶体被破坏，而成为有位错的单晶。碳的共价半径为 0.77Å，它取代了 1.17Å 的硅，会导致晶格收缩。在晶体横断面内，区熔硅中碳分布不均匀，如图 6 所示。这种不均匀产生的应变是 $\varepsilon=\dfrac{\Delta a}{a}=\beta N_{(c)}$，$\beta=\dfrac{1}{2}\left[1-\left(\dfrac{R_C}{R_{Si}}\right)^3\right]\Big/ N_{[Si]}$，$R_C$ 和 R_{Si} 分别是碳和硅的共价半径，Δa、a 分别为晶格常数变化量和晶格常数。碳浓度为 $5\times10^{17}cm^{-3}$ 时，产生的应变为 2.38×10^{-6}。如果是位错均匀成核，则要求应力为 $G/30$，G 为硅的切变模量。失配应力不足以产生位错均匀核化所需之量，即位错产生不是碳分布不均匀产生的失配引起。很可能是 SiC 颗粒在生长界面上引起的位错。我们的电镜实验也看到沉淀物。

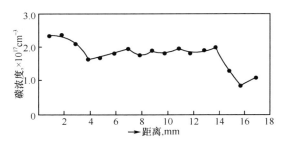

图 6　FZ 硅晶体内碳的径向浓度分布（侧—半径距离）

五、结　　论

（1）用气相掺杂法求得低氧区熔晶体中熔点附近碳的固溶度为 $8.6\times10^{17}cm$。

（2）碳在硅中含量小于 $5\times10^{17}cm^{-3}$ 时，在低氧情况下，不影响漩涡缺陷的出现与否，它只与生长条件有关。

（3）当碳含量大于 $5\times10^{17}cm^{-3}$ 时，无位错单晶被破坏。单晶结构仍可保持。当碳含量为 $6\sim8.6\times10^{17}cm^{-3}$ 时，区熔单晶被破坏出现多晶。

（4）在 $1423K\leqslant T\leqslant1573K$ 范围内找到碳的固溶度可以用式 $[C]=3.0\times10^{26}\exp\cdot(-66kcal/RT)$ 代表，这式外推到硅熔点时和固相线正好衔接。

（5）求得 Si-C 相图的硅侧。

参考文献

［1］M.J.Hill et. al., Semicond. Silicon, 1977, 715.

［2］N. Akiyam et al., Appl. Phys. Lett., 1973, 22, 630.
　　C.E.Jones et.al., J. Appl. Phys., 1981, 52, 5148.

［3］R.Baron et. al., Appl. phys. Lett., 1979,34,257.

［4］J. R. Davis et. al., IEEE Trans ED-27. 1980, 677.

［5］Y. Tarui, JJAP, 1980, 19, Supplement, 19-1,615.

［6］梁骏吾等,1981 年第二届全国大规模集成电路与硅材料会议论文。

［7］M.Tajama et. al., Semicond. Silicon, 1981,72.

［8］R.N.Hall, J.Appl.phys., 1958, 29, 914.

［9］ R.I.Scace, J.Chem. Phys., 1959, 30,1551.

［10］ T.Nozaki et. al., JECS, 1970, 117, 1566.

［11］ A. R.Bean et. al., J.Phys. Chem. Solids, 1971, 32, 1211.

［12］ R.W. Voltmer, Semicond. Silicon, 1973, 75.

［13］ Y. Endo et. al., Anal. Chem., 1972, 44, 2258.

［14］ C.A.Chang et. al., J. Appl. Phys., 1975, 46, 3402.

T.W.Heas et. al., J.Appl. phys., 1972,43,1853.

［15］ 梁骏吾等,1979 年第一届全国大规模集成电路与硅材料会议论文。

［16］ O.Kylasehewski et. al., Metallurgical Thermochemistry, 1958.

［17］ H.Föll et. al., Semicond. Silicon,1977,565.

掺氮区熔硅单晶深能级的研究

栾洪发　梁骏吾　邓礼生　郑红军　黄大定

（中国科学院半导体研究所，北京）
1986 年 12 月 30 日收到

摘要：DLTS 测量发现，在原生掺氮区熔硅单晶中，除 $E_c-0.20eV$、$E_c-0.28eV$ 与氮相关外，$E_c-0.57eV$ 能级也与氮相关。此三能级在低于 400℃、经 0.5 小时退火均消失，同时测得三个与氮相关的新能级 $E_c-0.17eV$、$E_c-0.37eV$ 和 $E_c-0.50eV$，并研究了它们的退火行为。

主题词：深能级，硅材料，氮杂质

一、引　　言

近年来人们发现少量氮杂质存在于硅中可显著提高材料的机械强度，因此氮在硅中的行为引起了人们的广泛重视，其溶解度为 $4.5\times10^{15}cm^{-3}$，分凝系数为 7×10^{-4}[1].Tokume-ru 等[2] 和 Nauka 等[3] 对掺氮区熔硅的深能级进行了研究.文献[4-6]报道了我们对其力学性能、光学性能和电学性能的研究结果.

本文对氮在硅中引入的深能级及其退火行为进行了研究.

二、实　　验

本实验所用样品为 n 型掺氮区熔硅单晶，电阻率为 45Ω·cm 左右，氮杂质浓度由 FTIR 测定为 $1.3\times10^{15}cm^{-5}$，Schottky 势垒二极管由表面蒸金得到.我们在 77—400K 温度范围内，分别进行了原生掺氮区熔硅单晶样品，300—900℃、0.5 小时等时退火样品和 0.5—10 小时、750℃ 等温退火样品的 DLTS 谱的测量.

三、实验结果和讨论

图 1 为原生样品的 DLTS 谱，出现四个能级峰，由 $\ln c_n T^{-2}\sim 1/T$ 曲线可确定其能级位置分别为 $E_c-0.14eV$、$E_c-0.20eV$、$E_c-0.28eV$ 和 $E_c-0.57eV$.与文献[2]对比，可知 $E_c-0.14eV$ 能级与氮无关是由氧引起的，而与氮相关的两个能级 $E_c-0.19eV$ 和 $E_c-0.28eV$ 均在我们的样品中观察到，所不同的是我们还观察到 $E_c-0.57eV$ 的能级，由于不掺氮样品中未观察到这一能级，因此可判定与氮杂质相关.

将样品分别在温度为 300、400、500、…900℃ 条件下，进行 0.5 小时等时退火；在时间为 0.5、1、2、5 和 10 小时条件下，进行 750℃ 等温退火，之后进行 LDTS 测量.图 2 给出了

原载于：半导体学报，1988，9（3）：312-314.

等时退火后与氮相关能级变化,表 1 给出了等温退火后与氮相关的能级数据.

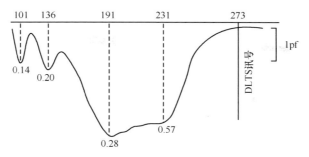

图 1　原生掺氮样品的 DLTS 谱

原生晶体	300℃退火	400—750℃退火	800℃退火	900℃退火
——0.20		——0.17		
——0.28	0.28	——0.37	——0.37	
		——0.50		
——0.57	——0.57			

图 2　掺氮样品 0.5 小时等时退火与氮相关能级的变化,单位 eV

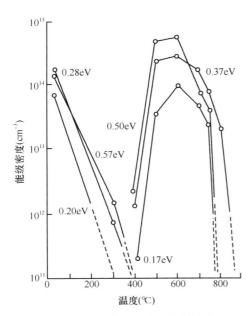

图 3　能级密度随退火温度的变化

表 1　掺氮样品 750℃等温退火后的能级数据

退火时间 (小时)	能级位置 $E_c - E_T$(eV)	能级密度 N_T(cm^{-3}) *
	0.17	2.1×10^{13}
0.5	0.37	7.0×10^{13}
	0.50	3.5×10^{13}
	0.17	1.7×10^{13}
1	0.37	4.4×10^{13}
	0.50	2.9×10^{13}
2.5.10	无能级峰	

图 3 给出了与氮相关能级密度在 0.5 小时等时退火下随退火温度的变化.由上可见,经 300℃、0.5 小时退火,能级 $E_c - 0.20\text{eV}$ 消失,400℃、0.5 小时退火,$E_c - 0.28$ 和 $E_c - 0.57\text{eV}$ 两能级均低于检测极限,同时形成三个新能级 $E_c - 0.17$、$E_c - 0.37$ 和 $E_c - 0.50\text{eV}$,与未掺氮样品对比,可知此三能级均与氮杂质相

---

* 由于样品电阻率为 $45\Omega \cdot \text{cm}$,这里和图 3 所列浓度值只具有相对意义.

关.其能级密度随温度上升而增加,600℃时均达极大,而后随温度上升而减小,800℃、0.5小时退火,只观测到 $E_c-0.37eV$ 一个能级,经900℃、0.5小时或750℃、2小时以上退火,所有能级均消失.因此氮在硅中引入的深能级均可经高温退火消除。

四、结　　论

（1）在原生掺氮 n 型区熔硅单晶中存在 $E_c-0.20$、$E_c-0.28$ 和 $E_c-0.57eV$ 三个与氮相关的能级,他们在低于400℃、经0.5小时退火均可消除.

（2）在温度高于400℃退火又出现 $E_c-0.171$、$E_c-0.37$ 和 $E_c-0.50eV$ 三个与氮相关的新能级,它们在900℃以下、经0.5小时退火或750℃、2小时以上退火均可消除.因此氮引入的所有深能级均可通过退火消除.

作者感谢本所深能级组和中国科技大学研究生院半导体教研室的大力协作.

参考文献

[1] Y. Yatsurugi, N.Akiysms, Y.Endo and H.Nozaki *J.Blectrochem*.Soc., 120, 975, (1973).

[2] Y.Tokumaru, H.Okushi, T.Masui and T.Abe *Jpn.J.Appl.Phys*., 21, L443(1982).

[3] K.Nauka, M.S.Goorsky, H.C.Gatos and J.Lagowski, *Appl.Phys.Lett*. , 47, 1341(1985).

[4] 梁骏吾、邓礼生、范缇文、郑红军、刘风祥,第三届全国半导体集成电路、硅材料学术会论文集,p.30,(1983).

[5] 梁骏吾、邓礼生、栾洪发、郑红军,第四届全国半导体集成电路、硅材料学术会论文集,p.48,(1985).

[6] J.W.Liang, L.S.Deng, H.F.Luan and H.J.Zheng proceeding of the International Conference on Semiconductor and Integrated circuit Technology, eds.x.y.Wang and B.X.Mo, p.771, (1986).

Deep Level Investigation of N-Doped FZ Si Crystals

Luan Hongfa, Liang Junwu, Deng Lisheng
Zheng Hongjun and Huang Dading

(*Institute of Semiconductors, Academia Sinica, Beijing*)

Abstract: The deep levels related to nitrogen in N-doped FZ Si crystals were studied by DLTS.Level located at $E_e-0.57$ eV related to nitrogen was observed besides the two levels, $E_e-0.20$ eV and $E_e-0.28$ eV, observed by others.After annealing at 400℃ for 0.5 hr., the three levels vanished and three new levels related to nitrogen were formed.They were located at $E_e-0.17$ eV, $E_e-0.37$ eV and $E_e-0.50$ eV.Their annealing behavior was studied.

Keywords: Silicon, Deep levels, Nitrogen impurity

Ge 在 GaAs 液相外延中的行为

杨　辉　梁骏吾

（中国科学院半导体研究所,北京）

1987 年 2 月 25 日收到

摘要:本文用霍耳、SIMS、电化学 C-V 和光致发光等方法,研究了在 550℃ 至 950℃ 生长温度范围内 LPE GaAs 中 Ge 的分凝行为以及占 Ga 位 Ge 原子与占 As 位 Ge 原子的占位比. 得到 Ge 的分凝系数随生长温度降低而增大,占位比 Ge_{Ga}/Ge_{As} 随生长温度降低而减小。

关键词:分凝,砷化镓,晶体生长,液相外延

一、前　　言

在 GaAs 液相外延工艺中,由于 Ge 的蒸汽压低,扩散系数小,可避免多层外延时由于气氛产生的源溶液的相互沾污以及层与层间杂质互扩散的影响,因此 Ge 成为多层、薄层异质结器件的重要的 P 型掺杂剂. 研究 Ge 在 GaAs 液相外延时的分凝系数及其随生长温度的变化关系以及两性掺杂元素 Ge 的占位情况,对器件材料的生长及掺杂控制都具有重要意义,对研究生长过程中杂质与材料的相互作用也具有重要意义. 许多作者研究了 Ge 在 LPE GaAs 中的分凝系数以及与掺杂量的关系[1-6],但分凝系数与生长温度的关系以及占位比与生长温度的关系研究比较少. 文献报道的两篇文章得到的分凝系数与生长温度的关系完全相反[6,7],数值上有数量级的差别.

本工作在更广的温度范围(550—950℃)研究 Ge 在 LPE GaAs 中的分凝系数,以及 Ge 的占位情况. 通过大量重复性实验,包括液相外延生长,变温霍耳测量和数据分析,电化学 C-V 测量,二次离子质谱,光致发光实验,使结果的可靠性得到进一步的保证.

二、实　验　方　法

我们的两个生长系统都是滑动石英舟开管生长系统,这种石英系统比石墨系统更易获得高纯度外延层. 整个生长过程中反应管内部都通有一定流量的经钯管净化的高纯氢气. 生长前先对生长溶液在高温下进行烘烤. 生长溶液是过饱和的,初始过冷度控制在 5℃ 左右,降温速率为 0.5℃/min,降温范围 15℃.〈100〉掺铬半绝缘衬底. 生长前需经化学腐蚀以去除表面的机械损伤和氧化层. 掺杂剂锗是以元素锗的形式直接溶解于生长溶液中的. 我们分别在两个系统上作了十几个系列样品,初始生长温度从 550℃ 变化到 950℃. 同一系列样品生长溶液中锗浓度不变,只改变生长温度. 不同系列相比较以保证结果的重复性.

原载于:半导体学报,1988,9(4):429-434.

三、结果与分析

1. 系统与纯度

外延层中杂质锗的浓度主要是通过电学方法确定的. 当外延层中含有除锗外的其它电活性杂质时, 就要对锗的能级进行补偿. 因此其它杂质的存在会影响杂质锗浓度的确定. 为此我们进行了不掺杂的空白实验, 观察背景杂质的浓度.

我们分别在两个系统上做了实验. 两系统的主要差别为系统清洁度不同. 在系统 I 上, 557℃ 时可以得到 $n = 2.7 \times 10^{15}\,\text{cm}^{-3}$, $\mu_{300} = 6710\,\text{cm}^2/\text{V} \cdot \text{s}$, $\mu_n = 3.8 \times 10^4\,\text{cm}^2/\text{V} \cdot \text{s}$ 的外延层, 而我们的掺杂样品掺杂量都大于 $2 \times 10^{17}\,\text{cm}^{-3}$, 本底杂质浓度与锗的浓度相差两个数量级, 因此我们可以认为样品中的载流子主要是由杂质锗决定的, 而本底杂质的影响可忽略. 系统 II 的清洁度比系统 I 稍差, 但在 720℃ 左右仍可以重复得到 $n = (1.4 - 1.5) \times 10^{15}\,\text{cm}^{-3}$, $\mu_{300} = 6600 - 6950\,\text{cm}^2/\text{V} \cdot \text{s}$, $\mu_{77} = (4.8 - 5.3) \times 10^4\,\text{cm}^2/\text{V} \cdot \text{s}$ 的外延层.

从掺杂样品的迁移率与理论值迁移率的比较也可以看出本底杂质的影响. 生长前对生长母液进行高温处理后生长的样品本底杂质浓度低, 迁移率接近甚至超过了理论值[a], 如图 1 所示. 而不对母液进行高温处理生长的样品, 迁移率就要低得多, 这说明样品中本底杂质有严重的补偿. 分析文献[6]的数据可得, 他们的样品迁移率与我们的未经母液高温处理生长的样品迁移率相近.

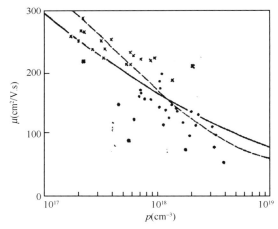

图 1   霍耳迁移率与载流子浓度的关系   实线是[8]的理论值, 虚线是[12]的理论值. 实验点是我们的测量结果

×　系统 I 样品 ⎫
○　系统 II 样品 ⎭ 溶液经高温处理　　● 系统 II 样品, 溶液未经高温处理

2. Ge 在 GaAs 中的占位情况及其温度关系

测量用的掺杂样品都是严格控制本底杂质浓度生长的样品, 掺杂量比本底杂质浓度

大两个多数量级. 因此,用电学方法测量到的杂质浓度就是杂质锗的浓度,补偿度 N_d/N_a 就是占 Ga 位和占 As 位的 Ge 原子数之比.

通常用 B-H 公式计算补偿度时是假设在室温时杂质是全部电离的,即总杂质浓度 N 等于

$$N = (N_a^- + N_d^+)_{300K}$$

其中 N_a^- 和 N_d^+ 分别是 300K 时的电离受主和施主. 由于 Ge 在 GaAs 中的受主电离能比较大,300K 时受主杂质不能全部电离,实际测量发现,从 300K 至 500K 载流子浓度增大了 1.4 倍左右,即只电离了 60%—70%. 因此需要考虑受主电离能的影响. 我们是用 B-H 公式结合杂质电离的统计分布,根据 77K 和 300K 时的载流子浓度和迁移率数据来计算占位比和杂质总浓度的. 由于受主电离能 E_a 与杂质浓度 N 有关[9]

$$E_a = 0.0398 - 1.80 \times 10^{-8} N^{1/3} (eV)$$

因此具体计算是用计算机迭代的办法来逐步逼近,最后得到总杂质浓度和占位比.

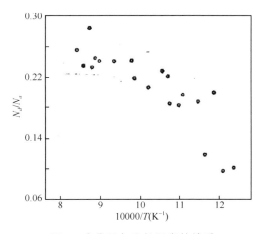

图 2　占位比与生长温度的关系

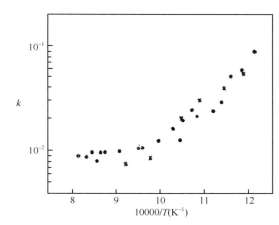

图 3　SIMS 和电学测量得到的 $k(T)$ 关系的比较
●为电学测量结果,×为 SIMS 测量结果

图 2 是如上方法得到的不同温度下生长的样品的占位比 N_d/N_a. 从图中可以看出,在 550℃至 950℃范围内,占位比随生长温度升高而增大,从 0.1 增大到 0.28,这与文献 [6]的结果是不同的.

3. 分凝系数 k 随生长温度的变化关系

分凝系数的定义为固相和液相中杂质锗的摩尔浓度之比. 液相中杂质锗是以元素锗的形式直接加到生长溶液中去的,掺锗量可用分析天平直接测量. 固相中锗的浓度是通过电学测量 N_a 和 N_d 得到的. 由于我们严格控制了生长条件,外延层中除锗外的其它杂质浓度都比锗浓度低两个数量级,因此电学测量得到的杂质浓度就等于锗的浓度.

分凝系数与生长温度的关系如图 3 所示. 我们得到的分凝系数与生长温度的关系是比较平滑的,变化趋势是分凝系数随生长温度的上升而下降. 这种变化趋势与文献 [6]的结果相反而与[7]的结果相同,但[7]的变化率比我们的结果大得多,我们的曲线在 800℃以上趋于平缓,而[7]的结果在 850℃至 950℃下降了一个数量级. 文献[4][5]

报道的结果与我们的结果符合得非常好,他们的实验点非常好地落在我们的曲线上.

4. SIMS 测量结果和电化学 *C-V* 测量结果

我们将不同温度下生长的样品在相同的条件下测量了 SIMS,得到各样品中外延层锗浓度的相对值,图 3 中的 SIMS 实验点是用电学测量结果定标后计算的分凝系数.可见用 SIMS 测出的外延层中的锗的分凝系数也是随温度的升高而下降,变化趋势与电学测量结果完全符合. SIMS 测量直接证明了我们的分凝系数随温度升高而下降的这一结果.

分凝系数与生长温度的这种变化趋势的另一个证明是电化学 *C-V* 测量结果.沿外延层生长方向,不同深度的外延层的生长温度是不同的,由于分凝系数不同,因此进入到外延层中的锗浓度也不同,载流子浓度有一个深度分布.我们用电化学 *C-V* 一边腐蚀一边测量,得到载流子的深度分布.如图 4 所示.外延层表面对应的生长温度低,分凝系数大.随深度增加,对应的生长温度升高,分凝系数减小,这与前面得到的变化趋势相同.图 4 中虚线是从已经得到的分凝系数与生长温度的变化关系计算出的载流子的浓度深度分布.可见与实际测量结果符合的非常好.这种符合也反回来证明了 $k(T)$ 关系.

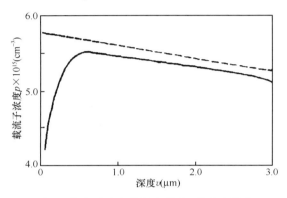

图 4 载流子浓度的深度分布,其中实线为
电化学 *C-V* 测量结果

我们用低温光致发光检测了部分样品,得到 Ge 在 GaAs 中的能级为 39.3meV,这与文献报道的结果相接近[13,14]. 我们同时测出了 Ge 受主发光峰的一级声子伴线,它与 Ge 受主发光峰的能量差为

$$E_{\mathrm{pho}} = 36.6\mathrm{meV}$$

该值与已知的 GaAs 中纵光学声子能量 36meV[13] 相一致.声子伴线与 Ge 受主峰的峰高之比约为 1/26.

我们的样品中除了 Ge 的发光峰外,没有发现其它杂质的发光峰,这说明在我们的样品中主要杂质确实是 Ge.

四、讨   论

在实验温度范围 550—950℃ 得到了分凝系数与生长温度的关系曲线 $K(T)$,随生长温度升高,分凝系数降低.由于分凝系数是通过电学测量来确定的,因此当系统不够清洁时,外延层中其它杂质的补偿严重,实验规律就不明显,甚至有相反的规律.在系统Ⅱ生长时,生长前不对溶液进行高温处理得到的几个系列实验数据,重复性很差,而且有随温度升高分凝系数增大的趋势,这是由于在生长前溶液未经高温处理,外延层本底杂质浓度较高,我们实验发现本底杂质可以达到与掺杂水平同一个数量级.因此对 Ge 受主补偿严重,尤其是当生长温度较低时,氧施主杂质的分凝系数比高温大[10]，补偿更严重．而生长前先对生长溶液进行高温处理，同样是系统Ⅱ生长的几个系列的样品，结果实验规律完全相同，分凝系数随温度上升而下降，重复性很好，且与较清洁的系统Ⅰ结果符合．

图5中给出了我们的实验结果与文献结果的比较．为了避免由于确定杂质浓度方法不一致造成的区别掩盖实验规律，图中的分凝系统都换算成载流子浓度与液相杂质浓度之比，我们称之为空穴分凝系数，记为 k_p．从图中可以看出，文献[4]，[5]的结果与我们的结果符合的非常好，他们的样品迁移率相对理论值都比较高，说明他们的样品中本底杂质引起的补偿是较低的．而文献[6]与我们的结果完全相反，他的样品迁移率都比较低，与我们的不经高温处理母液生长的几个系列样品的迁移率值接近，因此，文献[6]的结果与我们不同，除了实验条件不同引起的变化外，还可能是他们的样品本底杂质浓度较高引起的补偿造成的．文献[6]的 $k(T)$ 关系与我们未经高温处理生长的几个系列实验规律一致，都是随温度降低，分凝系数减少，这很可能是氧施主补偿的结果，生长温度越低，氧的分凝系数越大，补偿越严重，使外延层中载流子浓度

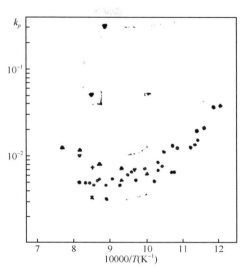

图5 分凝系数与生长温度的关系
〇和●是我们的结果，分别对应系统Ⅰ和系统Ⅱ，
+Ref.[1]，×Ref.[2]，▼Ref.[4]；▲Ref.[5]，
△Ref.[6]，▽Ref.[7]

降低．如前所述，系统不清洁时，本底杂质浓度可达与掺杂水平同一数量级，这就造成了分凝系数随温度降低而减小的假象．

文献[11]从热力学理论解释了 Ge 在 GaAs 中液相外延时的分凝行为，他的理论中使用了文献[6]的结果，即占位比不随生长温度而变化，为一常数．得到了与文献[6]符合的理论关系 $k(T)$，我们的实验发现占位比是生长温度的函数，且 $k(T)$ 关系也与文献[6]不同，因此应重新考虑理论上的解释．

五、结　论

本工作在 550—950℃ 范围内进行了掺锗液相 GaAs 外延实验，可重复得到高迁移率的外延片．用霍耳分析，SIMS，电化学 $C\text{-}V$ 等方法测量和分析了掺锗 GaAs 外延样品中杂质锗的掺杂行为，Ge 在 GaAs 中的占位比与生长温度有关，随生长温度升高，占位比也增大．Ge 的分凝系数在 550—950℃ 范围内随生长温度升高而减小．

本工作是在梁骏吾导师全面指导下完成的，龚秀英具体地指导了大部分工作，向贤碧，吴让元，李瑞云，王万年以及本所电化学 $C\text{-}V$ 测量组，光致发光组的同志也对本工作给予很大帮助，在此致以衷心的感谢．

参考文献

[1] C. R. Constantinescu and I. Petrescu-Prahova, *J. Phys. Chem. Solids*, **28**, 2397 (1967).

[2] F. E. Rosztoczy and K. B. Wolfstirn, *J. Appl Phys.*, **42**, 426 (1971).

[3] H. Kressel, F. Z. Hawrylo and P. LeFur, *J. Appl. Phys.*, **39**, 4059 (1968).

[4] J. Vilms and J. P. Garrett, *Solid State Electronics*, **15**, 443 (1972).

[5] D. R. Ketchow, *J. Electrochem. Soc.*, **121**, 1237 (1974).

[6] H. Neumann, K. Jacobs, Nguyen Van Nam. W. Koj and C. Krause, *Phys. Stat. Sol.*, (a) **44**, 675 (1977).

[7] V. N. Romanenko and V. S. Kheifets, *lsv. Akad. Nauk* SSSR Ser. Neorg. *Mater.*, **11**, 736 (1978).

[8] C. Hilsum, Progress in Semiconductors, Vol. 9, Ed. by A. F. Gidson London Heywood, (1965).

[9] 杨辉, 硕士论文, 中国科学院半导体研究所, 北京 (1985).

[10] Mutsuyuki Otaubo, Kazuaki Segawa and Hidejiro Miki, *Jpn. J. Appl. Phys.*, **12**, 791 (1973).

[11] D. T. J. Hurle, *J. Phys. Chem. Solids*, **40**, 647 (1979).

[12] J. D. Wiley, Semiconductors and Semimetals. Vol. 10, 91. Ed. R. K. Willardson and Alrest, C. Beer, (1975).

[13] F. E. Rosztoczy. F. Ermanis, I. Hayash, and B. Schwartz, *J. Appl. Phys.*, **41**, 264 (1970).

[14] P. D. Green, *J. Phys. Chem. Solids* **36**, 1041 (1975).

Behavior of Ge during LPE Growth of GaAs

Yang Hui and Liang Junwu

(*Institute of Semiconductors, Academia Sinica, Beijing*)

Abstract: The incorportion behavior and the ratio of Ge of Ga site to Ge on As site during GaAs LPE growth have been studied in a temperature range of 550—950℃ by means of Hall measurement, SIMS, electrochemical *C-V* and photoluminescence. The segregation coefficient of Ge rises as the temerature decreases and the ratio of Ge_{Ga}/Ge_{As} increases with temperature in the range of 550—950℃. A comparison between out data and those in literatures is given.

Keywords: Segrag. . . ion, Gallium arsenide, Crystal growth, LPE

杂质在硅和砷化镓中行为

梁骏吾

（中国科学院半导体研究所）

一、引　言

　　材料是半导体器件的基础,纯净的本征半导体不能直接满足器件需要,必须在纯净材料中掺入一定浓度,具有特定分布的特定杂质。从而具有器件所要求的电学、光学、力学等性质。

　　杂质与缺陷决定了半导体的非本征性质。杂质的性质与其在半导体中状态有关,此外,杂质间以及杂质与缺陷的相互作用使材料又呈现一些特别性质,这些作用和状态与温度、气氛等因素有关[1]。杂质的行为这一题目的范围十分广泛。本文从材料科学观点,阐述杂质在硅和 GaAs 中行为研究中几个最活跃的问题,着重于杂质间以及杂质与缺陷间相互作用。

二、杂质在硅和砷化镓中引入的能级

1. 硅中杂质引入能级

　　各种杂质在 Si 中能级已有许多著作[2],本文将不重复. 此文介绍的是杂质与杂质或缺陷作用后出现的结果。

　　Ⅲ族和Ⅱ族元素在 Si 能隙中引入浅受主和浅施主,其浓度可在 10^{12}—10^{21} cm^{-3} 范围变化,使 Si 的电阻率在 10^{-3}—10^{4} Ω·cm 范围变化。杂质浓度低时可以忽略其原子间作用。当浓度足够大时,杂质原子靠近,其电子轨道发生作用,分立能级展宽为杂质能带,甚至与导带或价带叠交。电离能与浓度 C 的关系为

$$Ea = Eao - AC^{1/3}$$

式中 Ea=电离能,Eao=C 极小时电离能,a=实验常数。如 Si 中硼的电离能 Ea = 0.045 - $4.5×10^{-8}C^{1/3}$ eV。

　　杂质的能级与其存在状态有关。硅中 Ge 和 C 是等电子杂质呈中性。但离子注入的 Ge 则有施主能级(Ec-0.55eV)和受主能级(Ec-0.14eV)。这二能级经550℃退火后消失。硅中 C 处代位是中性。处间隙态时具有 Ec-0.12eV 能级。间隙氧是中性,经~450℃热退火出现施主能级 Ec-0.060eV 和 Ec-0.130eV。常温下氮仅约百分之一电离,在深能谱可探测到 Ec-0.20eV,Ec-0.28eV 和 Ec-0.57eV 三个与氮相关能级[1,3,4](图1)

原载于:第二届中国材料研讨会论文集(上册),1988,17-29.

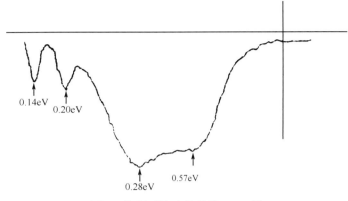

图1 掺氮区熔硅单晶的 DLTS 谱

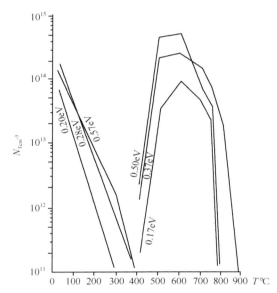

图2 氮相关的深能级在退火过程中的变化

经30℃半小时热处理以后,这三能级密度下降。Ec-0.20eV 能级已低于检测限。经400℃半小时退火以上能级均低于检测限,同时生成三个新能级,它们分别位于导带下 0.17eV,0.37eV 和 0.50eV 处,其密度在 400℃—300℃范围内随温度上升而上升。在 600℃ 达极大值。温度再继续上升,能级宽度减小,900℃半小时退火后所有深能级均消失(图2)。

杂质络合物常被命名。如图一中 Ec-0.14eV 是 O—V 络合物叫 A 中心。氧的新施主则可能是含有氧和碳的络合物。碳与Ⅲ-A 元素形成受主,即 X 中心[5],它们是 Al-C (Ev⁻ + 0.0563eV),Ga-C (Ev + 0.0563eV), In-C (Ev + 0.111eV)。E 中心则是 V 族杂质与单空位络合物[6],P-V(Ec-0.40eV),As-V(Ec-0.47eV),Sb-V(Ec-0.44eV)。我们的分析表明图的 Ec-O、eV 是 N-V 络合物。Fe 与Ⅲ族络合:FeB 呈深施主(Ev+0.1eV)和深受主(Ec-0.55eV)Fe-Al 呈深施主(Ev+0.16eV)和深受主(Ev+0.21eV)。碳在硅中是有害杂质,其行为在工作[7,8]中有详细研究。

2. GaAs 中杂质引入能级

GaAs 中浅施主电离能约为 58meV,彼此十分靠近(<0.2meV),难用 Hall 测量区分。但可用远红外光电导或光致发光来检测。Ⅵ族 S,Se,Te 是浅施主,占 As 位。

GaAs 中浅受主电离能一般为 20—40meV。相差几个到十几 meV,用低温 PL 容易检测,可察知 10^{13}cm⁻³ 的杂质。由于电子跃迁可以在导带至受主能级也可在施主与受主能级之间,所以对应每一受主有两个峰。Ⅱ族 Be,Mg,Zn,Cd 占 Ga 位,是浅能级 P 型杂质。

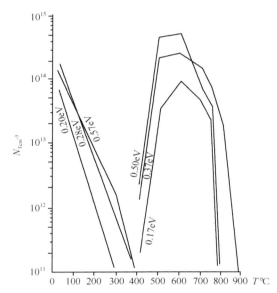

过渡元素除 V 是深施主外($Ec-0.22eV$),其余大都是深受主。如 Mn,Co,Ni,Fe,Cr 是 +2 价,取代 Ga 形成受主。按照应力模型[9]其能级为 $E = 1.78R_M\delta R(eV)$ 式中 $\delta_R = R_F - R_M$,R_M 是金属的原子半径,R_F 是外推 d 层填满时的原子半径。此模型计算一个能级有一定程度符合。但Ⅷ族有多重能级,情况比较复杂。

Ⅵ族元素是两性杂质,占 Ga 位时是 n 型杂质,占 As 位时是 P 型杂质(表1)。占 As 位与占 Ga 位的比例将在下面讨论。

表 1　两性杂质在 GaAs 中电离能[10]

	Ei(meV)(n 型)	Ei(meV)(p 型)
C	5.937	26
Si	5.854	34.5
Ge	5.908	40
Sn	5.817	167

杂质浓度高时,分立能级也将展宽为能带。例如我们测得 Ge 在 GaAs 中受主电离能等于

$$Ea = 0.0398 - 1.0 \times 10^{-8} C^{1/3} eV$$

GaAs 的热点缺陷种类比 Si 要多,所以杂质与点缺陷的络合物种类也复杂得多。例如 Si 只有一种空位。GaAs 中则有两种:形成 Si-Vga 受主中心,(332meV)Ge-Vga(受主中心,312meV),Sn-Vga(受主中心,315meV),S-Vga(受主中心,314meV),Se-Vga(受主中心,287meV),Fe-Vga(受主中心,295meV)。而与 V_{As} 形成辐射中心的有 Zn-V_{As}(143meV 光吸收),Cd-V_{As}(148meV)Ge-V_{As}(57meV)[10]等等。

3. 半绝缘 GaAs(SI GaAs)

将 GaAs 中残余浅施主(Si)或浅受主(C)补偿可以得到电阻率达 ~$10^8\Omega\cdot cm$ 的 SI GaAs。早期用水平方法(HB)生长 GaAs。由于石英和 Ga 反应所以晶体中主要残留杂质是施主 Si,可以掺深受主 Cr 来补偿 Si,当〔Cr〕>〔Si〕>〔浅受主〕时,费米能级被 Cr 钉在能隙中间,只有 Cr 能级上的电子激发到导带,而 Cr 的能级深达 0.76eV,所以电阻率可以高达约 $10^8\Omega\cdot cm$。

掺 Cr 的 SI GaAs 用于外延衬底或离子注入。外延时 Cr 向外扩散导致电阻率下降,注入层中有 Cr 和 Si 使迁移率不高,从而降低电路的速度。

1978 年用 B_2O_3 覆盖于直拉法(LEC)及用热鲜 BN 坩埚减少 Si 污染,不掺 Cr 也得到了 SI GaAs[11,12]。开始对这种不掺 Cr 的 SI GaAs 的研究。这种材料的主要剩余杂质已不是 Si,因为 BN 坩埚不引入 Si 沾污。即使用石英坩埚,如果覆盖的 B_2O_3 含有一定水(1000ppm)则熔体内含足够的氧,抑制 Ga 与 SiO_2 的反应。但干 B_2O_3 则不能。这种材料主要剩余杂质是受主碳,用红外法测得含量为 $10^{15}-10^{16} cm^{-3}$。补偿碳受主的是深施主 EL-2,其表现电离能为 $Ec-0.825\pm0.01eV$,表观俘获截面为 $\delta = 1.5\pm0.5\times10^{-18}cm^{-2}$ 纯度 SI GaAs 性能良好,850℃ 热处理(有保护层)后可保持半绝缘,离子注入分布理想,掺杂到 $10^{17}cm^{-3}$ 迁移率可达 $5000cm^2v^{-1}S^{-1}$,做成的 FET 管夹断电压一致性好。

由于 SI GaAs 的重要性,对 EL-2 进行了大量研究。开始以为 EL-2 是氧引起的。但

精确测量表明 EL-2 浓度比〔O〕大。所以这一看法被否定。EL-2 与化学比有关。HB，LEC，VPE，MBE，MOCVD-GaAs 中都有存在，但富 Ga 生长的 LPE-GaAs 中没有。生长 SI-GaAs 必需〔As〕大于 0.475。EL-2 的浓度随〔As〕下降而减少[13]，Wagner[14] 等用 EPR 观察到 ASga 缺陷。于是有人认为 EL-2 是孤立 ASga。亦有人[15] 计算出 ASga V_{As} 能级为 Ev +0.8 和 0.14eV。还有其它模型如 ASgaVga[16]，（ASga）n，[17]（A）$_4$ 和 VgaV$_{As}$[18] 模型。我国邹元烯的模型是 Asga V_{As} Vga[19] 这一问题仍在研究中。

三、杂质在 Si 和 GaAs 中的分凝系数

熔体生长和液相外延时杂质进入半导体的特征参数是分凝系数 K。K 值关系杂质分布的宏观均匀性，也关系着微观均匀性，与杂质的过饱和，成核及沉淀紧密联系。

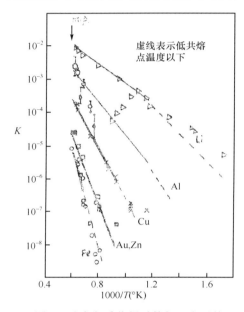

图 3　硅中杂质分凝系数与温度系数

1. 分凝系数与温度

结果结晶速度极慢，液相杂质分布均匀，杂质浓度很低，即得到平衡分凝系数 K_0。

只考虑 Si 和一种杂质的二元体系，并用理想溶液和理想固体液体近似，则 K_0 的表达式为[20]

$$LnK_0 = \frac{\Delta H}{K}\left(\frac{1}{T}-\frac{1}{T_A}\right)$$

式中 T_A 是杂质熔点，ΔH 为杂质的熔化热，此式说明 LnK_0 与 $\frac{1}{T}$ 是线关系，实验证明[21]对于低固溶度杂质在 Si 或 Ge 中都遵守这一规律。如图 3 所示。随温度上升 K_0 也增大，显然，降低生长温度可能减少杂质进入 Si 或 Ge 晶体的数量。

上述规律与 GaAs 中杂质分凝系数的温度关系却不一致，对于Ⅳ族两性杂质 LnK~1/T 关系曲线并非直线，最小值出现在~850°K[22]。Ⅳ族 Te 的 K 值随温度上升而下降，正好与 Si，Ge 中杂质相反[23]。其过程是：

GaAs 结晶或熔化　　　　　　$GaAs \xrightleftharpoons{K_1} Ga_1 + As_1$

$$K_1 = r_{Ga}[Ga][Y_{AS}[As^1] \tag{1}$$

V_{AS} 的生成　　　　　　$As_{AS} \xrightleftharpoons{K_2} A_{S1} + V_{AS}$

$$K_2 = r_{AS}[As^1][V_{AS}{}^S] \tag{2}$$

V_{ga} 的生成　　　　　　$Ga_{Ga} \xrightleftharpoons{K_3} Ga_1 + V_{ga}$

$$K_3 = r_{ga}[G_a{}^1][V_{ga}{}^S] \tag{3}$$

Te 进入晶体并电离　　　　　　$Te_1 + V_{AS} \xrightleftharpoons{K_4} Te_{AS} + e^- \tag{4}$

$$K_4 = \frac{r_{Te^s}[T_{e^s}]r_n n}{rTe^1[T_{e^1}][V_{As}]}$$

T_e 的分凝系数为

$$K_{Te} = \frac{K_2 K_1}{K_1} \cdot \frac{rT_3{}^1 rGa^1 [Ga^1]}{r_n n} \tag{5}$$

式中 ri 为 i 组元活度系数,〔i〕为 i 组元浓度,l 和 s 表液相和固相。实验得到 K_{Te} 与温度关系如图 4 所示:K_{Te} 随温度上升而下降,正好与 Si,Ge 中相反。

2. K 与化学配比的关系

化合物半导体存在化学配比的问题,液相中〔As^e〕的大小影响〔V_{Ga}〕和〔V_{As}〕,也就影响 K。Erice[24] 得到 In,C,S,Al 等杂质的 K 值随〔As〕的变化而变化(图 5)。

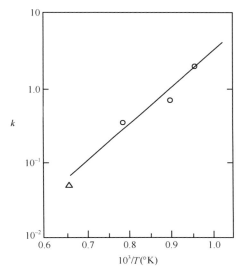

图 4　Te 在 GaAs 中的分凝系数

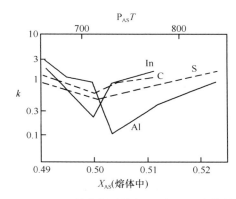

图 5　In,C,S,Al 的分凝系数与 As 的原子分数的关系

由图 5 可以看出当接近等化学比时分凝系数最小,而偏离化学配比时,无论是富 As 或富 Gs 都使这些杂质的 K 变大。应该注意的是出现这一现象的既有两性杂质 C,也有等电子杂质 In,Al,还有Ⅳ族 S。

3. Ⅳ族两性杂质在 GaAs 中的分凝

Ⅳ族 C,Si,Ge,Sn,在 GaAs 中占 As 位为受主,占 Gα 位为施主,其浓度分别为〔N_A〕和〔N_D〕,以 Ge 为例,则分凝系数有两个:$K_A = N_A / [Ge^1]$ 和 $K_D = N_D / [Ge^1]$ 总的分凝系数为

$$K = K_A + K_D$$

我们以 Ge 为例,对Ⅳ族两性杂质的分凝系数进行了实验和计算:[22]

Ge 进入 A$_s$ 位 　　　　　$Ge^1 + Ga^1 \xrightarrow{k_6} GaGe^s$ 　　　　　(6)

Ge 进入 Ga 位 　　　　　$Ge^1 + As^1 \xrightarrow{k_7} AsGe^s$ 　　　　　(7)

GaAs 结晶 　　　　　$Ga^1 + As^1 \xrightarrow{k_8} GaAs$ 　　　　　(8)

则
$$K_A = K_b r_{Ga}^{-1} \left[Ga^1 \right] r_{Ge}^{-1} \left(1 + \frac{1}{g_A} e \times P \left[(E_F - E_A)/K_T \right] \right) / 2 r_{GaGe}^s \qquad (9)$$

$$K_D = K_7 r_{As}^{-1} \left[As^1 \right] r_{Ge}^{-1} \left(1 + \frac{1}{g_D} e \times P \left[(E_D - E_F)/K_T \right] \right) / 2 r_{AsGe}^s \qquad (10)$$

(9),(10) 两式考虑了杂质能级占有情况的统计分布,式中 g_A 和 g_D 是受主和施主杂质能级的简并度,E_A 和 E_D 是占 A_s 位和占 G_a 位杂质 G_e 的电离能。要解(9),(10) 两式必须知道活度系数 K_8 和 K_7。K_1 和 K_2 的推导可以用固液相化学势平衡关系。此外将 Ga—As—Ge 三元溶液看做是规则溶液;将固相看作 GaAs—GaGe—AsGe 三元规则溶液:

$$RTln r i = \sum_{\substack{i=1 \\ i \neq j}}^{m} \alpha_{ij} X_j^2 + \sum_{\substack{k=1 \\ k<j, j \neq i, i \neq k}}^{m} \sum_{j=1}^{m} X_k X_j (\alpha_{ij} + \alpha_{ik} - \alpha_{jk}) \qquad (11)$$

式中 i,j,k 表组成,α_{ij} 表 i 与 j 的相互作用参数 X_i 表 i 组分的分子分数

经简化后得 GaGe 和 AsGe 的活度系数为:

$$RTln r_{GaGe}^s \cong \alpha^s \text{ GaAs-GaGe} \qquad (12)$$

$$RTln r_{AsGe}^s \cong \alpha^s \text{ GaAs-AsGe} \qquad (13)$$

由化学势平衡:
$$K_8 = \frac{4}{r_{Ga}^{s1} r_{Ge}^{s1}} exp \left[\Delta S_{GaGe}^F (T_{GaGe}^F - T)/RT \right] \qquad (14)$$

$$K_7 = \frac{4}{r_{As}^{s1} r_{Ga}^{s1}} exp \left[\Delta S_{AsGe}^F (T_{AsGe}^F - T)/RT \right] \qquad (15)$$

一般体系中 α 是温度的线性函数。我们发现在 GaAs—GaGe—AsGe 体系中相互作用参数不是温度的线性函数,由模拟方法我们得到下式关系:

$$\alpha_{GaAs-GaGe}^S = 21860 - 80.7T + 0.0378T^2 \text{Cal/mcle} \qquad (16)$$

$$\alpha_{GaAs-AsGe}^S = 8942 - 41.3T + 0.0211T^2 \text{Cal/mcle} \qquad (17)$$

由(12)—(17)再考虑 GaAs 能带表面弯曲确定 $E_F - E_A$ 和 $E_D - E_F$ 的温度函数,得到 K_A 和 K_D,并求得 Ge 占 Ga 位与占 As 位的比与温度关系(图6)。

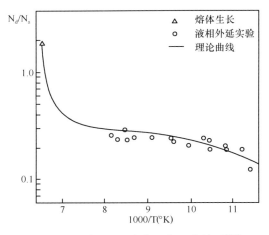

图 6　GaAs 中 Ge 的占位比与温度关系[22]

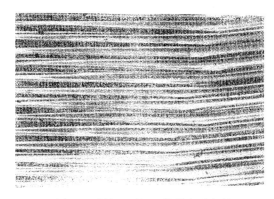

图片 1　重掺 Sb 的 Si 单晶杂质条纹

随温度上升,P_{As} 上升,V_{As} 减少,V_{Ga} 增加,占 Ga 位的 Ge 增加即施主浓度增高。计算

表明由 P 型到 n 型的转变温度是 ~1235℃。在熔点温度(1513°K)我们求得 Nd/Na = 1.59，Ge 的分凝系数为 K = 0.0483，这时晶体是 n 型。一般 LPE—GaAs 都是 P 型。

3,4. 分凝系数与生长参数波动

K_0 是平衡分凝系数。实际熔体或溶液生长时液相搅拌并不充分，固液界面有杂质堆积，杂质浓度与液体内的浓度并不相等，所以有效分凝系数 K_{eff} 并不等于 K_0，而等于

$$K_{eff} = K_0 / [K_e + (1 - K_0) \exp(-Vd/D)]$$

式中 V = 生长速度，d = 扩散层厚，D = 杂质在液相扩散系数。

实际热场是不均匀的，晶体各部分生长速度 V 不一致，对于 $K_0 < 1$ 的杂质，V 上升，K_{eff} 上升，于是引起杂质的不均匀，如上晶体旋转，于是形成了杂质条纹如图片 1 所示为重掺 Sb 的硅单晶的杂质条纹。

四、杂质与晶体完整性

1. 杂质原子失配引起应力

杂质原子半径与 Si 或 GaAs 中的 Ga 或 As 原子半径的差异可以引起应力，σ。

且 $\sigma = \left[1 - \left(\frac{ri}{rs} \right)^3 \right] \frac{Cs}{Cl} \frac{r}{1-V}$ 式中 ri 为杂质共价半径，rs 是半导体的共价半径(代位杂质)或空隙的半径(间隙位杂质)；Cs 为杂质浓度，Cl 为半导体晶体晶体原子密度，r 为杨氏模量，V 为泊松比。当应力足够大时可以引起失配位错。杂质 B，P 在 Si 中高浓度扩散时出现失配位错纲络重掺 Sb 的硅单晶自熔体生长时比较容易产生位错。K<1 的杂质在拉晶过程中逐步富集导致超过溶解度析出，这时单晶会破坏。

硅中的氧含量可达 ~$1.5 \times 10^{18} cm^{-3}$，比一般电活性杂质含量高，在热处理过程中氧会出现过饱和而沉淀，硅生成 SiO_2 时体积增大约一倍。氧沉淀是层错的核心，冲击完全位错环，发射自间隙。但是如果控制适当，可以利用这些缺陷来吸取重金属杂质从而提高器件的成品率[1]。

2. 杂质与低位错或无位错 GaAs 单晶

实验发现加入杂质对降低位错是有明显效果的[25]（图 7）。

图 7 表示(111)生长 GaAs 的位错坑密度与杂质种类以及浓度的关系。N 型杂质如 S 可以有效地减少位错，浓度达 $6-7 \times 10^{18} cm^{-3}$ 时位错可以消失，当 n $>7 \times 10^{18} cm^{-3}$ 时出现沉淀和错位密度上升。

这些杂质是电学活性的，如果单晶要求载流子浓度低或高阻，则加入等电子杂质。实验证实加入 10^{-2} 的 In 可以使 GaAs 中位错降至 $10^2 cm^{-2}$ 以下。许多工作包括[26]用杂质溶解硬化来解释此现象，并作了定量估计。In 在 GaAs 中处 Ga 位，根据扩展 X—射线精细结构 EXAFS 的数据，提出模型，认为 GaAs

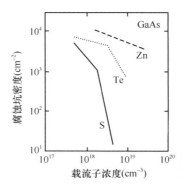

图 7 载流子浓度与晶体完整性关系

掺 In 后晶格畸变:GaAs 距离短,In—As 距离长。GaAs 母体中有五原子的 InAs 四面体单元。键膨胀 $(a_{InAs}-a_{GaAs})/a_{GaAs}=7\%$,则体膨胀为 21%。这数值比代位杂质在金属中引起的形变要大。失配的原子团球与棱位错之间的弹性作用能是:

$$E(R.\theta)=\left(\frac{\mu+(1+v)}{3\pi(1-v)}\delta V\right)\frac{\sin\theta}{r}=\beta\frac{b}{r}\sin\theta$$

式中 μ = 切变模量,b = 柏式矢量,r 为位错与球距离,θ 是 $\vec{b}$ 与指向原子团球体矢量的夹角。

$$\delta V=0.21\left(\frac{4}{3}\pi r_0^3\right)$$

根据 GaAs 的力学特性数据,求得 $\mu=48.7GPa$,$v=0.23$
$$所以\ \beta=0.666eV$$

$\theta=\frac{\pi}{2}$ 时,相互作用力最大并等于

$$F\backsimeq\frac{W(b)}{b}\frac{\beta}{b}$$

这也是杂质对位错的钉扎力。必须克服方能使位错运动。设 T 为位错线张力(图 8)按简单模型 $T=\mu b^2/2$。位错线受力后成弓形并被撑而拱高。临界角为 ϕ_c,则

$$F=\frac{\beta}{b}=2T\cos\frac{\phi_c}{2}$$

求得 $\phi_c/2=88.0°$
在滑移面 YZ 上应力 Y 向分向为 σ,则临界值为 σ_c。
$F=\sigma cbL$, L 为钉扎原子的距离。

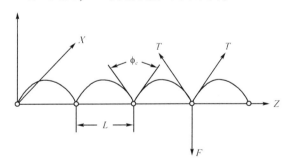

图 8 杂质钉扎位错线示意图

如果加入 3% 的 In,则 L=4b,由此得到临界应力为 420MPa。不掺杂 GaAs $\sigma\backsimeq$ 100MPa(实验值外推到室温)。说明加 3% In 后受位错运动的临界应力增加到 4.2 倍。

其它,如 Si 中氧和氮[2]也有明显的钉扎位错的效果。氮的钉扎效应十分明显,只要 $\sim10^{18}cm^{-3}$ 浓度即可抑制位错的产生和繁殖,这种低浓度即产生明显效果是十分有意义的。

五、杂质扩散与点缺陷

杂质在 Si 中扩散系数(图 9)相差很大,氢的扩散最快,不但超过任何其它元素也超过点缺陷。工作[27]得到 $D_H=0.0094cm^2/s\times exp(-0.48eV/KT)$。过渡金属在 Si 中溶解是既有代位态又有间隙态。如果金属同时占据二种位置,则温度升高时占间隙态的比例上升。快扩散过渡金属(包括 Cr,Fe,Co,Ni,Cu,Zn,Pt,Au)的扩散过程主要靠间隙扩散。

Li 是次于 H 的快扩散元素,其熔解度高达 $6×10^{19}\mathrm{cm}^{-3}$,其扩散和溶解都是间隙位。Na 的扩散速度次于 Li。

点缺陷扩散十分迅速,硅中空位尤其快,$D_v \cong 10\mathrm{cm}^2/s × exp(-1.47eV/KT)$[28] ,而自间隙的扩散系数为 $D_J = 4.2×10^{-3} × exp(S_J/K) × exp(-H_I/KT)$,式中 $570°\mathrm{K}$ 时 $S_J = 1.00K$,$H_I = 1.50eV$,$1320°\mathrm{K}$ 时 $S_J = 5.69K$,$H_I = 1.86eV$,$1650°\mathrm{K}$ 时 $S_I = 6.96K$,$H = 2.02eV$[29] 。

Ⅲ、V 族代位杂质的扩散比较慢,它们靠点缺陷。以常见的晶体管内基区硼扩散与发射区磷扩散为例:

如图 10 所示:首先在 N 型 Si 片扩硼到虚线处。左边有 Si_3N_4 保护,右边又进行浓磷扩散。扩散进行时表面有氧化层的生成。氧化层的厚度不一样,磷扩区的厚度最大。虽然硼扩散的时间是一样的,但是深度却不一致:磷扩区下面的基区扩散最快,用 Si_3N_4 保护区下面的硼扩散最慢,这一事实可以用扩散的空位和自间隙机制得到解释。Ⅲ 和 V 族杂质扩散可以通过空位机制也可以通过间隙机制如图 11 所示:[30]

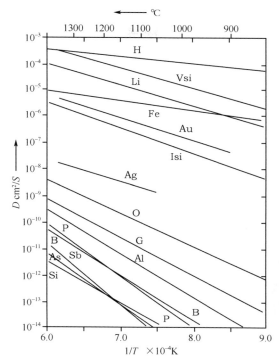

图 9　杂质知点缺陷在 Si 中扩散系数图

图 11(a)是空位型机制,(b)是通过与硅自间隙反应的扩散机制。二者浓度即 $[Vsi]$ 与 $[SiI]$ 是随温度指数上升,所以扩散速度也随滴度指数上升。在 Si 中 $[V_{si}]$ 与 $[SiI]$ 均有相当数量[1] ,它们影响扩散。

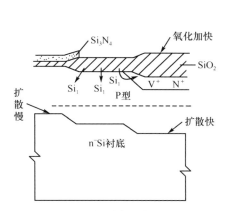

图 10　Si 中杂质扩散氧化与点缺陷的关系

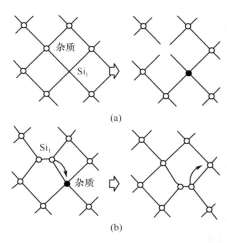

图 11　硅中杂质扩散机理(a)空位型(b)间隙型

·207·

当 Si 氧化成 SiO$_2$ 时体积膨胀一倍,有 Si$_1$ 放出所以未被 Si$_3$N$_4$ 覆盖区域氧化能不受阻碍 SiO$_2$ 形成后放出较多 Si$_1$,于是硼扩散比 Si$_3$N$_4$ 覆盖区要快。在浓磷区除有较多的 Si$_1$ 外还有高浓度电子。V$_{si}$ 有不同荷电状态;V$_{si}^-$,V$_{si}^-$,V$_{si}^+$ 和 V$_{si}^{++}$。在高掺杂区,E$_F$ 不在能隙中央,于是〔V$_{si}^-$〕和〔V$_{si}^-$〕上升(N$^+$材料)或〔Si$_1^+$〕上升(P$^+$材料)在工艺温度约 ~1000℃时本征载流子浓度 n$_i$ ≈ 10^{19}cm^{-3},所以当浓磷或浓硼扩散的浓度高于 ni 时可以发生图 11 所示的加速扩散反应。即在图 10 中 N$^+$ 区下硼扩散最快。

另一方面,硅氧化时要放出 Si$_1$,所以空位浓度高可以吸收 Si$_1$,从而加速 SiO$_2$ 生长。浓磷区的空位浓度高,所以 SiO$_2$ 也最厚。这种效应在制造 VLSI 的亚微米级器件是要考虑的。

六、氢在硅中钝化作用

作为杂质间相互作用的例子很多。H 在硅中的钝化作用是受到重视的。在 H 等离子处离 Si 以后,Si 中一些电活性杂质的作用被钝化,减少 P-N 结漏电。

H 可以钝化浅受主[31]Si 中(表面 1μm 区域)99%的 B 受主经 270℃,4 小时等离子体氢处理后失去电活性。早期有 B$^-$H$^+$时对模型解释[32]。1986 年还发现氢等离子体处理可以钝化浅施主,减少电子浓度并提高迁移率。此外 H 等离子退火还可以钝化深能级。

含 H 的 a-Si 或 a-SiC 膜对器件也有钝化作用可以降低界面态减少复合电流。

七、结　　语

杂质是研究的中心问题之一。研究杂质在半导体中的行为,不能限于孤立的杂质,特别要深入研究不同条件下杂质状态的变化以及杂质间,杂质与缺陷间的相互作用。

参考文献

[1] 梁骏吾、黄大定,第一届中国材料研讨会学术交流论文　Al—6(1986).

[2] M. Schulz in Landolt-Börnstein. New Serice Vol. 17 Semiconductors Subvolume a Physics of Group Ⅳ Elements and Ⅲ—Ⅴ Compounds Ed. O. Madelung,Springer-Verlag Berlin 1982,P. 50.

[3] Liang Jun-Wu,Den Lisheng,Luan Hongfa and Cheng Hongjun,The Proceeding of the Int. Conf. On Semiconductor and I. C. Technology,world Scientific,P. 771(1986).

[4] 栾洪发、梁骏吾,半导体学报第九卷(1988)排印中.

[5] W. Scott,Appl. Phys. Lett,32,540(1978)W. Scott,J. L,Schmit,Appl. Phys. Lett,33,294(1978).

[6] D. Kendall,D. devries,in Semiconductor Silicon,Princeton 1969 P. 358;参考文献〔2〕.

[7] 梁骏吾、黄大定、汪光川等,半导体学报,5,No. 1,26(1984).

[8] 梁骏吾、邓礼生、郑红军,稀有金属,11,No. 5,336(1987).

[9] D. L. Partin,et. al,Solid Sfafe Elecfronics,22,455(1979).

[10] L. Hollan,et. al,in Current Topics in Maferials Science Vol. 5,Cpt. 5,E. Kaldis Ed. North-Holland(1980).

[11] E. M. SWiggand,et. al,"Gallium Arsenide and Related Compounds 1978"(Inst. Phys. Conf. Ser. 45,P125,1979).

[12] T. R. Aucoin,et. al,Solid State Technology,22,No. 1,59(1979).

[13] O. E. Holmes,et. al,Appl. Phys. Lett,40,46(1982).

[14] J. R. Wagner,et. al,Solid State Commun,36,141(1980).

［15］ C. W. Myles and O. F. Sankey, Phys. Rev, B, 29, 6810(1984).

［16］ A. Goltzene, et. al, J. Appl. Phys, 56, 3394(1984).

［17］ W. Frank, "Gallium Arsenide and Related Compounds 1986"(Inst. Phys Conf. Ser. 79, P. 217, 1985).

［18］ P. J. Lin-Chung and T. L. Reinecke, Phys. Rev. B. 27, 1101(1983).

［19］ Zou Yuanxi, et. al, Gallium Arsenide and Relafed Compouncs(Inst. Phys Conf. Ser. 65, P. 49 1982).

［20］ C. D. Thurmond, in Semiconductors N. B. Hannay Ed. Cpt. 4 Reinhold, 1959.

［21］ R. N. Hall, J. Phys. Chem. Solids, 3, 63(1957).

［22］ 杨辉, 梁骏吾, 半导体学报, 第九卷(1988)排印中.

［23］ H. C. Casey, Jr. and M. B. Panish, Heterostructure Lasers, Part B, P. 98 Academic Press. 1978.

［24］ J. C. Brice in D. Shaw, Atomic Diffusion in Semiconductors Plenum, New York Cpt. 3(1973).

［25］ Y. Seke, H. Watanabe and J. Mafsui, J. Appl. Phys. 49, 822(1978).

［26］ H. Ehrenreich and J. P. Hirth, Appl. Phys Letters, 46, No. 7, 668(1985).

［27］ Van A. Wieringen, N. Warmoltz, Physica. X XII, 849(1956).

［28］ B. J. Masters, E. F. Gerey, J. Appl Phys. 49, 2717(1978).

［29］ A. Seeger, et. al, Radiation Effects in Semiconductors, 12(1976)Inst. PhYs. Conf. Ser. 31, 1(1977).

［30］ J. D. Plummer, Solid State Technology, 29, No. 3, 61(1986).

［31］ J. I. Pankove, J. Y. C. Sun, J. J. T, Tzou, Appl, Phys. Letters, 43, 204(1933).

［32］ N. M. Johnson, C. Herring, D. J. Chadi, Phys. Rev. Letters, 56, 769(1986).

两性杂质锗在 LPE GaAs 中分凝系数
和占位比的计算

杨 辉 梁骏吾

(中国科学院半导体研究所,北京)

1988 年 8 月 9 日收到

摘要:将三元相图理论推广到Ⅲ-Ⅴ族化合物及两性Ⅳ族元素杂质组成的赝四元体系,推导了Ⅳ族元素 Ge 在 GaAs 液相外延时的分凝系数的温度关系以及占位比与温度的关系,理论计算与实验相符合.并用拟合的方法确定了 Ga-Ge-As 固相体系中的相互作用参数是温度的二次函数.

关键词:液相外延,分凝系数,相图,砷化镓

一、引 言

由于相图理论在晶体生长等方面的重要作用而受到了广泛重视,许多作者研究了二元,三元甚至四元相图理论,并成功地用于计算化合物半导体生长及其掺杂情况,如Ⅲ-Ⅴ族化合物 GaAs 及掺入各种Ⅱ,Ⅵ族杂质的情况已有不少报道.但由于Ⅳ族元素在Ⅲ-Ⅴ族化合物中的复杂性,例如Ⅳ族元素在Ⅲ-Ⅴ族化合物中既可以占Ⅲ族元素的位置又可以占Ⅴ族元素的位置,起两种杂质的作用,即可成为施主又可成为受主,而且两种占位情况的Ⅳ族元素还可以相互转变,因此这是一个赝四元系统,但又比普通的四元系统复杂.因此有关这种情况的报道比较少.Hurle[1]曾计算了在液相外延 GaAs 时杂质 Ge 的分凝系数与生长温度的关系.他是根据固相与液相达到平衡,用质量作用定律和电中性条件导出Ⅳ族杂质 Ge 在 GaAs 中的分凝系数与外延生长温度的关系,并根据 Neumann[2] 报道的占位比与生长温度无关且恒等于 0.18 的实验结果,确定了待定参数.Hurle 的计算结果与 Neumann 的实验结果相一致.但现在有新的实验证据表明占位比是与生长温度有关的[3],而且否定了 Neumann 的分凝系数与生长温度关系的实验.因此有必要重新考虑 Ge 在 GaAs 中的占位情况和分凝系数与生长温度的变化关系.

二、Ge 在 GaAs 液相外延生长时的分凝

在 LPE GaAs 中,如果主要掺杂剂是 Ge,则掺杂剂进入外延层的反应可用下式代表

$$Ge^l + Ga^l \xrightleftharpoons{K_1} GaGe^s \tag{1a}$$

$$Ge^l + As^l \xrightleftharpoons{K_2} GeAs^s \tag{1b}$$

原载于:半导体学报,1989,10(10):725-732.

$$Ga^1 + As^1 \xrightleftharpoons[]{K_{GaAs}} GaAs^s \qquad (1c)$$

其中(1a)式代表 Ge 由液相分凝进入固相并占 As 位的反应,(1b)式代表 Ge 由液相分凝进入固相并占 Ga 位的反应,而(1c)式是 G_2 和 As 形成 GaAs 的反应. 这里将固相看做是 GaAs-GaGe-GeAs 的三元溶液,GaGe 表示 Ge 占 As 位 Ga 占 Ga 位,GeAs 表示 Ge 占 Ga 位 As 占 As 位. 由质量作用定律可得

$$K_1(T) = \gamma_{GaGe}^s [GaGe^s]/\gamma_{Ga}^1 [Ga^1] \gamma_{Ge}^1 [Ge^1] \qquad (2a)$$

$$K_2(T) = \gamma_{GeAs}^s [GeAs^s]/\gamma_{As}^1 [As^1] \gamma_{Ge}^1 [Ge^1] \qquad (2b)$$

式中 $K_1(T)$ 和 $K_2(T)$ 是平衡常数,γ_i 是 i 组元的活度系数,[GaGe]表示 GaGe 在固相三元溶液中的摩尔浓度,其它符号类似. 如果用 $[Ge_{Ga}^s]$ 和 $[Ge_{As}^s]$ 表示固相中占 Ga 位和占 As 位 Ge 的摩尔浓度,按浓度定义有

$$[Ge_{Ga}^s] = 占 \ Ga \ 位 \ Ge \ 原子数/(Ga \ 原子数 + As \ 原子数)$$

$$\therefore \quad [Ge_{Ga}^s] = \frac{1}{2}[GeAs^s]$$

同样

$$[Ge_{As}^s] = \frac{1}{2}[GaGe^s]$$

以上固相中 Ge 的浓度都是未电离的中性 Ge 的浓度,计算分凝系数 k 要用固相中 Ge 的总浓度. 杂质能级电子占有率服从费米统计分布,用 N_A 表示占 As 位的总 Ge 受主摩尔浓度,N_D 表示占 Ga 位的总 Ge 施主摩尔浓度,则

$$[Ge_{As}^s] = N_A \left(1 + \frac{1}{g_a} \exp[(E_F - E_a)/kT]\right) \qquad (3a)$$

$$[Ge_{Ga}^s] = N_D \left(1 + \frac{1}{g_d} \exp[(E_d - E_F)/kT]\right) \qquad (3b)$$

其中 E_a 和 E_d 分别为占 As 位 Ge 和占 Ga 位 Ge 的电离能,g_a 和 g_d 分别是受主和施主杂质能级简并度. 根据分凝系数定义 $k = \dfrac{固相中杂质摩尔数}{液相中杂质摩尔数}$ 结合(2)(3)式可分别得到占 As 位和占 Ga 位的杂质 Ge 的分凝系数 k_A 和 k_D:

$$k_A = \frac{N_A}{[Ge^1]} = K_1(T) \gamma_{Ga}^1 [Ga^1] \gamma_{Ge} \left(1 + \frac{1}{g_a} \exp[(E_F - E_a)/kT]\right) / 2\gamma_{GaGe}^s \qquad (4a)$$

$$k_D = \frac{N_D}{[Ge^1]} = K_2(T) \gamma_{As}^1 [As^1] \gamma_{Ge} \left(1 + \frac{1}{g_d} \exp[(E_d - E_F)/kT]\right) / 2\gamma_{GeAs}^s \qquad (4b)$$

杂质 Ge 的分凝系数 $k(T) = k_A + k_D$ \qquad (5)

因此只要求出(5)式中各参数即可得 $k(T)$ 的温度关系.

应用多元简单溶液近似[4],

$$RT\ln\gamma_i = \sum_{\substack{i=1 \\ i \neq j}}^{n} n_{ij} X^i + \sum_{\substack{k=1 \\ k<i, i\neq 1}}^{m} \sum_{\substack{i=1 \\ i \neq k}}^{l} X_k X_j (\alpha_{ij} + \alpha_{ik} - \alpha_{ik}) \qquad (6)$$

式中 α_{li} 表示组分 i 与 j 的相互作用参数,X_j 表示组分 j 的克分子分数,将 Ge-Ga-As 三元溶液看做是规则溶液,可得下列活度系数

$$RT\ln\gamma_{Ge}^1 = \alpha_{GaGe}[Ga^1]^2 + \alpha_{GeAs}[As^1]^2 + [Ga^1][As^1](\alpha_{GaGe} + \alpha_{GeAs} - \alpha_{GaAs}) \tag{7}$$

$$RT\ln\gamma_{Ga}^1 = \alpha_{GaGe}[Ge^1]^2 + \alpha_{GaAs}[As^1]^2 + [Ge^1][As^1](\alpha_{GaGe} + \alpha_{GaAs} - \alpha_{GaAs}) \tag{8}$$

$$RT\ln\gamma_{As}^1 = \alpha_{GeAs}[Ga^1]^2 + \alpha_{GaAs}[Ge^1]^2 + [Ga^1][Ge^1](\alpha_{GaAs} + \alpha_{GeAs} - \alpha_{GaGe}) \tag{9}$$

将固相看作 GaAs-GaGe-GeAs 的三元规则溶液有:

$$RT\ln\gamma_{GaGe}^1 = \alpha_{GaAs-GaGe}^1[GaAs^s]^2 + \alpha_{GeAs-GaGe}^1[GeAs^s]^2 + [GaAs^s][GeAs^s]$$
$$\cdot (\alpha_{GaAs-GaGe}^1 + \alpha_{GeAs-GaGe}^1 - \alpha_{GaAs-GeAs}^1)$$

由于 Ge 的掺杂量一般很小,$[GeAs^1]$ 和 $[GaGe^s] \ll [GaAs^s]$ 所以 $[GaAs^s] = 1 - [GeAs^1] - [GaGe^s] = 1$,即可忽略 $[GeAs^s]$ 和 $[GaGe^s]$ 项,这样上式可以简为

$$RT\ln\gamma_{GaGe}^s = \alpha_{GaAs-GaGe}^s \tag{10}$$

同样可得 GeAs 的活度系数

$$RT\ln\gamma_{GeAs}^s = \alpha_{GaAs-GeAs}^s \tag{11}$$

三、分凝反应的平衡常数的表达

平衡时对应分凝反应(1a-1c)式分别有固相和液相的化学势平衡关系

$$\mu_{Ge}^1 + \mu_{Ga}^1 = \mu_{GaGe}^s \tag{12a}$$

$$\mu_{Ge}^1 + \mu_{As}^1 = \mu_{GeAs}^s \tag{12b}$$

$$\mu_{Ga}^1 + \mu_{As}^1 = \mu_{GaAs}^s \tag{12c}$$

其中 μ_i 是表示 i 组元的化学势,角标 1 和 s 分别表示液相和固相. 对任意两个温度 T_1 和 T_2,由(12a)式可得下列关系

$$\mu_{Ga}^0(T_2) - \mu_{Ga}^0(T_1) + \mu_{Ga}^0(T_2) - \mu_{Ge}^0(T_1) - \mu_{GaGe}^{10}(T_2) + \mu_{GaGe}^{10}(T_1) \equiv \Delta\mu^0$$

$$= -RT_2\ln\left[\frac{\gamma_{Ga}^1(T_2)[Ga^1](T_2)\gamma_{Ge}^1(T_2)[Ge^1](T_2)}{\gamma_{GaGe}^1(T_2)[GaGe^2](T_2)}\right]$$

$$+ RT_1\ln\left[\frac{\gamma_{Ga}^1(T_1)[Ga^1](T_1)\gamma_{Ga}^1(T_1)[Ge^1](T_1)}{\gamma_{GaGe}^1(T_1)[GaGe^2](T_1)}\right] \tag{13}$$

如果 $S_{Ga}^0(T)$ 表示纯 $[Ga]$ 的熵,C_{pO}^0 表恒压下纯镓的热容,则

$$\mu_{Ga}^0(T_2) - \mu_{Ga}^0(T_1) = -\int_{T_1}^{T_2} S_{Ga}^0(T)\,\mathrm{d}T = -\int_{T_1}^{T_2}\left\{S_{Ga}^0(T_2) + \int_{T_1}^T \frac{C_{pGa}^0}{T'}\mathrm{d}T'\right\}\mathrm{d}T$$

$$\mu_{Ga}^0(T_2) - \mu_{Ga}^0(T_1) = -S_{Ga}^0(T_2)(T_2 - T_1) - \int_{T_1}^{T_2}\int_{T_1}^T \frac{C_{pGa}^0}{T'}\mathrm{d}T'\mathrm{d}T \tag{14a}$$

同理

$$\mu_{Ga}^0(T_2) - \mu_{Ga}^0(T_1) = -S_{Ga}^0(T_2)(T_2 - T_1) - \int_{T_1}^{T_2}\int_{T_2}^T \frac{C_{pGe}^0}{T'}\mathrm{d}T'\mathrm{d}T \tag{14b}$$

$$\mu_{GaGe}^0(T_2) - \mu_{GaGe}^0(T_1) = -S_{GaGe}^0(T_2)(T_2 - T_1) - \int_{T_1}^{T_2}\int_{T_2}^T \frac{C_{pGaGe}^0}{T'}\mathrm{d}T'\mathrm{d}T \tag{14c}$$

$$\therefore \qquad \Delta\mu^0 = -\Delta S^0(T_2)(T_2-T_1) - \int_{T_1}^{T_2}\int_{T_1}^{T}\frac{\Delta C_p^0}{T'}\mathrm{d}T'\mathrm{d}T \qquad (15)$$

其中 $\Delta S^0 = S_{Ga}^0 + S_{Ga}^0 - S_{GaGe}^0$ 表示固体 GaGe 的熵与液态纯 Ga 和纯 Ge 的熵之差. $\Delta C_p^0 = C_{pGa}^0 + C_{pGe}^0 - C_{pGaGe}^0$，与其它项相比很小，所以(15)式中积分项可忽略[5]. 令 $T_2 = T^F$ 为 GaGe 的熔点温度，$T_1 = T$ 为任意温度，在该 T^F 温度下 $[Ga^1]=[Ge^1]=0.5$，$\mu_{GaGe}^s = \mu_{GaGe}^{10}$，即 $[GaGe^s]=1$，则由(13)和(15)式可得

$$-\Delta S^0(T^F)(T^F-T) = -RT^F\ln\frac{\gamma_{Ga}^{s1}\gamma_{Ge}^{s1}}{4} + RT\ln\frac{\gamma_{Ga}^1[Ga^1]\gamma_{Ge}^1[Ge^1]}{\gamma_{GaGe}^s[GaGe^s]} \qquad (16)$$

式中 γ_{Ga}^{s1}，γ_{Ge}^{s1} 表示等化学配比时的活度系数值，即 $[Ga^1]=[Ge^1]=0.5$ 时的值，由(7)(8)两式可知

$$RT\ln\gamma_{Ga}^{s1}\gamma_{Ge}^{s1} = \alpha_{GaGe}^1/2$$

α_{GaGe}^1 表示液相中 Ga 和 Ge 间的相互作用参数. 对 III-V 族二元系液相诸组元实验找到 $\alpha(T)$ 有线性温度关系，$\alpha=a+bT$，将其推广到 IV-V 族及 III-IV 族二元液相系统，有

$$a_{GaGe}^1 = a_{GaGe} + b_{GaGe}T$$

$$RT\ln\gamma_{Ga}^{s1}(T)\gamma_{Ge}^{s1}(T) = (a_{GaGe} + b_{GaGe}T)/2$$

$$RT^F\ln\gamma_{Ga}^{s1}(T^F)\gamma_{Ge}^{s1}(T^F) = RT\ln\gamma_{Ga}^{s1}(T)\gamma_{Ge}^{s1}(T) + \frac{1}{2}b_{GaGe}(T^F-T)$$

将此式代入(16)式得到

$$(\Delta S^0(T^F) + R\ln4 - b_{GaGe}/2)(T-T^F) = RT\ln\frac{\gamma_{Ga}^1[Ga^1]\gamma_{Ge}^1[Ge^1]}{\gamma_{GaGe}^s[GaGe^s]} - RT\ln\frac{\gamma_{Ga}^{s1}\gamma_{Ge}^{s1}}{4} \qquad (17)$$

将 GaGe 也看做是规则溶液，则上式左端的 $R\ln4 + \Delta S^0(T^F)$ 正好是理想熔化熵，$-b_{GaGe}/2$ 正好是在 T^F 下的过剩溶化熵[5]，所以

$$\Delta S_{GaGe}^F = \Delta S^0(T^F) + R\ln4 - b_{GaGe}/2 \qquad (18)$$

ΔS_{GaGe}^F 是 GaGe 的熔化熵. 用(18)式将(17)式化简可得在 Ga-Ge-As 体系中有

$$\frac{\gamma_{GaGe}^1[GaGe^s]}{\gamma_{Ga}^1[Ga^1]\gamma_{Ge}^1[Ge^1]} = \frac{4}{\gamma_{Gs}^{s1}\gamma_{Ge}^{s1}}e^{\Delta S_{GaGe}^F(T_{GaGe}^k-T)/RT} \qquad (19)$$

其中 T_{GaGe}^F 即为(18)式中的 T^F，是 GaGe 的熔点. 将(19)式与(2a)比较可以看出，上式左端即为平衡常数，所以

$$K_1(T) = \frac{4}{\gamma_{Gs}^{s1}\gamma_{Ge}^{s1}}e^{\Delta S_{GaGe}^F(T_{GaGe}^F-T)/RT} \qquad (20a)$$

同理可得

$$K_2(T) = \frac{4}{\gamma_{Ge}^{s1}\gamma_{As}^{s1}}e^{\Delta S_{GeAs}^F(T_{GeAs}^F-T)/RT} \qquad (20b)$$

四、表面能带弯曲、相互作用参数以及熔化熵

在 LPE 生长过程中，如果在外延层中杂质扩散快，而且生长速度较慢，则有可能在固

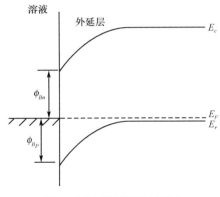

图 1　固液界面能带的弯曲

体体内和液相建立热力学平衡,按[6],其条件是 $D/L_1v>10$,其中 D 是杂质扩散系数,L_1 是 Debye 长度,v 是生长速度,如果 $D/L_1v<0.1$ 则是固相表面和液相建立平衡. GaAs 掺 Ge 外延的典型条件是 $v\sim10^{-6}$cm/s,$L_1=(RT\varepsilon/q^2n)^{1n}=10^{-5}\sim10^{-6}$cm,$D\leqslant10^{-13}$cm^2/s[7],则 $D/L_1v<0.1$,所以在 GaAs 掺 Ge 的生长条件下固相表面与液相建立平衡,而不是整个固相体内与液相建立平衡. 外延层与液体的界面处能带的弯曲使体内和界面处的化学势不同,所以必须考虑 GaAs 表面能带的弯曲的影响[6].

半导体固相和与之接触的液体的界面可以看做是金属-半导体接触,有一肖特基势垒,如图所示,在界面处,E_F 被钉钆在禁带中与价带顶距离保持常数[8]即

$$\phi_{B_p}(T)=常数$$

对 p 型 GaAs,我们取

$$\phi_{B_p}(T)=0.60\text{eV}^{[9]}$$

因为施主和受主电离能都非常小,可忽略

$$E_F-E_A\approx E_F-E_V=\phi_{B_p}=0.60\text{eV}$$

$$E_D-E_F\approx E_C-E_F=\phi_{B_n}=Eg-\phi_{B_p}$$

ϕ_{B_p} 与温度无关,而 E_g 是温度的函数[8]

$$E_g(T)=1.519-5.405\times10^{-4}T^2/(T+204)$$

所以 ϕ_{B_n} 也是温度的函数,所以

$$E_D-E_F=0.919-5.405\times10^{-4}T^2/(T+204)$$

至于受主和施主的简并度 g_A 和 g_D,导带考虑电子两个自旋取向,简并因子 $g_D=2$,而 GaAs 价带顶是轻重空穴的简并态,故简并因子 $g_A=4$[10].

剩下的未知参数只有相互作用参数和熔化熵以及熔点了,求出这些参数就可以得到分凝系数和温度的关系. 实验发现,对许多二元系统 α 与温度是线性关系,即 $\alpha(T)=a+bT$,Thurmaod[11]曾研究了许多二元系统包括 GaGe 和 GeAs,得到了

$$\alpha_{\text{GaGe}}=-150\text{cal/mole}$$

$$\alpha_{\text{GaAs}}=(-5600+4.16T)\text{cal/mole}$$

Casey 等[8]也得到了

$$\alpha_{\text{GaAs}}=(5160-9.16T)\text{cal/mole}$$

在平衡常数的表达式中 ΔS^F 和 T^F 分别是熔化熵和熔点,从 Thunmand 给出的二元系统的实验数据可推出 GaGe 和 GeAs 的 T^F,即液相线上等化学配比浓度的温度:

$$T^F_{\text{GaGe}}=1000\text{K},\ T^F_{\text{GaAs}}=950\text{K}$$

在缺乏实验数据的情况下,我们对 ΔS^F 的取值进行估计. Panish[12]曾用下列两式

$$\Delta S^F_{\text{III-V}}=\Delta S^F_{\text{IV}}+\Delta S^F_{\text{IV}}+6.95$$

或

$$\Delta S^F_{\text{III-V}} = \Delta S^F_{\text{III}} + \Delta S^F_{\text{V}} + R\ln 4$$

来估算Ⅲ-Ⅴ族化合物的熔化熵. 在我们这里,我们取Ⅲ-Ⅴ族化合物的熔化熵来近似Ⅲ-Ⅳ和Ⅳ-Ⅴ族化合物熔化熵,即取

$$\Delta S^F_{\text{GaGe}} = \Delta S^F_{\text{GeAs}} = \Delta S^F_{\text{GaAs}}$$

[8]中给出 $\Delta S^F_{\text{GaAs}} = 16.64\text{cal/mole} \cdot \text{K}$,因此

$$\Delta S^F_{\text{GaGe}} = \Delta S^F_{\text{GeAs}} = 16.64\text{cal/mole} \cdot \text{K}$$

固相中的相互作用参数 $\alpha^s_{\text{GaAs-GaGe}}$ 和 $\alpha^s_{\text{GaAs-GeAs}}$ 也是温度的函数,许多作者在计算中都未考虑该参数的影响. 我们通过对[3]的实验数据拟合来考虑固相中的相互作用参数. Thurmond[11]由实验得出在许多二元溶液中, α 是温度的线性函数,我们发现将该结果推广到固相中 GaAs 和 GaGe 以及 GaAs 和 GeAs 间的相互作用参数是不适当的. 如果假设 $\alpha^s_{\text{GeAs-GaGe}}$ 和 $\alpha^s_{\text{GaAs-GeAs}}$ 都是温度的线性函数,则无法得到与实验一致的结果,$\ln k - 1/T$ 关系在[3]的实验温度范围内550℃至950℃近似为一条直线,无法与实验点拟合. 若保留相互作用参数中温度的二次项,即设 α^s 是温度的二次函数,则可以非常好地拟合实验数据了. 由此可见,不能将液相中相互作用参数的线性关系简单地推广到固相中的相互作用参数,固相中相互作用参数是温度的更为复杂的函数.

五、实验曲线的拟合

如前所述,固相中相互作用参数 $\alpha^s_{\text{GaAs-GaGe}}$ 和 $\alpha^s_{\text{GaAs-GeAs}}$ 不能近似为温度的线性函数,要保留温度的二次项. 这里我们具体拟合是设

$$\alpha^s_{\text{GaAs-GaGe}} \approx a_1 + a_2 T + a_3 T^2$$
$$\alpha^s_{\text{GaAs-GeAs}} \approx b_1 + b_2 T + b_3 T^2$$

将他们分别代入(4a)和(4b)中,用[3]的实验数据分别拟合 k_A 和 k_D 得到

$$\begin{cases} a_1 = 21860 \\ a_2 = -80.7 \\ a_3 = 0.0378 \end{cases} \qquad \begin{cases} b_1 = 8942 \\ b_2 = -41.3 \\ b_3 = 0.0211 \end{cases}$$

实际拟合结果如图2所示,图中虚线是将 α^s 作为温度的线性函数的拟合结果. 由图可见,将固相中的相互作用参数作为温度的二次函数是非常好的近似,可以很好地与实验结果一致. 图3是拟合结果求出的占位比与温度的关系以及实验结果,可见符合的也是很好.

从我们的理论可以推测出在[3]的实验温度以外的液相外延以及熔体生长的 Ge 的掺杂特性. 将熔点温度 $T = 1513\text{K}$ 代入 k_A 和 k_D 的表达式中可求出熔体生长时杂质 Ge 的分凝系数 k 和占位比 N_D/N_A:

$$k = 0.048 \qquad N_D/N_A = 1.59$$

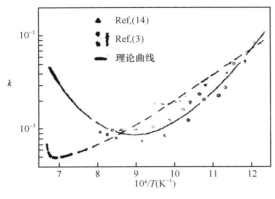 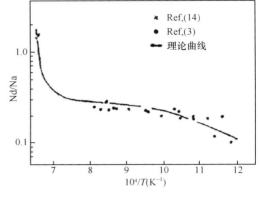

图 2　分凝系数 k 与温度倒数的关系　　　　图 3　占位比与温度倒数的关系

　　这说明熔体生长时 Ge 在 GaAs 中主要占 Ga 位成为施主,而不是像液相外延时主要占 As 位,即熔体生长掺 Ge 的 GaAs 材料是 n 型而不像液相外延得到 P 型材料. 熔体生长时占 Ga 位的 Ge 和占 As 位的 Ge 原子浓度之比为 1.59. 这与已有的文献报道的实验结果符合的很好. 表示出了我们的理论推测结果与文献报道的实验结果是一致的.

　　从拟合结果还可以预言,Ge 在 GaAs 中从主要占 Ga 位至主要占 As 位的转变,即生长出的材料从 n 型到 P 型的转变大约发生在生长温度为 1235℃ 左右,即液相外延的生长温度比熔点低不到 10℃ 就出现了转变. Hurle[1] 预言转变温度在熔点以下不到 100℃,而 Teramoto 估计转变温度比熔点低 120℃,但 Hurle 和 Teramoto 均未考虑固相的活度系数. 但他们的结果与我们的计算结果还是比较接近的. 得到的转变温度都比较高,因此,从液相外延生长的掺 Ge 的 GaAs 外延层总是 P 型的.

六、结　　论

　　我们将三元相图理论推广到 III-V 族化合物及两性 IV 族杂质组成的赝四元体系,考虑 IV 族杂质 Ge 的两性占位情况,GaAs 表面能带弯曲,以及杂质能级占有情况的统计分布,推导了 Ge 在 GaAs 液相外延时的分凝系数的温度关系以及占位比与温度的关系,理论计算与实验相符合,并可推出高温一直到熔点时的分凝系数和占位比.

　　用拟合的方法确定了 Ga-Ge-As 固相体系中的相互作用参数的温度函数 $\alpha^1_{GaAs-GaGe}(T)$ 和 $\alpha^1_{GaAs-GeAs}(T)$,与二元 III-V 族液相体系中的相互作用参数的温度函数不同,不能用线性关系表达,固相中的相互作用参数是温度的二次函数. 并拟合确定了该参数.

参考文献

[1] D. T. J. Hurle, *J. Phys. Chem. Solids.* **40**, 647(1979).

[2] H. Neumann, K. Jacobs. Nguyen Van Nam. W. Koj and C. Krause, *Phyt. Stetms. Solidi(a)* **44**, 675(1977).

[3] 杨辉,梁骏吾,半导体学报,**9**(4),429(1988).

[4] A. S. Jordan, *J. Electrochem. Soc.* 119, 123(1972).

[5] O. Kubaschewski, E. L. Evans and C. B. Allock, Metallorgicol Thermochemistry, (1967).

[6] K. H. Zachauer and A. Vogel, Gallium Arsenide:1970 Symp. Proe. p. 100(Inst. of Phys. London. 1971).

[7] T. T. Lavrishchev, L. P. Vasilevs. R. K. Zayatov, and S. S. Khludkov, Arsenid Galliya 2. 129(1969).

[8] H. C. Casey, Jr, M. B. Panish, Heterostructure Laters, Part B, p. 71(1978).

[9] S. M. Sze, "Physics of Scmiconductor Devices" 2nd ed. New York, Jobs Wiley & Sent, 1981.

[10] K. Seeger, "Semiconductor physics" ; an introduction, 2nd corrected and updated ed. Berlin, Springer Verlag, 1982.

[11] C. D. Thurmood and M. Kowalchik, *Bell sytt. Tech*, *J.* 89, 169(1960).

[12] M. B. Paoith and M. Hegems. Progress in Solid State Chemistry, 7, p. 39(1972).

[13] I. Teramote, *J. Phys. Chem. Solids.* 33, 2089(1972).

[14] L. R. Weisberg, F. D. Rosi and P. G. Heckart, Properties of Elemental and Compound Semiconductors (edited by H. C. Gatos, Interscience, New York, 1960) p. 25.

Calculation of the Segregation Coefficient and the occupation Ratio GaGe/GeAs of the Amphoteric Impurity Ge in LPE-GaAs

Yang Hui and Liang Junwu

(*Institute of Semiconductors, Academia Sinica, Beijing*)

Abstract: A theoretical temperature dependence of Ge segregation coefficient by is proposed extending ternary alloy theory to pseudo-quaternary alloy system consisting of III - V compound and the amphoteric impurity of group IV element. The temperature dependence of the occupation ratio of Ge on Ga site to Ge on As site is also obtained. The calculated results are in agreement with the experimental data. Using iterative method, the quadric temperature dependence of the interaction parameters in the Ga-Ge-As solid phase system is determined.

Keywords: LPE, Segregation, Phase diagram, GaAs

半 导 体

（目　录）

梁骏吾　王守武

中国科学院半导体研究所(1,2,3,4,5,6,7)；中国科学院半导体研究所(1,2,5)

原载于：化工大百科全书(第一卷),1990,193-262.

水平式矩形硅外延系统的计算机模拟[*]

Computational Modelling of Horizontal and Rectangular Silicon Epitaxial Reactor

梁骏吾　郭予龙　杨　辉

(中国科学院半导体研究所)[**]

摘要：本文针对水平式矩形硅外延系统,在分析其物理化学过程的基础上,不做滞流层或发展边界层模型的假设,把系统的温度发展分为两个阶段,即温度发展阶段和温度充分发展阶段。考虑到温度对速度分布的影响,混合气体物性对温度的强烈依赖性以及热扩散和表面反应速率的因素,分阶段进行求解,得到了生长速率分布与生长温度、基座倾角、气体流量以及反应物浓度的关系,并与实验进行比较,取得较为满意的结果。

Abstract：Based on the physical analysis of the horizontal and rectangular silicon epitaxial reactor, we have abandoned the stagnant and boundary sublayers assumption. In this work, various temperature zones and effects of temperature on velocity distribution and physical properties of mixed gases are considered. In addition, the thermodiffusion is taken into account. The distributions of temperature, velocity and concentration are calculated and the dependence of the growth rate distribution along the susceptor on the reactor geometry and technological conditions is obtained. Calculating results are also compared with experimental data.

一、引　言

硅外延技术的发展已有 20 多年的历史,前人在模型建立及分析方面已做了许多工作[1~11]。但由于生长过程的化学动力学及流体力学复杂性,因而做了许多假设,然而这些假设与物理真实性存在差距。

发展边界层模型[2]及滞流层模型[1]假设能够定性地解释生长速率沿气流方向逐渐减少的趋势,以及解释了基座倾角对提高生长速率均匀性的作用,但都不符合物理真实性,计算结果也不够定量准确。在一般的硅外延生长系统中,上下边界层在距入口几厘米处就已相交了[12],实验上也证实了滞流层是不存在的[12]。随着模型假设的发展,有人假定气体流速充分发展与气流方向无关,并假设一定的温度分布进行处理[4,5],他们忽略了物性参数对温度的强烈依赖性,也没有考虑到热扩散的强烈影响。J. Jüza[6]比较全面地考虑了这些问题,但由于物性参数较多,表达式也很复杂,没有给

原载于:化工出版社,1990,193-262.

* 1990 年 1 月收到,同年 5 月修改定稿.

** Liang Junwu,Guo Yulong,Yang Hui(Institute of Semiconductors,Academia Sinica,Beijing).

出具体的算法。

在硅外延反应系统中,实验与理论都证明了气流为层流[12]。由于气流上下边界层在气流入口处几厘米已开始相交,因此,可以把气流看作到达基座前沿已充分发展,即流速呈抛物线型分布。由于气体在入口处处于室温,而基座温度高达1400K左右,上管壁也由于热辐射及传导的影响,温度高达800K左右。因此,气体进入生长区后产生剧烈热膨胀,流速显著加快。我们显然必须考虑到流速由于气体膨胀而加快,气体速度场与温度场发展相互作用的因素。气体流经长度为$L_t = 0.1 HR_eP_r$后,温度达到充分发展,L_t称为热进口长度[13],其中H为基座与上管壁之距离,R_e和P_r为雷诺数和普朗托数。由于上管壁距基座一般只有几厘米,而温差却高达几百K,生长方向的温度梯度很大,热扩散的影响很大,因此模型的建立必须考虑到热扩散的影响。对于氢气携带$SiCl_4$进行外延的系统,人们发现生长温度在1200℃以上时,生长速率由反应扩散机制控制,而生长温度低于1200℃时,生长速率由反应速率常数控制[6]。

本工作在分析了系统的物理化学过程的基础上,不作滞流层或发展边界层假设,考虑到物性参数对温度的强烈依赖关系,考虑了热扩散的影响,采用生长速率控制机制进行计算,并与实验进行比较,得到了较为满意的结果。

到目前为止,还未发现有这个问题的三维模型处理,把这种方法推广到三维模型,能使三维模型的求解变得方便得多,也比较符合物理真实性。

二、模型的建立及求解

1. 基本假设

对于感应加热矩形硅外延系统,建立如图1所示的坐标系,并作如下假设:①气流为层流,气流速率分布为抛物线型,平均流速与Y方向平均温度成正比。忽略Y方向速度分量;②气流经$L_t = 0.1 HR_eP_r$后温度达到所谓充分发展,即气流方向温度梯度可以忽略;③气相无反应,只在固气界面发生化学反应,生长速率由反应速率常数控制,$SiCl_4$在生长表面转化为Si而淀积的转化率为70%;④系统内浓度变化不影响物性参数,物性参数由入口处浓度及温度分布决定,并忽略浓度变化对温度分布的影响;⑤忽略气流方向的扩散及热扩散;⑥系统宽度方向各量均匀,即二维模型;⑦系统石墨基座及上管壁温度恒定且均匀。

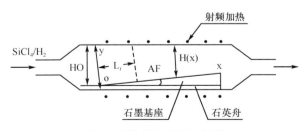

图1 系统的构成及坐标系

基于如上假设,我们得到了系统的动量、能量、质量守恒方程及其边界条件:

连续性 $\quad \dfrac{\partial \rho u}{\partial x}=0 \hfill (1)$

动量守恒 $\quad \rho u\dfrac{\partial u}{\partial x}+\dfrac{\partial \rho}{\partial x}=\dfrac{\partial}{\partial y}\left(\mu\dfrac{\partial u}{\partial y}\right) \hfill (2)$

能量守恒 $\quad \rho C_p u\dfrac{\partial T}{\partial x}=\dfrac{\partial}{\partial y}\left(K_T\dfrac{\partial T}{\partial y}\right)+\dfrac{\partial}{\partial x}\left(K_T\dfrac{\partial T}{\partial x}\right) \hfill (3)$

质量守恒 $\quad \rho u\dfrac{\partial w}{\partial x}=\dfrac{\partial}{\partial y}\left(\rho D\dfrac{\partial w}{\partial y}\right)+\dfrac{\partial}{\partial y}\left(1.34\rho D\dfrac{1}{T}\dfrac{\partial T}{\partial y}w\right) \hfill (4)$

边值条件：$x=0$ 处　$T=TE, W=WO, Q=QO$

$$y=O_2 \quad T=TO, \quad \rho D\dfrac{\partial w}{\partial y}+1.34\rho D\dfrac{1}{T}\dfrac{\partial T}{\partial y}W=KW$$

$$y=H(x)_1 \quad T=T1, \quad \rho D\dfrac{\partial w}{\partial y}+1.34\rho D\dfrac{1}{T}\dfrac{\partial T}{\partial y}W=0$$

其中：$H(x)=[HO-x\sin(AF)]/\cos(AF)$；$\rho$ 为混合气体密度；μ 为混合气体粘滞系数；HO 为入口处反应管上管与基座的距离；QO 为入口处气体总流量；AF 为基座倾角；TE 为气体入口处温度；TO 为生长温度；$T1$ 为上管壁温度；WO 为入口处 $SiCl_4$ 百分比浓度；W 为 $SiCl_4$ 百分比浓度。

参数选取如下：

（1）反应速率常数 $K^{[6]}$ $\quad K=7.2\times10^4 e^{-23345/TO}\cdot TO\cdot\rho$

（2）定压热容[5] $\quad C_P=x_{H_2}C_{pH_2}+x_{SiCl_4}\cdot C_{pSiCl_4}$

其中 $\quad C_{pH_2}=14534-0.4023T+9.816\times10^{-4}T^2$

$$C_{pSiCl_4}=561.4+6.417\times10^{-2}T-8.64\times10^{-6}T^2$$

在这里我们将 C_p 近似为不随温度变化，取其平均温度时的值 $C_p(T)=C_p\left(\dfrac{TO+T1}{2}\right)$

（3）扩散系数 $D^{[5]}$ 在考虑到 $SiCl_4$ 和 H_2 混合气体复合势参数为：$\sigma_{12}=4.31\text{Å}, e_{12}/K_B=144K$ 时可得

$$D(T)=2.11\times10^{-5}\times T^{1.674}\text{cm}^2/\text{s}$$

（4）热导系数 K_T 的选取，我们用了两元混合物热导系数关系[5,16]

$$K_T=\dfrac{K_{T1}}{1+G_{12}x_2/x_1}+\dfrac{K_{T2}}{1+G_{21}x_1/x_2}$$

其中 $\quad G_{ij}$ 为瓦西耳耶瓦常数。

（5）热扩散系数 D_T，在 $x_{SiCl_4}\ll x_{H_2}$ 的近似下，我们在 1100K 温度下计算得

$$DT=1.34x_{SiCl_4}\cdot D$$

2. 方程的求解

用平行及垂直于基座的线段把反应器分成规则的网格，x 方向格点间距为 DD；y 方向格点间距为 DH，其关系为：$DH=DD\cdot\text{tg}(AF)$。为了计算方便，应使上管壁取在格点上，将反应器分为温度发展区和温度充分发展区两部分进行计算，由热进口段长度的关系式 $L_t=0.1HR_eP_r$，计算热进口段 x 方向的网格数，由系统生长区长度减 L_t 计算热充分发

展区网格数。

由于气体可达基座前沿速度分布已充分发展,呈势物线型分布,考虑到热膨胀,速度分布为

$$u = \frac{6QO}{H(x)Z} \cdot \frac{\overline{T}(x)}{TE} \cdot \left(\frac{Y}{H(x)} - \frac{Y^2}{H(x)^2} \right) \tag{5}$$

为计算温度分布,先考虑温度发展区,在这里能量方程变为

$$u \frac{\partial T}{\partial x} = GG \frac{\partial^2 T}{\partial y^2} + GG \frac{\partial^2 T}{\partial x^2} + \frac{5}{8} GG \frac{1}{T} \left(\frac{\partial T}{\partial y} \right)^2 + \frac{5}{8} GG \frac{1}{T} \left(\frac{\partial T}{\partial x} \right)^2 \tag{6}$$

由于速度与温度分布相互影响,需联立求解。可采用迭代法,将能量方程变成差分方程,并设一初始温度分布,用此温度分布代入式(5)计算出速度分布的一级近似。用求出的速度分布的一级近似可以求出温度分布的一级近似。由迭代法可解在一定误差范围内的速度温度分布。

在温度充分发展区,考虑到定压热容与温度关系不大,能量方程变为

$$\frac{\partial}{\partial y} \left(K_T \frac{\partial T}{\partial y} \right) = 0 \tag{7}$$

考虑到边界条件解得

$$T(x,y) = \left(\frac{T_1^{13/8} - TO^{13/8}}{H(x)} \cdot y + TO^{13/8} \right)^{8/13} \tag{8}$$

该式与速度无关,因此在温度充分发展区,求得温度分布后就可以求得速度分布、至此我们已求得整个区间各格点的温度的速度分布。这为求解浓度分布并进而求出生长速率分布打下基础。

质量方程在考虑到 $\rho \propto 1/T$ 之后变为

$$\frac{1}{T} u \frac{\partial \omega}{\partial x} = \frac{\partial}{\partial y} \left(\frac{D}{T} \frac{\partial w}{\partial y} \right) + 1.34 \left(\frac{D}{T^2} \frac{\partial T}{\partial y} \omega \right) \tag{9}$$

边值条件

$$D \frac{\partial \omega}{\partial y} \bigg|_{y=0} + 1.34 \frac{D}{T} \frac{\partial T}{\partial y} \omega \bigg|_{y=0} = \frac{K}{\rho} \omega \bigg|_{y=0}$$

$$D \frac{\partial \omega}{\partial y} \bigg|_{y=H(x)} + 1.34 \frac{D}{T} \frac{\partial T}{\partial y} \omega \bigg|_{y=H(x)} = 0$$

这是一个稳定的初值问题,可以在解得各格点速度、温度和温度梯度后,采用 Crank-Nicolson 差分格式把式(9)变为差分方程进行数值求解。

生长速率在求得浓度分布以后可以得到

$$G(X) = \frac{M_{Si}}{M_{SiCl_4}} \cdot \frac{0.7}{d_{Si}} \cdot K \cdot W(X)$$

式中,M_{Si} 为硅原子原子量;M_{SiCl_4} 为 $SiCl_4$ 分量;d_{Si} 为单晶硅密度。

三、结果与讨论

我们 MICRO VAX-Ⅱ/VM-S 上作了数值计算,得到了速度分布,温度分布、浓度分布曲线。计算了生长速率随基座倾角,生长温度,气体流量,$SiCl_4$ 浓度的变化,如图 2 所示。

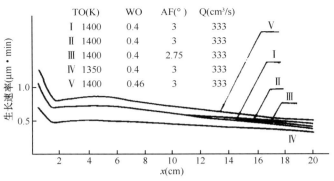

図2 不同生长条件下生长速率的分布

我们固定系统的几何尺寸,取反应管内壁宽度 $Z=10cm$,基座与上管壁在入口处距 $H=2cm$,计算得到生长速率随生长条件变化的关系。图2中曲线 I 和曲线 II 分别为气体流量为 $367cm^3/s$ 和 $333cm^3/s$ 时得到的生长速率分布,可见当气体流量增大时,可以改善生长速率均匀性。而曲线 II 和曲线 III 是在相同流速等条件下,不同基座倾角下得到的生长速率分布。可见倾角增大有利于生长速率均匀性。但当倾角过大时,会使尾部上管壁温度升高,产生淀积并掉楂,影响外延层质量。因此,对于一定的冷却条件,倾角也不应过大。从曲线 II 与曲线 IV 的对比看出在满足外延生长的温度范围内,温度较低时生长速率均匀性较好。这是因为生长温度低,生长速率就小,因此在基座前部分消耗的 $SiCl_4$ 就相对减少,使得基座的后部分仍有较高 $SiCl_4$ 含量,生长速率减小也相对较少。当然,温度过低,晶体完整性下降,上述结果只能在一定温度范围内运用。曲线 II 与曲线 V 的比较显示出生长速率随生长源混合气体中 $SiCl_4$ 浓度的变化。

图3为两组实验与计算结果的比较曲线。可以看到,计算结果与实验结果符合的相当好。

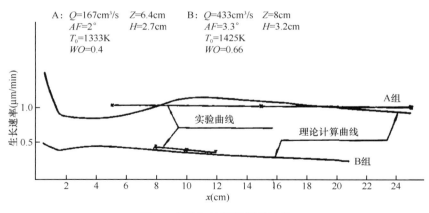

图3 实验与计算结果的比较

图4对比了三种机制下的生长速率分布:即①考虑到热扩散,且生长速率由扩散机制控制;②忽略热扩散,生长速率由表面反应速率控制;③考虑热扩散,生长速率由表面反应速率控制。我们看到,忽略热扩散后,基座前部分生长速率的起伏消失了。可见这种起伏是由于热扩散引起的。由于在入口处附近温度梯度很大,$SiCl_4$ 热扩散非常剧烈,

使表面浓度降低较多,但随着气体流动,热扩散减小了,因此出现了生长速率在入口处附近的起伏。我们从图中还可以看出忽略热扩散时的生长速率要比考虑到热扩散时的生长速率大得多。从这里我们可以看出热扩散的影响是不能忽略的。由于热扩散与温度梯度成正比,而系统的温度梯度在生长方向是很大的,因此热扩散对生长速率的影响很厉害。当考虑生长速率为扩散机制并考虑到热扩散时,我们可以看出计算得到的生长速率均匀性很差,在基座前部分生长速率很大而尾部生长速率相对的又较小。这是由于考虑生长速率为扩散控制机制时把表面反应速率算的很大,造成基座前部分生长速率的提高,致使后部分 $SiCl_4$ 浓度大大降低,生长速率相应地有很大减少,生长速率均匀性计算结果比较差。实际上生长速率均匀性与考虑到热扩散且为表面反应速率控制的情况比较相符,如图 3 所示。

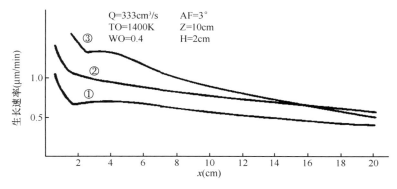

图 4 热扩散及生长速度控制机制对生长速率的影响

我们在与实验的比较中,还发现计算结果与实验结果还存在一定范围的偏差,如图 3 所示,计算得到的生长速率的均匀性要比实验结果低一些。这可能是由于上壁温度均匀的假设及认为反应器宽度方向各参数均匀有关。尽管上管壁温度分布大部分为恒温,但在前部和后部,温度会有所偏低和偏高。考虑到热扩散与温度梯度的关系,这样实际生长速率均匀性要比计算结果好一些。而实际基座并不能布满整个反应管底面积,会造成基座前部分的浓度消耗比计算结果小一些,这样实际上的均匀性也要比计算结果好一些。

四、结 论

本文分析了水平式由氢携带 $SiCl_4$ 进行外延生长的硅外延系统的物理化学机制,提出了把反应系统分为温度发展区及温度充分发展区两部分,考虑到混合气体的物性参数与温度的依赖关系,进行必要的化简、并考虑到热扩散的影响,采用一定的差分格式,数值计算了系统的速度、温度,浓度分布,计算了基座倾角、气体流量、生长温度及 $SiCl_4$ 浓度对生长速率的影响,计算结果与实验基本相符。讨论了热扩散对生长速率的影响,指出生长速率控制机制考虑为表面反应速率控制时与实验比较相符。并提出了提高生长速率均匀性的几种可能途径,即可以通过适当增加基座倾角,提高气体流量和在保持晶格完整性的范围内,降低生长温度,提高混合气体中 $SiCl_4$ 的浓度来改善生长速率均匀性。

参考文献

[1] F. C. Eversteyn et al. : J. Electrochemical Soc. , Vol. 117, p. 925, 1970.

[2] V. S. Ban : J. Crystal Growth, Vol. 97, p. 45, 1978.

[3] P. C. Rundle : J. Crystal Growth, Vol. 6, p. 11 1971.

[4] E. Fujii et al. : J. Electrochemical Soc. , Vol. 119, p. 1106, 1972.

[5] C. W. Manke, L. F. Donaghey : J. Electrochemical Soc. , Vol. 124, p. 561, 1977.

[6] Jiñ Júza, Jan Cenmák : J. Electrochemical Soc. , Vol. 129, p. 1627, 1982.

[7] W. H. Shephercl : J. Eleetrochemical Soc. , Vol. 112, p. 988, 1965.

[8] S. E. Bradshaw : Int. Electronics, Vol. 21, p. 205, 1966.

[9] R. Takahashi : J. Electrochemical Soc. , Vol. 119, p. 1406, 1972.

[10] R. W. Andrews et al. : Solid State Technol. , Vol. 61, p. 12, 1969.

[11] D. W. Hess et al. : Rev. in Chemical Engineering, Vol. 3, p. 97, 1985.

[12] L. J. Giling : J. Eectrochemical Soc. , Vol. 129, p. 624, 1982.

[13] 钱壬章等 : 传热分析与计算, 高教出版社, p. 179, 1987.

[14] H. Schlichting : Boundary-layer Theory, 6th ed. , p. 177.

[15] 金希卓等 : 第一届全国固体薄膜会议论文集, p. 32, 1988.

[16] E. R. G. 埃克尔特等 : 传热与传质, 科学出版社, p. 534, 1963.

[17] J. O. Hirschfelder et al. : Molecular Theory of Gases and Liquids, 1954, p. 541.

[18] 郭予龙, 梁骏吾 : Proc Second Inter. Conf. Solid State and IC Technology, ed. Mo Bangxian, p. 44, 1989.

低压 MOCVD 生长的 InGaAs/InP 量子阱的光致发光谱线线宽及量子尺寸效应的测量分析

陈德勇　朱龙德　李　晶　熊飞克

徐俊英　万寿科　梁骏吾

中国科学院半导体研究所,北京　100083

(1992 年 1 月 28 日收到;1992 年 4 月 2 2 日收到修改稿)

摘要:用低压 MOCVD 方法生长了 InGaAs/InP 单量子阱及多量子阱结构.用低温光致发光方法研究了量子阱样品困量子尺寸效应引起的激子能量移动以及激子谱线线宽同量子阱阱宽的关系.7Å 阱宽的激子能量移动达 370meV.选取 $Q_c = \Delta E_c/\Delta E_g = 0.4$,采用修正后的 Kronig-Penny 模型,考虑能带的非抛物线性,拟合了激子能量移动和阱宽的关系曲线.用有效晶体近似方法(VCA)分析了激子尺寸范围内界面不平整度以及合金组分无序对激子谱线线宽的影响.以界面不平整度参量 δ_1 和 δ_2,合金组分无序参量 r_c 为拟合参数.拟合了激子线宽对阱宽的关系曲线.取 $\delta_1 = 2.93\text{Å}$,$\delta_2 = 100\text{Å}$,$r_c = 3\text{ML}$,理论拟合值与实验值符合较好.

PACC:7855,7865,8115H

一、引　言

量子尺寸效应和室温下二维激子的存在是量子阱结构的两个基本特征.由于量子阱结构的特有的物理特性,晶格匹配的和应变的 InGaAs/InP 量子阱材料,在长波长光纤通信用的激光器、探测器及调制器方面,在高速电子器件方面都有着十分重要的应用前景.有关这类量子阱材料的研究和器件应用已成为一个十分活跃的研究课题,引起了广泛的兴趣.

MOVPE(低压[1-3]和常压[4-5])及 CBE 是生长 InP 系材料的主要方法[6].低压条件更有利于突变陡峭异质结构的生长.低温光致发光是研究量子尺寸效应和界面特性的一种简单而重要的手段.D.Grützmacher 等人用 LPMOCVD 方法获得了窄至 0.5nm 的 InGaAs/InP 量子阱,低温(2K)激子能量移动达到 528meV,阱宽涨落<1ML,10nm 阱宽的激子荧光峰线宽为 3me V.本文利用瑞典进口的 MOCVD 仪器,生长出了标定阱宽为 0.7nm 的量子阱,其激子能量移动达 362meV(10K),达到国际上八十年代中期的水平.有关 InGaAs/InP 量子阱低温光致发光谱线线宽的分析,就我们所知,工作不细致,大多只考虑阱宽涨落引起的谱线展宽,而忽视了 InGaAs 合金组分无序造成的影响.Singh 等人提出了三维体材料中合金组分无序以及不均匀余相导致激子谱线加宽的理论模型[7].本文考虑量子阱

原载于:电子学报,191,19(3):30-35.

中激子的准二维特性以及激子局域于阱层内的几率.发展了上述模型,选取合适的模拟参数,得到了符合实验结果的理论曲线.此外,在计算激子能量移动过程中,运用了 Kane 的三带模型理论[8],考虑了能带的非抛物线修正,也获得了较好的结果.

二、实　验

样品生长是在水平式反应器内进行的.沉积碳化硅的石墨基座由高频感应加热,反应管方形内管的截面积为 $6.0 \times 1.5 \mathrm{cm}^2$.使用的反应源为 TMG,TM I,100% 的 AsH_3 和 PH_3,经钯管纯化的氢气为载体.总的气流为 11SLM.各源占的摩尔分数是 TMI:5.1×10^{-5}.TMG:3.1×10^{-5},PH_3:1.4×10^{-2},AsH_3:4.4×10^{-3},TMI 源温度为 15℃,源瓶压力 150mbar,TMG 源温度为 -10℃,源瓶压力为 1.2atm.系统压力为 50mbar.生长温度为 640℃,衬底为 (001) 取向 S 掺杂 N 型 InP.在以上生长条件下,生长了 InGaAs/InP 近匹配的体材料,根据生长的厚度和时间确定的生长速率为 InGaAs:6.41Å/s,InP:3.52Å/s.

量子阱的生长分为两类,一类是多个不同阱宽的单量子阱(QWs 1—4),另一类是多量子阱(SL1—10).所有样品的生长均由计算机控制.首先在 InP 衬底上生长一层 InP 缓冲层,然后再根据需要生长多个单量子阱或多量子阱.表 1 是多个单量子阱样品的生长安排(从左到右为生长顺序),表 2 是多量子阱样品的生长安排.

表 1　多个单量子阱样品的生长安排

样品	参数	缓冲层	参考层	势垒层	量子阱				顶层
QWS-2	生长时间(s)	900	180	90	18	11	6	3	600
	厚度(Å)	3600	1154	360	115	70	38	19	2400
QWS-3	生长时间(s)	1500		140	18	11	6	4	2	600
	厚度(Å)	6000		560	115	70	38	26	13	2400
QWS-4	生长时间(s)	900	180	140	18	8	4	1	600
	厚度(Å)	3600	1154	560	115	51	26	7	2400

表 2　多量子阱样品的生长安排

样品	参数	缓冲层	势垒层	阱层	顶层	周期数
SL-1	生长时间(s)	900	60	15	900	10
	厚度(Å)	3600	240	96	3600	
SL-4	生长时间(s)	300	27	5	4800	20
	厚度(Å)	1200	108	32	19200	
SL-8	生长时间(s)	900	28	5	4800	30
	厚度(Å)	3600	112	32	19200	

具体的 LP-MOCVD 生长工艺条件参见文献[9].

低温光致发光实验用 Ar^+ 激光器作激发源,激发波长是 5145Å.典型的激发功率为 100mW,只对 QWS-4 进行变化激发强度的实验(40—200mW)样品置于制冷器冷指上,温度为 15K. 采用双光栅 0.5m 单色仪分光, 液氮制冷锗探测器接收信号, 经锁相放大器放大后输出, 驱动记录仪记录谱线.

三、理 论 计 算

1. 量子尺寸效应

当量子阱的厚度可以与电子或空穴的德布罗意波长相比拟时, 载流子(电子或空穴)在垂直于界面方向即 z 方向上的运动是量子化的, 可近似用一维方势阱的有效质量 Schrö-dingez 方程描述, 利用边界上波函数 φ 及 $\dfrac{1}{m}\dfrac{d\varphi}{dz}$ 连续, 得到单量子阱中受限载流子的能量本征方程是

$$\frac{m_W}{K_W} = \frac{m_h}{K_b} \text{tg} \frac{K_W d}{2},$$

$$K_W = \sqrt{\frac{2m_W E}{\hbar^2}}, \quad K_b = \sqrt{\frac{2m_b(V-E)}{\hbar^2}}. \tag{1}$$

其中 m_w, m_b 是载流子在势阱区和势垒区内的有效质量, V 是势阱高度, d 是势阱宽度.

根据 Kane 的三带模型理论[8], 导带与价带及自旋分裂带三带之间耦合, 导致导带、轻空穴价带非抛物线性. 重空穴价带因不与其它带耦合而维持抛物线性. 有效质量的具体表达式是:

$$m_{hh}^*(E) = m_h,$$

$$m_e^*(E) = m_e \frac{3Eg+2\Delta}{Eg(Eg+\Delta)} \cdot \frac{(E+Eg)(E+Eg+\Delta)}{3(E+Eg)+2\Delta}, \tag{2}$$

$$m_{ch}^*(E) = m_l \cdot \frac{6Eg+2\Delta}{Eg(2Eg+\Delta)} \cdot \frac{(E+Eg)(E+2Eg+\Delta)}{3(E+2Eg)+2\Delta},$$

其中 m_h, m_e, m_c 为 $E=0$ 时即在 Γ 点的重空穴、电子和轻空穴的有效质量, Eg 是带隙, Δ 是自旋轨道分裂值. 不同的半导体材料取不同的 Eg 和 Δ 值. 在 InGaAs/InP 量子阱中, 阱中载流子有效质量由(2)式给出, $Eg, \Delta, m_k, m_e, m_i$ 取 InGaAs 的值, 势垒中载流子的有效质量除相应参数取 InP 值以外, (2)式中的 E 换成 $V-E$.

对电子 $V=\Delta E_c$(导带失调), 对重空穴, $V=\Delta E_v$(价带失调). $\Delta E_c+\Delta E_v=\Delta E_g$ 是两种半导体材料的带隙差. 关于 $\Delta E_c/\Delta E_g=Q_c$ 的取值, 一般文献上取 40%[4]. 在我们的计算中采用这一值, 其它用到的参数值见表 3.

表 3 计算中用到的参数值

	E_g(eV)	Δ_0(eV)	m_e(emμ)	m_g(emμ)	α_0(Å)
InP	1.424	0.11	0.079	0.606	5.8603
GaAs	1.519	0.34	0.067	0.341	5.6416
InAs	0.418	0.37	0.023	0.400	6.0501

$In_xGa_{1-x}As$ 量子阱的有关参数除 Eg 外, 由线性插值(vegard 定律)求出. Eg 为抛物线

插值

$$Eg(x) = 1.519 - 1.597x + 0.496x^2 \qquad (3)$$

由以上参数,在不同阱宽 d 下,对电子和重空穴分别用计算机程序求解方程(1)的最小数值解,得到电子和重空穴在量子阱中的基态能量 E^e 和 E^h,量子阱带隙能量移动为 $E^e + E^h$. 从而得到一条能量移动对量子阱阱宽的理论拟合曲线.

2. InGaAs/InP 量子阱光致发光激子谱线线宽的分析

在量子阱材料中存在二维激子. 激子跃迁的光谱线宽由均匀线宽和非均匀线宽迭加而成,在低温下,均匀展宽可忽略不计[10]. 不均匀展宽主要是由量子阱宽度的原子层量级的涨落引起的,在势阱为合金半导体时,合金组分无序也是引起谱线加宽的主要原因. 有效晶体近似方法[7,11,12]就是在激子尺寸范围内考虑异质界面的不平整以及合金组分涨落对晶体势的影响,用统计方法计算合金组分涨落及阱层界面不平整发生的几率来确定激子能量的扰动,从而获得相应的谱线宽度.

1) 合金组分无序引起的谱线加宽

在 $In_{\lambda n}Ga_{1-xu}As$ 合金中,设 V_c 为产生组分无序的合金团体积. 球形近似下 $V_c = \frac{4}{3}\pi r_c^3$. r_c 是合金团半径,在激子体积 V_{ex} 范围内,In 组分浓度为 x 的几率由下式给出

$$P(x) = \exp\left[-\frac{V_{ex}}{V_c}\left(x\ln\frac{x}{x_0} + (1-x)\ln\frac{1-x}{1-x_0} \right) \right]. \qquad (4)$$

当 $V_{ex}/V_c \gg 1$ 时,将上式展开得

$$P(x) = \exp\left(-\frac{V_{ex}}{V_c} \cdot \frac{(x-x_u)^2}{2x_0(1-x_u)} \right). \qquad (5)$$

其半宽

$$\sigma = 2\sqrt{2\ln 2}\left[\frac{V_c}{V_{ex}}x_0(1-x_0) \right]^{1/2}. \qquad (6)$$

在量子阱中激子波函数在 z 方向(生长方向)上受到限制,激子体积会收缩,变成准二维激子[14].

$$V_{ex} = \frac{4}{3}\pi R_{ex}^2 \cdot \frac{d}{2}, \qquad (7)$$

式中 R_{ex} 是激子半径,d 是阱宽

考虑激子局域于阱中的几率,因组分无序引起的激子谱线线宽为[15]

$$\Gamma_a = \left| \frac{dE_g}{dx} \right| \cdot \sigma \cdot P_{ex}, \qquad (8)$$

$$P_{ex} = \langle \psi_e | \psi_e \rangle_{\text{well}} \cdot \langle \psi_h | \psi_h \rangle_{\text{well}} \qquad (9)$$

是激子局域在量子阱中的几率.

由(4-9),给定 r_c, d, x_0 值即可求得激子谱线的线宽 Γ_a.

2) 界面不平整引起的谱线加宽

在异质外延生长中,界面上会出现原子层厚度的岛和谷[16],这些岛和谷的存在引起量子阱的有效阱宽发生变化,从而影响激子能量,导致谱线加宽.

设外延生长方向上岛和谷以及平坦区的横向尺寸分别是 $\delta_{2a}, \delta_{2b}, \delta_{2c}$,平均密度是 C_a^0,

C_b^0, C_c^0 . 岛和谷的深度为 δ_1 , 则在激子尺寸范围内岛和谷以及平坦区密度为 C_a , C_b , C_c 的几率[11]

$$P(C_a, C_b, C_c, R_{ex}) = \exp\left[-\left(\frac{2R^2}{\delta_{2a}^2}C_a\ln\frac{C_a}{C_a^0} + \frac{2R_{ex}^2}{\delta_{2b}^2}C_b\ln\frac{C_b}{C_b^0} + \frac{2R_{ex}^2}{\delta_{2c}^2}C_c\ln\frac{C_a}{C_c^0}\right)\right]. \qquad (10)$$

忽略平坦区 $C_c^0 = 0$,并假定 $C_a^0 = C_b^0 = \frac{1}{2}$,展开上式.

$$P(C_a, C_b, R_{ex}) = \exp\left[-\frac{2R_{ex}^2}{\delta_2^2} \cdot \frac{(C_a - C_a^0)^2}{2C_a^0 C_b^0}\right]. \qquad (11)$$

其半高宽

$$\sigma = 2\sqrt{\ln 2 \cdot C_a^0 C_b^0} \cdot \delta_z / R_{ex} = \frac{\sqrt{\ln 2} \cdot \delta_2}{R_{ex}}. \qquad (12)$$

阱宽的变化 $\Delta d = 2\delta \cdot \sigma$

由 Δd 引起的激子能量改变即线宽

$$\Gamma_t(d, \delta_1, \delta_2) = \Delta d \cdot \left|\frac{\alpha E_{ex}}{\partial d}\right| d = dn\Big|, \qquad (13)$$

总的线宽 $\Gamma = \Gamma_a + \Gamma_l$.

四、实验结果及讨论

对所有的多个单量子阱样品(QWS1-4),和部分多量子阱样品进行低温($T = 15\text{K}$)光致发光实验,图 1 是样品 QWS-4 的低温光致发光谱图.

InGaAs 参考层发出的荧光峰出现双峰结构.峰的位置较区配的 InGaAs 体材料向长波方向红移,表明 InGaAs 层发生正的失配 $\Delta a/a$.所有量子阱激子能量移动都是相对于这一参考层的峰位,最大的能量移动是 370meV,相应于生长 1s(大约 7Å)的量子阱,阱宽越大,能量移动越小.图 2 画出了所有量子阱样品的激子能量移动随阱宽变化的实验点,以及从方程(1)计算的能量移动对阱宽的关系曲线,阱宽较窄时(<20Å)实验点位于理论曲线下面.可能是由于阱宽误差所致.另外在计算中所采用的参数,比如 $V_c E_g \text{InGaAs}$,以及应变等都影响了激子能量的移动? 总的说来,符合较好.

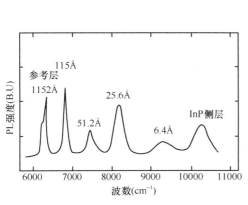

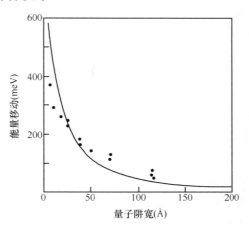

图 1　样品 QWS-4 的低温光致发光光谱($T = 15\text{K}$)　图 2　激子能量移动与量子阱宽的关系曲线

衡量异质界面陡度的一个重要指标是量子阱光荧光峰的半宽 FWHM.我们求出了所有单量子阱样品的线宽,并描出了线宽对阱宽的实验点,见图 3.

阱宽越大.半宽越小,最小的半宽是参考层荧光峰的,只有 3.1meV(激发强度 40mW),最大值属于 7Å 量子阱,在 100mW 激发强度下达 60meV 根据第三部分的理论推导,我们采用合适的参数 $\delta_1 = 2.93$Å,$\delta_2 = 100$Å,$r_c = 8.79$Å.拟合了 $\Gamma(d)$ 曲线见图 3.在窄阱情况下量子阱阱宽的原子层涨落是谱线加宽的主要因素.在本实验中,阱宽的平均涨落小于 1ML = 2.93Å,而在较大的阱宽下(>30Å),合金组分无序引起的加宽不容忽视.造成合金组分无序的原因.可能是由于在生长 InGaAs 过程中,温度较低,因合金相图中的非混溶隙(miscibility gap).会产生相的分离,出现两相或多相结构.将导致荧光谱线的加宽,以及峰位的移动.图 1 中的参考峰的移动以及双峰结构与文献[17]中两相结构效应一致,这支持了前面讨论的组分不均匀导致谱线加宽的结论.

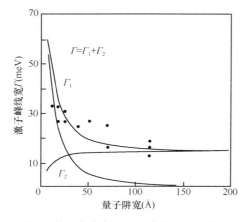 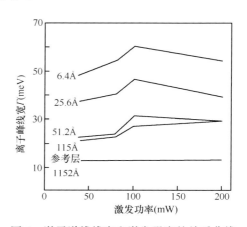

图 3　激子峰线宽和量子阱宽的关系曲线　　　图 4　激子谱线线宽和激发强度的关系曲线

此外,激光照射到量子阱样品中产生的载流子(电子和空穴对)以及持续光电导效应造成的载流子也会引起谱线加宽[17].但是这种载流子效应在一定程度上达到饱和.我们的变化激发强度实验证实了这一点.图 4 是不同激发强度下 QWS-4 样品各个阱的荧光峰的半宽曲线,当激发强度增加时线宽增加.到 100mW 后变化很小,甚至有所降低.

五、结　论

本文系统研究了 LP-MOCVD 生长的 InGaAs/InP 量子阱结构的低温光致发光特性.对量子尺寸效应及低温光荧光峰的展宽机理进行了理论分析.7Å 宽的量子阱荧光峰的能量移动达 370meV.取 $Q_1 = 0.4$,考虑有效质量的修正,拟合了激子能量移动对阱宽的关系曲线,与实验值符合较好,在 InGaAs/InP 量子阱中,低温下激子谱线的展宽是由 InGaAs 合金组分无序以及异质界面不平整两种因素造成.对于窄阱(<20Å)界面不平整的贡献是主要的,而宽阱(>80Å)则主要是合金组分无序的贡献.所有这两种因素直接取决于 MOCVD 生长条件,因此,要生长高质量的 InGaAs/InP 量子阱材料.优化生长条件以减小合金组分无序及界面不平整程度十分重要.而这正是我们所追求的目标.

参考文献

［1］ D.Grutzmacher,K.Wolber,H.Jurgensen and P.Balk.*Appl.Phys.Lett.*,52.872(1988).

［2］ P.Wiedemann,M.Klenk,W.Korber,U.Koerner,R.Weinmann.E.Zielinski and P.Sperer.*J.Crystal Growth*,107,573(1991).

［3］ J.Camassel,J.P.Laurenti,S.Juillaguet.F.Reinhardt,K.Wolter,H.Kurz and D.Grutzmacher.*J.Crystal Growth*, 107,543(1991).

［4］ B.I.Miller,E.F.Schubert,U.Koreo.A.Ourmazd.A.H.Dayem and R.J.Capic,*Appl.Phys.Lett.*,49,1384(1986).

［5］ T.Y.Wang.K.L.Fry,A.Persson.E.H.Reihlen and G.B.Stringfellow,*J.Appl.Phys.*,63,2674(1988).

［6］ W.T.Tsang and E.F.Schubert.*Appl.Phys.Lett.*,49,220(1986).

［7］ J.Singh and K.K.Bajaj.*Appl.Phys.Lett.*,44.1075(1984).

［8］ E.O.Kane,J.Phys.*Chem.Solids*,1,249(1957).

［9］ 朱龙德,李晶,陈德勇,熊飞克,半导体学报,14(4),(1993).

［10］ J.Lee,E.S.Koteles and M.O.Vassell,*Phys, Rev.*,B33.5512(1986).

［11］ J.Singh.K.K.Bajaj and S.Chaudhuic.*Appl.Phys.Lett.*,44,805(1984).

［12］ 徐强,徐仲英,郑宝真,许继宗,半导体学报,11(6),404(1990).

［13］ E.F.Schubert,E.O.Gobel,Y.Horykoshi,K.Ploog and H.J.Queisser,*Phys.Rev.*,B30,813(1984).

［14］ W.Stolz,J.C.Maan,M.Altarelli,L.Tapfer and K.Ploog,*Phys.Rev.*,B36,4301(1987).

［15］ M.Sugawara,T.Fujii,M.Kondo,K.Kato,S.Domen,S.Yamazaki and K.Nakajima,*Appl.Plys*,*Lett.*,53,2290(1988).

［16］ C.Weisbuch,R.dingle,P.M.Petroff,A.C.Gassard and Wiegmann,Appl.*Phys*,*Lett.*,38,840(1981).

［17］ S.J.Bass,S.J.Barnett,G.T.Brown,N.G.Chew,A.G.Cullis,M.S.Skoinick and L.L.Taylor,*NATO ASI Series*, *Physics* 163, 137(1986).

Investigation of PL Linewidth and Quantum Size Effect of InGaAs/InP Quantum Wells Grown by LP-MOCVD

Chen Deyong,Zhu Longde,Li Jing,Xiong Feike,

Xu Junying,Wan Shouke and Liang Junwu

(*Institute of Semiconductors*, *Academia Sinica*, *Beijing* 1000083)

(*Received* 28 *January* 1992;*reuised manuscript received* 22 *April* 1992)

Abstract:Single and multiple InGaAs/InP quantum well structures were grown by MOCVD at 50mbar.Photoluminescence method was used to characterize the relation between the exciton energy shift and the well width caused by quantum size effect.The energy shift of a 7Å quantum well was as high as 370meV.Considering the nonparabolic nature of the bands, we took $Q_c = \Delta E_c/\Delta E_g = 0.4$, and got a curve about energy shift and width, which was a good fit for the experimental points.Virtul Crystal Approximation (VCA) method was applied to discuss the dominant mechanism for the linewidth broadening over the extent of exciton.With the interface microscopic fluctuations $\delta_1 = 2.93\text{Å}$,$\delta_3 = 100\text{Å}$,and the radius of the cluster in the alloy $R_c = 3\text{ML}$, variation of the exciton photoluminescence linewidth Γ as a function of well width d was obtained, which was also a very good approximation to the experimental results.

PACC:7885,7865,8115H

GaAs/Si 外延层 X 射线双晶衍射摇摆曲线的动力学模拟和位错密度的测量

郝茂盛　　王玉田　　梁骏吾

(中国科学院半导体研究所；国家光电工艺中心，北京，100083)

摘要：利用 X 射线衍射动力学理论和位错的小角晶界模型，分析了 GaAs/Si 外延层中位错对 X 射线双晶衍射摇摆曲线的影响，认为 GaAs/Si 外延层并不是严格取向一致的完整单晶膜，而是存在着许多小角晶界的镶嵌晶体，并推导出了其中镶嵌块的晶向分布函数和晶格应变分布函数，模拟出了 GaAs/Si 外延层 X 射线双晶衍射摇摆曲线，由此曲率计算出了 GaAs/Si 外延层中的位错密度。同时还得到了 Si 衬底上 GaAs 外延层中镶嵌块的大小。为分析高失配外延材料的双晶衍射摇摆曲线提供了新的方向。

关键词：X 射线双晶衍射　小角晶界模型　镶嵌晶体　异质结

GaAs/Si 异质外延生长由于其可能的应用前景，得到了高度重视。首先它为我们实现光电集成提供了一条途径，同时，作为衬底的 Si 单晶本身也体现出许多显著优点，它不但质量轻，而且导热性能、机械性能均优于 GaAs 单晶，另外，Si 工艺的发展已相当成熟，很容易得到质量高、面积大的 Si 衬底。这一切对 GaAs/Si 器件非常有利。但是，由于 Si 是非极性晶体，GaAs 是极性晶体，Si 和 GaAs 的晶格常数以及热膨胀系数都相差很大，所以，GaAs/Si 外延层中必然存在大量位错。位错对半导体器件，特别是光电器件是非常有害的，因此如何精确测量 GaAs/Si 外延层中的位错密度是一个十分重要的问题。

透射电镜横截面测量法（TEM）和腐蚀坑测量法（EPD）作为测量位错密度的两种方法，都是破坏性的。用 TEM 测量位错密度，不但制样麻烦，而且由于其视场很小，只能用于测量高缺陷样品中的位错密度。EPD 法对于亚微米级的薄层样品十分困难，而且对于高位错密度（$5 \times 10^6 \mathrm{cm}^{-2}$）的样品还有位错腐蚀坑重叠等问题，所以其测量结果不够准确。用 X 射线双晶衍射摇摆曲线测量位错密度的技术作为 TEM 和 EPD 的补充，有很多优点，它不需要任何复杂的制样过程，是一种理想的非破坏性测量方法。有人[1]利用近似公式 $D = \beta^2/9b^2$ 来估计晶体中的位错密度，式中 D 是位错密度，β 是 X 射线双晶衍射摇摆曲线的半高宽，b 是位错的 Burgers 矢量，这种计算显然不够精确。最近，Ayers[2]把 Hordon[3]等人提出的关于有位错金属晶体的 X 射线双晶衍射摇摆曲线的加宽理论应用到了闪锌矿结构的半导体晶体，推导出了利用 X 射线双晶衍射摇摆曲线的半高宽（FWHM）计算其中位错密度的方法。Ayers 只考虑了位错导致的晶体偏转和位错产生的应变对 X 射线双晶衍射摇摆曲线 FWHM 的加宽，忽略了镶嵌块尺寸效应对 FWHM 的加宽作用，更重要的是它没有考虑 X 射线双晶衍射摇摆曲线的峰形，并且在最后的计算中把 GaAs/Si 系统中的 60° 位错当做螺旋位错来处理。到目前为止，利用动力学理论模拟双晶衍射摇摆曲线，从而

原载于：半导体学报，1995，16（3）：188-194.

求出位错密度、镶嵌块大小的工作还没有.在本文中,我们利用 X 射线双晶衍射动力学理论,将位错导致的镶钳块偏转、位错引入的应变、镶嵌块尺寸效应统一考虑,模拟出了 GaAs/Si 外延层的 X 射线双晶衍射摇摆曲线,并由此精确地求出了 GaAs/Si 外延层中的位错密度.

1. 理论分析

众所周知,GaAs/Si 外延层 X 射线双晶衍射摇摆曲线的 FWHM 一般在 200s 左右,比完整 GaAs 晶体的 FWHM((004)衍射的本征宽度为 7.9s)大许多,由于 GaAs/Si 失配很大(4%),GaAs 外延层存在大量位错,而且这些位错不可能均匀地分布,位错的堆集会形成亚晶界.从而形成镶钳晶体,使 GaAs 外延层的 X 射线双晶衍射 FWHM 加宽.

1.1 单个镶嵌块对 X 射线的反射率

设外延层的厚度为 T_0,当 X 射线相对于整个外延层晶体表面的掠射角为 θ 时,则 X 射线相对于某一个镶嵌块的掠射角为 $\theta' = \theta + \xi$(ξ 为某一个镶钳块晶向偏离平均晶向的角度).根据 X 射线衍射动力学理论[4],从 Maxwell 方程组出发,按照平面波、双光束近似,就可以推导出,对于对称 Bragg 衍射,不存在应变的单个镶嵌块的反射率在 Bragg 角 θ'_B 附近的分布为:

$$R'(\theta' - \theta'_B) = \frac{\sinh^2\left[A\sqrt{1-y^2}\right]}{|1-y^2| + \sinh^2\left[A\sqrt{1-y^2}\right]} \tag{1}$$

其中

$$A = -\frac{1+|\cos 2\theta'_B|}{2}\frac{k_0\pi e^2 F_H d_0}{\varepsilon_0 m w_0^2 a^3 \sin\theta'}, y = \frac{\dfrac{e^2 F_0}{\varepsilon_0 m w_0^2 a^3} + (\theta' - \theta'_B)\sin 2\theta_B}{\dfrac{1+|\cos 2\theta'_B|}{2}\dfrac{e^2 F_H}{\varepsilon_0 m w_0^2 a^3}}$$

k 为 X 射线的波矢, ω_0 为 X 射线的角频率, m 为电子的质量, F_H 为相应 Bragg 衍射的结构因子, d_0 为镶钳块的大小, a 为镶钳块垂直于衍射面方向的晶格常数, ε_0 为真空介电常数.

1.2 存在应变的单个镶嵌块对 X 射线的反射率

考虑到应变的存在,任意一个镶嵌块垂直于衍射面方向的晶格常数 a 在平均晶格常数 a_0 附近有个随机分布 $P(a)$,所以存在应变的单个镶嵌块对 X 射线的反射率在平均晶格常数 a_0 的 Bragg 角 θ_B 附近的分布应为:

$$R(\theta' - \theta_B) = \int_{a_0-\tau}^{a_0+\tau} R'(\theta' - \theta_B)P(a)\,\mathrm{d}a, \tag{2}$$

上式的积分上下限分别为 $a+\tau$ 和 $a-\tau$,τ 是一个正常,当 τ 大到一定程度时 $P(a_0+\tau)$ 接近于 0,实际计算时 τ 取 0.2nm 就可达到精度.

现在来求晶格常数 a 的分布函数 $P(a)$.

设由位错导致的垂直于衍射面方向的应变分布函数 $P(\varepsilon)$ 为 Gauss 分布

$$P(\varepsilon) = \frac{1}{\sqrt{2\pi}\,c}\mathrm{e}^{\varepsilon^2/2c^2}, \tag{3}$$

这里 $\varepsilon = (a - a_0)/a_0$ 为位错导致的应变,c 为应变的均方根,a 为垂直于衍射面方向的晶格常数.

因为在(001)面的 GaAs 外延层中,位错主要是 60° 位错,所以,Ayers[2] 根据位错理论[5]和文献[3]的推导结果,计算出:

$$c^2 = 0.28\left(\frac{b^2 D}{\pi^2}\right)\ln\left(\frac{5 \times 10^6}{\sqrt{D}}\right), \tag{4}$$

其中 D 的单位为 cm^{-2},b 的单位用 cm.

将(4)式代入(3)式,就可得导用 D 表示的晶格应变分布函数.如果再将(3)式中的变量 ε 用 $(a - a_0)/a_0$ 代替,就可以得到 a 在 a_0 附近的分布,归一化后的结果为:

$$P(a) = \frac{1}{\sqrt{2\pi}\, c a_0}e^{-(a-a_0)^2/2c^2 a_0^2}. \tag{5}$$

将(5)式代入(2)式就可具体求得存在应变的单个镶嵌块对 X 射线的反射率在 Bragg 角 θ_B 附近的分布.

1.3 一层镶嵌块对 X 射线的反射率

在 X 射线双晶衍射中,镶嵌晶体中有许多镶嵌块参与衍射.设这些镶嵌块的晶向分布函数 $W(\xi)$ 为 Gauss 分布,且可以用一个参数表示,则

$$W(\xi) = \frac{1}{\sqrt{2\pi}\,\eta}e^{-\xi^2/2\eta^2}, \tag{6}$$

其中 ξ 为任意一个镶嵌块晶向偏离平均晶向的角度,η 为标准偏差.

设外延层中镶嵌块的平均大小为 d_0,根据小角晶界模型[6],当镶嵌块间的夹角为 φ,位错 Burgers 矢量为 b 时,由此决定的位错密度为:

$$D = \frac{\varphi}{b d_0}. \tag{7}$$

由(6)式可以得到,相邻两个镶嵌块夹角为 $\varphi(\varphi > 0)$ 的几率为:

$$W'(\varphi) = \int_{-\infty}^{+\infty} W(\xi)\left[W(\xi + \varphi) + W(\xi - \varphi)\right]d\xi = \frac{1}{\sqrt{\pi}\,\eta}e^{-\varphi^2/4\eta^2}. \tag{8}$$

整个外延层中的位错密度 D 应为:

$$D = \int_0^{\infty} W'(\varphi)\frac{\varphi}{b d_0}d\varphi = \frac{2\eta}{\sqrt{\pi}\,b d_0} \tag{9}$$

这样就把镶嵌块的晶向分布函数 $W(\xi)$ 用外延层中的位错密度 D 和镶嵌块的平均大小 d_0 来表示:

$$W(\xi) = \frac{\sqrt{2}}{\pi b d_0 D}e^{-2\xi^2/\pi(b d_0 D)^2}. \tag{10}$$

如果认为 GaAs 外延层中主要是 60° 位错则 $b = (\sqrt{2}/2)a_0$.

因为不同镶嵌块的晶向分布是随机的,它们对 X 射线的散射是非相干的,所以,一层镶嵌晶块,也就是厚度为 d_0 的外延层对 X 射线的反射率 r 也可以表示成积分形式,即:

$$r = \int_{-\infty}^{+\infty} R(\theta' - \theta_B)W(\xi)d\xi. \tag{11}$$

此外延层中厚度为 dT 的薄层对 X 射线的反射率 δdT 可表示成:

$$\delta \mathrm{d}T = \frac{r}{d_0}\mathrm{d}T. \tag{12}$$

1.4 整个外延层对 X 射线的反射率

根据双光束近似[4],仍然假设在晶体中只存在一束入射光和一束反射光.设距外延层表面 T 处,入射光束的强度为 $P_0(T)$,反射光束的强度为 $P_H(T)$,外延层的线吸收系数为 μ_0,则穿过 $\mathrm{d}T$ 的薄层后,两束光的强度变化为:

$$\mathrm{d}P_0(T) = -\mu_0 P_0(T)\frac{\mathrm{d}T}{\sin\theta} - \delta P_0(T)\mathrm{d}T + \delta P_H(T)\mathrm{d}T,$$

$$\mathrm{d}P_H(T) = \mu_0 P_H(T)\frac{\mathrm{d}T}{\sin\theta} + \delta P_H(T)\mathrm{d}T - \delta P_0(T)\mathrm{d}T. \tag{13}$$

这是一个微分方程组,其边界条件为:

当 $T = O$,也就是在外延层表面处,$P_0(T) = P_0(O)$,

当 $T = T_0$,也就是在外延层与衬底交界面处,$P_H(T_0) = O$.

求解这个微分方程组可以得到整个外延层对 X 射线的反射率:

$$\frac{P_H(0)}{P_0(0)} = \frac{\delta + \dfrac{\mu_0}{\sin\theta} - U}{\delta} - \frac{U\left(\delta + \dfrac{\mu_0}{\sin\theta} - U\right)\mathrm{e}^{-UT_0}}{\delta\left[\left(\delta + \dfrac{\mu_0}{\sin\theta}\right)sinh(UT_0) + Ucosh(UT_0)\right]},$$

其中

$$U = \sqrt{\left(\delta + \frac{\mu_0}{\sin\theta}\right)^2 - \delta^2}.$$

上式中除变量 θ 和 δ 外,均为常数.当外延层中的位错密度 D 和镶嵌块的大小 d_0 已知时,δ 也只是 X 射线平均掠射角 θ 的函数,对每一个掠射角 θ,根据(12)式和(11)式就可以求出一个 δ 值.外延层的厚度 T_0 可以通过其它方法(如台阶仪)测量,GaAs 的线吸收系数 μ_0 为 403.9cm^{-1}.因此,根据(14)式,就可以求得整个外延层对 X 射线的反射率在 Bragg 角 θ_B 附近的分布.反过来如果测得外延层的 X 射线的反射率在 Bagg 角 θ_B 附近的分布.反过来如果测得外延层或 X 射线双晶衍射摇摆曲线,就可以通过对其模拟计算,求得外延层中的位错密度 D 和其中镶嵌块的大小 d_0.具体计算中使用 $\Delta\theta(\Delta\theta = \theta - \theta_B)$ 作变量.

2. 结果分析

文中所用的 GaAs/Si 样品是使用 MOCVD 生成的,样品在出反应室前在 As 压下 850℃退火 30min.外延层厚度经台阶仪测量为 $T_0 = 2\mu m$.X 射线双晶衍射摇摆曲线的实验曲线由理学双晶衍射仪测得,使用的是 Cu 靶,$\lambda = 0.154nm$,第一晶体为非对称的 Ge(004).

图 1 是某一 Si 上 GaAs 样品(004)摇摆曲线的实验结果和模拟结果的比较,从中可以发现模拟结果和实验结果符合的很好.这里得到的外延层位错密度 D 等于 $1.65 \times 10^8 cm^{-2}$.镶嵌块的大小 d_0 等于 1 050nmA.为了验证这个结果,我们使用通过模拟(004)摇摆曲线得到的 D 值和 d_0 值,反过来计算出了该样品的(006)摇摆曲线,发现它和实验结果也符合的很好(见图 2).

大量实验事实表示[7],在 Si 上直接外延生长 GaAs,刚开始一定是三维岛状生长,所

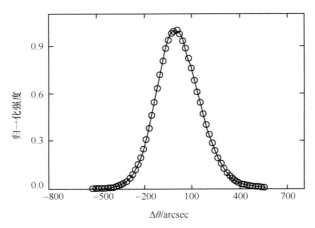

图 1 Si 上 GaAs 的 (004) 摇摆曲线

○ 为实验曲线   —— 为理论曲线

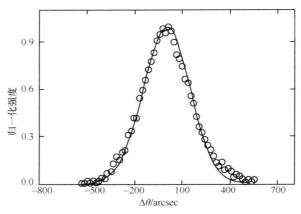

图 2 Si 上 GaAs 的 (006) 摇摆曲线

说明同图 1

以,现时一般采用两步生长法[8],先在 Si 衬底上低温(400℃左右)生长大约 20nm 厚的 GaAs,比较平整地覆盖 Si 衬底,然后再进行第二步生长.因为第一层 GaAs 本身质量很差,由很多晶粒组成,这些晶粒在第二次生长中逐渐合并长大,形成最终的镶嵌晶体.镶嵌块的大小和外延层的生长条件密切相关,因此通过模拟 GaAs/Si 外延层的双晶衍射摇摆曲线,还可以研究 GaAs/Si 外延的生长机理.

3. 结论

本文第一次应用 X 射线动力学理论结合小角晶界模型,考虑了取向差、位错引入的应变和镶嵌块尺寸对失配体系 GaAs/Si 外延层的双晶衍射摇摆曲线的影响,并对其进行了计算机模拟.模拟曲线与测量结果符合的很好,说明本文提出的计算方法是正确的,GaAs/Si 外延层确实是镶嵌晶体结构.作为通过 X 射线双晶衍射摇摆曲线计算 GaAs/Si 外延层中的位错密度的方法.本文还给出了 GaAs/Si 外延层中镶嵌块的大小,为分析高失配外延材料的双晶衍射摇摆曲线提供了新的方法.

参考文献

[1] Chand N, Allam J.Gibson J M et al.GaAs avalanche photodiodes and the effect of rapid thermal annealing on crystalline quality of GaAs.J Vac Sci Technol, 1987.B5(3):822—826.

[2] Ayer J E.The measurement of threading dislocation densities in semiconductor crystals by X-ray diffraction.Journal of Crystal Growth 1994.135:71—77.

[3] Hordon M J, Averbach B L.X-ray measurements of dislocation density in deformed copper and aluminum single crystals. Acta Met, 1961, 9:237—245.

[4] Pinsker Z G.Dynamical Scattering of X-rays in Crystal.2nd ed.Berlin:Springer Verlag, 1978.82—176.

[5] Nabarro F R N.Theory of Crystal Dislocations.2nd ed.New York:Dover, 1987.51—56.

[6] 许顺生.金属 X 射线学.上海:上海科学技术出版社,1962.40—80.

[7] Biegelsen D K.Ponce F A, Smith A J et al.Initial stages of epitaxial growth of GaAs on(100)silicon.Mat Res Soc Symp Proc, 1986, 67:45—48.

[8] Akiyama M, Kawarada Y, Kaminish K.Growth of single domain GaAs layer on (100)oriented Si substrate by MOCVD. Jpn J appl Phys, 1984, 23(Ⅱ):L843—L845.

SIPOS 膜的结构组成[*]

谭 凌 雷沛云 梁骏吾

(中国科学院半导体研究所,北京,100083)

摘要:采用常压化学气相淀积(APCVD)方法.生长了不同氧含量的 SIPOS(半绝缘含氧多晶硅)膜,研究了 SIPOS 膜的结构组成.SIPOS 膜是微晶,多晶和非晶共存的结构.其晶态物中含有缺氧的 α-Cristobalite(方石英)结构.膜中含氧量可变,以 SiO_x($x<2$)表示.随着氧含量的增加或减少,其结构向非晶或多晶方向移动.膜中氧原子分布不均匀,局部有氧原子微区集中或缺少现象,使 $x=0$ 或 1 或 2.

PACC:7360H;**EEACC**:2520M,2550E

1. 引 言

SIPOS(半绝缘含氧多晶硅)是七十年代中期出现的新型钝化材料,并以其电中性和半绝缘性等特点已成功地应用于器件工艺中[1-3].

大量实验表明,SIPOS 膜中的氧含量是一个重要的参数,它直接影响着 SIPOS 膜的生长,结构,各种物理化学性质以及在器件工艺中的应用等等.

关于 SIPOS 膜的结构组成,目前文献报道众说纷纭.根据 W.R.Knolle[4] 的统计模型,它是 $Si(Si_yO_{x-y})$ 形式的四面体结构,在各种氧化物形式中 SiO_2 的几率最小 M. Hamasaki[5] 的"镶嵌"模型则认为在 SIPOS 膜中包含了硅的微晶粒和硅的各种氧化物,它们"镶嵌"在非晶硅中.但这一模型被 James N.的实验否定了,他的理由是在实验中未观察到渗透阈值;而 James Ni[6] 提出的"壳"模型,即 SIPOS 膜中每一个硅粒都被一层薄的 SiO_2 所包围着,彼此是隔离的.氧主要以 SiO_2 的形式存在.这一模型很好地解释了 SIPOS 膜的电子输运机制;此外还有 B.Greenberg[7] 的 c-Si/a-Si/SiO_2 结构和 J.H.Thomas[8] 所认为的其中至少有硅以及硅的氧化物两个分离的相等等.这些观点,由于分析问题的出发点和角度以及手段不同,往往各有疏漏,无法统一.关于 SIPOS 膜的 Raman 谱的报道更是很少.目前见到的观点[9] 认为它反映了膜中晶态硅与非晶态硅的体积比.本文采用 X 射线衍射分析.TED 与 TEM 分析及 Raman 谱分析等测试方法.从不同侧面全面分析了 650℃ 下. APCVD 生长的各种氧含量的 SIPOS 膜的结构组成.得到了比较可靠的与实验相符的结论.

原载于:半导体学报,1993, 14(6):345-352.

*国家自然科学基金资助项目.

谭凌 女,1968 年生,助理工程师,从事半导体硅材料研究和分析工作,现在工作单位为北京有色金属研究总院半导体工程中心(100088).

雷沛云 男,1937 年生,高级工程师,从事集成电路工艺和半导体材料理化分析工作.

梁骏吾 男,1933 年生,研究员,从事半导体材料研究.

2. 实 验 结 果

2.1 SIPOS 膜的生长(样品制备)

目前 SIPOS 膜的生长主要有三种方式:APCVD. LPCVD 和 PECVD.本文采用 APCVD 法.在硅单晶衬底上生长不同氧含量的 SIPOS 膜,其化学气相反应可概括为:

$$SiH_4 + xN_2O \xrightarrow[650℃]{Ar} SiO_x + xN_2 \uparrow + 2H_2 \uparrow \tag{1}$$

实验表明.N_2O 和 SiH_4 的流量比 η 是一个很重要的参数,调节它可以严格控制 SI-POS 膜中的氧含量.生长条件见文献[12-14].

SIPOS 膜中氧含量的测定采用称重-红外法.利用下式[1,11]得到氧的原子百分比

$$at\%(O) = 2.63 \times 10^{-5}\alpha + 0.099 \tag{2}$$

其中,α 为红外吸收系数.

2.2 SIPOS 膜的结构组成

2.2.1 X 射线衍射分析结果

图 1 给出了氧含量为 30at% 和 45at% 的 SIPOS 膜的 X 射线衍射图谱,可以看到,二者衍射峰位置略偏移.相对强度育变化.

下面我们考虑衍射角的偏移与 SIPOS 膜组分的关系,通过 SIPOS 膜的 X 射线衍射谱无法检测到相应于 SIPOS 膜面间距的物质,说明在测量的 SIPOS 膜中不存在定态的 Si, SiO 或 SiO_2.可假定 SIPOS 膜样品是成分和结构都介于 Si 和 α-Cristobalite 之间.晶体结构相同,如果在 —Si—Si— 结构中加入氧原子成为 —Si—O—Si— ,则由硅晶体转化为 α-Cristobalite.这样,我们得到的将是一种面间距为 d_{Si} 和 d_{SiO_2} 的线性组合结果的物质,即是一种缺氧的 α-Cristobalie 结构.假定 SIPOS 膜成分为 $SiO_x(x<2)$,其面间距 d_{SIPOS} 与 SiO_2 和 Si 的面间距服从 Vigard 定理,那么对于 30at%(O) 和 45at%(O) 的 SIPOS 膜,实验得到的 d_{SIPOS} 与按照 Vigard 定理用 d_{Si} 和 d_{SiO_2} 数据计算的理论数值 d'_{SIPOS} 列于表 1.可以看到,理论值与实验值十分接近,可以认为上述线性组合的假定是符合实际的.说明 SIPOS 膜含有类 α-Cristobalite 结构,但结构中缺氧.

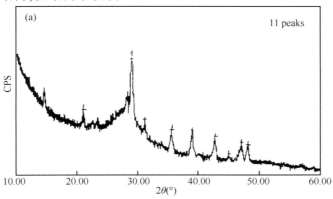

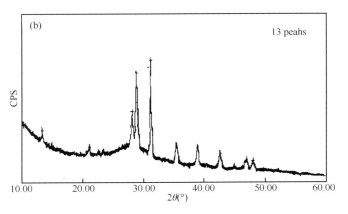

图 1　SIPOS 膜 X 射线衍射谱

(a)氧含量 30at% ;(b)氧含量 45at%

表 1　SIPOS 膜各沂射峰对应的晶面指数

晶面指数	晶面间距 $d(\text{Å})$					
	Si	SiO_2 *	30at%		45at%	
			理论	实验	理论	实验
001	5.44	6.90	6.08	6.01	6.40	6.63
101	3.84	4.04	3.94	4.19	3.96	4.19
011	3.84	4.02	3.92		3.95	3.92
110	3.84	3.53	3.71		3.64	3.77
111	3.14	3.14	3.14	3.14	3.14	3.15
002	2.72	3.45	3.07	3.07	3.22	
012	2.43	3.43	2.85	2.86	3.08	3.08
020	2.72	2.44	2.52	2.51	2.50	2.52
102	2.43	2.82	2.62		2.72	2.86
210	2.43	2.23	2.30	2.31	2.26	2.30
121	2.22	2.11	2.17	2.11	2.15	2.12
211	2.22	2.12	2.16	2.01	2.14	2.01
122	1.81	1.86	1.89	1.93	1.87	1.92
212	1.81	1.87	1.86	1.88	1.86	1.89

＊注:数据取自 ASTM(11—695)卡片,SiO₂/Cristobalite syl

2.2.2　TED 与 TEM 分析结果

图 2(见图版 I)给出了 SIPOS 膜的 TED 图像,其中(a)(b)(c)分别对应着氧含量为 23at% ,33at% 和 45at% 的 SIPOS 膜.由图可见,SIPOS 膜的 TED 图像明显为多晶的衍射环状.同时其衍射环的形态又明显随着氧含量的不同而不同:氧含量越低.衍射环数目越多,衍射环越锐;随着氧含量的增加.衍射环数目减少.并变得弥散.当氧含量增至 45at% 时,衍射环弥散为三个亮带,说明此时样品更接近于非晶态了.图 3 为 SIPOS 膜的 TEM 图像(见图版 I)亦有很好的说明:氧含量较低时.形貌具有很清晰的晶粒间界,呈明显的多晶形

貌;随着氧含量的增加,晶粒间界逐渐模糊,当氧含量达到45at%时.晶粒间界逐渐消失,已经很接近于非晶形貌了.表2是图2之衍射环的数值计算结果.

表2　图2之 TFM 衍射环的数值计算结果

衍射环半径 r(cm)	0.83	0.94	0.99	1.02	1.44	1.50	1.63	1.69	1.77	2.04	2.17	2.50	2.65	3.05
晶面间距 d(Å)	2.49	2.18	2.08	2.01	1.43	1.37	1.26	1.22	1.16	1.01	0.95	0.82	0.78	0.67
ASTM 卡片晶面间距	2.50	2.17	2.114	2.01	1.43	1.36	1.25	1.21	1.17	1.04	0.96	0.83	0.79	0.68
ASTM 卡片物质	SiO_2 (110)	SiO_2 (200)	SiO_2 (004)	SiO_2 (201)	SiO_2 (300)	SiO	Si (331)	SiO_2 (213)	SiO_2 (303)	St (511)	Si (440)	St (533)	SiO	SiO
氧含量 23at%	+			+	+		+	+	+	+	+	+	+	+
氧含量 33at%	+	+		+	+		+							
氧含量 45at%	+		+		+	+								

注:"+"表示该衍射环出现

由以上可以得到,SIPOS 膜是含氧硅的微晶、多晶和非晶共存的膜,它的组成随氧含量的不同而不同:随着膜中氧含量的提高,Si 晶粒逐渐被氧化,并且氧化物向高氧转化,结构则转向非晶.

我们注意到,在45at% O 的 SIPOS 膜中有许多一团团的大颗粒.分析结果表明,它是许多颗粒的团聚,嵌在几乎是非晶的背底上.TED 数值分析表明,大颗粒是膜中大量 SiO_2 团聚的结果.电子束轰击后颗粒明显晶化,即电子束轰击 SIPOS 膜.使 SiO_x 发生再结晶.

2.2.3　Raman 光谱分析结果

图4是不同氧含量的 SIPOS 膜的 Raman 光谱.并对光谱的数值分析结果列于表3.由图2及表3可以看到,对于氧含量为20at%的样品,出现了对应于 c-Si 的 520cm^{-1} 的峰,当氧含量增大时,该峰逐渐减弱,到了含氧45at%时,c-Si 峰消失;对所有的样品均有 Si 的 480cm^{-1} 的峰,表明 SIPOS 膜中无定形硅的存在;与 SiO(498cm^{-1}) 及 SiO_2(467cm^{-1}) 相比,SIPOS 膜略有偏移,分别位于 500—502cm^{-1} 和 444—446cm^{-1} 处;在含氧量有为 33at% 和 45at% 的样品中,均出现了 474cm^{-1} 的峰.目前尚未查找到能够与之很好对应的谱蜂,但可以推断它是介于 SiO 和 SiO_2 之间的某种硅的氧化物,即2.2.1节中得到的缺氧的 α-Cristobalite 结构.

表3　SIPOS 膜的 Raman 光谱数值分析结果

氧含量(at%)	频移(cm^{-1})				
45	464	474	480	–	–
33	466	474	480	502	520
20	466	–	482	500	520
物质	SiO_2		无定形硅	SiO	单晶硅
峰位[11]	467		480	498	520

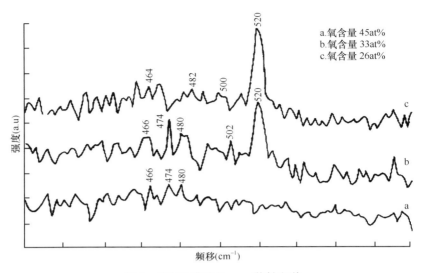

图 4　SIPOS 膜的 Raman 散射光谱

由 Raman 谱分析得知,SIPOS 膜由 SiO_x 代表,由 x 不同可得到所含物质种类有 SiO、SiO_2、Si,c-Si 和 SiO_y($1<y<2$),这比文献[9]所认定的种类要多.它认为 SIPOS 膜的 Rman 谱只有 520cm^{-1} 的峰和 480cm^{-1} 的波包,而把它等同于晶化非晶硅的谱,将膜中氧化物的振动归并到非晶硅的振动中,并以此计算膜中晶态硅与非晶态硅的体积比.

2.2.4　X 射线衍射分析与 TED 分析讨论

综合以上对 SIPOS 膜结构及组成的分析,可以看到,X 射线衍射分析与 TED 分析可相互补充.X 射线衍射分析得到 SIPOS 含有缺氧的 α-Cristobalit 结构,其面间距是 d_{Si} 和 d_{SiO_2} 的线性组合.对于电子衍射来说,由于其波长短,测量的是微区(本实验可以看到 $10^{-2}\mu m$ 数量级的质点),所以它得到的是某一微区的成分,如 Si、SiO 和 SiO_2 等等.我们可以得到如下结论:SIPOS 膜微晶,非晶和多晶共存的结构,它随着膜中氧含量的不同而略有差异,即随着氧含量的增加,结构向非晶方向转化.SIPOS 膜是由硅及硅的氧化物组成,晶态物质中含有缺氧的 α-Cristobalite 结构,以 SiO_x 表示($x<2$),局部氧分布均匀,可以有小颗粒.SIPOS 中硅有晶态和无定形态两种存在形式,并且随氧含量的提高,晶态硅的成分逐渐减少以至消失.以上讨论弥补了文献中关于 SIPOS 膜结构与组成讨论中的含混.

2.3　SIPOS 膜中微昌粒大小的计算

由 X 射线多晶衍射谱测定微晶粒的大小是根据衍射线变宽的放应来进行的.当晶粒小于 1000Å 时,晶体的 X 射线衍射峰开始弥散,随晶粒的减小.衍射峰越来越宽.因此由 X 射线衍射谱的半宽度.利用 Deby-Scherrer 公式:$L=K\lambda/\beta \cdot \cos\theta$,即可对样品晶粒大小进行计算.其中,$L$ 为晶粒直径,K 为 0.9 附近的固定常数.β 为弧度表示的半宽度.λ 为 X 射线波长.θ 为衍射角.本实验采用铜靶.根据图 1 的计算结果列于表 4.

可见,在我们的实验范围内,不同氧含量的微晶粒大小略有差别,而同一样品中,不同晶向的微晶粒大小相差较大,并且从晶粒大小可以看出,SIPOS 膜是微晶、多晶和非晶共存的结构.

表 4　SIPOS 微晶粒计算结果

氧含量 (at%)	（111）晶向			（020）晶向			（132）晶向		
	β 弧度×10^{-3}	20°	$L(\text{Å})$	β 弧度×10^{-3}	20°	$L(\text{Å})$	β 弧度×10^{-3}	20°	$L(\text{Å})$
30	3.06	28.39	467.21	9.18	35.67	158.60	19.85	47.13	75.80
45	2.45	28.36	583.36	7.34	35.52	198.28	25.93	47.19	58.33

目前文献中多以 SIPOS 膜的 TEM 形貌直接观测晶粒的大小.但实验中发现,这只是膜中颗粒的大小.它一般由几个甚至很多微晶粒团聚而成的,因此所得到的并不是微晶粒的真正尺寸.本文上述方法才真正计算了膜中微晶粒的大小.这在文献中很少涉及到.

3. 结　　论

SIPOS 膜是微晶、多晶和非晶共存的结构,是由含氧量可变的 $SiO_x(x<2)$ 组成,随着膜中氧的增多或减少,其结构向非晶或多晶方向转化,膜中含有缺氧的 α-Cristobalite 结构,膜中氧原子分布不均匀,存在局部氧原子微区集中或缺少现象,使得 $x=0$ 或 1 或 2,随膜中氧含量的提高,氧化物向高氧方向转化,用电子束轰击后,发生再结晶现象.

参考文献

[1] Takeshi Motsushtta et al.,Jpn J.Appl.Phys.,1976.15:35.
[2] Yablonvltch and T.Gmitter.1EEE Electron Device Lett.,1985.EDL-6:597.
[3] R.M.Swansan and Y.H.Kwark,SoLid State Electron.1987.30:1121.
[4] W.R.Knolle and H.R.Maxwell.Jr,J.Electroehem.Soc:Solid-State Science and Technology,1980.127(8):2254.
[5] M.Hamasaki et al.J.Appl.Phys.,1978,49:3987.
[6] James Ni.et al.,Appl.Phys.Left.1981,39(7):5.
[7] B.Greenbetg et al.,J.Electronchem.Soc:Solid-State Sctence and Technology,1988.135(9):3295.
[8] J.H.Thomas I.et al..J.Electrochem.Soc.,Solid-State Science and Technology,1979,126(10):1766.
[9] 王云珍,等,半导体学取,1989,10(7):534.
[10] 郑红军.等.全国固体薄膜学术会议论文集,河北承德.1990 年 9 月.
[11] 硅的氧化物 Raman 散射图谱(清华大学).
[12] 雷沛云.等,第三届全国固体薄膜学术会议论文集.1992 年,11 月,桂林.
[13] 谭凌.等,1994 年硅材抖学术会议论文集,P134.
[14] 谭凌,等,第八届全国半导体与集成技术会议论文集.1993 年 10 月,杭州,P196.

Structure and Composition of SIPOS Film

Tan Ling, Lei Peiyun and Liang Junwu

(*Institute of Semiconductors, The Chinese Academy of Scrences, Beijing* 100083)

Received 22 July 1994, revised manuscript received 6 October 1994

Abstract：SIPOS(Semi-Insulting Polycrystalline Silicon) films with different exygen concentration were grown by using APCVD.Their composition and structure were studied by means of X-ray diffractometry, TED, TEM and Raman Scattering Spectrometry, It was found that the film grown at 650℃ was a coexistent structure of microcrystallite, polycrystals and amorpha, and oxygen deficient a-Cristobalite exists in it.The structure of the SIPOS film $SiO_x(x<2)$ will change into amorsphous or polycrystalline, with the increasing or decreasing of o'xygen content respectively.The distribution of oxygen atoms in the film was not uniform.Oxygen content varried with x value from 2 to 0.

PACC:7360H;**EEACC**:2520M ,2550E

半导体材料与器件生产工艺尾气中砷、磷、硫的治理及检测

闻瑞梅* 梁骏吾 邓礼生 彭永清

摘要:本文研究了化合物半导体材料、器件生产工艺过程中排出的有毒物质砷、磷、硫及其化合物的治理方法.还研究了这些有毒物质的低温富集取样及快速、灵敏的分析监测方法,并与其它经典的方法作了对比。

PACC:8670;**EEACC**:7720

1. 前　　言

当今世界各国面临的重大社会问题,一般认为集中表现在粮食、能源、人口、资源、环境等五个方面.

环境问题主要由人类的生活和生产活动迅速发展所引起,反过来又对生产和生活发生重大影响.人类每年将大约 5 亿吨的颗粒物,2 亿吨二氧化硫,百亿吨二氧化碳,2.5 亿吨一氧化碳,数千亿吨氮氧化物,以及数百亿吨的固体废弃物,千亿吨废水排放到大气、水体、土壤中,造成严重的环境污染,破坏了生态平衡.我国的大气污染也是很严重的,就拿降尘量和排 SO_2 来说,我国降尘量是全球其它陆地降尘量的一倍多;排 SO_2 量高出全球其它陆地降 SO_2 量的 40%.我国降尘量 1985 年为 7512 万吨,SO_2 排放量为 1505 万吨;1990 年测算,降尘量为 10439 万吨,SO_2 排放量为 1991 万吨.

随着高技术的发展,也给环境带来新的污染,由于它新,因而还不能广泛地被环保部门了解和重视.就拿我国公布的"13 种有毒物质的排放标准"来说,就没有砷、磷的标准.由于电子工业飞速发展,半导体器件、材料制造中所用有毒气体种类繁多,毒性大,易燃、易爆、易水解,加之低浓度致害力极强,因此给治理和检测带来很大的困难.

随着高技术的发展,近 8 年来某单位大气中砷的含量逐年增加:1984 年工艺尾气中砷平均含量$<0.001mg/m^3$;1989 年为 $0.03mg/m^3$;1992 年上升到 $0.12mg/m^3$.这些事实应该引起人们的高度重视.

砷及其化合物是溶血性剧毒物质,砷化物被吸入体内能引起许多病症[1],如损害消化系统,肝、脾肿大.皮肤接触砷化物,引起表皮脱落,皮肤角质化等;与黏膜接触会出现咳嗽,气喘等.更严重的是损害神经系统,引起意识障碍,神经混乱,呼吸衰竭而致死.

众所周知,成人每天需呼吸空气量平均为 14—16kg,而需生理消耗的水 1.5—2.0kg,吃的食物如按干固体计不超过 0.7kg,可见空气对人的重要性是显而易见的.因此保护大

原载于:半导体学报,1995,16(12):890-896.

闻瑞梅　女,1933 年生,研究员。当前从事各种水处理,高纯水,气的制备及检测,以及环境污染综合治理及检测等科研、开发工作.

气不受污染是每个公民应尽的义务.

2. 化合物半导体制造及砷、磷的污染

化合物半导体制造方法有水平布利奇曼法(Horizontal Bridgman Method)和液封直拉法(LEC),分子束外延生长法(MBE),化学束外延法(CBE),液相外延法(LPE),金属有机化学气相外延法(MOVPE)以及氧化物淀积法等.在上述过程中通常要用下述的源气和掺杂剂:元素包括 As、P、Ga、Al、In;氯化物包括:$AsCl_3$,PCl_3,氢化物包括:AsH_3,PH_3,H_2Se,金属有机化合物包括 $Ga(CH_3)_3$,$Ga(C_2H_5)_3$,$Al(CH_3)_3$;$Al(C_2H_5)_3$,$Zn(CH_3)_2$,$In(C_2H_5)_3$ 和 $Zn(C_2H_5)_2$.工艺中还需用各种的化学试剂和大量的有机溶剂,显然这些有毒物质在工艺过程中随着各种炉子的尾气和腐蚀间通风管道,排放到大气中,造成严重的环境污染,给人类和生态平衡造成极大的危害.

以 MOVPE 生长工艺来说明:

有机金属化学气相外延是近几年来发展起来的生长电子材料的新工艺,由于用该技术生长的半导体材料、包括Ⅲ-Ⅴ族和Ⅱ-Ⅵ族以及高温超导体薄膜材料等,在纯度和界面过渡以及均匀性上都具有优越的特性.特别是可以生长量子阱和超晶格超薄层材料,用它制造新一代高速电子器件、激光器、探测器等.因此 MOVPE 工艺目前使用的很多.

在整个的 MOVPE 生长过程中将伴随着大量的有毒气体排放出来.

其总反应为:

$$Ga(CH_3)_3 + AsH_3 \longrightarrow GaAs + CH_4$$
$$In(CH_3)_3 + PH_3 \longrightarrow InP + CH_4$$

其分反应[2]为:

$$Ga(CH_3)_3 \xrightarrow{\text{衬底表面}} Ga(CH_3)_{3\text{衬底表面}}^*$$
$$AsH_3 \xrightarrow{\text{衬底表面}} AsH_{3\text{衬底表面}}^*$$
$$Ga(CH_3)_3^* + AsH_3^* \longrightarrow (CH_3)_2GaAsH_2 + CH_4$$
$$(CH_3)_2GaAsH_2 \longrightarrow (CH_3)GaAsH + CH_4$$
$$(CH_3)GaAsH \longrightarrow GaAs + CH_4$$

根据 Chadwick[3] 的分析,在使用 $Ga(CH_3)_3$-AsH_3-H_2 体系的 MOVPE 生长中,在 1000K 左右,砷存在的最多状态为 As_2 和 As_4,镓存在最多的状态是 $Ga(CH_3)_3$,碳存在最多的形态是 CH_4,含量较少的还有 AsH_3,As_3,AsH_2,所以衬底上发生反应的应该是 As_2(或 As_4),即有以下模型:

$$As \Longrightarrow 2As_{ads}$$

或

$$As_4 \Longrightarrow 4As_{ads}$$
$$Ga(CH_3)_{ads} + As_{ads} \Longrightarrow GaAs + CH_{3ads}$$
$$CH_{3ads} \Longrightarrow CH_3$$
$$CH_3 + H \Longrightarrow CH_4$$

式中 ads 表示吸附在表面的分子式自由基.

由于 MOVPE 是冷壁系统,所以在远离衬底处 AsH_3 和 $Ga(CH_3)_3$ 的浓度比衬底处要

高得多,反应时 AsH_3 大大过量,所以大量的含砷物进入尾气,排放到大气中.

在反应管中 AsH_3 过量,三甲基化合物基本耗尽,尾气中主要含 AsH_3,PH_3,CH_4,H_2Se,GaAs,InP 等.这些工艺排放的尾气,多数单位是不经处理直接排放到大气中,造成严重的污染.环境中的砷化物以蒸气态及气溶胶态稳定地存在于空气中,MOVPE 工艺流程示意图见图1.

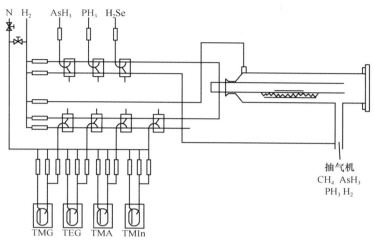

图1 MOVPE 流程示意图

3. 治 理 方 案

国内外常用的治理方法[4]有湿法:喷淋吸收;干法:吸附,化学吸附或催化吸附;燃烧法和分解法四种.我们根据半导体工艺排放的毒气,采用两种治理方法.

3.1 热解法和溶液吸收法

热解法原理:

$$2AsH_3 \xrightarrow{\triangle} 2As + 3H_2$$

$$2PH_3 \xrightarrow{\triangle} 2P + 3H_2$$

单质 As、P 收集后集中处理.

溶液吸收:用 $KMnO_4$,NaOH,H_2O_2 或它们的混合液吸收尾气.

3.2 填充塔喷淋

利用溶液和有毒气体之间的作用,喷淋吸收各种含酸的尾气如:$AsO_4^=$,$PO_4^=$,$SO_4^=$,Cl^-,F^- 等,效果很好.

根据北京市环保部门对大气污染的协商标准,40m 高烟筒排放口 As 的浓度为 $0.04mg/m^3$.我们用 $KMnO_4$,KOH,KIO_3,H_2SO_4,H_2O_2 等不同溶液喷淋吸收和用活性炭吸附,对工艺尾气进行了模拟试验.不同吸收液对尾气处理前后对比试验结果如表1所示.

表 1   不同吸收液对 As、P 吸收效果对比数据

有毒成分	吸收溶液	处理前 mg/m³	处理后 mg/m³	去除率%
AsH_3	5% $KMnO_4$+1% NaOH	2.54	0.03	98
	5% H_2O_2+1% NaOH	0.42	0.03	92
	2% NaOH	0.49	0.022	95.4
	5% HIO_3	0.11	0.01	90.7
	①+②串联	6.54	0.038	99.4
	活性炭和 $KMnO_4$ 碱液	0.172	0.01	94.7
	活性炭吸附	0.018	0.01	44
	2% H_2SO_4 吸收	0.44	0.32	27
PH_3	5% $KMnO_4$+1% NaOH	0.06	0.003	95
	5% H_2O_2+1% NaOH	0.047	0.003	93.6
	2% NaOH	0.13	0.005	96.1
	5% HIO_3	0.04	0.003	92.9
	活性炭和 $KMnO_4$ 碱液	0.045	0.002	95.5
	活性炭吸附	0.015	0.004	73.3
	2% H_2SO_4	0.14	0.08	42.8

4. 治 理 效 果

考虑到 HIO_3 太贵,活性炭不易再生,H_2SO_4 效果不理想,根据模拟实验将某单位实验大楼 10 个处理塔排放的不同毒气,分别加入 KM_nO_4,H_2O_2,NaOH 溶液或它们的混合液喷淋处理尾气.图 2 为 10 个尾气处理塔工艺流程示意图.表 2 为工作时 10 个处理塔治理效果,治理前后 As,P.S、F、Cl 含量对比.

通过以上处理,基本上符合排放标准,说明治理是很有效的.

5. 检 测 方 法

我们还研究了用低温($-80℃$)富集或溶液吸收取样,高温氢还原后用气相色谱测定半导体工艺废气中砷、磷、硫及其化合物的分析新方法.对于废气中的 AsH_3,PH_3,H_2S 等气相杂质,采用低温富集取样,直接进入气相色谱仪检测.对于废气中的固相单质及其化合物,用 1% NaOH+3% H_2O_2 吸收,吸收液在通风柜中用红外灯烘干后在还原炉中经 950℃用 H_2 还原成砷、硫的氢化物 AsH_3,H_2S,再用双火焰检测器进行气相色谱检测[5]方法灵敏可靠,不需复杂的样品前处理.

对不同物质的检测极限和相对偏差列于表 3.根据误差统计,AsH_3,PH_3,H_2S 测试方法均能满足分析化学的要求.该方法快速、准确,可用于测定半导体生产过程中 As、P、S 对周围环境的污染,以及 As、S 固液相样品的测试.

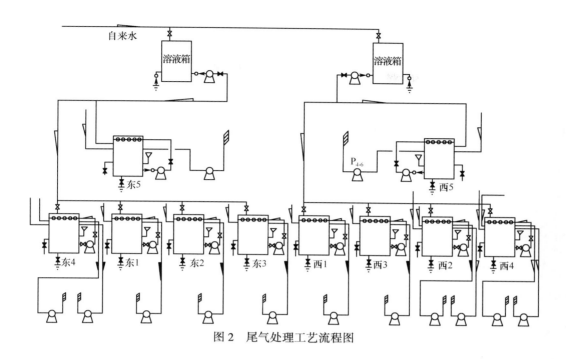

图2 尾气处理工艺流程图

表2 10个尾气处理塔工作效果对比

有毒物质	结果 塔号	西1	西2	西3	西4	西5	东1	东2	东3	东4	东5
As（mg/m³）	处理前	0.46	0.23	0.01	0.18	0.32	<0.01	<0.01	0.31	0.175	0.164
	环理后	0.016	0.04	<0.01	0.025	0.034	<0.01	<0.01	0.021	0.011	0.023
	去除率	96.5%	81.7%		86.1%	89.4%			93.2%	93.7%	85.9%
P（mg/m³）	处理前	0.022	0.052	<0.003	<0.003	0.091	0.048	0.017	0.047	<0.003	0.130
	处理后	<0.003	<0.003	<0.003	<0.003	0.004	<0.003	<0.003	0.004	<0.003	0.004
	去除率	86.3%	94.2%			95.6%	93.7%	93.7%	91.4%		96.2%
SO₄⁼（mg/m³）	处理前	0.32	0.20	0.23	0.20	0.23	1.10	0.91	0.51	0.90	3.15
	处理后	0.11	0.10	0.14	0.12	0.12	0.16	0.12	0.11	0.12	0.30
	去除率	70%	50%	40%	40%	48%	96%	87%	80%	87%	99%
F⁻（mg/m³）	处理前	0.650	0.560	0.044	0.915	0.650	0.030	0.026	0.600	0.125	0.180
	处理后	0.021	0.016	0.020	0.015	0.013	0.018	0.015	0.022	0.002	0.010
	去除率	96.7%	97.1%	55%	98.3%	98%	40%	42%	96.3%	98.4%	94.4%
Cl⁻（mg/m³）	外理前	0.45	0.23	0.24	0.52	2.40	1.04	1.02	0.50	0.68	1.52
	处理后	0.12	0.04	0.14	0.10	0.08	0.15	0.10	0.13	0.15	0.02
	去除率	73.3%	83%	42%	81%	97%	85.5%	90%	74%	78%	98.6%

注：As用二乙基二硫代氨基甲酸银分光光度法测定；P用钼锑抗比色法测定；SO₄⁼、F⁻、Cl⁻用离子色谱法测定

表 3　色谱法对不同物质的检测极限和相对偏差

有毒物质	AsH_3	PH_3	As(溶液取样)	H_2S
检测极限	0.01ppm	0.03ppm	0.013ppm	0.02ppm
相对偏差	6.2%	8.6%		0.3%

我们在 5 个单位,用 4 种不同的测试方法对 As 进行了测试,其结果列于表 4.

表 4　四种测试方法对 As 的测试数据对比(mg/m³)

样品号 \ 测试单位结果	A	B	C	D	E
1	0.020	0.021			
2	0.459	0.460		0.457	
3	0.335	0.320		0.340	
4		0.007	0.005		
5		0.007	0.004		
6	0.122	0.120	0.130		0.130
7	0.160	0.140			
8	0.093	0.100			
9	0.060	0.062			
10	0.100	0.110			

注:As 的测试方法　A:气相色谱法;B,C:二乙基二硫代氨基甲酸银分光光度法;D:等离子质谱法;E:原子吸收分光光度法

某单位实验大楼尾气中 As、P、S 处理前后两种不同分析方法数据对比列于表 5.

表 5　某单位实验大楼尾气 As、P、S 处理前后两种分析方法数据

样品号	As(mg/m³) A 单位		As(mg/m³) B 单位		P(mg/m³) A 单位		P(mg/m³) B 单位		$SO_4^=$(mg/m³) A 单位		$SO_4^=$(mg/m³) B 单位	
	处理前	处理后	处理前	处理后	处理前	处理后	处理前	处理后	处理前	处理后	处理前	处理后
1	0.18	0.048	0.23	0.04	0.05	0.04	0.05	0.03	0.2	0.1	0.2	0.1
2	0.12	0.02	0.18	0.025	0.10	0.012	0.091	0.01	0.12	0.1	0.2	0.2
3	0.15	0.02	0.164	0.02	0.13	0.005	0.15	0.004	3.6	0	3.15	0.30
4	0.2	0.09	0.175	0.011	0.02	0.01	0.017	0.01	1.0	0.1	0.9	0.12
5	0.31	0.04	0.32	0.034	0.12	0.05	0.09	0.04	0.23	0.1	0.3	0.12

注:A 单位 As、P、S 均为气相色谱法测定;B 单位 As 为二乙基二硫代氨基酸银法测定;P 为钼锑抗比色法测定; $SO_4^=$ 为离子色谱法测定.

北京市环境保护监测中心对实验楼排放气体进行了 As、P、S、Cl 的监测,1992 年 12 月的结论为实验大楼废气净化装置比较完善,房顶排气筒排放的砷和氯化氢等废气污染物低于排放标准,而且排气筒高度较高,为 42 米,不会对周围环境造成大的影响.附近区域空气与北京市近效区一般环境一致,未发现有砷和氯化氢等的污染.我们研究的分析方

法,快速、灵敏、可靠.与其它方法对比结果非常理想.鉴定认为治理方法填补了国内空白,分析检测方法国内外领先.

环境空气质量评价执行国家《大气环境质量标准》,国家大气环境质量标准未作规定的,执行国家《工业企业设计卫生标准》居住区大气中有害物质的最高容许浓度限值.

参考文献

［1］高千穗化学工业株式会社编,陈志君译"半导体制造中气体使用",化工部信息情报中心站,1987.

［2］D.J.Schlyer and M.A.Ring,J.Electrochem,Soc.,1977,124:569.

［3］B.K.Chadwick,J.Crystal Growth,1989,96:693.

［4］Richard Bvookman,Semiconductor International,Oct.,1988,p88.

［5］闻端梅,彭永清等,劳动保护科学技术,1993,13(2):29.

Abatement and Detection of Arsenic, Phosphoric and Sulphuric Pollution during Semiconductor Material and Device Processes

Wen Ruimei, Liang Junwu, Deng Lisheng and Peng Yongqing

(*Institute of Semiconductors*, *The Chinese Academy of Sciences*, *Beijing*, 100083)

Received 17 September 1993, Revised manuscript received 21 February 1994

Abstract: The abatement technology of toxic arsenic, phosphoric and sulphuric pollution during semiconductor material and device processes has been studied. Sampling methods with low temperature concentration of these toxic species and their rapidly and sensitively analytical methods have been proposed. A comparison between our analytical method and the conventional ones has been shown.

PACC: 8670; **EEACC**: 7720

GeSi CVD 系统的流体力学和表面反应动力学模型[*]

A Kinetics and Transport Model of Ge_xSi_{1-x} Chemical Vapor Epitaxy.

金晓军　　梁骏吾

(中国科学院半导体所,北京,100083)[**]

摘要:本文首次提出了一个用以分析 Ge_xSi_{1-x} 合金 CVD 生长的流体力学和表面反应动力学的统一模型.利用流体力学的偏微分方程组计算了反应管内的速度场、温度场和浓度场.讨论了反应管中的质量传输对生长速度的影响和生长过程中锗和硅的不同的生长速度控制机制.从生长的初始条件出发同时模拟了 Ge_xSi_{1-x} 合金外延层的生长速度和外延层中的锗组分.计算结果和实验结果符合得很好.本文还定量地解释了外延速度及薄膜中锗组分随 GeH_4 浓度的变化规律.

关键词:化学气相外延,Ge_xSi_{1-x},外延机制

Abstract:A model that combines mass transportation process and surface kinetics is firstly applied to analyze the Ge_xSi_{1-x} CVD process. The temperature, velocity ad concentration distributions in the reactor are calculated by the partial different equations of fluid dynamics. The surface kinetics is used to discuss the deposition of Si and the mass transportation process is used to discuss the deposition of Ge. The theoretical relationship between the initial conditions and the Ge composition x in the solid has been established. The calculated result of the growth rate and the Ge composition in the solid agree with the experiment data. The increase of the growth rate and Ge composition x with the increase of initial GeH_4 concentration is explained quantitatively by our model.

Key words:Chemical vapor ep. taxy, Ge_xSi_{1-x}, Mechanism of epitaxy

一、引　　言

近年来,Ge_xSi_{1-x} 异质结外延层的研制引起了人们的广泛兴趣,主要原因是其在高速器件,微波探测器等方面的广泛应用前景以及其与传统的硅工艺的兼容性.各种外延方法都用来生长 Ge_xSi_{1-x} 外延层,如分子束外延(MBE),化学气相沉积(CVD)等[1~3].CVD 的沉积温度范围从500℃到1000℃,沉积压强范围由 1 到 $1×10^6$Pa.对于 Si-Ge-H-Cl 系统,人们做了许多研究工作[4~5],主要原因是由于 Si-H-Cl 系统生长 Si 外延层在工业生产应用中取得了很大成功.特别是对于 $SiH_2Cl_2+GeH_4+H_2$ 系统,由于 SiH_2Cl_2 的沉积温度较低且与 SiH_4 相比,其对系统的要求较宽容,更适合于工业生产,低压生长和常压生长 Ge_xSi_{1-x} 合金外延层都已见诸报道.

原载于:电子学报,1996,24(5):7-11.1996.

*1995 年 3 月收到,1995 年 7 月修改定稿.

**Jin Xiaojun, Liang Junwu(Institute of Semiconductors, Chinese Academy of Sciences, Beijing 100083).

很多人对 Ge_xSi_{1-x} 的沉积机理进行了研究.他们的研究工作集中在表面反应机制上,这主要是因为锗硅合金外延层的沉积温度较低,一般都认为其生长速度由表面反应控制.在他们的模型中,反应气体的吸附速度认为是由衬底表面氢原子的解吸速度控制.衬底表面的反应一般都认为是 $MH_4 = (H-MH_3)^* \longrightarrow H(a) + MH_3$,$M = Si$ 或 Ge.$(H-MH_3)^*$ 代表气体与表面碰撞并发生反应而被吸附.衬底表面附近的反应气体浓度被简单地假设等于初始输入的反应气浓度.外延层中锗的组分由输入的锗源和硅源的比例确定,外延层中锗组分和初始条件(包括各种气体的初始浓度、生长温度等)的理论关系尚待建立.这些工作未考虑 Ge 在高温($T>650℃$)是扩散控制,在 $T<650℃$ 是反应控制这一事实[4].

我们的分析表明,沉积过程中反应管内不同的温度分布会造成反应管内反应气体浓度分布的不同,这将对 Ge_xSi_{1-x} 生长产生很大的影响,如果在计算中考虑反应管内的气体组分分布,将会使模型更加接近反应管内真实的物理过程.Kamins 等人通过实验对 Ge_xSi_{1-x} 的生长机理进行了研究[4].他们的实验结果表明:在生长温度大于 650℃ 时,Ge_xSi_{1-x} 外延中锗的生长速度由扩散过程所控制,而在温度小于 650℃ 时,Ge 生长速度由表面反应速度所控制.纯锗外延生长的实验数据表明,在 $T>500℃$ 范围内是由扩散速度控制的.所以,在建立 Ge_xSi_{1-x} 生长模型时要考虑在不同温度下 Ge 生长机制的不同.

在本文中,我们首次将流体力学和表面反应动力学模型应用于 Ge_xSi_{1-x} 合金生长过程的模拟.在模型中,流体力学的偏微分方程和表面反应动力学一起用来分析 Ge_xSi_{1-x} 的生长过程.Navier-Stokes 方程组用于计算反应管中的速度场、温度场和浓度场.表面反应动力学用于讨论硅的生长,而扩散过程用于讨论锗的生长.并且建立了生长的初始条件和外延层中锗组分的理论关系.由模型计算出来的生长速度和外延层中的锗组分与实验结果符合得很好.并且我们用该模型定量地解释了外延速度及薄膜中锗组分随 GeH_4 浓度的变分规律.据我们所知,在有关 Ge_xSi_{1-x} 合金外延的理论工作中,这是第一次从初始条件出发,从理论上同时计算出外延层的生长速度和锗组分.另外,我们用表面反应动力学机制解释硅的沉积、用扩散机制解释锗的淀积的作法也是已知的第一次尝试.鉴于锗烷的生长活化能比所用硅源低得多,因此,我们认为在 Ge_xSi_{1-x} 生长的 650~1000℃ 的温度范围内,锗的淀积主要由扩散控制,硅的生长则由表面反应控制,因此采用上述处理方法更接近生长过程的物理实质,且上述处理方法也和目前已知的实验结果相符合.

二、实　　验

在 Ge_xSi_{1-x} 的生长实验中,我们采用水平矩形石英反应管,用卤钨灯加热.衬底为 Si(100),硅源为 SiH_2Cl_2,锗源为 GeH_4,氢气为载气,生长温度为 800~1000℃,生长压力为常压.外延层厚度用 Rutherford 背散射谱(RBS)测得,Ge_xSi_{1-x} 外延层中锗的组分由 X 射线双晶衍射和 RBS 确定.

三、理论模型

对于光加热矩形外延系统,建立二维坐标系,x 轴沿石墨舟方向,$x=0$ 表示石墨舟的入口处;y 轴垂直于石墨舟方向,$y=0$ 表示在石墨舟表面,$y=H(x)$ 表示在反应管的上管壁处.我们假定反应管中的气流为稳定的层流且在达到衬底前其速度已充分发展.气相中无化学反应,只在固气界面发生化学反应.流量场可用连续方程(1)和动量守恒方案(2)来描述,方程(3)是能量守恒方程.方程(5)和(6)分别是 SiH_2Cl_2 和 GeH_4 的质量输运方程.

$$\rho \frac{\partial u_x}{\partial x} + \rho \frac{\partial u_y}{\partial y} = 0 \tag{1}$$

$$\rho u_x \frac{\partial u_x}{\partial x} + \rho u_y \frac{\partial u_x}{\partial y} = \frac{\partial}{\partial y}\left(\mu \frac{\partial u_x}{\partial y}\right) - \frac{\partial P}{\partial x} \tag{2}$$

$$\rho u_x c_P \frac{\partial T}{\partial x} + \rho u_y c_P \frac{\partial T}{\partial y} = \frac{\partial}{\partial x}\left(k_T \frac{\partial T}{\partial x}\right) + \frac{\partial}{\partial y}\left(k_T \frac{\partial T}{\partial y}\right) \tag{3}$$

$$\rho = \sum \frac{P_\iota}{RT} m_\iota \tag{4}$$

$$u_x \frac{\partial w_{SiH_2Cl_2}}{\partial x} + u_y \frac{\partial w_{SiH_2Cl_2}}{\partial y} = \frac{\partial}{\partial y}\left(D_{SiH_2Cl_2} \frac{\partial w_{SiH_2Cl_2}}{\partial y}\right) + \frac{\partial}{\partial y}\left(D_{SiH_2Cl_2} a_{SiH_2Cl_2} w_{SiH_2Cl_2} \frac{\partial T}{\partial y}\right) \tag{5}$$

$$u_x \frac{\partial w_{GeH_4}}{\partial x} + u_y \frac{\partial w_{GeH_4}}{\partial y} = \frac{\partial}{\partial y}\left(D_{GeH_4} \frac{\partial w_{GeH_4}}{\partial y}\right) + \frac{\partial}{\partial y}\left(D_{GeH_4} a_{GeH_4} w_{GeH_4} \frac{\partial T}{\partial y}\right) \tag{6}$$

其中 ρ 是气体密度,u_x 是 x 方向的气流速率,u_y 是 y 方向的气流速率,P 是气体的压强,T 是温度,w 是反应气体的浓度,μ 是粘滞系数,D 是各反应物的扩散系数,a 是热扩散比,c_P 是定压热容,k_P 是热导率在求解过程中,应该联立求解方程(1)~(6),从而获得速度场、温度场和浓度场的耦合解,但是 K.L.Knutson 等人的研究表明:在实际的锗硅外延中,SiH_2Cl_2 的流量一般为总流量的1%左右,锗烷的流量更小,在这样的条件下,非耦合解和耦合解的误差很小,可以忽略.所以,在我们的模型中为了节省计算机机时,我们采用非耦合的计算.由于速度与温度分布相互影响,并且要考虑热膨胀对速度分布的影响,所以温度场和速度场需要联立求解.首先将方程(1)~(4)差分格式化,并设一初始温度分布,计算出温度场的一级近似,然后反复叠代可求出所需精度的温度场和速度场,如图1、图2所示.然后用方程(4)~(6)按基本类似的方法计算反应管中 SiH_2Cl_2 和锗烷的空间分布.速度场、温度场的边界条件已由梁骏吾等在文献[12]中进行了详细的讨论.物性参数的选取和计算方法也类似于文献[12]中的讨论,但在我们的计算中考虑了反应管内的各点不同的温度和浓度对物性参数的影响.SiH_2Cl_2 和 GeH_4 浓度分布的边界条件将在下面讨论.

SiH_2Cl_2 浓度场的边界条件由下式给出:

$$D_{SiH_2Cl_2} \frac{\partial w_{SiH_2Cl_2}}{\partial y} + D_{SiH_2Cl_2} a_{SiH_2Cl_2} w_{SiH_2Cl_2} \frac{\partial T}{\partial y}\bigg|_{y=0} = R_{Si} \tag{7}$$

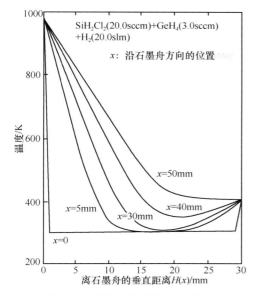
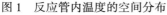
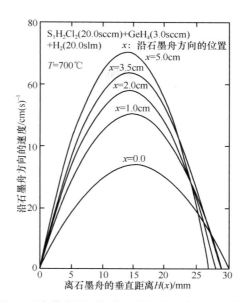

图1 反应管内温度的空间分布   图2 反应管内沿石墨舟方向气流速度的空间分布

$$D_{\mathrm{SiH_2Cl_2}}\frac{\partial w_{\mathrm{SiH_2Cl_2}}}{\partial y} + D_{\mathrm{SiH_2Cl_2}}a_{\mathrm{SiH_2Cl_2}}w_{\mathrm{SiH_2Cl_2}}\frac{\partial T}{\partial y}\bigg|_{y=H(x)} = 0 \qquad (8)$$

式中 y 表示垂直生长表面的方向, $y=H(x)$ 表示在反应管壁上, $y=0$ 表示在衬底表面. 方程(7)的表示: 表面反应所消耗的 $\mathrm{SiH_2Cl_2}$ 质量等于由气相向生长表面输运的 $\mathrm{SiH_2Cl_2}$ 质量. 对于锗的沉积, 由于其反应速度由扩散速度所控制, 表面反应速度远大于扩散速度, 所以我们可以假定生长表面锗烷的浓度为零.

$$D_{\mathrm{GeH_4}}\frac{\partial w_{\mathrm{GeH_4}}}{\partial y} + D_{\mathrm{GeH_4}}a_{\mathrm{GeH_4}}w_{\mathrm{GeH_4}}\frac{\partial T}{\partial y}\bigg|_{y=H(x)} = 0 \qquad (9)$$

$$w_{\mathrm{GeH_4}}\big|_{y=0} = 0 \qquad (10)$$

由于硅的生长速度由表面反应机制所控制, 所以我们必须讨论衬底表面氢原子的吸附与解吸, 方程(10)描述了衬底表面的吸附与解释.

$$\mathrm{H_2 \Leftrightarrow 2H} \qquad (11)$$

氢的吸附过程为: (1)气机中的 $\mathrm{H_2}$ 输运到生长表面, 其速率为:

$$R_c = \frac{P_{\mathrm{H_2}}}{(2\pi mkT)^{1/2}} \qquad (12)$$

上式中 $P_{\mathrm{H_2}}$ 为混合气体中 $\mathrm{H_2}$ 的分压, m 为分子量, k 为玻尔兹曼常数, T 为生长表面的温度. (2)输运到表面的 $\mathrm{H_2}$ 被表面的空位吸附形成生长表面的 H 原子. 其速率为:

$$R_a = R_c(1 - \theta(\mathrm{H}))^2\exp\left(-\frac{19\mathrm{kcal/mol}}{RT}\right) \qquad (13)$$

上式中 $(1-\theta(\mathrm{H}))$ 表示生长表面空位浓度, 上式中的平方项表示吸附一个 $\mathrm{H_2}$ 分子需要 2 个表面空位. 19kcal/mol 为表面 H 原子吸附的活化能.

$\mathrm{Ge_xSi_{1-x}}$ 合金上氢原子的解吸与硅上氢原子的解吸不同, 因为 Ge-H 键比 Si-H 键更容易打开, 所以 $\mathrm{Ge_xSi_{1-x}}$ 合金上氢原子解析的速度比硅上氢原子的解析速度快. 按 Garone 等人[6]的研究结果，Ge_xSi_{1-x}合金上氢原子的解析速度可由下多表示：

$$R_d = N_S \theta(H)^2 v \left[x \exp\left(-\frac{E_{dG}}{RT}\right) + (1-x) \exp\left(-\frac{E_{dS}}{RT}\right) \right] \tag{14}$$

式中 x 是薄膜中 Ge 的组分，N_s 为生长表面悬挂键的密度，$\theta(H)$ 为表面 H 原子浓度，它的平方表示从表面解吸一个 H_2 需 2 个表示 H 原子. v 为频率因子，它的值取为 $8 \times 10^{11} s^{-1}$，E_{ds} 和 E_{dG} 分别为氢原子从硅和锗上解析的活化能. 按照参考文献[7]中的讨论，在我们的模型中，E_{ds} 和 E_{dG} 分别取为 47kcal/mol 和 37kcal/mol. 在稳定生长的条件下 H_2 的吸附速率和解吸速率应该相等：

$$R_a = R_d \tag{15}$$

解方程(14)可求出生长表面空位的浓度 $(1 - \theta(H))$.

生长表面硅的生长可以看成是按如下步骤进行的：(1)气相中的 SiH_2Cl_2 输运到生长表面. (2)输运到表面的 SiH_2Cl_2 一部分分解为表面的 Si 原子，另一部分被解吸. 这一过程可以表示为：

$$SiH_2Cl_2(g) + 2 \underset{k_d}{\overset{a}{\rightleftharpoons}} (H-SiHCl_2)^* \overset{k_r}{\longrightarrow} (\underline{H} + \underline{SiHCl_2}) \tag{16}$$

上式中 $SiH_2Cl_2(g)$ 为气相中的 SiH_2Cl_2 分子. $*$ 表示生长表面的空位. $(H-SiHCl_2)^*$ 为吸附在生长表面的 SiH_2Cl_2 分子. a 为冷凝系数. k_d, k_r 分别为解吸速率常数和反应速率常数. Si 的生长速率可以表示为：

$$R = G \frac{P_{SiH_2Cl_2}}{(2\pi m_{SiH_2Cl_2} kT)^{\frac{1}{2}}} (1 - \theta(H))^2 S_0 \tag{17}$$

上式中 G 是几何因子，S_0 是 SiH_2Cl_2 的吸附几率. 按照式(15)的讨论，S_0 的表示式为：

$$S_0 = \frac{a k_r}{k_d + k_r} = \frac{a}{1 + \frac{k_{d0}}{k_{r0}} \exp[-(E_d - E_r)]} \tag{18}$$

$$k_r = k_{r0} \exp\left(\frac{-E_r}{RT}\right), k_d = k_{d0} \exp\left(\frac{-E_d}{RT}\right) \tag{19}$$

Coon 等人对在 Si(111)生长表面由 SiH_2Cl_2 为源生长 S 外延层的机制进行了探讨[14]，根据对实验结果的分析，他们得出 S_0 的表达式为：

$$S_0 = \frac{0.36}{1 + 600 \exp[-(E_d - E_r)/RT]} \tag{20}$$

对于 Ge_xSi_{1-x}(100)表面上 Si 的生长，S_0 表达式(17)中各参数的取值目前尚不清楚，在我们的模型中，以 Coon 等人的结果式(20)为参考，对其中的参数略作调整使计算结果与实验结果符合得最好.

当生长温度大于 650℃时，锗的生长速度由扩散机制控制. 在 GeH_4 的浓度分布确定以后，我们可以通过下式来计算 Ge_xSi_{1-x} 合金外延生长中 Ge 的生长速率：

$$R_{Ge} = GK\left(D_{GeH_4} \frac{\partial w_{GeH_4}}{\partial y} + D_{GeH_4} a_{GeH_4} w_{GeH_4} \frac{1}{T} \frac{\partial T}{\partial y}\right) \tag{21}$$

式中 w_{GeH_4} 表示气相中 GeH_4 的浓度，G 为几何因子，K 为由锗烷生长锗的反应效率，在模型中我们取为 90%.

分别计算生长中硅和锗的生长速度后,合金的生长速率和薄膜中锗的组分可由下面两式求得:

$$R_{Ge_xSi_{1-x}} = R_{Si} + R_{Ge} \tag{22}$$

$$x = R_{Ge}/(R_{Si} + R_{Ge}) \tag{23}$$

四、结果与讨论

图 1 给出了反应管内的温度的空间分布.在反应舟的入口处气流的温度等于室温,沿石墨舟方向气流温度逐渐升高,温度梯度逐渐下降显示出气流沿石墨舟方向被加热,这将对系统的速度场、浓度场、质量输运和外延生长产生影响.

图 2 为沿石墨舟方向气流速度的空间分布.如图 2 所示,气流速度沿石墨舟方向逐渐增加.引起这种增加的原因有两个:(1)沿石墨舟方向气流温度逐渐升高,气流的热膨胀导致气流速度增加.(2)由于石墨舟的倾斜使得沿石墨舟方向的横截面积逐渐减少,从而导致气流速度增加.

图 3 为反应管内 SiH_2Cl_2 浓度的空间分布.如图 3 所示,生长表面($H(x) = 0$)的 SiH_2Cl_2 的分压比气流中的 SiH_2Cl_2 的分压小,沿石墨舟方向,表面的 SiH_2Cl_2 分压略有上升.这是因为表面附近的分压较低是由于生长表面向气相中的热扩散造成的,沿石墨舟方向温度梯度逐渐减少(如图 1 所示),导致了热扩散的降低从而使表面附近 SiH_2Cl_2 分压增大.这种沿石墨舟方向的分布将会对外延层的均匀性产生影响.所以,在 Ge_xSi_{1-x} 生长的模型中一定要考虑质量传输对生长的影响.

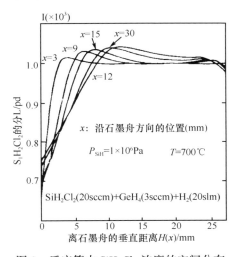

图 3　反应管内 SiH_2Cl_2 浓度的空间分布

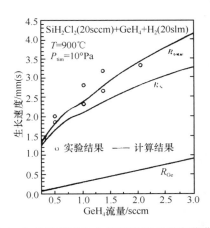

图 4　生长速度随输入的锗烷流量的变化曲线

图 4 给出了 Ge_xSi_{1-x} 的生长速率随输入的锗烷流量的变化曲线.生长速度随 GeH_4 流量的增加而显著增加.图中的实验数据由 RBS 测得.由图可知,计算结果和实验结果符合得很好.图 4 中的理论计算结果表明,Ge_xSi_{1-x} 生长速度的增加由两部分组成,硅的生长速度以及锗的生长速度皆随 GeH_4 流量的增加而增加.图 4 给出了硅和锗的生长速度随输

入锗烷流量的变化曲线.当 GeH_4 流量较小时,硅的生长速度随 GeH_4 流量增加得较大,当 GeH_4 流量较大时,随 GeH_4 流量的变化较小.锗的生长速度随 GeH_4 流量的增加而几乎成线性增加.

图 5 给出了薄膜中锗组分随锗烷流量的变化曲线,实验数据由 RBS 和 X 射线双晶衍射测理,理论计算的结果和实验数据非常吻合.如图 5 所示,当锗烷流量较低时,固相中锗的组分随锗烷流量的增加而增加得很快,当锗烷的流量较大时,薄膜中锗的组分随气相中锗烷流量的增加而增加较慢.

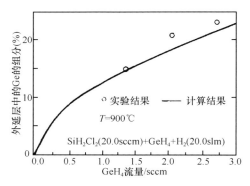

图 5　外延层中 Ge 组分随输入 GeH_4 流量的变化曲线

五、结　　论

综上所述,我们提出了一个用以分析 Ge_xSi_{1-x} 合金化学气相外延生长的流体力学和表面反应动力学的统一模型.从生长的初始条件出发同时模拟了 Ge_xSi_{1-x} 合金外延层的生长速度和外延层中的锗组分.计算结果和实验结果符合得很好.据我们所知,这在 Ge_xSi_{1-x} 合金外延生长的理论工作中尚属首次.我们还首次从理论上定量地解释了外延层的生长速度和组分随混合气体中 GeH_4 浓度的变化规律.

在本项工作中,RBS 的测试工作由中科院物理所的殷士端教授完成,中科院半导体所的王雨田高级工程师帮助进行了 X 射线双晶衍射的测量,在此我们表示衷心的感谢.

参考文献

[1] B.S.Meyerson, K.J.Uram, and F.K.LeGous. Appl. Phys. Letts, 1988,53:2555—2559.

[2] W.B.de Boer and D.J.Meyer. Appl. Phys. Letts, 1991, 58:1286—1290.

[3] J.C.Beam, L.C.Feldman, A.T.Fiory, S. Nakahara and I.K. Robinson. J. Vac. Sci. Technol. A, 1984,2(2):436—441.

[4] T.I. Kamins and D.J. Meyer. Appl. Phys. Letts, 1991,59:178—182.

[5] T.I. Kamins and D.J. Meyer. Appl. Phys. Letts, 1992,61:90—93.

MOVPE 生长 $Ca(CH_3)_3$—AsH_3—H_2 体系中砷的形态转化及砷的治理[*]

The Transformation of Arsenic in $Ga(CH_3)_3$—AsH_3—H_2 System during MOVPE Growth and Arsenic Abatement

闻瑞梅　梁骏吾

（中国科学院半导体研究所，北京，100083）[**]

摘要：在热力学分析的基础上，计算了在 $Ca(CH_3)_3$—AsH_3—H_2 体系中在 500K—1200K 的温度范围内，可能的含砷及砷化物的形态和浓度.同时通过大量的模拟实验找出了去除尾气中砷的最好方法，还研制出用三级逆向喷淋法的治理设备，对尾气进行治理.治理后的尾气中砷的含量符合国家排放标准.

关键词：气相外延，热力学分析，砷的治理

Abstract：Based on thermodynamic analysis, the possible species containing arsenic and their concentrations at temperature from 500K to 1200K are calculated for $Ca(CH_3)_3$—AsH_3—H_2 system. A new method for arsenic abatement has been proposed through numerous simulation experiments. In order to improve the efficiency of arsenic abatement a three stage, counter flow shower—bath has been inverstigated. The arsenic concentration in gases meets the State Standard for arsenic emission.

Key words：Vapor phase epitaxy, Thermodynamic analysis, Arsenic pollution

一、引　言

有机金属气相外延是近几年来发展起来的生长电子材料的新工艺，由于用这种工艺技术生长的半导体材料、包括Ⅲ-Ⅴ族及其固溶体半导体材料等，在纯度、界面过渡区的陡峭性以及均匀性上都具有优越性，特别是可以生长量子阱和超晶格薄层材料，制造新一代高速电子器件、激光器、探测器等.用 MOVPE 技术相对于其他的技术容易扩大为工业生产，所以 MOVPE 工艺有很大的吸引力.因此有机金属气相外延工艺目前被广泛地使用.但是 MOVPE 生长技术的主要缺点是使用大量剧毒的砷烷气体，随着工艺尾气排放到大气中，严重危害人们的健康，污染环境.所以需要研究一种控制砷污染的有效技术.为此对使用砷烷的 MOVPE 过程中砷的污染需要进行全面的热力学分析，弄清在 MOVPE 过程中砷的形态和浓度，并提出对砷污染的有效治理技术.

原载于：电子学报，1997，25(2)：76-78.

* 1996 年 7 月收到，1996 年 11 月定稿.

** Wen Ruimei, Liang Junwu(Institute of Semiconductors Chinese Academy of Sciences, Beijing 100083)

二、MOVPE 中 Ca(CH₃)₃—AsH₃—H₂ 体系的热力学分析

在 500K—1200K 的温度范围内,在 Ga(CH₃)₃—AsH₃—H₂ 体系中,我们考虑了下列物种[1]:Ga、GaAs(S)、As₂、As₃、As₄、H₂、H、AsH₂、AsH₃、GaH、GaH₂、GaH₃、Ga(CH₃)₃ 和 CH₄。在 Ga(CH₃)₃—AsH₃—H₂ 体系中存在着下列独立的方程式:

$$\text{GaAs(S)} \xrightleftharpoons{k_1} \text{Ga+As} \tag{1}$$

$$\text{GaAs(S)} \xrightleftharpoons{k_2} \text{Ga+1/2As}_2 \tag{2}$$

$$\text{GaAs(S)} \xrightleftharpoons{k_3} \text{Ga+1/3As}_3 \tag{3}$$

$$\text{GaAs(S)} \xrightleftharpoons{k_4} \text{Ga+1/4As}_4 \tag{4}$$

$$\text{As+H}_2 \xrightleftharpoons{k_5} \text{AsH}_2 \tag{5}$$

$$\text{H}_2 \xrightleftharpoons{k_6} \text{2H} \tag{6}$$

$$\text{Ga+H} \xrightleftharpoons{k_7} \text{GaH} \tag{7}$$

$$\text{GaH+H} \xrightleftharpoons{k_8} \text{GaH}_2 \tag{8}$$

$$\text{GaH}_2\text{+H} \xrightleftharpoons{k_9} \text{GaH}_3 \tag{9}$$

$$\text{Ga(CH}_3)_3\text{+AsH}_3 \xrightleftharpoons{k_{10}} \text{GaAs(S)+3CH}_4 \tag{10}$$

$$\text{AsH}_2\text{+H} \xrightleftharpoons{k_{11}} \text{AsH}_3 \tag{11}$$

以上共有十一个方程式,用通式表示:

$$mA+nB=uC+vD$$

每个方程式均有相应的反应平衡常数

$$K = P_C^u \times P_D^v / (P_A^m \times P_B^n) \tag{12}$$

表示 K 的方程共有十一个,即由 K_1,K_2,$\cdots K_{11}$,

例如:对反应(1)有 $K_1 = P_{Ga} \times P_{As}$

对反应(2)有 $K_2 = P_{Ga} \times P_{As_2}^{1/2}$ 等等,

化学反应的标准平衡常数与标准状态下的吉布斯自由能变化 ΔG 之间有关系式

$$\Delta G = -RT\ln K \tag{13'}$$

标准状态下的吉布斯自由能变化 ΔG 可以由反应的 ΔH_{298},ΔS_{298} 和 ΔC_p 求出即按下式:

$$\Delta G = \Delta H_{298} + \int_{298}^{T} \Delta C_p dT - T\Delta S_{298} - T\int_{298}^{T} \frac{\Delta C_p}{T} dT \tag{13}$$

反应物和生成物的热容 C 可由通式求出:

$$C = a + bT + cT^{-2} + dT^2 \tag{14}$$

式中,a,b,c,d 为常数,可由热力学手册查出[2,3],然后将诸生成物热容的代数和减去诸反应物热容的代数和可求出 $\Delta C(T)$。根据反应的 ΔH_{298} 和 ΔS_{298},利用式(13')可求出不同温度的反应平衡常数 $K_1 - K_{11}$。这样表示 K 的方程一共是十一个,但是未知数有 P_{Ga},

$P_{As}, P_{As_2}, P_{As_3} P_{As_4}, P_{H_2}, P_H, P_{AsH_2}, P_{AsH_3}, P_{GaH}, P_{GaH_2}, P_{GaH_3}, P_{Ga(CH_3)_3}$ 和 P_{CH_4}, 共 14 个, 所以还要有另外三个独立的关系式, 这三个独立方程式是:

（1）所有物种的分压和为一个大气压, 即

$$P_{Ga} + P_{As} + P_{As_2} + P_{As_3} + P_{As_4} + P_{H_2} + P_H + P_{AsH_2} + P_{aAsH_3} + P_{GaH_2} + P_{GaH_3}$$
$$+ P_{Ga(CH_3)_3} + P_{CH_4} = 1 \qquad (15)$$

（2）H 原子和 C 原子守恒

令 $R\left(\dfrac{H}{C}\right)$ 表示 H 原子数和 C 原子数之比

$$R\left(\frac{H}{C}\right) = 2P_{AsH_2} + 3P_{AsH_3} + P_{GaH} + 2P_{GaH_2} + 3P_{GaH_3} + 2P_{H_2} + P_H + 9P_{Ga(CH_3)_3} +$$
$$4P_{CH_4}/3P_{Ga(CH_3)_3} + 4P_{CH_4} \qquad (16)$$

（3）Ga 原子和 As 原子守恒

令 $R(Ga/As)$ 表示 Ga 原子数和 As 原子数之比

$$R\left(\frac{Ga}{As}\right) = \frac{P_{Ga} + P_{GaH} + P_{GaH_2} + PP_{GaH_3} + P_{Ga(CH_3)_3}}{2P_{As_2} + 3P_{As_3} + 4P_{As_4} + P_{AsH_2} + 2P_{AsH_3}} \qquad (17)$$

加上式(15)-(17)三式以后, 可以用计算机编程将十四个方程式编程求解, 并将每种物种的分压对温度的依赖关系作图, 得出不同温度下, 反应物种的分压曲线, 见图 1:

由图 1 看出, 在 500K-1200K 时, $Ga(CH_3)_3$—AsH_3—H_2 体系中, 主要气态物种是 H_2、AsH_3、CH_4、As_2、As_4、GaH_3、GaH、Ga、GaH_2 等, 其它物种的分压很小.

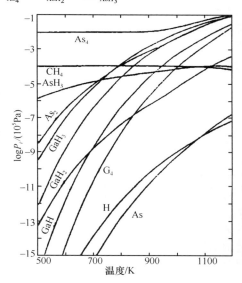

图 1 不同温度下, 在 $Ga(CH_3)_3$—AsH_3—H_2 体系中, 各物种的分压

三、砷污染的治理

如上所述在 $Ga(CH_3)_3$—AsH_3—H_2 体系中, 含砷的物种主要以 As_4、As_2 的形态存在, AsH_3 的分压较小, 而 As 的分压更小($10^{-3}Pa$), 显然我们应将它们转化为 V 价的砷酸而溶解; 例如用硫酸介质中的 KIO_3 作氧化剂.

$$As_4 + 4IO_3^{3-} + 4H_2O = 4AsO_4^{3-} + 2I_2 + 8H^+$$

$$As_2 + 2IO_3^3 + 2H_2O = 2AsO_4^{3-} + I_2 + 4H^+$$

$$5AsH_3 + 8IO_3^{3-} = 5AsO_4^{3-} + 4I_2 + 4H_2O + 7H^+$$

$$As + IO_3^{3-} + H_2O = AsO_4^{3-} + 1/2I_2 + 2H^+$$

碱性介质中的 $KMnO_4$ 和酸性介质中的 $CuSO_4$ 也能起同样的氧化作用, 我们用了三级不同的吸收剂.

第一级: 用 $KIO_3 + H_2SO_4 + KI + H_2O$ 溶液逆向鼓泡喷淋吸收.

第二级:用 $CuSO_4+H_2SO_4+H_2O$ 溶液逆向喷淋吸收.

第三级:用 $KMnO_4+NaOH+H_2O$ 溶液逆向喷淋吸收.

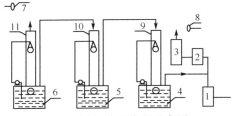

图 2　尾气治理流程示意图

1. 油分离装置;2. 过压保护及报警;3. 活性炭装置;
4. 第一级处理箱;5. 第二级处理箱;6. 第三级处理箱;
7. 排放尾气毒性监测及报警装置;8. 过压报警装置;
9. 第一级逆向喷淋装置;10. 第二级逆向喷淋装置;
11. 第三级逆向喷淋装置

将 As_4、As_2、AsH_3、As 充分转化为 AsO_4^{3-} 为溶液吸收. 我们还进行了一系列的模拟砷吸收的实验[4,5],选择了最佳的吸收剂,对尾气中的砷进行吸收,并制定出合理的净化流程. 设计、制造了一种治理设备,安装在 MOVPE 生长系统的设备尾气出口处,让尾气在排放到大气前进行处理见图 2.

用低温(−80℃)富集或溶液吸收取样,高温氢还原后,用气相色谱法测定尾气中砷的含量[6,7],结果见表 1,表 1 为治理前后砷含量的两种不同分析方法对比数据.

由表 1 看出治理后的 MOVPE 工艺尾气,其砷含量全部达到国家排放标准[8].

表 1　尾气治理前后的砷含量

治理前砷的含量, mg/m³		治理后砷的含量, mg/m³	
比色法*	色谱法**	比色法	色谱法
0.61	0.69	0.04	0.04
0.49	0.51	0.03	0.04
0.91	0.93	0.05	0.04
0.32	0.33	0.04	0.05
0.26	0.31	0.03	0.05
0.18	0.13	0.04	0.05
0.15	0.16	0.03	0.02

* 为二乙基二硫代氨基甲酸银分光光度法,由中科院生态环境中心测试

** 为高温氢还原一气相色谱法,由中科院半导体研究所测试

四、结　论

在热力分析的基础上,从理论上阐明砷存在的形态和转化规律,在 900K−1050K 范围内,半导体 MOVPE 尾气主要的含砷物种为 As_4,As_2,AsH_3,尾气用高价的碘盐、铜盐、锰盐在不同的酸、碱介质中的治理技术是非常有效的,未经治理的尾气全部超标,治理后的尾气全部达到国家排放标准.

闻瑞梅　中科院半导体所研究员.1955 年毕业于武汉大学化学系.三十多年来一直从事水化学基础、水处理、表征技术的研究,设计高纯水系统工程以及设备的研制与开发,高纯气和环境中痕量杂质分析和环境治理及检测.主持的科研项目先后获国家级,中科院级,北京市级各种科技进步奖十二次、国家级及院级重大成果七项专著两本,约 100 多万字,完成中英文论文 100 多篇.专利五项.

参考文献

［1］Yang Hui, Liang Junwu, et al. In First Pacific Rim Int. Conf. on Adv. Mater and Proccessing, Eds. Shi, C.D；Scott. A. TMS, 1992,541~545.

［2］I. Barin. O. Knacke and O. Kubachewski. Thermochemical Properties of Inorganic Subatances(Springer, Berlin, 1991).

［3］J.A. 迪安.《兰氏化学手册》. 北京：科学出版社,1991.

［4］闻瑞梅等. 半导体学报. 1995,16(3):188.

［5］Wen Ruimai. Journal of Environment Sciences. 1994, 6(1):123.

［6］闻瑞梅等. 劳动保护科学技术. 1993,13(2):29.

［7］Wen Ruimei, Journal of Environment Sciences. 1995,7(2):229.

［8］国家《大气环境质量标准》GB 3095-82 和国家《工业企业设计卫生标准》TJ36-79.

用固相外延方法制备 $Si_{1-x-y}Ge_xC_y$ 三元材料[*]

于 卓　李代宗　成步文　黄昌俊　雷震霖　余金中　王启明　梁骏吾

（中国科学院半导体研究所集成光电子国家重点联合实验室，北京，100083）

摘要：分析了 $Si_{1-x-y}Ge_xC_y$ 三元系材料外延生长的特点，指出原子性质上的巨大差异使 $Si_{1-x-y}Ge_xC_y$ 材料的制备比较困难.固相外延生长是制备 $Si_{1-x-y}Ge_xC_y$ 的有效方法，但必须对制备过程各环节的条件进行优化选择.通过实验系统地研究了离子注入过程中温度条件的控制对外延层质量的影响以及外延退火条件的选择与外延层结晶质量的关系，指出在液氮温度下进行离子注入能够提高晶体质量，而注入过程中靶温过高会导致动态退火效应，影响以后的再结晶过程，采用两步退火方法有利于消除注入引入的点缺陷，而二次外延退火存在着一个最佳退火温区.在此基础上优化得出了固相外延方法制备 $Si_{1-x-y}Ge_xC_y/Si$ 材料的最佳条件.

关键词：$Si_{1-x-y}Ge_xC_y$ 材料；固相外延

PACC：6150C；8110

中图分类号：TN 304 2+4　**文献标识码**：A　**文章编号**：0253-4177（2000）09-0862-05

Preparation of $Si_{1-x-y}Ge_xC_y$ Alloy Layers by SPER [*]

YU Zhuo，LI Dai-zong，CHENG Bu-wen，HUANG Chang-jun，LEI Zhen-lin，
YU Jin-zhong，WANG Qi-ming and LIANG Jun-wu

（*State Key Laboratory on Integrated Op toelectronics，Institute of Semiconductors，The Chinese
A cademy of Sciences，Beijing 100083，China*）

Received 25 August 1999，revised manuscript received 14 December1999

Abstract：The epitaxial growth of $Si_{1-x-y}Ge_xC_y$ materials，which is very difficult because of the great difference between the characteristics of C，Si and Ge atoms，is studied.The Solid Phase Epitaxial Recrystallization（SPER）is proved to be an effective method to make this kind of semiconductors，though the conditions during the preparation process must be optimized. Experimental results show that the film qualities are greatly affected by the ion-implantation temperature as well as the epitaxial annealing temperature. The ion-inplantation executed at liquid nitrogen temperature will improve the quality of the materials，while a higher ion-inplantation temperature leads to an active annealing effect that may obviously affect the quality of the epitaxial layers.Two-step annealing is favorable to diminish the point defects introduced by ion-implantation，and there exists the best

---

原载于：半导体学报，2000，21（9）：862-866.

* 国家自然科学重大基金资助项目，编号 69876260[Project Supported by National Natural Science Foundation of China Under Grant NO.69876260].

于卓，男，1966 年出生，博士，现从事 Si 基材料生长与特性分析研究.

成步文，男，1967 年出生，助研，现从事 Si 基材料与器件研究.

李代宗，男，1972 年出生，博士生，现从事 Si 基材料与器件集成研究.

temperature region for recrystallization during the second annealing step.The optimized conditions for the formation of ternary $Si_{1-x-y}Ge_xC_y$ alloy layers by SPER is finally obtained

Key words：$Si_{1-x-y}Ge_xC_y$ alloys；SPER

PACC：6150C；8110

Article D：0253-4177(2000)09-0862-05

1. 引　言

$Si_{1-x-y}Ge_xC_y$ 三元系是一种具有巨大发展潜力的新型半导体材料,其独特的性质是对 $Si_{1-x}Ge_x$ 二元材料固有性质的有益补充或改进.C 原子的加入不但能有效地改变 $Si_{1-x}Ge_x$ 材料的晶格常数,补偿 Ge 原子带来的晶格内部应变,而且还能够明显地影响 $Si_{1-x}Ge_x$ 的能带结构,对材料能带的人工改性有重要意义.不过,由于 C 与 Si 和 Ge 的原子半径差别很大,$Si_{1-x-y}Ge_xC_y$ 材料的制备就显得更为复杂.因此,深入了解 $Si_{1-x-y}Ge_xC_y$ 材料制备过程中存在的困难,探索行之有效的制备方法,是研究这一材料的基本问题.

目前用于 $Si_{1-x-y}Ge_xC_y$ 材料外延生长的方法包括固相外延[1-5]（SPE）、分子束外延（SS-MBE[6]、GS-MBE[7]）和化学气相沉积（RTCVD[8]、PECVD[9]、UHV/CVD[10]、CMD[11]）等多种,它们各具特色,互相补充,很难说哪一种更好.但不论哪一种方法,都面临着如下生长过程中的困难：

（1）C 与 Si、Ge 在原子半径上的较大差别会导致产生强烈的局部应变,严重影响外延层的完整性.根据 A tzmon[12] 等人的研究,C 组分小于 4at%,$Si_{1-x-y}Ge_xC_y$ 外延层的质量可以很好；C 组分为 4%—10at%,外延层中出现大量堆垛层错和孪晶等缺陷；C 组分大于 10at%,则无法获得单晶层.可见,C 的组分越高,外延生长越困难.

（2）C 存 Si 中体固溶度小于 $2×10^{-3}$at%,而存 Ge 中几乎是不溶的[13].为使材料中溶入更多的 C,必须从生长过程入手,寻求摆脱热平衡限制的方法.如果生长过程遵循二维生长模式,就应通过动力学限制的生长过程,设法提高 C 原子的表面固溶度.

（3）在大约 2000℃ 以下,等原子比的 β-SiC 为稳定的相,而混溶的 $Si_{1-y}C_y$ 材料为亚稳态.因此,必须选择较低的生长温度,以抑制 C 的扩散,避免出现 β-SiC 相.

采用固相外延(Solid Phase Epitaxy Regrowth)生长是制备 $Si_{1-x-y}Ge_xC_y$ 材料的一种可取手段.该方法的第一步是要获得含 Si、Ge、C 的非晶层,一般是通过 C 离子（或 C 离子和 Ge 离子）注入来实现.由于 C 离子是强行注入进去的,不受固溶度的限制,C 的组分可以做得比较高（可达 1.5%—2at%）.采用适当退火工艺可以有效地抑制 β-SiC 的出现.整个 SPE 工艺过程比较简单,易于形成大批量生产,且与 Si 工艺兼容性很好.

SPE 的典型工艺有两种,一种是材料中的 C 和 Ge 组分全部采用注入的办法来加入[1,2],另一种是利用 CVD 或 MBE 先生长出 $Si_{1-x}Ge_x$ 材料层,再向其中注入 C 离子[3-5].两种方法最终都要通过高温退火实现固相外延.

固相外延制备 $Si_{1-x-y}Ge_xC_y$ 样品要注意以下两点：

离子注入过程中,C 离子的注入水平至少要达到 10^{15}cm^{-2}.如果热量不能及时扩散,衬底温度将明显升高,造成注入层的动态退火效应.一般来说,用液氮冷却靶体对动态退火效应能够起到抑制作用.

在外延生长过程中,退火条件的选择也十分重要.C 原子在 Si 中迁移的激活能比较高,所以,退火温度偏低就不能使 C 原子迁移到替位格点位置;但同时,过高的退火温度又会导致 β-SiC 相的出现.为解决这一问题,我们采用两步退火的办法:首先在较低温度退火,以消除离子注入过程带来的一些位错和点缺陷,使晶格损伤得到部分恢复;第二步在较高温度进一步退火,实现注入层的再结晶生长.

2. $Si_{1-x-y}Ge_xC_y$ 样品的制备过程

根据不同的实验目的,$Si_{1-x-y}Ge_xC_y$ 样品的制备采用了不同的条件,在后面的实验中还要具体给出.但总体的制备原则为:

(1) 所用衬底均为 n-Si(001) 衬底,电阻率为 3—5Ω,离子注入前经严格的清洁处理.

(2) 离子注入顺序为首先进行 Ge 离子注入,然后进行 C 离子注入.

(3) Ge 离子注入能量为 110keV,注入剂量为 $4\times10^{16}/cm^2$,相应的投影射程 R_{PGe} 为 65nm,标准偏差 ΔR_{PGe} 为 23nm.注入过程在 LN_2 温度(77K)下进行.C 离子的注入能量为 20keV,投影射程 R_{PC} 为 63nm,比 R_{PGe} 略小,标准偏差 ΔR_{PC} 为 24.3nm,反而略大于 R_{PGe}.注入过程分别在 LN_2 温度(77K)和室温下进行.

(4) 退火外延生长是在 UHV/CVD 生长室中进行的,退火方式为两步退火,第一步在 450℃ 退火 1h,以消除注入带来的点缺陷和位错,使晶格得到部分恢复,第二步在 650—900℃ 退火 1h 实现固相外延生长.

3. $Si_{1-x-y}Ge_xC_y$/Si 外延层制备条件的优化选择

3.1 离子注入过程温度条件对外延层晶体质量的影响

对于固相外延生长的 $Si_{1-x-y}Ge_xC_y$ 样品,离子注入条件的选择对材料质量的影响非常大.除了要适当选取注入能量和剂量外,注入过程温度条件的控制也直接影响下一步的退火外延效果.为了研究这一现象,我们选择不同温度进行离子注入,然后对注入样品进行相同条件的退火处理,用卢瑟福背散射谱(RBS)测试整个样品制备过程,比较测试结果的异同.

1# 样品的 Ge 离子注入是在 77K 下进行的,通过 RBS⟨100⟩ 沟道谱可知注入直接形成了约 150nm 厚的非晶层(图 1(a)),C 离子也是在 77K 下注入的,由于其质量较轻,所引起的沟道产额被 Si 背底信号覆盖,在背散射谱中很难分辨出来;450℃ 退火 1h 后,晶格损伤得到部分恢复,沟道产额略有下降,750℃ 退火 1h 实现了固相外延生长.相对随机谱而言,外延生长的 $Si_{1-x-y}Ge_xC_y$ 层的沟道产额 χ_{min} 比衬底略高,这一结果与 Lu 等人[14]的结果基本相当,表明外延层结晶质量比较好,不过注入后样品晶格质量不可能恢复到原来水平.在 Si 表面处,可以明显观察到表面峰的存在,反映了表面具有较多的杂质和较大的晶格缺陷,在 $Si_{1-x-y}Ge_xC_y$/Si 界面位置也存在一个界面峰,它反映了异质结处晶格缺陷较为严重,这种缺陷一是缘于晶格的失配,更与注入损伤有密切关系.

$2^\#$样品的 Ge 离子注入也是在 77K 下进行的,但 C 离子注入过程靶温控制在 100℃,注入对$\langle 100 \rangle$沟道谱的影响并不十分明显,但可以观察到沟道产额略有下降,经历了与 $1^\#$ 样品相同的退火处理后,其最小沟道产额却明显偏高(图 1(b)),而且界面峰也更高.下表比较了两个样品沟道谱的最小产额 χ_{min} 及界面峰的高度 H.

样品号	$\chi_{min}/(\%,Si)$	$\chi_{min}/(\%,Ge)$	$H/(counts)$
$1^\#$	7.9	7.8	85
$2^\#$	14.4	16.3	122

$2^\#$样品的 χ_{min} 比 $1^\#$ 样品增大了约 1 倍,界面峰增大了 0.5 倍.这一结果完全是 C 离子注入过程中的动态退火效应造成的.在注 C 过程中,Si 衬底的温度比较高,注入的离子比较容易与反冲原子结合形成复杂的络合物,并使部分原子保持在间隙位置[15,16].这种络合物结构是在注入过程形成的,且一旦形成很难再把它打开.由于动态退火效应,间隙原子的比例增大,退火后外延层的沟道产额相应提高.

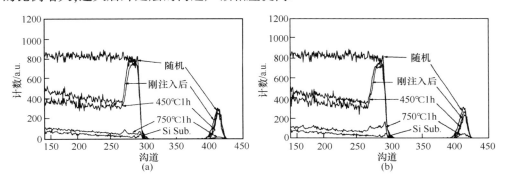

图 1 $Si_{1-x-y}Ge_xC_y$ 样品制备过程的 RBS 谱(a)$1^\#$样品,(b)$2^\#$样品

Fig. 1 RBS Spectra of $Si_{1-x-y}Ge_xC_y$ Samples During Fabrication.(a)Sample $1^\#$,(b)Sample $2^\#$

由此可见,在离子注入过程中,对注入层的温度进行控制,防止动态退火的发生,是实现高质量外延生长的重要前提.

3.2 退火条件对外延层晶体质量的影响

固相外延生长是通过退火方式实现的.$Si_{1-x-y}Ge_xC_y$ 材料的 SPE 过程中,退火条件的优化对提高外延层质量显得尤为重要.按一般的外延退火规律,材料的熔点越高,退火温度也越高.C 的熔点比 Si 和 Ge 都高得多,C 原子的加入使 $Si_{1-x-y}Ge_xC_y$ 层的再结晶温度有所提高,所以应适当提高外延生长的退火温度,不过,退火温度过高又容易导致 β-SiC 的产生,只有适当地选择退火条件,才能获得高质量的 $Si_{1-x-y}Ge_xC_y$ 外延层.

不同研究小组采用的固相外延退火条件不尽相同,但几乎都没有给出退火条件的选择过程.Lu[14]等人注意到退火温度对注入前沿位错团的作用,而 Goorsky 等人[17]研究了实现外延生长后的样品的热稳定性,但这些都不是对退火生长条件的优化研究.因此我们利用自己的注入样品,考察了退火温度对外延层生长质量的影响,优化了外延生长的退火条件.

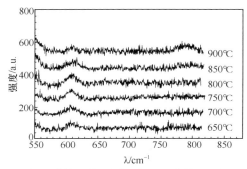

图2 1#样品在不同温度下退火外延后的
Raman 光谱

Fig.2 Raman Spectra of Sample 1# After Epitaxial
Annealing Under Different Temperature

实验选用 1#注入样品,根据 Strane[18] 的研究,首先在 450℃ 退火 1h,减少注入造成的部分点缺陷等晶格损伤.第二步退火外延则分别在不同的温度下进行,时间也为 1h.利用 Raman 谱观察退火的效果(图2).

Raman 光谱能反映样品内部 C 原子的成键特征.当 C 原子处于替位位置,并与 Si、Ge 原子形成合金态时,其局域振动模式(LVM)会在 610cm^{-1} 附近产生一个振动峰;如果 C 原子与 Si 原子化合形成了 β-SiC 沉淀相,就会在 790cm^{-1} 附近出现一个较宽的振动峰.较为理想的 $Si_{1-x-y}Ge_xC_y$ 外延层应保证 C 原子基本处于替位位置且没有形成 β-SiC 沉淀相,因此,我们希望 Raman 光谱中 610cm^{-1} 附近具有明显的振动峰,同时在 790cm^{-1} 附近观察不到振动峰.

样品低于 600℃ 退火,没有观察到替位 C 原子的振动峰,说明在这一温度下不能实现再结晶生长.温度提高到 650℃,存 608cm^{-1} 处出现一个很弱的峰,到 700℃ 该峰已经变得较强,并在 750℃ 达到极大.说明在 750℃ 进行退火,能够使大多数 C 原子占据格点位置,外延效果最为理想.进一步提高退火温度该峰并不再继续增强,反而存 900℃ 开始有所减弱.在这一温度下,790cm^{-1} 附近开始出现一个新的峰,它标志着 β-SiC 沉淀相已经开始产生.沉淀相的产生很不均匀,一般出现在缺陷附近,所以引起的振动峰比较宽,显得非常平缓.正是由于有更多的 C 原子与 Si 原子形成了 β-SiC 沉淀相,使得替位 C 原子的比例相应减小,所以出现在 608cm^{-1} 处的替位 C 原子振动峰随之减弱.

根据以上结果,我们认为采用我们这种离子注入方法制备的 $Si_{1-x-y}Ge_xC_y$ 材料,外延再结晶的最佳二次退火温度为 700—800℃.

值得注意的是,理想的退火外延温区是由多方面的因素共同决定的.温度过低就不能使原子获得足够的动能运动到格点位置,而过高的温度不但会导致 β-SiC 沉淀相的产生,而且还会造成晶格内部位错的滑移和攀升,使晶体质量下降.事实上,单就 $Si_{1-x}Ge_x$ 材料而言,有人采用快速退火(RTA)方法来提高 GS-MBE 生长的 $Si_{1-x}Ge_x$ 样品的发光性能,得到的理想退火温区与我们的结果基本一致[19].

4. 结　　论

本文用固相外延方法制备了 $Si_{1-x}Ge_xC_y$ 三元系材料,并对制备条件进行了优化选择.实验结果表明,在液氮温度下进行 C 离子注入能有效地抑制注入过程的动态退火效应.而采用两步退火法既能有效消除离子注入引入的点缺陷又能避免产生 β-SiC 沉淀相.第二步外延退火的最佳温区为 700—800℃.

参考文献

[1] S.Lombardo,J.Priolo,S.U.Campisano and S.Lagomarsino,Appl Phys Lett,1993,**62**:2335.

［2］ S.Lombardo,K.K.Larsen,V Raineri et al.,J.Appl Phys,1996,**79**:3456.

［3］ J.Menendez,P.Gopalan,G.S.Spencer et al.,Appl Phys Lett,1995,**66**:1160.

［4］ M.J.Antonell,K.S. Jones and T.E. Haynes,J.Appl Phys,1996,**79**:7646.

［5］ A.Fukami,K Shoji,T.Nagano and C.Y.Yang,Appl Phys Lett,1990,**57**:2345.

［6］ K.Eberl,S.S.Iyer,S.Zollner et al.,Appl Phys Lett,1992,**60**:3033.

［7］ A.R.Powell and S.S.Iyer,Jpn.J.Appl Phys,1994,**33**:2388.

［8］ P.Boucaud,C.Francis,F.H.Julien et al.,Appl Phys Lett,1994,**64**:875.

［9］ J.Mi,P.Warren,P.Letoumeau et al.,Appl Phys Lett,1995,**67**:259.

［10］ M.Hiroi and T.Tatsumi,J.Cryst Growth,1995,**150**:1005.

［11］ N.Herbots,P.Ye,H.Jacobsson et al.,Appl Phys Lett,1996,**68**:782.

［12］ Z. Atzmon,A.E.Bair,E.J.Jaquez et al.,Appl Phys Lett,1995,**65**:2559.

［13］ R.W.Olesinki and G.J.Abbaschian,Bull Alloy Phase Diagrams,1984,**5**:484.

［14］ X.Lu and N.W.Cheung,Appl Phys Lett,1996,**69**:1915.

［15］ T.E.Haynes and O.W.Holland,Appl Phys Lett,1992,**61**:61.

［16］ J.S.William s,M.C.Ridgeway,R.G.Ellin an et al.,Nucl Instrum.Methods Phys Res B,1991,**59/60**:572.

［17］ M.S.Goorsky,S.S.Iyer,K.Eberl et al.,Appl Phys Lett,1992,**60**:2758.

［18］ J.W.Strane,H.J.Stein,S.R.Lee et al.,Appl Phys Lett,1993,**63**:2786.

［19］ 司俊杰,滕达,王红杰,等,半导体学报,1999,**19**:477［SI Jun-jie,TENG Da,WANG Hong-jie et al.,Chinese Journal of Semiconductors,1999,**19**:477(in Chinese)］.

兴建年产一千吨电子级多晶硅工厂的思考

梁骏吾

(中国科学院半导体研究所,北京,100083)

摘要:文章简要评述了世界以及中国的电子级多晶硅的生产能力和市场需求。在 2000 年和 2010 年中国对多晶硅的需求分别是 736t/a 和 1304t/a。但近几年中国的多晶硅生产仅达到 80t/a,所以在中国建设一座年产 1000t 电子级多晶硅的工厂是很合理的。然而由最新统计数据可知,自 1997 年以来,世界多晶硅生产能力连年均超过市场需求,而且在最近的将来,这一趋势将会继续。为了占领国内多晶硅市场,未来的多晶硅工厂将面临挑战,产品质量和生产成本是应当考虑的最重要指标。为了占领国内市场,在保证多晶硅产品纯度的前提下,生产成本只能略微超过 20 美元/kg。

关键词:多晶硅;半导体工业;规模生产

半导体材料是半导体工业的基础材料。在半导体材料中用量最大和用途最广泛的是半导体硅。当今 95% 以上的半导体器件是用硅材料制造的,集成电路的 99% 以上是硅集成电路。硅材料支撑着种类繁多、意义重大的半导体工业。电子级多晶硅是单晶硅片的起始材料,因此多晶硅的重要性是十分明显的。

我国早在 20 世纪 50 年代即开始了电子级多晶硅的研制,60 年代中期开始批量生产。现在仍然是世界上少数(含日、美、德、俄、乌、意等国)能生产电子级多晶硅的国家之一。然而我国的多晶硅生产工艺与设备严重落后,不符合现代化大生产的要求,产量、质量和价格均不具备竞争力,所以兴建一个年产 1000t(即达到现代化生产的临界产量)的大硅厂一直是人们关注的项目。许多单位提出项目可行性报告。一个千吨级多晶硅工厂的投资约为 1 亿美元以上。因此在考虑项目上马时应当十分慎重,需仔细分析全球电子级多晶硅的生产和销售形势,特别要注意由于资料来源和时间不同往往分析的结果有很大差别。本文将根据一些最新的数据提出以下背景形势分析和千吨级多晶硅厂的建立应考虑的标准。

1. 有利形势——半导体工业迅速增长

以半导体器件为主的世界电子产品的产值在 1998 年达到 9300 亿美元,而且增长速度很高——1999 年、2000 年至 2001 年的增长率分别为 9.1% 、15.2% 和 18.2%。与这样大的增长率相适应的是世界集成电路市场迅速上升,1996 年为 1153 亿美元,2001 年将达到 2110 亿美元。世界多晶硅需求也相应上升,1996 年世界电子级多晶硅需求为 14 300t,而 2000 年和 2001 年分别上升为 16 100t 和 17 800t(见表 1)[1,3]。

原载于:中国工程科学,2000,2(6):33-35.

表 1　世界电子级多晶硅的市场需求、生产能力和库存量/t·a^{-1}

Table 1　Production capacity, market demand and stock of the electronic
grade polysilicon in the world/t·a^{-1}

年份	1996	1997	1998	1999	2000	2001	2002	2003
生产能力	12 995	16 950	22 450	24 110	26 060	26 585	26 635	26 635
需求	14 300	15 600	13 800	14 500	16 100	17 800	19 400	21 100
需求-能力	1 305	−1 350	−8 650	−9 610	−9 960	−8 785	−7 235	−5 535
库存	1 720	2 400	5 800	5 510				

数据来源:德国 Wacker 公司(1999 年 8 月 30 日);数据不包括太阳能级多晶硅

2. 严峻的现实——多晶硅生产能力大于市场需求

表 1 的数据是由多晶硅主要生产厂家 Wacker 公司统计和推测的,是最新数据。在引用数据时要特别注意其准确性;如有疏忽则会得出错误结论。例如根据 1996~1997 年日本稀有金属新闻和日本金属时评[2]的资料推断得 2000 年世界多晶硅需求量高达 25 508t。比表 1 中的 2000 年需求量高了 58%,显然过高了,不能反映真实情况。

我国电子级多晶硅市场 2000 年和 2010 年需求量可根据 1998 年实际产量进行预测(表 2)。

由表 2 可知,建设一个年产千吨的电子级多晶硅厂与中国市场的需求量大体上一致。

表 2　国内多晶硅市场需求[4]

Table 2　Polysilicon demand in China

年份	1996	2000	2010
需求/t·a^{-1}	242	736	1304

我国在 1983 年有 18 家工厂生产多晶硅,生产能力为 150t/a。由于市场竞争,到 1987 年剩下 7 个工厂,生产多晶硅能力下降为 112t/a。1998 年只剩下两个多晶硅厂,生产能力进一步下降到 80t/a。

多晶硅缺额很大,所以我国需求的多晶硅由国外进口,许多单晶厂家为了降低成本向国外收购含石墨的多晶料。总之,目前我国多晶硅主要依赖外国。

另一方面,我国多晶硅生产规模小(仅为 30~50t/a),公认的多晶硅生产临界规模为 1000t/a。所以新建一个年产 1000t,质量与价格均有竞争力的电子级多晶硅厂,从而满足国内以及周边地区的需求已成为半导体界的一个共识,也是半导体工作者多年来的心愿。

但是在考虑项目的可行性时,一定要全面而准确地判断世界多晶硅生产与销售形势。表 1 的数据说明,世界多晶硅市场固然在扩大,然而生产能力也在扩大,结果在 1998 和 1999 年世界多晶硅的生产能力分别超出当年市场需求的数量为 8650t 和 9610t;并分别造成库存 5800t 和 5510t。预计到 2000 年和 2003 年时生产能力分别将超过市场需求为 9960t 和 5535t。这意味着新建的千吨级硅厂将面临激烈的竞争。

竞争是不可避免的,要占领中国多晶硅市场必须通过竞争。不过在竞争中我们要做到知己知彼,否则会陷入盲目性。

3. 必须在产品质量和价格两方面均有竞争力

电子级多晶硅的生产经过 40 多年的发展,已经取得很大进步。目前国外工厂均以闭环三氯氢硅法为主(也有少数工厂用硅烷法)。由于工艺先进,国外每生产 1kg 多晶硅的物质消耗(含原料硅、液氯、氢等)和能耗(还原电耗和总电耗)远比国内的低。这样,国外的生产成本远低于国内生产成本。通常工厂的生产成本是不轻易公开的。但据 Rogers 估算,一个年产 200t 多晶硅工厂的多晶硅成本如表 3 所示[5]:

表3　闭环三氯氢硅工厂的运行成本

Table 3　Operating costs of a trichlorosilane plant using closed loop system

项目	费用(美元/kg)
原材料	7.31
设备	2.23
劳力	2.45
运行	1.74
废物处理	0.20
折旧(十年)	6.40
合计	20.63

按表 3,多晶硅的运行成本为 20.63 美元/kg,折合人民币为 172 元/kg。当工厂运行 10 年之后,折旧费已扣完,运行成本降至 14.23 美元/kg,折合人民币为 114 元/kg。当然,工厂运行 10 年以后要维持生产还需投入资金。上述计算有些偏低。

我国多晶硅生产的工艺比较落后,过去未采用闭环生产。多晶硅原料消耗为国外的 3.5 倍,液氯消耗为 13 倍,氢消耗为 21 倍,电消耗为 4.2 倍。因此,我国的多晶硅成本远高于世界其它硅厂。中国多晶硅售价为 500 元/kg,明显高于外国进口料。

新的多晶硅厂的能耗和物耗必须达到国际先进水平,否则无法竞争。

即使应用十分先进的生产工艺,电耗仍然在成本中占重要部分。新的多晶硅厂必须能得到廉价的电力。全年电价起码不能超过 0.25 元/kW·h。否则成本不可能下降。

我国四川峨眉半导体厂的年产 100t 多晶硅闭环生产线通过鉴定,其技术指标先进,诸如物耗、能耗、硼、磷杂质含量均有突破,为建立规模化大生产提供了设计依据。但是从 100t/a 试制到 1000t/a 的大生产仍然有一过程。

在我国国产多晶硅短缺情况下,国外进口多晶硅的价格为 40 美元/kg(直拉)和 60 美元/kg(区熔)。随着竞争激烈,国外多晶硅仍在降价:直径 20~65mm 的多晶料降至 20 多美元/kg,直径 20~150mm 多晶料降至 28 美元 kg,所以新建的多晶硅工厂的生产成本只能接近于 20 美元/kg 才有竞争力。

电子级多晶硅的纯度要求十分严格。表 4 列出国际上最新的多晶硅纯度指标[3,6]。可以看出,对高纯硅除要求很低的施主、受主、碳、金属杂质外,对表面金属杂质也有很高要求。

表4　多晶硅质量指标

Table 4　Purity characteristics of polysilicon

	杂质	浓度*	电阻率/Ω·cm
体纯度	施主杂质(P,As,Sb)	最高 150ppta	最低 500
	受主杂质(B,Al)	最高 50ppta	最低 1500
	碳	最高 100ppba	
	体多属总量	最高 500pptw	
	(Fe,Cu,Ni,Cr,Zn)		
表面金属	Fe	最高 500pptw/250ppta	
	Cu	最高 50pptw/25ppta	
	Ni	最高 100pptw/50ppta	
	Cr	最高 100pptw/55ppta	
	Zn	最高 100pptw/130ppta	
	Na	最高 800pptw/980ppta	

* 在半导体硅材领域,杂质含量的国际通行表示法仍为 ppb,ppt 等"非标准",为方便读者,此处未予更改

** 为表面酸洗后的值

我国多晶硅的硼、磷、碳含量一般能达到国际质量水平。但是体金属杂质含量往往不注意,表面金属杂质含量也未列入指标。另一方面,优品率的提高也是工厂盈亏的重要条件。如果能提供超高纯多晶硅,即质量指标优于表 4 的产品(硼杂质含量小于 0.03 ppb)供区熔单晶使用,则价格可提高到 60 美元/kg,经济效益立即上升。即多晶硅厂的产品质量除满足表 4 指标外,还应能生产优级产品。

4. 结　语

综上所述,中国在 2000 年和 2010 年分别有 736t 和 1304t 电子级多晶硅的市场,但多晶硅厂的建设必须考虑国际竞争,必须考虑全球多晶硅生产能力过剩这一现实。要取得中国乃至周边地区的多晶硅市场,必须保证产品质量为第一流,生产技术也必须是第一流的,能耗和物耗等指标应处于世界先进行列,有廉价电力供应,其生产成本只能接近于 20 美元/kg;建成的工厂应能生产区熔硅用的高纯多晶硅。

参考文献

[1] Wacker Siltronic A G.Polysilicon Production,1995-2003[R].1999.
[2] 中国硅材料工业发展研究课题组.中国硅材料工业发展研究[R].1997,11:52.
[3] 宋大有.上海有色金属,2000,21(1):31.
[4] 万群.中国信息产业领域相关重点基础材料科技发展战略研究[M].北京:电子工业出版社,2000.
[5] Rogers L C.Handbook of Semiconductor Silicon Technology[M],Eds,O'Mara W C,Herring R B.Hunt L P.Noyes Publ. New Jersey,1990,60.
[6] Product Specification of Wucker-Chemie GmbH,1999,No.PCA-CH4;1998,No.PCA-AE4.

Thoughts on the Construction of an Electronic Grade Polycrystalline Silicon Plant with Annual Production of 1000t in China

Liang Junwu

(*Institute of Semiconductors,Chinese Academy of Sciences,Beijing* 100083,*China*)

Abstract: This paper briefly reviews the electronic grade polysilicon production capacity and market demand in the world as well as in China,It is estimated that in the year of 2000 and 2010 the polysilicon demand in China will be 736t/a and 1304t/a,respectively.

In the recent years, the gross polysilicon production in China is only 80t/a, so the construction of an eleetronic grade polysilicon plant in China with a 1000t/a production capacity should be resonable.However, referring the newest statistical data since 1997, the world polysilicon production capacity has being exceeded the market demand and the trend will continue in the near future. In order to occupy the domestic polysilicon market the future polysilicon plant will face challenge. The quality of the product and the manufacturing cost are the most important criteria to be considered.Ensuring the polysilicon product purity,the manufacturing cost should be near 20 dollars per kilogram for competition in domestic market.

Key words:polycrystalline silicon;semiconductor;production

电子级多晶硅的生产工艺

梁骏吾

（中国科学院半导体研究所, 北京, 100083）

摘要:就建设1000t电子级多晶硅厂的技术进行了探讨。对三氯氢硅法、四氯化硅法、二氯二氢硅法和硅烷法生产的多晶硅质量、安全性、运输和存贮的可行性、有用沉积比、沉积速率、一次转换率、生长温度、电耗和价格进行了对比;对还原或热分解使用的反应器即钟罩式反应器、流床反应器和自由空间反应器也进行了比较。介绍了用三氯氢硅钟罩式反应器法生产多晶硅三代流程。第三代多晶硅流程适于1000t/a级的电子级多晶硅生产。

关键词:多晶硅;三氯氢硅法;硅烷法;流程;生产

笔者在文献[1]中讨论了电子级多晶硅的需求,世界及中国电子级多晶硅的生产能力,市场竞争形势,多晶硅的体纯度和表面纯度以及生产成本。提出了占领市场必须具备的质量标准,能源消耗和材料消耗指标以及最终生产成本。

本文将进一步讨论目前电子级多晶硅的各种关键技术和这些技术对比,从而提出在建设我国1000t电子级多晶硅工厂的技术建议。

1. 多晶硅技术的特殊性及我国的差距

1.1 多晶硅技术的特殊性

电子级多晶硅的发展经历了将近50年的历程。各国都在十分保密的情况下发展各自的技术。国外有人说参观一个多晶硅工厂甚至比参观一个核工厂还要难,可见其保密性之严。电子级多晶硅的特点是高纯和量大,其纯度已达很高级别:受主杂质的原子分数仅为 5×10^{-11},施主杂质的原子分数为 15×10^{-11}(国外的习惯表示法分别为50ppt和150ppt)。其生产能力于1965年达30t/a,1988年上升到5 500t/a,2000年已达到26 000t/a,这在凝聚态物质中是首屈一指的。生产如此大量的超纯材料是经过了几代的改进,淘汰了许多工厂。只有那些掌握了大规模生产技术和亚ppb级纯度多晶工艺的12家工厂在竞争中生存下来并且发展壮大。

1.2 世界和中国多晶硅技术的比较

世界多晶硅的生产技术以 SiH-Cl$_3$ 法为主,并已进入第三代闭环大生产。我国的生产也用 SiH-Cl$_3$,但尚处于第一代小规模生产,第三代闭环技术尚处于100t的试验阶段。我国生产能力约100t/a,而国外工厂如德山曹达为4 000t/a,Wacker为4 200t/a,Hemlock

---

原载于:中国工程科学,2000,2(12):34-39.

为 6 200t/a[2]，差距甚大。从生产多晶硅的反应器来看，我国只有小型钟罩式，国外钟罩式反应器直径已达 3m，并且还有流床反应器和自由空间反应器，大大提高了生产效率。我国尚未开展后两者的研究。国外有完善的回收系统，生产成本低，氢耗、氯耗、硅耗、电耗均优于国内。一般直拉硅用多晶有相当数量由国外进口，区熔用特别高纯多晶硅原料更依赖进口。我国多晶硅的质量和成本均落后于先进水平，因此未来的我国大型电子级多晶硅厂必须采用世界先进技术。

2. 主要的多晶硅生产技术选择

经过数十年的研究和生产实践，许多方法被淘汰，如以 Ca，Mg 或 Al 还原 SiO_4；Zn，Al 或 Mg 还原 $SiCl_2$ 法等；剩下的是硅烷分解法和氯硅烷还原法。下面我们讨论这几种方法的优劣[3]。

2.1 $SiCl_4$ 法

氯硅烷中以 $SiCl_4$ 法应用较早，所得到的多晶硅纯度也很好，但是生长速率较低（4~6μm/min），一次转换效率只有 2%~10%，还原温度高（1200℃），能耗高达 250kW·h/kg，虽然有纯度高安全性高的优点，但产量低。早期如我国 605 厂和丹麦 Topsil 工厂使用过，产量小，不适于 1000t 级大工厂的硅源。目前 $SiCl_4$ 主要用于生产硅外延片。

2.2 SiH_2Cl_2 法

SiH_2Cl_2 也可以生长高纯度多晶硅，但一般报道只有~100Ω·cm，生长温度为 1000℃，其能耗在氯硅烷中较低，只有 90kW·h/kg。与 $SiHCl_3$ 相比有以下缺点：它较易在反应壁上沉淀，硅棒上和管壁上沉积的比例为 100：1，仅为 $SiHCl_3$ 法的 1%；易爆，而且还产生硅粉，一次转换率只有 17%，也比 $SiHCl_3$ 法略低；最致命的缺点是 SiH_2Cl_2 危险性极高，易燃易爆，且爆炸性极强，与空气混合后在很宽的范围内均可以爆炸，被认为比 SiH_4 还要危险，所以也不适合做多晶硅生产。

2.3 SiH_4 法

我国过去对硅烷法有研究，也建立了小型工厂，但使用的是陈旧的 Mg_2Si 与 NH_4Cl 反应（在 NH_3 中）方法。此方法成本高，已不采用。用钠和四氟化硅或氢化钠和四氟化硅也可以制备硅烷，但是成本也较高。适于大规模生产电子级多晶硅用的硅烷是以冶金级硅与 $SiCl_4$ 逐步反应而得。此方法由 Union Carbide 公司发展并且在大规模生产中得到应用，制备 1kg 硅烷的价格约为 8~14 美元。

硅烷生长的多晶硅电阻率可高达 2 000Ω·cm（用石英钟罩反应器）。硅烷易爆炸，国外就发生过硅烷工厂强烈爆炸的事故。

现代硅烷法的制备方法是由 $SiCl_4$ 逐步氢化：$SiCl_4$ 与硅、氢在 3.55MPa 和 500℃下首先生成 Si-HCl_3，再经分馏/再分配反应生成 SiH_2Cl_2，并在再分配反应器内形成 SiH_3Cl，SiH_3Cl 通过第三次再分配反应迅速生成硅烷和副产品 SiH_2Cl_2。转换效率分别为 20%~

22.5%，9.6%及14%，每一步转换效率都比较低，所以物料要多次循环。整个过程要加热和冷却，再加热再冷却，消耗能量比较高。硅棒上沉积速率与反应器上沉积速率之比为10∶1，仅为$SiHCl_3$法的1/10。特别要指出，SiH_4分解时容易在气相成核。所以在反应室内生成硅的粉尘，损失达10%～20%，使硅烷法沉积速率仅为$3～8\mu m/min$。硅烷分解时温度只需800℃，所以电耗仅为$40kW \cdot h/kg$，但由于硅烷制造成本高，故最终的多晶硅制造成本比$SiHCl_3$法要高。用钟罩式反应器生长SiH_4在成本上并无优势，加上SiH_4的安全问题，我们认为建设中国的大硅厂不应采取钟罩式硅烷热分解技术。

硅烷的潜在优点在于用流床反应器生成颗粒状多晶硅。

2.4 $SiHCl_3$法

$SiHCl_3$法是当今生产电子级多晶硅的主流技术[4]，其纯度可达N型2000Ω·cm，生产历史已有35年。实践证明，$SiHCl_3$比较安全，可以安全地运输，可以贮存几个月仍然保持电子级纯度。当容器打开后不像SiH_4或SiH_2Cl_2那样燃烧或爆炸；即使燃烧，温度也不高，可以盖上。$SiHCl_3$法的有用沉积比为1×10^3，是SiH_4的100倍。在4种方法中它的沉积速率最高，可达$8～10\mu m/min$。一次通过的转换效率为5%～20%，在4种方法中也是最高的。沉积温度为1100℃，仅次于$SiCl_4$（1200℃），所以电耗也较高，为$120kW \cdot h/kg$。$SiHCl_3$还原时一般不生成硅粉，有利于连续操作。为了提高沉积速率和降低电耗，需要解决气体动力学问题和优化钟罩反应器的设计。反应器的材料可以是石英也可以是金属的，操作在约为0.14MPa的压力下进行，钟罩温度≤575℃。如果钟罩温度过低，则电能消耗大，而且靠近罩壁的多晶硅棒温度偏低，不利于生长。如果罩壁温度大于575℃，则$SiHCl_3$在壁上沉积，实收率下降，还要清洗钟罩。国外多晶硅棒直径可达229mm。国内$SiHCl_3$法的电耗经过多年的努力已由$500kW \cdot h/kg$降至$200kW \cdot h/kg$，硅棒直径达到100mm左右。

要提高产品质量和产量，必须在炉体的设计上下工夫，解决气体动力学问题，加大炉体直径，增加硅棒数量。

$SiHCl_3$法的最终多晶硅价格比较低，其沉积速率比$SiCl_4$法约高1倍，安全性相对良好。多晶硅纯度完全满足直拉和区熔的要求，所以成为首选的生产技术。世界上11家大公司均采用$SiHCl_3$法，只有一家美国ETHYL公司使用SiH_4法。我国的多晶硅厂也以$SiHCl_3$为宜。硅烷和氯硅烷法生产电子级多晶硅的比较示于表1。

表1　硅烷法和氯硅烷法生长电子级多晶硅的比较

Table 1　Comparison of rankings of silane and chlorosilanes methods to produce electronic grade polysilicon

参数	$SiCl_4$	$SiHCl_3$	SiH_2Cl_2	SiH_4
多晶硅纯度*	优***	优****	良	优
安全性	优	良	差	差
运输	可行	可行	不可	不可
存贮	可行	可行	不可	少量
有用沉积比**	1×10^4	1×10^3	1×10^2	10
沉积速率/$\mu m \cdot min^{-1}$	4～6	8～12	5～8	3～8
一次通过转换率/%	2～10	5～20	17	/

参数	SiCl$_4$	SiHCl$_3$	SiH$_2$Cl$_2$	SiH$_4$
生长温度/℃	1 200	1 100	1 000	800
电耗/kW·h·kg^{-1}				
钟罩反应器	250	120	90	40
流床反应器	—	30	—	10
价格				
钟罩反应器	较低	较低	高	高
流床反应器	—	—	—	最低

＊指钟罩反应器生长的多晶硅；＊＊有用沉积比＝棒上沉积量/钟罩上沉积量；＊＊＊基磷含量高而基硼含量低；
＊＊＊＊基硼含量高而基磷含量低

3. 电子级多晶硅流程

三氯硅烷法经历了数十年的历史,许多工厂关闭;有竞争力的工厂经过几度改造生存下来,提高了产量,有的年产量达到了 4 000~6 000t,成本价格降至 20 美元/kg 左右;其关键技术是由敞开式生产发展到闭环生产。

3.1 第一代 SiHCl$_3$ 的生产流程

适用于 100t/a 以下的小型硅厂以 HCl 和冶金级多晶硅为起点,在 300℃和 0.45MPa 下经催化反应生成。主要副产物为 SiCl$_4$ 和 SiH$_2$Cl$_2$,含量分别为 5.2% 和 1.4%,此外还有 1.9% 较大分子量的氯硅烷[4](图 1)。生长物经沉降器去除颗粒,再经过冷凝器分离 H$_2$,H$_2$ 经压缩后又返回流床反应器。液态产物则进入多级分馏塔(图 1 只绘出 1 个),将 SiCl$_4$、SiH$_2$Cl$_2$ 和较大分子量的氯硅烷与 SiHCl$_3$ 分离。提纯后的 SiHCl$_3$ 进入储罐。SiHCl$_3$ 在常温下是液体,由 H$_2$ 携带进入钟罩反应器,在加温至 1100℃的硅芯上沉淀。其反应为:

$$SiHCl_3 + H_2 \rightarrow Si + 3HCl \tag{1}$$

$$2SiHCl_3 \rightarrow Si + SiCl_4 + 2HCl \tag{2}$$

式(1)是使我们希望唯一发生的反应,但实际上式(2)也同时发生。这样,自反应器排出气体主要有 4 种,即 H$_2$、HCl、SiHCl$_3$ 和 SiCl$_4$。第一代多晶硅生产流程适应于小型多晶硅厂。回收系统回收 H$_2$、HCl、SiCl$_4$ 和 SiHCl$_3$。但 SiCl$_4$ 和 HCl 不再循环使用而是作为副产品出售,H$_2$ 和 SiHCl$_3$ 则回收使用。反应器流出物冷却至-40℃,再进一步加压至 0.55MPa.深冷至-60℃,将 SiCl$_4$ 和 SiHCl$_3$ 与 HCl 和 H$_2$ 分离。后二者通过水吸收:H$_2$ 循环使用;盐酸为副产品。SiHCl$_3$ 和 SiCl$_4$ 混合液进入多级分馏塔,SiCl$_4$ 作为副产品出售,高纯电子级的 SiHCl$_3$ 进入贮罐待用。

第一代多晶硅生产的回收和循环系统小,所以投资不大。但是 SiCl$_4$ 和 HCl 未得到循环利用,生产成本高,当年生产量仅为数十吨以下时还可以运行;而年生产量扩大到数百吨以上时,则进展到第二代。

3.2 第二代多晶硅的生产流程

提高多晶硅的产量可以走两条途径:一是提高一次通过的转换率,另一种是维持合

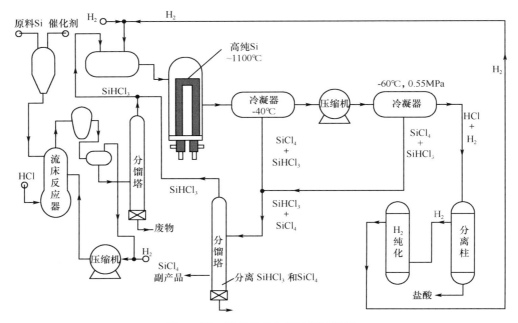

图 1　第一代多晶硅生产流程示意图

Fig.1　Flow chart of the first generation electronic grade polysilicon plant

理的一次通过转化率的同时,加大反应气体通过量,提高单位时间的硅沉积量。第一种途径可以节约投资,但是生产产量提高不大。第二种途径可以加大沉积速率,从而扩大产量,但要投资建立回收系统。第二代多晶硅生产流程就是按第二途径而设计。流程中将 $SiCl_4$ 与冶金级硅反应,在催化剂参与下生成 $SiHCl_3$(见图2)。其反应式为:

$$3SiCl_4 + Si + 2H_2 \rightarrow 4SiHCl_3 \tag{3}$$

式(3)应在高压下进行,例如 3.45MPa 压力和500℃的温度。所得产物主要是 $SiCl_4$ 和 $SiHCl_3$。分离提纯后,高纯 $SiHCl_3$ 又进入还原炉生长多晶硅,$SiCl_4$ 重新又与冶金级硅反应。由于 $SiCl_4$ 的回收可以增加沉积速度,从而扩大生产。

3.3　第三代多晶硅生产流程

第二代多晶硅生产流程中虽然 $SiCl_4$ 得到利用,但 HCl 仍然未进入循环。

第一代和第二代多晶硅生产流程中,H_2 和 HCl 的分离可以用水洗法,并得到盐酸。而第三代多晶硅生产流程(图3)中不能用水洗法,因为这里要求得到干燥的 HCl。为此,用活性炭吸附法或冷 $SiCl_4$ 溶解 HCl 法回收,所得到的干燥的 HCl 又进入流床反应器与冶金级硅反应。在催化剂作用下,在温度300℃和压力0.45MPa 条件下转化为 $SiHCl_3$,经分离和多级分馏后与副产品 $SiCl_4$、SiH_2Cl_2 和大分子量氯硅烷分离。$SiHCl_3$ 又补充到储罐待用,$SiCl_4$ 则进入另一流床反应器,在500℃和3.45MPa 的条件下生产 $SiHCl_3$。

第三代多晶硅生产流程实现了完全闭环生产,适用于现代化年产 1000t 以上的多晶硅厂。其特点是 H_2、$SiHCl_3$、$SiCl_4$ 和 HCl 均循环利用。还原反应并不单纯追求最大的一次通过的转化率,而是提高沉积速率。完善的回收系统可保证物料的充分利用,而钟罩反应器的设计完善使高沉积率得以体现。反应器的体积加大,硅芯根数增多,炉壁温度

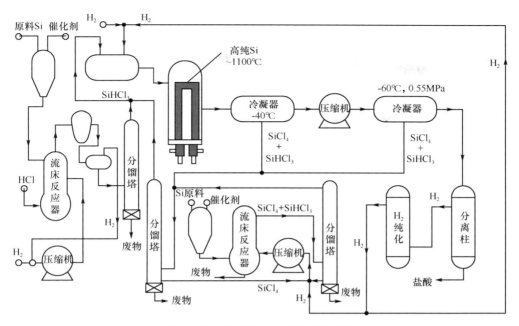

图 2　第二代多晶硅生产流程示意图

Fig.2　Flow chart of the second generation electronic grade polysilicon plant

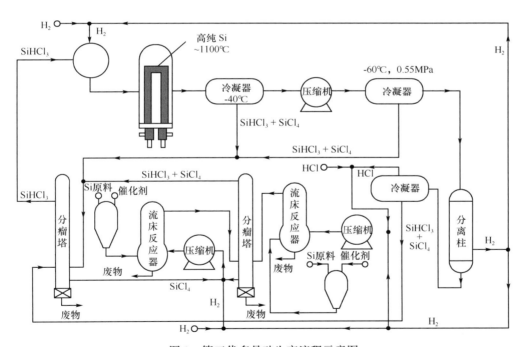

图 3　第三代多晶硅生产流程示意图

Fig.3　Flow chart of the third generation electronic grade ploysilicon plant

在≤575℃的条件下尽量提高;多硅芯温度均匀一致(~1100℃),气流能保证多硅棒均匀迅速地生长,沉积率已由 1960 年的 100g/h 提高到 1988 年的 4kg/h,现在已达到 5kg/h,

数十台反应器即可达到千吨级的年产量。

成功运行第三代多晶硅生产的关键之一是充分了解反应物和生成物的组成,另一关键是充分了解每步反应的最佳条件,才能正确地设计工厂的工艺流程及装备。

现代多晶硅生产已将生产 1kg 硅的还原电耗降至 $100 \sim 120$kW·h,冶金级硅耗约 1.4 kg,液氯耗约 1.4kg,氢耗约 0.5m^3,综合电耗为 ~ 170kW·h。

多晶硅的纯度也是至关重要的[5],施主杂质容许的最高原子比为 15×10^{11}(150ppta),受主杂质浓度为 5×10^{-11}(50ppta),碳浓度为 1×10^{-7}(100ppba)。体金属总量也应控制在 5×10^{-10}(500pptw)以下。此外对表面金属也有严格要求[1]。

4. 流床反应器和自由空间反应器

如前所述,在全钟罩式反应器中,SiHCl$_3$ 一次通过率转换仅有 5%~20%,这是相当低的数值。SiH$_4$ 容易分解,但由于有用沉积比仅为 10,为了不致产生过多粉尘和减少钟罩上的沉积物,沉积速率限制在 $3 \sim 8$μm/min,这也是相当慢的。如果使用流床反应器生长颗粒状多晶硅,一次通过转换率和沉积速率均可以大大提高,由此可以有效地降低能耗[6]。

如果用 SiH$_4$ 为气源,流床温度为 $575 \sim 685$℃,SiH$_4$ 与 H$_2$ 的分子比为 1:21 时可以得到 99.7% 的转化率,也就是说接近 100% 的转化率。生长时需要很小的硅籽晶,多晶硅沉积在籽晶上,大约长到直径 $150 \sim 1500$μm 时落下。流床反应器可以连续工作,从而减少反应器的清洗次数。加大流床的直径,可以使生产能力上升;提高 SiH$_4$ 与 H$_2$ 的比率,提高温度,也能增大产量,但后二者过高则产生硅粉尘。用 SiH$_4$ 流床法生产的能耗已降至 10kW·h/kg,前景十分诱人。

流床反应器法生产的多晶硅是粒状,不可能直接提供区熔使用,但可作为连续直拉硅的原料。目前在产量和质量方面都远不及 SiHCl$_3$ 钟罩法。流床反应器的操作条件很苛刻,温度和压力均要准确控制,要在解决能经受温度冲击的同时,又能保证多晶硅纯度的反应器内壁材料。SiH$_4$ 流床反应器法还不能作为中国大多晶硅工厂的方案。

自由空间反应器的结构十分简单,只有一个空腔,硅源气体用 SiH$_4$,用等离子体加热到 800℃,生成很细的硅粉,直径约为 $0.3 \sim 0.4$μm,转化率接近 100%。

自由空间反应器可以进一步降低多晶硅成本。但是此法得到的硅粉太细,在直拉炉内操作不方便,到处是硅粉;纯度也不够,导电类型有时是 n 型,有时是 p 型;拉晶后电阻率可达 55Ω·cm。在目前,自由空间反应器比流床反应器法更不成熟。

5. 结 论

对三氯氢硅法、四氯化硅法、二氯二氢硅法和硅烷法生产电子级多晶硅的纯度、安全性、运输和存贮的可行性、有用沉积比、沉积速率、一次转换率、生长温度、电耗、价格等进行了对比分析。对钟罩反应器、流床反应器以及自由空间反应器生产电子级多晶硅进行了优劣比较。三氯氢硅钟罩反应器法优越性明显,适用于 1 000t/a 级的电子级多晶硅工厂,同时应采取全部回收 SiCl$_4$ 和 HCl 的三代多晶硅流程。

参考文献

[1] 梁骏吾.兴建年产一千吨电子级多晶硅工厂的思考[J].中国工程科学,2000,2(6):33.

[2] Wacher Sitronic A G.Polysilicon production 1995—2003.1995.

[3] Rogers L O.Handbook of semiconductor silicon technology[M].Noyes Publ.New Jersey,1990,33—93.

[4] Conventional polysilicon process(Siemens Technology) report,DOE/JPL-954343-21,Nat Tech Inform Center Springfield, 1981,208.

[5] Product specification of Wacker-Chemie GmbH,1999,PCA-CH4;1998.PCA-AE4.

[6] Union Carbide Corp.Final report,DOE/JPL-954334-21,Nat Tech Inform Center,Springfield,1981.

The Production Technology of Electronic Grade Polycrystalline Silicon.

Liang Junwu

(*Institute of Semiconductors, Chinese Academy of Sciences, Beijing* 100083, *China*)

Abstract: The technology of construction of an electronic grade polycrystalline sihcon plant with annual production of 1000 tons is explored. The product qualities, safety, transportation, storage, useful deposition ratios, deposition rates, one pass conversions, deposition temperatures, electrical energy consumption and manufacturing costs are summarized for silane, dichlorosilane, trichlorosilane and tetrachlorosilane methods. The bell jar, fluidized bed and free-space polysilicon reactors for polysilicon deposition are compared with each other. In addition, the flow charts of polysilicon production are described. The trichlorosilane method of third generation using bell jar reactors is suitable for a plant with an annual production of 1 000 tons of electronic grade polysilicon.

Key words: polysilicon; trichlorosilane method; silane method; flow chart; production

中国信息产业领域相关重点基础材料科技发展战略研究

梁骏吾[1]　郑敏政[2]　袁　桐[2]　段维新[1]

（1　中国科学院半导体研究所,北京,100083）　（2　信息产业部,北京,100846）

Study on the Development Strategies of Fundamental Materials Related to China's Information Industry

Liang Junwu[1]　Zheng Minzheng[2]　Yuan Tong[2]　Duan Weixing[1]

（1　Institute of Semiconductors,Chinese Academy of Science）　（2　Ministry of Information Industry）

Abstract：In this paper the present state and problems of the fundamental materials related to China's information industry are reviewed. These information materials include elemental, compound,low-dimensional and widegap semiconductors,magnetic and magneto-optical storage materials,sensor materials,laser materials,materials for non-linar optics,display materials,prezoelectrical materials and light transmitting optical fibers.The strategic thoughts and aim of the development of the information materials toward the 21st century are proposed.The materials fields which should be preferentially promoted and policies and proposals to speed up the development of information materials are given.

0. 序　言

信息产业领域包括信息的发射、传输、接收、运算、处理、存储、显示以及敏感等。这些领域的兴起和发展都以相关的信息材料为基础,例如微电子产业的核心——集成电路就是以半导体硅和 GaAs 为其基础材料。自 1947 年发明晶体管,1958 年发明集成电路以来,半导体技术的发展就是物理、材料、器件三者相互促进的结果。又如,光电子技术的核心是激光技术,激光器的工作物质是某些半导体、激光晶体、有机染料等。

信息材料可以按信息发射、传输、接收等功能来区分,也可以按材料在信息技术中的功能并结合材料的物理特性来区分。而后者与实际产业的划分比较一致。因此,将本项研究的对象分为元素半导体材料、化合物半导体材料、低维半导体材料、宽带隙半导体材料、磁记录材料、信息传感材料、激光材料、非线性光学材料、显示材料、压电及铁电材料。

1. 发 展 现 状

经过"八五"、"九五"的发展,我国在信息材料,包括半导体材料,各种记录材料,信

原载于:材料导报.2000,14(2):1-4.

息传输、显示、激光、非线性、光学、传感和压电、铁电材料等方面取得较大进步,建成了相应的研究、开发和生产中心,某些领域产品的产量已居世界前列。现就生产和研究水平予以介绍。

1.1 半导体多晶硅

我国多晶硅生产能力为 80t/年,产量约 40t/年;多晶硅生产工艺落后,成本高、规模小(世界水平生产多晶硅的临界规模为 1000t/年,远大于我国全国多晶硅产量)。世界年产量约为 14 500t,我国的多晶 Si 市场为 736t/年。

1.2 半导体单晶硅

我国生产的单晶硅直径范围为 50~200mm,并以 100mm 为主,能力为 200t/年,产量为 180t/年;抛光片直径为 50~150mm,以 100mm 为主,200mm 有样片,产量为 0.2 亿 in^2。抛光硅片世界产量约为 40 亿 in^2,以 Φ150~200 为主。我国抛光片产量约占世界产量 0.5%,直径以 Φ100 主,但国际上 Φ100 硅片比例<10%。而国际主流产品即 Φ200 抛光片在我国尚处于试制阶段。产品质量档次较低,在 IC 制造中只能作为陪片出口。全国单晶抛光片工厂的规模也远低于国外一个厂的临界经济规模——即 0.6 亿 in^2。

1.3 化合物半导体

我国化合物半导体 GaAs 单晶以 Φ50~75 为主,可提供 Φ100 单晶样品,生产能力为 600kg/年。主要为微波器件提供 GaAs 片,目前做不到"开盒即用"的水平。世界 GaAs 年产量约为 50 吨,GaAs 直径以 Φ75~100 为主,最大为 Φ150。我国的 HgCdTe 外延尺寸较小,衬底限制生长尺寸为 $20×20mm^2$。我国 InP 单晶直径 Φ50 已进入实用化,而国外 Φ 50~75 已工业化生产。

1.4 低维半导体材料

国内低维半导体材料已研制出 HEMT、PHEMT、HBT 等微电子器件和量子阱激光器、调制器、光学双稳态器件、光电子器件等。目前 GaAs 基量子阱微结构材料已达实用水平。InP 基量子阱材料尚处在实验室阶段.GeSi/Si 材料也正在研制中。目前,国际上毫米波通讯已从以军用为主走向以民用为主,工作频率已达几十 kMHz 到上百 kMHz。不同波长的量子阱激光器在光盘读出、磁光信息存储、全息显示、通讯和激光泵浦已广泛使用。GaAs 基量子微结构高频器件到 2000 年的产值将超过 6 亿美元。

1.5 宽带隙材料

我国对宽带隙材料——GaN 基、SiC 和金刚石等均已进行研究。目前,国外已有 GaN、SiC 的衬底材料,其中 SiC 衬底材料已商业化。我国尚无这些衬底单晶。我国已研制出六方相和立方相 GaN 基发光二极管,而且后者是我国率先在国际上做出来的。国际上蓝光激光二极管已形成产业。日本制备的 GaN 基蓝光激光器的寿命已超过一万小时,预计不久即可商品化。预计到 2006 年,氮化物器件市场将达 30 亿美元。SiC 也是制造高温、高速、耐高压、抗辐射、大功率器件的材料。我国已在硅衬底上生长了立方 SiC 的单晶外延材料。

1.6 固体激光材料和非线性光学晶体

固体激光材料包括晶体、玻璃、透明陶瓷和有机材料。激光晶体中以 Nd:YAG 最成熟,应用最广,产量最大。我国有数十台炉子生长 YAG,晶体尺寸最大 $\Phi60\times200mm^2$,商品化产品尺寸为 $\Phi40\sim60$,年产值为 0.2 亿～0.4 亿人民币。美国和俄罗斯有炉子 300 台,晶体尺寸最大 $\Phi100\times300mm^2$,商品化产品尺寸为 $\Phi50\sim75$,年产值为 0.3 亿～0.5 亿美元。由于 90 年代 LD 泵浦激光技术的发展,对 $Nd:YVO_4$ 要求大增,我国 $Nd:YVO_4$ 的产品占世界市场的 1/3。我国的 $Ho:Cr:Tm:YAG$、$Er:YAG$ 和 $Ho:Er:Tm:YLF$ 有小批量试制。美国在激光晶体研制处于领先地位,其次为俄罗斯、日本和中国。

非线性光学晶体包括各种变频晶体如 KDP、KTP、$LiNbO_3$、$KNbO_3$、$\beta-BaB_2O_4$(BBO)、LiB_3O_5 等。其中非线性光学晶体 BBO 和 LBO 是我国首创,在 80 年代末至 90 年代独占世界市场。近年来,其国际市场年销售额近千万美元。其余 LBO、BGO、$Fe:KNO_3$、$BaTiO_3$、KTP 和 LAP 也进入了国际市场。我国是激光晶体材料科研和生产的先进国家。

1.7 光传输材料

光传输材料指以波导方式传输光的光学纤维材料。目前世界上已有 80% 的信息业务由光传输,其重要意义不言而喻。

我国光纤生产企业有七家,以合资为主。1998 年光纤产量为 240 万 km,1999 年预测 430 万 km,其中仅一家有制棒能力,合 250 万 km。

从国内外光纤预制棒制造技术看,有 MVCD、OVD、VAD 和 PCVD 四种化学气相沉积方法。我国主要引进 MCVD,其次是 PCVD。但实际上 OVD 和 VAD 外沉积方法已是主流,其光纤质量好、成本低。

1.8 磁记录和磁光记录材料

半导体动态存储器(DRAM)提取时间短,多用于计算机的内存储器。外存储器则利用磁记录方式,做成磁带、软磁盘、硬磁盘。磁记录介质可以是颗粒($\gamma-Fe_2O_3$、$Co-\gamma-Fe_2O_3$、CrO_2、金属磁粉、钡铁氧体粉等),也可以是化学电镀钴镍合金或真空溅射蒸镀 Co 基合金。磁光记录和磁记录的主要不同点是记录读出信号所用传感元件是光头而不是磁头。

目前,国外存储密度为 $3\sim5Gb/in^2$ 的硬盘已商品化,130mm 单台硬盘的容量已突破 45GB。最近希捷已开发出 $23.8Gb/in^2$ 的硬盘,即 3.5″硬盘能存储 32GB 数据。磁带的性能也大大提高,QUANTUM DLT7000 线性记录磁带的压缩容量可达 $70\sim100GB$,但价格为同容量光盘的 1/10。90mm 磁光盘容量已从 128MB 提高到 640MB。最近 Sony 开发出 3.5″的 1.3GB 磁光盘。

磁粉有很大市场,世界年销售量估计近 10^5t,高性能磁粉(如 MP)需求不断增大。磁阻、巨磁阻等高性能磁头材料的研究生产发展很快。

国内原有磁盘生产厂四五家,已全部退出竞争,高校院所的研究也处于停顿状态。目前有外资、合资硬盘厂三家,年产硬盘驱动器 1000 万台;磁带、软盘生产严重萎缩,录像带涂布线全部停产,原有一百多家软盘生产厂大部分转产或停产,只有十家左右维持生产,年产量约 5 亿片,而且芯片主要依赖进口。原有十余家磁粉厂,目前只有几家小厂维持生产,年产量几百吨;国内研究单位研究开发成功钴改性氧化铁磁粉、金属磁粉、钡铁氧体磁粉,但尚未形成生产规模;国内金属磁头材料生产有一定规模,也开展了各种铁氧体、非晶和薄膜磁头材料以及磁阻、巨磁阻磁头材料和磁头的研究;现有合资和国有磁头厂 20 余家,1996 年的产量已达到 3.54 亿只,以深圳科技为代表的磁头厂已成为全球第三大磁头生产基地。

1.9 压电材料

压电材料主要用作 SAW 和 BAW 器件。用于信号发生、谐振、滤波、延迟、脉冲压缩和展宽。主要有 α-SiO_2、$LiNbO_3$、$LiTaO_3$ 等体材料和 ZnO、AlN、Ta_2O_5 和金刚石薄膜材料等。

我国已建成从事材料研究的开发体系,现已由军工转向民用。1998 年.全世界 α-SiO_2 的生产量为 $5000 \sim 8000t$,器件 50 亿~55 亿支。我国生产 1500t,器件 13 亿~15 亿支。虽然产量大,但高档材料仍要进口。1998 年世界 $LiNbO_3$ 和 $LiTaO_3$ 产量约为 300t,SAW 器件 7~9 亿支。我国生产 20t,SAW 器件约 4000 支,国外已有 ZnO/Al_2O_3 商品器件。我国从事压电材料器件的研究和生产厂家有近百个。研制和开发能力并不太低,但产业化水平低,相当国外 70 年代水平,而且规模小,低档品过剩。α-SiO_2,$LiNbO_3$ 和 $LiTaO_3$ 等晶体尺寸小,完整性较差:国内 mm 级包裹体,国外 μm 级;位错密度 $10^4 \sim 10^5 cm^{-2}$(国内),$10^2 \sim 10^3 cm^{-2}$(国际);$LiNbO_3$ 和 $LiTaO_3$ 仅可制成 400MHz SAW(国内),而国外产品可做 900MHz、1800MHz、1900MHz,可供手持电话用。我国 ZnO/Al_2O_3 材料处于实验室阶段。国外已有了 3GHz 以下的 ZnO/Al_2O_3 商品化的 SAW 器件。

1.10 显示材料

我国 LCD 工业起步于 80 年代初,现有 50 多条 TN-LCD 生产线,生产能力大于 500,000 M^2/年,90%以上的产品出口。"八五"期间 LCD 投资达 1.7 亿美元。1997 年产值为 30 亿元,2000 年预计为 60 亿~80 亿元。我国是世界 TN-LCD 生产大国。目前国内生产液晶的骨干企业有三家,年产液晶 12t 并即将达到 17t/年的能力。我国液晶主要是 TN 型,还不能生产室温低黏度 TN 显示用液晶。STN 型和 TFT 用液晶材料仍在研究中。

预计,2000 年前 TN-LCD 增长率为 5%以下,需求量约为 15~17t;TFT-LCD 增长率为 15%~20%,需求量为 13~15t。

目前世界 TN-LCD 生产正向中国转移。为了降低成本。中小尺寸的 STN-LCD 也有从日、韩向中国转移的趋势。预计 STN 用液晶材料用量将达 5t/年以上。

半导体发光二极管用外延材料是另一种类型的显示材料,它的应用面广,世界产量已达 500 亿支/年,波长由红外到紫外。可见光二极管所用材料主要是 GaP 和 GaAs 衬底上生长的 III-V 族半导体及其固溶体,如 GaP 掺 Zn、O 或 N,GaAlAs,GaAsP 等,蓝光则有 Al_2O_3,衬底上生长的 GaN 基材料。

我国目前发光二极管年产量为 50 亿支,但主要是用国外管芯进行装配。我国自己生长外延材料并做成管芯的只占其中的 10%,而且是低档产品,所用生长方法主要是液相外延,先进材料如 MOCVD 生长方法应用很少。我国已解决生产问题的有红、黄、橙三种颜色的发光二极管。绿色发光管未解决高亮度问题,蓝色发光管还处于实验室阶段。

1.11 信息传感材料

信息传感材料是指用作传感器中能获取信息并转换为可测信号(一般是电信号)的材料,输入信息可以是力学量、电学量、光学量、磁学量、化学量、生物量等。信息传感材料有:半导体材料(硅、硅基材料、III-V 和 II-VI 族化合物),陶瓷材料,高分子材料和光纤材料。

全世界传感器市场产值为 278 亿美元(1995 年),预计 2000 年将达到 380 亿美元。1998 年统计我国生产电压敏、光敏或热敏传感器超过 1000 万支/年的单位有 10 家。气敏传感器年产量超过 100 万支的有三家。1998 年产量为 3 亿多支,工业产值达 37 亿人民币,约有 1/5 的产品出口。

2. 信息材料领域发展指导思想和发展目标

指导思想:以企业技术创新为主,开发具有中国自己知识产权的信息材料。积极引进和消化国外先进材料制备技术,抓好科研基地和大公司集团的建设,努力形成规模生产,面向国内外两个市场。

总目标:以微电子和光电子材料为重点,注重发展量子结构材料,突破关键技术,逐步建成国际水平的研究和生产基地,形成规模经济,提高产品质量,2005 年使主要信息材料性能达到国际 90 年代中后期水平,初步满足微电子、光电子、通信、计算机、网络等科研和生产的要求。

具体目标为:

(1) 研究开发大直径硅片技术,满足 0.35~0.18μm 技术的要求。硅片生产规模要达到产业化水平。

(2) GaAs 单晶和外延片直径扩大至 Φ100~150mm,实现批量生产。满足微波器件和电路的要求。InP 单晶直径 Φ75~100mm,满足毫米波及亚毫米波器件需求。GaAs 片和 InP 片应达到"开盒即用"的质量标准。

(3) 重点解决 GaAs 基微电子材料和光电子材料、InP 毫米波电子器件和光电子器件材料。

(4) GaN 基蓝、绿二极管和紫外、蓝光激光二极管要实用化,并初步形成产业。解决 SiC 衬底单晶的生长和 SiC 外延的关键技术。满足高温、高频、大功率器件要求,并批量生产。在光电子器件基础上,形成这两种体系的量子微结构产业化生产。

(5) SiGe 异质外延材料应能满足 10~70GHz HBT 器件要求。

(6) SOI 的研制要跟上世界潮流,研制出满足低功耗、低电源电压、抗辐射、高性能集成电路要求,直径为 Φ200,解决生产工程化问题。

(7) 需求量最大的 Nd:YAG 晶体系列化,晶体质量达到国际先进水平,实现规模化生产,提高国际市场的竞争力。优选一批需求量大的激光材料,提高质量,面向国内外市场。

（8）HgCdTe 体材料和外延材料的质量全面满足红外探测器的要求并能批量生产。红外衬底材料 CdZnTe 技术成熟,达到批量生产程度。提高各种类型超晶格量子阱红外探测器材料的实用化水平。

（9）提高 TN 型液晶材料的技术水平,增加品种,满足室温低黏度显示的要求,并实现商品化。STN 型显示用液晶材料和 TFT 用液晶显示材料进入商品化生产。

（10）半导体发光二极管管芯国产化。

（11）建设光纤预制棒产业。在创新基础上发展具有我国自己知识产权的光纤预制棒技术,扭转预制棒依靠进口的被动局面。

（12）磁记录材料应尽快摆脱受制于人的局面,建立自己的产业。掌握先进的颗粒介质制备技术,使涂层厚度达到亚微米水平。满足容量 100MB 以上软磁盘的需要。突破薄膜制造技术,开发面高密度 $1 \sim 10\text{Gb/in}^2$ 硬磁盘介质。建立我国自己的高性能磁头产业。

（13）攻克无宏观缺陷、低微缺陷的压电晶体生长及精密加工技术。重点以手机国产化所需的 900MHz/1800MHz 高频 SAW 滤波器为目标。完成大尺寸、高均匀性、高完整性的石英、$LiNbO_3$、$LiTaO_3$、$Li_2B_4O_7$ 等压电晶体的研制与产业化进程。开展新压电晶体及 ZnO、金刚石薄膜压电材料的研制工作,为新一代高性能、高频 SAW 及 BAW 器件发展奠定基础。

（14）实现汽车用传感器(如压力、加速度、角速度、喷油、空燃比测控器)所用的半导体和功能陶瓷的研究和实用化。

开展医疗(如温压、血压、尿样、血样等检测)用半导体材料、功能陶瓷、高分子传感材料的研究和实用化。

开展通信和广播领域传感器(高保真麦克风、角速度计)所用的半导体材料和功能陶瓷材料的研究和实用化。

3. 拟开展的重大研究课题

3.1 重大研究课题

拟开展的信息材料的重大研究课题是集成电路用高性能、大尺寸的半导体材料,光电子技术用化合物半导体材料和量子微结构材料,信息记录材料,信息传输材料和信息光学材料。

3.2 研究开发重点项目

（1）满足深亚微米集成电路用硅片的研究。单晶直径为 Φ200,无 A 缺陷、D 缺陷 $<200/\text{cm}^2$,控氧精度 ±1.5ppm。Si 片表面平坦度 $\leqslant 250\text{nm}$。表面杂质 $\leqslant 1 \times 10^{11} \text{ cm}^{-2}$, $\text{OISF} \leqslant 10\text{cm}^{-2}$,0.2μm 以下颗粒 $<50/$ 片,大直径 Si 外延片: Φ200、厚度不均匀性 $<\pm 15\%$,电阻率不均匀性 $<\pm 5\%$,微小缺陷密度 $\leqslant 0.1\text{cm}^{-2}$。

（2）满足超高速电路用 Φ150 ~ 200GaAs 单晶片和 Φ75 ~ 100InP 片。晶片表面加工精度、完整性、清洁度、电学指标满足器件要求,同时能达到"开盒即用"。晶片还应满足制造光电器件的衬底要求。

（3）满足超高速微电子器件（HEMT、PHEMT、HBT）的 GaAs 和 InP 基量子微结构材料。频率由 8mm 向 3mm 以下过渡，并产业化。满足不同波段的通讯用光电量子阱激光器等对低维半导体材料的要求。

（4）蓝、绿光 LED 用 GaN 基外延材料。在全色显示、白光照明、水下通信等领域产业化。

紫外、蓝光激光器用 GaN 基外延材料质量满足长寿命连续输出的实用要求。

SiC 衬底单晶直径可达 Φ25，管道缺陷降至 1cm^{-2} 以下。外延 SiC 材料能满足高频、大功率器件实用化要求，工作温度 >300℃。

（5）用于高频 HBT 器件的 $Si_{1-x}Ge_x$/Si 外延材料，器件频率 10~70GHz，用于红外探测器的量子阱结构 $Si_{1-x}Ge_x$/Si 材料。

（6）建立 SOI 材料的研究、开发和生产基地，解决制造中的关键技术（大剂量 O$^+$ 注入技术，Si 片键合技术，Si 片减薄-智能切割，背腐蚀或外延转移技术等），达到 Φ200 质量与国际 90 年代末相等的 SOI 材料。

（7）发展 Φ50 以上、Nd 分布均匀、低光学损耗的 Nd：YAG 晶体，开发新的 LD 泵浦激光材料，如 Yb：YAG 等和新波段激光晶体，包括 2~5μm 波段（军事、医疗、科研），1.5μm（通信和军事）蓝绿光波段（水下探测、通信）。开展非线性光学晶体（BBO、LBO、KBBF、SBBO、CBO）提高光学质量，加大尺寸，加快生长速度的研究和开发。

（8）红外探测器材料 HgCdTe、PbS、InSb 半导体单晶和薄膜以及 TGS、LiTaO$_3$、SBN 和 PVT 等热电材料实用化并形成产业。

（9）大直径光纤预制棒沉积技术如 OVD 工艺、VAD 工艺的研究和产业化。扩大特种光纤特别是光纤放大器用掺 Er 光纤系列和军用光纤陀螺用偏振光纤系列，高强度光纤等的研究和开发。

（10）宽温低黏度 TN 显示用液晶的开发和生产，STN 显示用液晶材料和 TFT 用液晶的开发和生产。

（11）适用于超高密度软盘、磁带的超薄涂层制备技术的研究（涂层厚 0.2~0.5μm）。100MB~1GB 容量的 3.5″软磁盘的研究和开发。

适用于大容量硬盘、磁光盘、薄膜磁头和巨磁阻磁头的薄膜制备技术的研究和开发。面记录密度为 1~10Gb/in^2 的低噪声硬盘介质的研究和开发。新型磁阻材料和磁头的研究。

（12）大尺寸（LN、LT 达到 Φ120~125，α-SiO$_2$ 达 Φ76~100，Li$_2$B$_2$O$_7$ 达 Φ76~100），低缺陷密度（位错 10^2~10^3），低尺寸包裹体（μm 级），低小角晶界（≤5′）的压电晶体生长技术，满足手持电话用 1900MHz SAW 滤波器的质量要求。开展新薄膜压电材料研究和开发，如 ZnO、Al$_2$O$_3$ 或金刚石/Si 材料研究，使频率扩展到 3GHz 以上。

4. 政策与建议

（1）加强自主开发能力，加强配套能力，自主掌握新型领域的关键技术，关键材料。

（2）通过竞争与联合，形成电子专用材料研究、生产基地，并逐步建成具有参与国际竞争能力的大公司或企业集团,形成规模经济。

(3)提高投资强度。对诸如微电子和光电子量大面广的电子专用材料,要加大投资力度,加快技术改造,尽快形成产业;对一些影响面广、难度大、技术含量高的关键材料,在组织科技攻关时要给以重点支持。

(4)制订扶植政策(如贷款、税收等),为独立自主的开发我国电子专用材料创造良好的环境。

(5)开展新材料研究,形成自己的知识产权。

(6)加强人才培养,充分发挥人的作用。技术创新的主体是人,要加强人才的培养,加强人才交流,引进高级人才,稳定材料专业人才队伍,防止人才流失。

中国硅材料工业的前景与挑战

中科院半导体所院士	梁骏吾
信息产业部电子信息产品管理司副司长	郑敏政
信息产业部电子信息产品管理司处长	袁桐
同济大学教授	戴自忠

我国半导体硅材料事业始于 20 世纪 50 年代末,现已经历了四十四个春秋。在这期间,我国建立了多晶硅、直拉单晶硅、区熔单晶硅、硅外延片和非晶硅的生产体系。此外,SiGe 材料、SOI、SiC 等硅基材料的科研也取得很大进展。我国现有硅材料厂 35 家,1999 年到 2000 年我国单晶硅增长率达到 33%,多晶硅增长率达到 39%。2001 年单晶硅和多晶硅的增长率分别为 25% 和 32%。虽然增长率有所下降,但在整个世界经济衰退期间,这仍然是极好的业绩。2001 年底中国正式加入 WTO,面对世界经济出现下滑,我国硅材料工业的前景如何?能否在世界经济不景气环境中继续发展?前进过程中将面临怎样的挑战和困难?本文将就以上问题进行分析和论述。

集成电路制造业的困难给我国硅材料行业带来机遇

2001 年世界感受了网络泡沫破灭的后果,电子信息产业投资下降,特别是在 9·11 事件以后,世界对电子信息产品需求下降。这些对我国集成电路制造业的影响是十分明显的。我国集成电路制造业在 2000 年 1 月至 11 月份利润上升到 17 亿元,而据经济日报报道,2001 年同期利润却下降到不足 1 亿元,降幅高达 94%,有的芯片企业出现严重亏损。从世界范围来说,2001 年世界集成电路销售额比 2000 年下降了 30% 以上,集成电路是硅片的最大用户,所以集成电路市场的下降将影响硅片的销售,这将给我国硅材料行业带来困难。但是我们也应看到,集成电路制造业的困难也给我们的硅材料工业的发展带来机遇。这是因为,集成电路芯片厂家利润下降或者亏损逼迫它们设法寻找对策以走出困境。重要对策之一就是寻求新的、价廉的硅片供应商。过去,中国境内的 8 英寸

原载于:中国集成电路,1994,34(5):36-38.

集成电路芯片厂使用进口硅片,6英寸集成电路芯片厂也主要使用进口硅片。现在,国内硅片厂用价廉质优硅片打入集成电路芯片制造厂,从而真正进入超大规模集成电路用硅片的大市场,为我国的硅片的发展提供了机会。

我国硅材料企业水平已经提高

过去,我国硅材料企业的产品档次较低,产品中集成电路用抛光片所占份额不多,小尺寸研磨片和分立器件用硅片占很大比例,所以产值不高。要提高产值,必需提升产品的档次,即提高集成电路用抛光片所占比例。在最近几年,我国硅材料企业的技术水平已经得到改造和提高,改造和提高的途径有两种:一种是直接采购国外的新设备,使技术水平上升。另一种则是瞄准机会,收购国外硅材料企业的设备。浙江和洛阳各收购了国外一个工厂,既节省资金,又缩短了建设期,收效显著。目前我国硅单晶年生产能力达到800吨以上,硅抛光片年生产能力至少达1亿平方英寸,供应我国境内集成电路芯片厂家已有富余。由于我国生产集成电路用硅片水平的提升,使我国在争夺高档次产品市场的能力上升,这是今后我国硅材料产业继续发展的重要基础。

电力电子器件和其它分立器件用硅材料仍然有发展空间

中国加入WTO以后,不同的硅材料所受的影响有所不同。竞争最激烈的首先是集成电路用硅材料,特别是大尺寸的硅外延片与抛光片。但是在电力电子器件和其它分立器件用硅材料领域的竞争却相对缓和一些。因为这些器件的生产向亚洲国家转移的同时,相应的硅材料也发生转移。美国是区熔硅单晶的发源地,但是在2001年,美国已停止区熔硅单晶的生产。与此相反,我国正在扩大区熔硅单晶的生产能力,并向丹麦大量订购区熔硅单晶炉,使我国即将能生产6英寸甚至8英寸区熔硅单晶,多年来我国一直生产和出售研磨硅片和腐蚀片等,虽然产值低一些,但是技术要求较低,不需要高额投资,作为发展中国家来说,在积累资金阶段也是可行的方式,这些产品在未来几年仍有发展空间,但是产品有待升级。

太阳能用硅材料出口势头不减

中国硅材料中太阳能级单晶硅占有较大比重,约占硅单晶生产量的25%。这么大的比重主要不是内销,而是出口。硅单晶的原料主要是进口多晶硅头和尾料,在中国拉成单晶,然后出口,利润很薄,对这种产品来说,在加入WTO后,出口势头不会衰减。与此同时,我们要大力开发国内市场,我国西北幅员辽阔,日照时间长,太阳能源丰富,具有广阔的市场需求,特别是随着西部开发步伐的加快,太阳能电池市场需求进一步扩大,从而带动我国太阳能用硅材料的发展。因此,我们必须要花大力气建立我国的太阳能电池用硅材料制造业。

大尺寸硅外延片有待开发

中国第一个 8 英寸集成电路生产线 (909 工程) 主要以 8 英寸硅外延片为基片。这种 8 英寸硅外延片,国内尚属空白,全部来自进口,今后要得到 8 英寸集成电路制造厂的订货单,8 英寸硅外延片是不可缺少的品种。当硅直拉单晶增大时,有一系列技术问题需要解决,采用外延片提高晶体质量是一种好方法。所以大尺寸硅外延片的开发和生产不仅是当前急需,而且是未来发展的趋势。从价值看,硅外延片的产值可提高一倍,硅外延片是硅材料的重要增长点。预计,能在硅外延产品上成功开发的硅材料厂将取得很大竞争优势。

中国的电子级多晶硅短缺为建立多晶硅厂提供了机遇

中国的单晶硅 2001 年已达到 500 吨左右,所需多晶硅为 1000 吨,而我国多晶硅年产量仅为 100 吨,二者相差甚大。严重短缺为我国建立新型多晶硅厂提供了机遇。但大量的进口多晶硅已充斥市场。所以新的多晶硅工厂在建设时必须考虑两个至关重要的问题——成本与质量。当前,多晶硅工厂的建设投资大约每公斤生产能力要超过 100 美元以上。如此高的建设费用,加上从国外引进先进的多晶硅技术还存在一些障碍,多年来,虽然不少地方想发展多晶硅,却始终未能如愿。国内的化工材料、各种分离技术和过程的理论计算都有了很大进步,而且,我们还有一批相当数量的人才,如果政府加以支持并适当组织,并通过对外合作,建设一个有竞争能力的现代化大型多晶硅厂是完全有能力的。

总之,在加入了 WTO 的环境下,面对国际经济下降的影响,我国硅材料企业既遭遇挑战,也得到了机遇。总体来说,2002—2005 年硅材料生产仍然会上升。我国单晶硅企业在过去二、三年内进行了扩产、改造,为争取高档产品市场提供了基础。要使这种机遇变为现实,还需要努力取得器件厂家的认可。大尺寸硅外延片的开发是重要的高档次产品。我国硅材料传统的分立器件市场仍然将会扩大,其中大尺寸区熔硅产品将有较大增长。随着我国太阳能电池制造能力的提高,太阳能电池用多晶硅及单晶硅的需求量也会不断加大。我国电子级多晶硅市场缺额甚大,急需建设大型多晶硅工厂,建设时要重视中国自身的技术力量。

＊中国工程院软课题 2/2001C

半导体硅片生产形势的分析

中国科学院半导体研究所中国工程院院士　　梁骏吾

中国信息产业部　　　　　　　　　　　　　郑敏政　袁　桐

同济大学　　　　　　　　　　　　　　　　闻瑞梅

　　半导体器件支撑着庞大的信息产业,而半导体器件93%以上是硅器件,它们以硅片为基础材料。本文将叙述半导体器件和硅片在世界与国内的生产状况和需求量[1~3],并对我国硅材料企业满足市场能力进行分析。

2001年世界半导体器件生产低落,世界期待其回升

　　2000年世界半导体销售额为2040亿美元,但是2001年下降了31.9%,仅达到1389亿美元。2001年是世界半导体生产最低落的一年。SIA预计2002年将增加6%,2003年和2004年都将有21%的连续回升。2004年全世界半导体销售额将达到2156亿美元(表1)。

表1　半导体销售额

年份	2000	2001	2002	2003	2004
销售额(亿美元)	2040	1389	1472	1782	2156
增长率(%)		-31.9	6	21	21

来源:SIA/WSTS

　　表1中的半导体器件包括三类产品:第一类是集成电路,这一类占的分量高达85%;第二类是分立器件,如:整流器、二极管等,所占比例不到10%;第三类是光电器件,所占比例约为5%,这一类主要由化合物材料制备。以2001年为例,这一年的1389亿美元销售额中集成电路占85.31%,分立器件占9.36%,光电器件占5.33%(图1)[4]。

　　2001年分立器件和集成电路销售额为1315亿美元,占94.67%。这些器件绝大多数是以硅片为基础材料制成的。2001年的硅片销售额为52亿美元。硅片制成集成电路、整流器和二极管后可以使产值增加25倍。

　　硅片是用于半导体器件制造的,因此,器件的需求决定了硅片的市场。

　　世界硅片的需求量是巨大的,2000年的销售

图1　世界半导体器件的组成(2001年)

原载于:中国集成电路.2003,44(1):34-37.

量达到 55.51 亿平方英寸,销售金额为 75.19 亿美元。由硅片量可以推算 2000 年单晶消耗量约为 11 100 吨(不计太阳能用硅单晶)。1996—2003 年世界硅片的需求量示于表 2 中,其中 2001 年有预测值和实际值,且前者大于后者,这是因为整个世界经济下滑所致。我国 2001 年生产的硅抛光片占世界生产量的 1.3%。世界各大硅片企业的生产能力可以满足市场的需求。根据世界半导体销售额的增长率(见表 1),可以预测 2002 年硅片市场将有 6% 的回升,2003 年和 2004 年则将有 21% 的增长。

表 2　世界硅片需求量

年份	1996	1997	1998	1999	2000	2001		2002	2003	2004
	实际	实际	实际	实际	实际	实际	预测	预测 *	预测 *	预测 *
硅片产量 (亿平方英寸)	36.91	39.55	36.13	44.69	55.51	39.40	58.16	41.76	50.53	61.14
晶片销售额 (亿美元)	70.57	70.23	54.43	58.89	75.19	52.00	81.55	58.46	70.74	85.60
晶片销售额增长率(%)	17.6	-0.48	-22.5	8.2	27.7	-30.8		6	21	21

SEMI/SEMI SMG 资料[5,6-10]

注 * :2002,2003,2004 年的预测值是本文作者做的

国 内 市 场

2000 年中国集成电路销售额为 200 亿元,半导体分立器件为 60 亿元,合计 260 亿元(相当于 31.3 亿美元)。同年世界半导体销售额为 2040 亿美元,中国占世界的 1.5%(见图 2)。

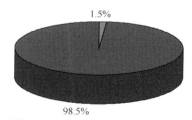

1.5%

98.5%

■全世界2040亿美元　■中国31.3亿美元

图 2　2000 年中国和世界的半导体销售额

国内 2000 年底有一条 200mm 集成电路芯片生产线(上海华虹 NEC),3 条 150mm 线(首钢 NEC、上海先进、华晶上华),6 条 125mm 线(上海先进、华晶、华晶上华、电子 58 所、华越、清华大学)和 15 条 100mm 芯片生产线[11]。现将六大集成电路厂家的生产能力换算成面积后可得知,现在的投片能力是 4000 万平方英寸/年,即将发展到 6000 万平方英寸/年。

近期还要建立 6 英寸(150mm)线 9 条,8 英寸(200mm)线 8 条。总共是 17 条 150mm 和 200mm 的集成电路生产线。保守估计,如果在 2005 年新增 1~2 条 300mm 生产线,月投 2 万~4 万片;3~5 条 200mm 生产线,月投 6 万~10 万片;2~3 条 150mm 生产线,月投 4 万~6 万片,新增投片量将为 7690 万~13 500 万平方英寸,则国内芯片厂在 2005 年投片量为 1.3 亿至 2 亿平方英寸。

我国硅抛光片生产迅速上升,但占世界份额仍很小

我国硅抛光片 1996 年产量为 1620 平方英寸,2001 年上升到 5183 平方英寸,为 1996

年的 3.2 倍,平均年增长率为 26.2%,抛光片的增长标志着国内硅片品技术的进步,预计在 2002 年将有 93% 的增长,而在 2003~2005 年期间仍将以 22% 的速度增长。1996 至 2001 年期间国内单晶硅的年均增长率为 27.5%。高于抛光片的年均增长率,说明我国硅产品的构成仍然以中低档产品为重点。

外延片是硅材料中的高档产品,随着器件性能的提高,外延片的使用比例愈来愈高。国内外延硅片生产由 1996 年的 229 万平方英寸增加到 2001 年的 998 万平方英寸。平均年增长率高达 34.2%,这说明我国外延片的使用在高速增长,预计 2002 年还将有 28% 的增长,产量将达 1275 万平方英寸。

虽然我国的抛光片和外延片发展迅速,然而绝对量仍然很低。2001 年国外抛光片和外延片的年产量分别为 29.72 亿平方英寸和 7.8 亿平方英寸。国内抛光片和外延片生产占世界份额分别为 1.7% 和 1.3%(图 3)。

(a) 硅抛光片(1.7%)　　　　(b) 硅外延片(1.3%)

图 3　2001 年国内生产硅抛光片(a)和硅外延片(b)所占世界份额

国内生产的主流仍是 100mm 和 150mm 硅抛光片

根据我们的调查,将浙江海纳、有研半导体材料、洛阳单晶硅、上海晶华、峨眉半导体材料、浙江硅峰、华晶、珠海南科、上海有色金属等企业的硅抛光片生产能力总和示于表 3。

表 3　国内企业硅抛光片生产能力(亿平方英寸)

	1999 年	2000 年	2001 年	2002 年预计
生产能力	0.8064	1.034	1.074	1.63

由表 3 可知,国内抛光片生产能力在 2000 年已达到 1 亿平方英寸,2002 年将达 1.63 亿平方英寸。从数量来说,可以供应国内企业。但是从品种和质量来说,要取得市场还要下很大气力。首先,国外主流产品是 200mm 和 300mm 硅片,而国内主流产品是 100mm 和 150mm 硅片。国内也花了很大力量建立了 200mm 硅抛光片生产线,但是华虹 NEC 的 200mm 线全部使用进口硅片(主要是外延片)。2000 年进口约 38 万片,合 1900 万平方英寸。国产 200mm 硅片尚未得到市场。150mm 硅片市场主要被进口货占据,但不是全部;2001 年首钢 NEC 的 150mm 陪片使用一些国产硅片。上海先进和华晶上华在 2001 年仍然使用进口 150mm 硅片。上海先进的 125mm 线全部使用进口片,华越用一部分国产 125mm 片。100mm 硅片则是国产片的市场。如华越和上海贝岭的 100mm 线使用国产硅片。

我国硅片在国内市场中主要是 100mm 及以下的小尺寸硅片。

SiGe/Si 和 SOI 材料在国内尚未生产

SiGe/Si 材料是近十年来硅基材料的又一新发展。SiGe/Si 的异质结晶体管和 CMOS

电路一般可在 1—20GHz 频率下工作。2001 年工作频率达到 210GHz 的 SiGe 晶体管问世。这样,可以在通讯领域替代一部分化合物半导体器件。

SOI 是指在绝缘体(通常用 SiO_2)上的单晶硅膜。用 SOI 制造的器件具有寄生电容小、工作电压低、功耗低、漏电小、无闩锁、抗短沟道效应、抗热电子效应、集成度高、速度快、工作温度高、抗辐照等优点。由于 SOI 材料的上述优点,各先进国家对此十分重视,发展了多种制造技术。目前,SOI 材料的尺寸和顶层硅单晶质量已接近体硅材料的水平。

国内的 SiGe/Si 和 SOI 材料尚未批量生产。

关于我国半导体硅片发展的几点思考

1. 制定发展战略必须正确定位

过去五年,我国硅材料发展速度很高,但绝对值不高。硅抛光片和外延片产量分别占世界的 1.7% 和 1.3%。集成电路用硅片的主流产品是 200mm 和 300mm 抛光片和外延片。我国硅片的主流产品是 100mm 和 150mm 片。150mm 硅抛光片的国内市场的主要部分还是进口货占领。国产 200mm 抛光片还未被芯片生产厂家采用。我国硅材料企业的技术水平比发达国家要落后约 10 年。这就是我国半导体硅材料的现状。在世界范围内,200mm 和 300mm 硅片仍然是少数几家硅片供应商的拳头产品,他们用自己的专有技术生产,为世界提供了大部分制造集成电路用的 200mm 和 300mm 硅抛光片和外延片。他们的产品已取得芯片制造厂家的信任,这种局面在相当长的时间内不会有根本的改变。一片 200mm 的抛光片价值不过 50 美元,做成 4M DRAM 后售价可达 3240 美元,升值 60 多倍。一条生产线月投片量通常是 2 万片。所以他们不会轻易冒险接受新的硅片供应商的产品。

目前,在国产 200mm 硅片尚未得到应用,市场全部为进口片占领的情况下,我国应当安排适当力量将 200mm 和 150mm 硅片市场开发做好。如果一味追赶国际潮流,很难收到良好效果。因此,政府有关部门在制订硅材料的科技规划和产业政策时,要充分考虑我国硅材料产业所处现状,不宜急于求成。

2. 抓住国内市场,发展集成电路用硅片和外延硅片

随着世界半导体制造业格局的重新调整,我国将逐渐成为世界半导体芯片的制造中心之一。这为发展我国的半导体硅产业提供了机遇。近期我国将形成规模较大的硅片需求。目前我国能够供应抛光片的厂家可以充分利用我国集成电路发展带来的新机遇,通过提供质优价廉的产品和周到的服务来占据国内市场。

双极型集成电路和至少有三分之二的分立器件是用外延硅片制造的,为了消除软误差和闩锁效应,CMOS 电路也有很大一部分采用外延片制造。随着硅片直径的不断增大,控制单晶的原生缺陷变得愈来愈困难,因此外延片会越来越多地被采用。在这种情况下,国外公司将外延片作为解决质量问题的办法。目前,合格的 300mm 硅片商品只有外延片[12]。我国的有关企业在进入该领域时要有正确的定位,避免一哄而上。国家有关部门应该支持有基础、有条件的企业扩大生产规模,并就关键的技术问题进行攻关。建议

国家有关部门制订有关外延片的科技攻关计划。

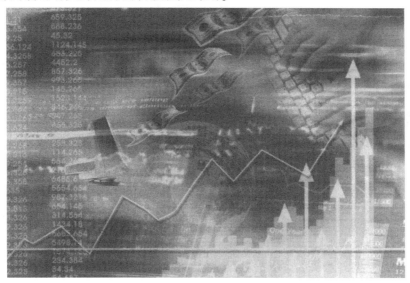

参考文献

[1] 梁骏吾、郑敏政、袁桐等."中国半导体硅材料发展战略研究".(中国科学院咨询报告).2002年6月.

[2] 梁骏吾、郑敏政、袁桐、段维新,"中国信息产业领域相关重点基础材料科技发展战略研究"材料导报,第14卷,第2期,1-4页,2000年.

[3] 电子信息材料咨询研究组编,"电子信息材料咨询报告"电子工业出版社,1-30;42-45;78-100;137-142;215-259页,北京2000年.

[4] R. Mathus,中国集成电路 总36期 No.5,11-14页,2002年.

[5] 稀有金属新闻(日)No. 2073(2002,2,24).

[6] 稀有金属新闻(日)No. 2003(2000.8.1).

[7] 稀有金属新闻(日)No. 2027(2001.2.16).

[8] 稀有金属新闻(日)No. 2048(2001.8.1).

[9] 金属时评(日)No. 1778(2000.8.15).

[10] 金属时评(日)No. 1815(2001.8.25).

[11] 朱贻伟 中国集成电路 34(3),第3-8页,2002年.

[12] Staff reports, Solid State Technology. May, pp91-94,96,(2001).

光伏产业面临多晶硅瓶颈及对策
Polycrystalline Silicon Bottleneck Confronting Photovoltaic Industry and the Countermeasures

梁骏吾/LIANG Jun-wu

(中国科学院半导体研究所,北京,100083)
(Institute of Semiconductors, Chinese Academy of Sciences, Beijing 100083, China)

摘要:叙述了世界以及中国光伏电池材料发展的形势。目前,世界光伏电池产业仍然以硅光电池为主,然而,自2004年以来,全球出现多晶硅短缺,中国的多晶硅也严重不足。这已成为光伏电池发展的瓶颈。因此,必须尽快完成下列紧迫任务:①国内已在建的多晶硅厂应早日建成、投产;②应改进多晶硅生产技术,降低硅生产的能耗、冶金硅消耗、氢耗和氯耗,每千克硅生产成本和环保指标都应该处于世界先进水平。从长远来看,流床技术将被一些工厂用来生产太阳能级多晶硅。薄膜太阳能电池(含非晶硅、微晶硅基及各种化合物半导体薄膜)具有相当大的潜力,但其产品性能还须改进,应努力使之形成规模生产。

关键词:太阳能电池;多晶硅;短缺　　**中图分类号**:TN304.1
文献标识码:A　　**文章编号**:1000-7857(2006)06-0005-03

Abstract: The actual conditions of the photovoltaic industry in the world as well as China were described. At the present time, the solar cells based on bulk crystalline silicon dominate the photovoltaic market. Silicon demand from photovoltaic application is increasing at unprecedented rates. However, since 2004 the global solar cell industry has been experiencing a severe polysilicon shortfall. The situation is even more serious in China and the polysilicon shortage has become the bottleneck of China's photovoltaic industry. In order to get rid of the trouble confronting the photovoltaic industry, the following tasks should be done: ①to complete the construction of polycrystalline silicon plants being still in construction in China; ②to improve the technologies of polysilicon production in order to reduce the energy, metallurgical silicon, chlorine and hydrogen consumption. The polysilicon production cost should be reduced and gain an avance in the competition. The processes should be environment friendly. In a long run, it is expected that fluid bed process will be adopted by a number of manufacturers to supply the photovoltaic industry. There is a big potential in switching over to thin film technology including amorphous silicon, microcrystalline silicon, and compound semiconductor films. However, the challenges of improving performance of the thin film products and scaling up production lie ahead.

Key Words: solar cell; polycrystalline silicon; shortage　　**CLC Number**: TN304.1
Document Code: A　　**Article ID**: 1000-7857(2006)06-0005-03

原载于:Solid-State Electronics,2005,49:847-852.

作者简介:梁骏吾,男,中国工程院院士,北京市海淀区清华东路甲35号中国科学院半导体研究所,研究员,主要研究方向为半导体材料;E-mail:junwuliang@163.com

太阳能电池及其材料的发展处在当今世界关注的两大问题——能源与环境的交汇点上。无论发达国家还是发展中国家对此都十分重视,仅2006年4月召开的有关光伏的国际或地区性会议就有15个,其重要议题之一就是如何发展光伏电池材料以解决太阳能多晶硅短缺问题。中国作为能源生产和消耗大国,环境问题十分突出,故对太阳能材料的发展必须予以充分关注。

1. 国内外太阳能电池生产需求概况

晶体管发明7年后的1954年,Chapin,Pearson 和 Fuller 成功制备了第一个硅光伏电池[1],转换效率(η)为6%;20世纪90年代 η 达到24.7%。目前大规模生产的硅光伏电池一般 $\eta = 14\% \sim 17.6\%$(单晶)或 $14\% \sim 16\%$(多晶)。1998年世界太阳能电池产量为155MW,之后以年增长率 30% ~ 40% 的高速度发展,2004年更以61%的速度增长到1195MW。其速度大大超过集成电路的增长(表1)。但由于多晶硅短缺,有些人悲观地估计,2006年太阳能电池的增长率可能下降到5% ~ 10%。

表1 世界太阳能电池产量

Tbl. 1 Global production of solar cells

年份	1998	1999	2000	2001	2002	2003	2004	2005	2006
产量(MW)	155	201	288	391	520	744	1 200	1 817	2 180
增长率(%)	2.3	30	43	36	33	43	61	51	20

世界光伏业尝试了各种半导体材料的光伏电池。太阳光谱覆盖紫外到红外波段($0.2 \sim 3\mu m$),理想的光伏电池应该能将这些光都利用起来。这样就应该设计多结太阳能电池,用不同带隙的半导体材料,分别收集不同波长的光。这种多结电池转换效率已达39%,但成本很高,只能应用于某些特殊场合,大量使用的是价格低廉的简单电池,如只有1个p-n结的简单电池。我们希望在一定的入射功率下得到最大输出功率 Pout,$Pout = Voc \cdot Isc \cdot FF$。式中:Isc 为短路电流;FF 为填充因子;Voc 为开路电压,$Voc = (nkT/q)\ln(I_L/I_0 + 1)$,$I_0$ 为暗态饱和电流,$I_0 \geq 1.5 \times 10^5 \exp(-Eg/kT)$。材料带隙 Eg 大,则 I_0 小,Voc 大。但 Eg 过大又不能吸收长波光能,于是存在一最佳的 Eg 值[2]。对理想的太阳能电池来说,Eg 最佳值范围较宽并在1.4eV附近。这样,GaAs 等材料比硅略微好一些(聚光度为1个太阳,理想的 GaAs 和 Si 太阳能电池的 η 分别为31%和29%)[3]。GaAs 太阳能电池已到 η 高于25%,Si 也达到 $\eta = 24.7\%$。硅的工艺成熟、材料质量好、原料丰富、不污染环境、价格低,所以大量生产的光伏电池材料仍然是硅。硅光伏电池占世界总产量的98.5%,其中多晶和单晶硅电池共占90.9%,非晶硅、带状电池占7.7%,化合物 CdTe 和 CIS 电池分别占 1.1% 和 0.4%。

表2 各种太阳能电池占百分比(%)

Tbl. 2 Composition of various solar cells(%)

电池种类	2002 年	2003 年	2004 年
单晶硅	36.4	32.2	36.2
多晶硅	51.6	57.2	54.7
片状硅	4.6	4.4	3.3

电池种类	2002 年	2003 年	2004 年
α-Si	6.4	4.5	4.4
CdTe	0.7	1.1	1.1
CIS	0.2	0.6	0.4

在研究中的还有各种电池材料,如染料敏化太阳能电池材料、光合电化学电池材料[6]、高失配混晶(HAMs)形成的多能隙半导体材料[7]等,但有的刚开始,有的距规模生产还有相当距离。

总之,晶体硅仍然是当今太阳能电池最主要的材料,其次是各种薄膜硅(非晶、微晶、多晶)和带状硅。集成电路生产的增长和光伏产业的高速增长,使多晶硅的用量增加,到2004年出现全球性多晶硅需求大于供给。2005年全世界光伏产业和微电子行业多晶硅需求分别为 15 000t 和 20 000t,多晶硅生产能力为 30 000t,缺额为 5000t。如果光伏产业按 30% 增长,微电子行业按 5.6% 增长,则到 2008 年多晶硅缺额将高达 8800t(表 3)。

表 3　世界多晶硅的需求产能与缺额(t)

Tbl. 3　Global demand, capacity and shortage of polysilicon(t)

		2005 年	2006 年	2007 年	2008 年	2009 年	2010 年
需求		35 000	40 000	46 000	53 600	62 400	72 000
产能	可能	30 000	33 600	38 000	44 800	48 000	62 400
	乐观				41 600	44 800	50 400
缺额	可能	5 000	6 400	8 000	8 800	14 400	9 600
	乐观				12 000	17 600	21 600

注:1. 需求 = 太阳能硅+电子级硅;2. 光伏产业按 30% 年增长率,微电子行业按 5.6% 增长率。

除非多晶硅生产技术出现突破性进展,否则这种不利局面将一直延续下去。中国的多晶硅局面则更将严峻,2005 年国内产量仅约 60t,按 2005 年的技术水平多晶硅的利用率为 12g/W,60t 硅仅能制造 5MW 太阳能电池,显然远远不够。2005 年中国太阳能单晶硅的生产能力为 2000t/年,则中国对多晶硅的需求为 2600t/年,这还未考虑微电子用多晶硅的需求。在全球多晶硅严重不足的情况下,价格飞涨,而且很难购买,于是多晶硅成为光伏产业的瓶颈。要解决多晶硅短缺问题,必须尽快完成下列任务。

(1)掌握 SiHCl₃ 法闭环生产多晶硅的工艺,使国内已在建的多晶硅厂早日建成、达产。国内正建和扩建的多晶硅厂有 3 个,都采用 SiHCl₃ 还原法和西门子还原炉;也都计划回收 H_2、$SiHCl_3$、HCl 和 $SiCl_4$,并进一步将 $SiCl_4$ 重新转化为 $SiHCl_3$ 并重新使用。

(2)使用世界先进多晶硅技术,建设质量指标每公斤能耗、冶金硅消耗、氢耗、氯耗、每公斤硅成本、环保指标都处于世界先进水平的新多晶硅生产线[4]。为此,我国应尽快掌握先进的西门子工艺。选择的标准是:①产品质量;②生产成本;③生产安全与环境保护。

集成电路级多晶硅的纯度要求:B、Al 含量<0.05 ppba;P、As、Sb 含量<0.15 PPb;金属总含量<0.5 ppbw。但是,有关太阳能级硅(SGS)纯度是 5N 或 6N 的说法仅适用于 B、P 杂质。假定用 0.6Ω·cm,p-Si 为基片,则掺硼后 [B] = $2.5 \times 10^{16} cm^{-3}$,相当 99.999 95%。而对金属杂质要求更高,金属杂质往往是复合中心,降低硅中少子寿命 τ

和少子扩散长度 L,而电池材料要求少子扩散长度 L=100μm,L=(Dτ)$^{1/2}$,D 为扩散系数,D=(kT/q)μ,μ 为迁移率。硅是间接带隙,光的吸收系数 α 小,硅片要有一定厚度才能充分吸收。光在空间电荷区被吸收后产生电子-孔穴对,其中一部分在未复合前就被内建电场分别扫至 n 区和 p 区而被利用,但 SGS 中有许多复合中心,于是有一部分光生电子-孔穴对重新复合而浪费了。在 n 型和 p 型中性区也产生光生孔穴和电子,它们要靠扩散进入空间电荷区被收集,但只有距空间电荷距离小于扩散长度的光生载流子才可以到达空间电荷区,其余距离大于扩散长度的光生载流子在扩散过程中复合,这部分光能被浪费了。所以,一定要将硅中起复合中心作用的杂质和缺陷减少。硅中的 Co、Fe、Nn、Cr 浓度超过 10^{15} cm^{-3}、Ti、V、Nb、Mo、W、Zr、Ta 杂质浓度超过 10^{13} cm^{-3} 后就影响电池的效率。这远远高于 5N 或 6N 的要求。基片掺杂浓度与电池性能有密切关系,浓度高则 μ 高,L 也高。而且 3 种复合寿命(复合中心复合、俄歇复合[>1×10^{19} cm^{-3}] 和辐射复合[>1×10^{21} cm^{-3}])都随浓度下降而上升,所以浓度低有利于 η 上升。但浓度过低则 Voc 下降,η 又下降,于是存在最佳浓度值范围(大约 3.2×10^{16} cm^{-3} 至 2.5×10^{15} cm^{-3},p 型)。

太阳能级硅通常为 p 型,单晶材料中[P]≤5×10^{15} cm^{-3},p 型电阻率为 0.5<-10Ω·cm,相应最高[B]=3.2×10^{16} cm^{-3},[O]<1×10^{18} cm^{-3},[C]<5×10^{17} cm^{-3},少子扩散长度 L=100μm,电池效率 η=14%~17.5%。

用西门子技术生产的多晶硅的质量能充分满足光伏电池的要求。这是因为液态的 $SiHCl_3$ 能用工艺成熟的精馏法提纯,塔板数可按要求增加,先进的精馏塔已达 30~40m。产品 $SiHCl_3$ 中 As、B 含量均≤0.03ppba,P≤0.3ppba。

西门子法的成本是比较低的[4],可以降到 20~30 美元/kg(与电价有关)。要降低成本必须掌握先进的西门子技术。

西门子法开始于 20 世纪 50 年代,已经历了 40 多年的改进,虽然仍称西门子法,但其内容细节与过去已不相同。它构成当今主流工艺,其还原能耗由 20 世纪 80 年代的 300kWh/kg 降至 90 年代的 95~110kWh/kg,现在先进的西门子技术更进一步降至 60~70kWh/kg,还解决了副产物 $SiCl_4$ 转化为 $SiHCl_3$ 的难题[5]。

其原理是将 $SiCl_4$、H_2 在催化剂作用下与冶金级硅反应生成 $SiHCl_3$。其反应为:$3SiCl_4+Si+2H_2 \rightarrow 4SiHCl_3$。反应条件为 3.45MPa 压力和 500℃ 温度;电耗为 20 kWh/kg。分离提纯后,高纯 $SiHCl_3$ 又进入还原炉生成多晶硅,形成闭环生产。降低还原电耗,就必须提高多晶硅的沉积速度。在大沉积速度条件下,$SiHCl_3$ 一次通过的转换效率不高,因此必须回收大量的 $SiCl_4$、$SiHCl_3$、HCl 和 H_2。先进的回收系统要求对这些物质的回收率达到 98%~99%。生产 1kg 硅的物耗指标为冶金级硅消耗 1.2kg、$SiCl_4$ 消耗 0.3kg、氢消耗 1.3m^3。此外,$SiHCl_3$ 工艺很安全,而 SiH_4 的安全性差。全世界生产多晶硅的工厂共有 10 家,使用西门子技术的有 7 家,西门子法硅产量占生产总量的 76.7%。

另一类多晶硅批量生产工艺就是 SiH_4 流床法。SiH_4 以 $NaAlH_4$ 还原 SiF_4 而制成,经纯化后在流床反应器分解:$SiH_4 \rightarrow Si+2H_2$,反应温度为 730℃ 即可,生成的粒状产品最后要脱氢处理。与西门子法比较,其能耗低,电耗仅为 30~40kWh/kg,投资低。此法一次转化率高达 98%,但缺点是生产物中有大量粉尘(微米直径)。目前,用 SiH_4 流床法批量生产的只有 MEMC Pasadena 公司一家,其产量占硅生产总量的 5.7%。

除上述 2 种技术外还有 2 家公司(ASiMl 和 SGS 公司)用 SiH_4 为原料在西门子式硅

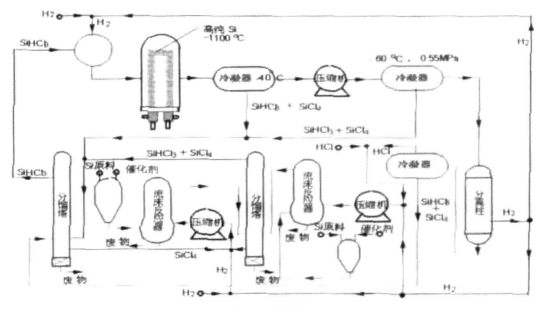

图 1 闭环生产多晶硅流程

Fig. 1 The close loop process for polycrystalline silicon production

沉积炉生长多晶硅,但制备 SiH_4 的方法和 MEMC Pasadena 公司不同。他们以 $SiHCl_3$ 为原料,首先经分馏/歧化反应生成 SiH_2Cl_2,后者再歧化生成 $SiHCl_3$,$SiHCl_3$ 通过第三次歧化反应生成 SiH_4。由于每一步骤转换效率都比较低,所以要多次循环,耗能量较高。其优点是多晶硅产品纯度高,适用于区熔生长高阻单晶,转化率高达 99%,副产物少,缺点仍然是粉尘多。此外,ASiMl 公司方法为了降低气相成核的几率,在反应室内引入许多冷却筒,结果其能耗高于西门子法,达到 140kWh/kg,导致成本高。

2. 光伏产业的扩产方案和新方案

由于光伏产业对多晶硅的需求,大多晶硅工厂纷纷扩产,许多新参加者也提出自己的技术方案。扩产方案和新方案如下。

2.1 现成方法的扩展

2.1.1 西门子法增加设备

对于有基础的大厂,这是一种最有把握、最现成的途径。世界第一和第二大多晶硅厂(HEMLOCK 和 Wacker 公司)都采用此方案。为了降低多晶硅的成本,可采取以下措施:①加快沉积速率;②在保证质量的前提下加快精馏塔产量;③减少一些分析检测环节等。这一方案预计扩产 6000~7000t。具体数字要看合同签订情况。Tokuyama 公司也考虑这个方案。

2.1.2 SiH_4 流床法增加设备

MEMC Pasadena 公司已有 1700t/年的生产能力,并打算将产量增加 1 倍。SGS 公司

也发展了 SiH_4 流床法,能 400h 连续工作,能耗为 30kWh/kg,预计 2008 年可以达到 4000t/年规模。此法应该解决的问题是降低金属污染,解决堵塞问题。

2.1.3 SiH_4 原料和西门子反应器扩产

ASiMl 公司一方面发展自己的 SiH_4 流床法,但仍计划用 SiH_4 原料和西门子反应器将产量扩大到 2600t/年,预计 2008 年完成。

2.2 新方法的发展

2.2.1 $SiHCl_3$ 氢还原方法,结合用"自由空间反应器"

西门子反应器内的沉积反应发生在气-固两相界面上,反应速度不可能太高。用自由空间可以提高反应温度到硅熔点以上,则可避免粉尘问题,可连续工作又可提高沉积速率至 10 倍。如 Tokuyama 公司发展了气相-液相沉积(VLD)法。VLD 法将沿着 10t-200t-2000t 规模前进,预计 2008 年投产。缺点是碳浓度高 100 倍达 100ppma,金属浓度高 20 倍,大于 200ppbw。目前,少子寿命达 $13\mu s$,电池效率为 15.6%。

2.2.2 $SiHCl_3$ 流床技术

使用 $SiHCl_3$ 氢还原流床技术,可提高反应效率并降低功耗。Wacker 公司发展了此项技术,反应效率为 65%,电耗 40kWh/kg,已连续运转 700h,目前已有 50t/年炉子 2 台,不过流床法产品的寿命和电池转化效率要低些。Wacker 公司可能在 2007 年建成 500t 的实验工厂。

2.2.3 SiH_4 在用硅管的西门子炉子热分解

使用此方案的是德国的 JSSI 公司,这也是一种在西门子炉和自由空间反应器的折中方案。炉温为 800℃,可降低成本。

2.2.4 用碳还原硅石(SiO_2)并结合若干物理化学提纯方法

1) 碳还原法使用电弧炉,实际反应比较复杂:

电极区上层温度 $\leqslant 1500℃$：$SiO+CO=SiO_2+C$ (1)

电极区中间层温度 $1500\sim1700℃$：$SiO+2C=SiC+CO$ (2)

电极区下层温度 $>1700℃$：$SiC+SiO_2=Si+SiO+CO$ (3)

(3) 式产生的液态硅流出电弧炉,冷却后就是冶金级硅产品。此法得到的冶金硅纯度可达 99%,不能满足太阳能电池需求,但能耗仅为 $12\sim14$kWh/kg。如能提高质量,当然人们是向往的。

SOLSILS 方法是用炭黑和硅石粉为原料,在对离子火焰中进行还原反应,得到的产品是 SiC,然后在电弧炉中将 SiC 与 SiO_2 反应,得到液体硅。

2) 另一类方案是将反应气体,如 H_2O 和 H_2 或惰性气体与硅液反应,或用等离子反应气体和液硅反应。还可以结合定向凝固,使杂质在尾部富集,而头部硅的纯度得到提高。Elkem 公司采用二步法[6]:第一步是成渣,除去某些杂质;第二步是浸取。生产硅的能耗仅为常规方法的 20%～25%。

2.2.5 用 $SiCl_4$ 为起点,使用金属还原

如用 Na 蒸气和 $SiCl_4$ 气体在 H_2+Ar 的等离子体中还原,选择合适的温度,使 NaCl 气化与液态硅分离,副产品 NaCl 再经电解得到 Na 和 Cl_2,后者用重复来产生 $SiCl_4$。

类似地,用 Zn 蒸气还原 $SiCl_4$ 生成 Si 和 $ZnCl_2$,既可以用西门子式反应器也可以用流

床反应器。

2.2.6　电解法

电解时将 SiO_2 在 1000℃ 的氟化物中溶解,然后将 SiO_2 电解得到硅和氧。杂质在渣中富集。以上这些方案都在试验之中,有的在 20 世纪 50 至 70 年代已开始试验。但到目前为止,有的只是小规模试验线,有的尚处实验室阶段,一般给出的日程表是到 2007—2008 年达到批量生产。中国是一个使用多晶硅的大国,对于各种创新应予以支持。至于项目的筛选可通过招标、评审,择优支持。

总之,当今太阳能电池仍然以硅为主,我国多晶硅的生产应以先进的西门子技术为骨干,其次是流床法。薄膜硅(含多晶、微晶、非晶)电池也是应关注的发展方向。对于生产太阳能电池的各种新材料、新方法要有适当安排,使我国的光伏事业走向健康发展之路。

参考文献

[1] CHAPIN D M,FULLER C S,PEARSON G Z. A new silic on p-n junction photocell for converting solar radiation into electrical power[J]. J ApPl Phys,1954(25):676—677.

[2] GREEN M A. In Modern Semiconductor Device Physics,Sze S. M. (Ed.)施敏主编. 现代半导体器件物理[M]. 北京:科学出版社,2001.

[3] HENRY C H. Limiting efficiencies of ideal single and multiple energy gap terrestrial solar cells[J]. J Appl Phys,1980(51):4494—4500.

[4] 梁骏吾. 兴建年产一千吨电子级多晶硅工厂的思考[J]. 中国工程科学,2000,2(6):33—35.

[5] 梁骏吾. 电子级多晶硅生产工艺[J]. 中国工程科学,2000,2(12):34—39.

[6] LAM K B,CHIAO M LINL. A micro photosynthetic electrochemical cell[C]. Proc. IEEE Conf. on Micro Electro Mechanical Syst. (MEMS Jan. 19-23,2003),Kyoto Japan,2003:391—394.

[7] YU K M,WALUKIEWICZ W,WU J,et al. Diluted ZnMnTe Oxide:a multi-band semiconductor for high efficiency solar cells[J]. Phys Stat Sol(b),2004,241(3):660—663.

"十五"期间中国半导体硅材料
发展战略思路和建议[28-30]

前面我们已叙述并分析了我国半导体硅材料发展情况。列举了我国半导体工业的特点、弱点、发展的有利形势以及在世界中的地位。并对国际半导体企业的特点、市场进行了分析。本章则分析十五期间中国半导体硅材料的发展战略思路,并以此章作为本报告的总结。

未来五年是我国半导体硅材料发展的关键时期,集成电路和半导体器件的快速增长为半导体硅材料的发展提供了广阔的市场需求,国务院(2000)18 号文和国办(2001)51 号函把单晶硅片列为优惠政策享受的范围,为硅材料的发展提供了良好的发展环境,国家有关部委又把硅材料列为重点发展的产品门类,在技术改造和科技攻关中予以支持,"十五"期间我国硅材料产业将迎来大的发展。

6.1　制定发展战略必须"知己知彼"

过去五年,我国硅材料的销售额以平均 26.38% 的高速发展。由 1996 年的 2.8 亿上升到 2001 年的 9.06 亿元。发展速度很高但绝对值不高,仅占世界的 2%。硅抛光片和外延片产量分别占世界的 1.7% 和 1.3%。中国生产的硅单晶中的 51% 是太阳能级硅。这些数据将我国定位于硅生产的发展中国家。集成电路用硅片的主流产品是 200mm 和 300mm 抛光片和外延片。我国硅片的主流产品是 100mm 和 150mm 片。150mm 硅抛光片的国内市场的主要部分还是进口货占领。国产 200mm 抛光片还未被生产芯片厂家采用。我国硅材料企业的技术水平比发达国家要落后约 10 年。这就是我国半导体硅的现状。在世界范围内 200mm 和 300mm 硅片仍然是少数几家硅片供应商(日本信越、住友、美国的 MEMC、德国的 WACKER 等)的拳头产品,他们有自己的专有技术生产,为世界提供了大部分制造集成电路用的是 200mm 和 300mm 硅抛光片和外延片。他们的产品已取得芯片制造厂家的信任,这种局面在相当长的时间内是不会有根本的改变。一片 200mm 的抛光片价值不过 50 美元,做成 4MDRAM 后售价可达 3240 美元,升值 60 多倍。一条生产线月投片量通常是 2 万片。所以他们不会轻易冒险接受新的硅片供应商的产品。

我国硅材料产业在技术水平、产业规模、创新能力都处于落后地位。在国际竞争中必须做到知己知彼方能制定正确战略。目前,在国产 200mm 硅片尚未得到应用,市场全部为进口片占领的情况下,我国应当安排适当力量将 200mm 和 150mm 硅片市场开发做好。如果一味追赶国际潮流,很难收到良好效果。因此,政府有关部门在制订硅材料的科技规划和产业政策时,要充分考虑我国硅材料产业所处现状,不宜急于求成。

原载于:中国工程院咨询报告(2002 年),2002.

6.2 抓住国内市场,发展集成电路用硅片

随着世界半导体制造业格局的重新调整,我国将逐渐成为半导体芯片的制造中心之一。这为发展我国的半导体硅产业提供了机遇。近期我国将可能拥有 13 条 150mm 和 9 条 200mm 生产线,加上已经拥有的近 15 条 100mm 和 6 条 125mm 生产线,已经形成了规模较大的硅片需求。目前我国能够供应抛光片的厂家可以充分利用我国集成电路发展带来的新机遇,通过提供质优价廉的产品和周到的服务来占据国内市场。不过,应该指出的是在我国境内新成立的芯片厂家大都具有外资背景,有着相对固定的原材料供应商,尤其对 200mm 的芯片厂家而言更是如此。因此,国内的硅片厂家在争取国内市场时同样面临首激烈的国际竞争。企业应充分利用国务院(2000)18 号文和国办(2001)51 号函所给予硅单晶的各项优惠政策,抓住机会,加快发展。

6.3 分立器件 用硅材料市场对中国十分重要

分立器件的销售额在全球来说远不如集成电路。根据 2001 年的统计,前者与后者比为 11:89。但是分立器件市场也是呈上升趋势。分立器促销售额为 130 亿美元(2001年),分立器件用硅材料产品比较适合中国的技术水平。其中,有相当份额是研磨片。与集成电路用抛光片相比,研磨片进入市场的难度低得多。所以,多年来我国硅片中的研磨片占相当比例。这部分市场是我们应当继续保持的。

近年来,在研磨硅片市场上竞争非常激烈,有些企业不惜亏本降价,这种方式不利于单晶硅产业的健康发展。市场上的竞争应该在合理的价格范围内以质量和服务求胜出。违背价值规律的价格战最终会使整个行业受损,因此建议相关企业遵守行业自律,共同维护良性的市场。

6.4 发展区熔硅片

大功率器件和电力电子器件也是分立器件。主要使用区熔硅片,其中功率小,耐压低的器件使用直接硅单晶片。其应用面虽然没有集成电路那么广,但它们在强电领域起着无可替代的作用,而且不像集成电路那样存在几年一次的低谷,因此,这些器件对硅片有一个稳定的需求。总的说来,国外公司重视区熔硅片的程度不如直接硅片,美国的公司甚至已经停止生产区熔硅单晶,这就为我国的企业提供了机会,应该抓住这个机会再上一个台阶。从整个产业来说,应该避免一哄而上和低水平重复建设,以免造成生产能力的过剩。

6.5 大力发展外延硅片

双极型集成电路和至少有三分之二的分立器件中是用外延硅片制造的,为了消除软误差和闩锁效应,CMOS 电路也有很大一部分采用外延片制造。随着硅片直径的不断增大,控制单晶的原生缺陷变得愈来愈困难,因此外延片会越来越多地被采用。在这种情

况下,国外公司将外延片作为解决质量问题的办法。目前,合格的 300mm 硅片商品只要外延片[31]。我国的有关企业在进入该领域时要有正确的定位,避免一哄而上。国家有关部门应该支持有基础、有条件的企业扩大生产规模,并就关键的技术问题进行攻关。建议国家有关部门制订有关外延片的科技攻关计划。

6.6　重视基本技术问题的研究,提高硅片质量

集成电路用硅片是高技术产品,随着直径的增大,对硅片质量的要求越来越高。硅片质量需要从控制晶体中的杂质和缺陷、控制表面沾污(颗粒和金属沾污)、保证几何尺寸(宏观的和微观的)片的包装等很多方面来保证。我国的单晶硅企业应该重视基本技术问题的研究,如:晶体生长中的缺陷控制技术、硅片的有蜡抛光技术、清洗技术和包装技术等。另外还要重视许多技术细节的研究,以硅片的包装为例,器件厂家一般要求包装的硅片 6 个月后表面质量稳定。这个要求对于硅片厂家而言并不是轻而易举就可以解决的。美国的 MEMC 公司就专门研究过包装好的硅片的时效性问题,从而找出影响包装的硅片的表面质量的各个因素。我国的大直径硅片至今没有过关,与没有彻底解决上述列举的一些基本技术问题有关。总之,我国单晶硅企业的发展不能简单地追求大直径,而必须在实实在在地解决一系列关键问题的基础上,给顾客提供有竞争力的产品。值得指出的是,在提高硅片质量方面,硅片厂家需要与器件厂家紧密协作,因为有些材料问题只有在器件制造过程中反映出来的。

6.7　中国半导体多晶硅短缺,应抓紧时机建设多晶硅厂

前面已叙述过,中国单晶硅在 2001 年已达 561.9 吨,所需多晶硅为 798.9 吨,2005年预计单晶硅将达 1400 吨,多晶硅市场将达 1983 吨,所以建立一至两个多晶硅工厂是有必要的。多晶硅工厂的建设必须解决好两个至关重要的问题——成本与质量。在建设多晶硅工厂时要注重国外先进技术的引进。同时要特别重视、依靠国内的技术力量。

6.8　继续发展太阳能用硅材料

太阳能用硅单晶是我国硅单晶的重要部分,十五期限间仍应继续发展。在扩大出口的同时要特别注重国内的太阳能电池的发展,使内需增长。
考虑多晶硅太阳能电池的优点,所以应研究和开发多晶硅太阳能材料。

6.9　重视设备和配套材料的开发与生产

硅材料的生产需要依靠先进的设备。如:多晶硅制造设备、提纯设备、单晶炉、外延炉、硅片加工设备、测试设备和硅装设备等。它们是材料创新的体现。硅材料生产还依靠配套材料,如:石英材料、石墨材料、高纯气体、高纯化学试剂、切磨加工材料和塑料等等。应当充分重视硅材料产业所需设备和配套材料的开发与生产。

薄膜光伏电池中的材料问题

梁骏吾

(中国科学院半导体研究所,北京,100083)

2009 年全世界光伏电池中薄膜电池产量为 1.9GW,占世界光伏电池总产量的 19.8%,比 2008 年 1.04GW 产量上升了 82.7%。其中 First Solar 公司的 CdTe 薄膜电池的产量超过所有生产晶硅和其它薄膜电池的厂家,取得世界第一。2009 年世界 CdTe 电池产量占全部薄膜电池产量的 62%。造成 CdTe 电池占市场主要份额的原因是多方面的,其中,薄膜电池材料的性质是必需着重分析的。

a-Si:H 是重要的薄膜材料。1976 年和 1977 年相继得到 $\eta = 2\%$ 和 $\eta = 5\%$ 的 a-Si:H 电池,这结果引发对 a-Si:H 电池的重视。a-Si:H 是长程无序的材料,电子跃迁不受准动量守恒限制,所以光吸收系数很大,(当入射光能量大于 Eg 时,α 大于 $10^2 cm^{-1}$),于是可以用很薄的 a-Si:H 吸收层,从而降低硅材料成本。非晶硅可以用 H、B、C、P、Ge 的掺杂量以及生产参数的变化来调节和控制 Eg、导电类型和相变。由于相变的限制,Eg 的上限为 1.9eV。Ge 加入可以降低 Eg,但同时 a-SiGe:H 中的缺陷增加,从而使 a-SiGe:H 的 Eg 下限为 1.3eV。在这范围内,可以设计多种叠层或多结电池,从而扩大波长响应范围,提高电池的转换效率。2010 年已有转换效率 14.8% 的记录。然而大规模生产的效率却仅为 6%—8%。

a-Si:H 的缺陷密度高。悬键有 D^0、D^- 和 D^+ 状态。高的隙态密度导致 a-Si:H 的扩散长度 $\sqrt{Dn\tau n}$ 或 $\sqrt{Dp\tau p}$ 低,所以 a-Si:H 电池用 p-i-n 或 n-i-p 结构,靠电场来增强载流子的收集,收集效率以漂移迁移率与寿命(μ,τ)乘积来描述。a-Si:H 中的 μ,τ 与电池的 η 关联。当前者从 $2\times10^{-9} cm^2/V$ 上升至 $5\times10^{-7} cm^2/V$ 时,电池的 η 可以由 1% 上升至 10%。

a-Si:H 中有 SW 效应—光照后材料的光电导和暗电导下降。电池使用后其转换效率下降。单结、叠层和三结电池的 η 可分别下降 18%~13%、12%~20% 和 12%~17%。所以长期稳定性是人们担心的问题。a-Si:H 电池生产线更新快,而且价格昂贵,这样又抵消了节约硅材料的好处。

CdTe 和 Cu(In,Ga)Se$_2$ 材料的带隙分别为 1.45eV 和 1.04-2.4eV(CIGS 电池最佳 η 对应 Eg 为 1.12eV)。两种材料都是直接带隙,都适于做太阳电池,世界光伏界对它们寄以很大的希望。

CIGS 可以用多种方法制备,但结果最好的是元素共蒸发法:在 550℃ 生长而且当 Ga/(Ga+In)= 0.2—0.3 时得到电池的效率为 18.8%。这一结果特别引人注目。

四元材料 CIGS 要十分注意控制其成分控制。生长时要有富 Cu 阶段,这样可以增大

原载于:2010 年第十二届全国固体薄膜学术会议,2010.

晶粒尺寸。材料的整体是富铟,这样可以得到好的电学性能。为了提高薄膜性能,还应掺入第五组分——Na。Na 可提高薄膜电导,减少 V_{Se} 施主浓度。生长时使用 Mo 覆盖的含 Na 玻璃,这样可以引入 Na,提高电池性能。CIGS 材料可以容忍很大的等化学比偏离——(In+Ga)/(In+Ga+Cu)= 0.52-0.64 范围变化,均可提到 $\eta>14\%$ 的电池。在 PV 器件级的 P 型 CIGS 材料中主要受主是 V_{Cu},其能级 $Ev+30meV$。而补偿施主是 V_{Se} 和 In_{Cu}。在 $CuInSe_2$ 中的本征缺陷数目多达 12 种——V_{Cu},V_{In},V_{Se},Cu_i,In_i,Se_i,In_{Cu},$CuIn$,Se_{Cu},CU_{Se},Se_{In} 和 In_{Se}。显然四元系将有更多的本征缺陷种类。所以材料难度大。

CIGS 生长后在空气中退火可以使 O 原子钝化 V_{Se} 施主,有利于提高器件效率。CIGS 组件的效率在生产中可达 12%,以共蒸发生长的结果最好。

二元化合物 CdTe 比四元化合物 CIGS 简单,它只有二种间隙缺陷——Cd_i 和 Te_i,二种空位缺陷——V_{Cd} 和 V_{Te} 和两种反位缺陷——Cd_{Te} 和 Te_{Cd}。所以 CdTe 比四元化合物容易处理。CdTe 中的 Cd 和 Te 之间有很高的结合能——5.75eV,不容易被破坏,与非晶材料相比,多晶 CdTe 材料是热力学稳定的,所以不存在性能衰退问题。

CdTe 材料可以用多种简单而有效方法生长,而在低压惰性气体下的窄间隔升华法取得了极好的效果。升华源用 CdTe,加热到 600℃ 时释放等量的 Te 和 Cd,并在 400—500℃ 的玻璃/TCO/CdS 衬底上结合为接近等化学比的 CdTe 薄膜。p-CdTe 材料中的 V_{Cd} 是主要的受主。在六方 n-CdS 和立方 p-CdTe 之间虽然失配高达 9.7%,但仍然可以得到高效率的太阳能电池。

p-CdTe/n-CdS 结形成后进行 $CdCl_2$ 活化,活化温度 400℃,活化后 CdS/CdTe 电池效率可以由 2% 提高到 16%。所以 $CdCl_2$ 活化工艺对提高 CdTe 电池效率具有神奇的效果。活化有三种作用:①使 CdTe 晶粒长大,从而提高收集效率;②CdTe 和 CdS 互扩散,从而降低 CdTe/CdS 晶间的失配影响;③使 CdTe 中的寿命值提高,从而提高光生电子的收集效率。

器件级 CdTe 材料的 τe 和 τh 可以达到 2ns,μe 和 μh 分别为 $800cm^2/Vs$ 和 $60cm^2/Vs$,则扩散长度分别为:$Le = 2.0\mu m$ 和 $L_h = 0.56\mu m$。所以 CdTe 中有较好的光生载流子收集效率。

由于 CdTe 光伏电池可以用价廉有效的方法生产,生长的 CdTe 材料能接近等化学配比,缺陷少,稳定性好,规模生产效率达 11%,而且用的是单结电池结构。设备投资低。这些因素使得成本降低。于是 First Solar 在 2008 年突破 $1/W_p$ 的生产成本壁垒。到 2010 年 2 季度生产成本降至 $ 0.76/W_p$。

CdTe 生产要用有毒性的 Cd,但可以回收 90% 的半导体材料,用于制造新电池,90% 的玻璃回收后移作它用。Te 在地壳中的含量仅 $10^{-7}\%$,大规模应用 CdTe 电池可能有资源问题。

光伏电池的胜出是与材料问题的成功解决密切联系的,由此预测 $CuInGaSe_2$ 光伏电池也将随着 CIGS 材料问题的解决而将扩大其生产。

总之,半导体材料问题是太阳能电池的关键部分,开发先进的工艺和设备,生产稳定而优良性能的材料是极其重要的任务。

降低超大规模集成电路用高纯水中总有机碳的能量传递光化学模型

闻瑞梅^1,梁骏吾^2

(1.同济大学,上海 200092;2.中科院半导体所,北京,100083)

摘要:本文提出用 185nn 紫外线降低高纯水中总有机碳(TOC)的能量传递光化学模型.计算了水的流量、TOC 的浓度、照射腔的尺寸与所需紫外光能量的关系,从而解决了在工程设计中 185nm 紫外灯的选择和计算方法.根据理论计算出的结果和实验十分一致,证实了本模型的正确性.使高纯水中的 TOC 由 4200μg/L 降至 0.3μg/L,是目前国内外高纯水中 TOC 浓度的最好水平.

关键词:超大规模集成电路;总有机碳;185 纳米紫外;光化学

中图分类号:TN405   **文献标识码**:A   **文章编号**:0372-21 12(2003)11-1601-4

An Energy Transfer Photochemical Model for the Abatement of Total Organic Carbon in High Purity Water Used in ULSI Fabrication

WEN Rui-Mei^1, LIANG Jun-Wu^2

(1.*Tongi University*,*Shanghai* 200092,*China*;2 *Institute of Semiconductcrs*,*Bejing* 100083,*China*)

Abstract: An energy transfer photochemical model for the abatement of total olganic carbon(TOC) in high purity water using 185mm Ultraviolet(UV) irradiations is proposed. The dependence of 185mm UV irradiation energy on the water flow rates, TOC concentrations and size of irradiation cell has been established. The models of selection of 185nm UV source and calculation in engineering design have been solved. The theoretical calculation agrees with experiments, which proves the model to be eorrect. The TOC concentrations in high purity water were decreased from 4200μg/L to 0.3μg/L, which is the lowest concentration of TOC.

Key words: ULSI; total organie carbon; 185nm UV; photochemistry

1. 引　　言

高纯水的质量是影响超大规模集成电路(ULSI)成品率的重要因素[1],水中总有机碳(TOC)含量高,导致器件漏电流上升,TOC 中碳残留物会引起硼、磷、砷等杂质扩散或离子注入时的内部结深变化.TOC 的残留会影响光刻胶的覆盖,显影时导致针孔,造成缺陷.含碳的有机物污染能在硅片表面分解,在硅片上呈蓝灰色的雾状物,这些有机污染可使

原载于:电子学报,2003,31(11):1601-1604.

硅片增加局部氧化速度,能生长几十 Å 的无定型氧化硅,使氧化层不均匀.对于薄栅氧化(10nm),更要严格控制高纯水的 TOC.当高纯水中 TOC 高达 800μg/L 时,则在栅氧化过程中会造成 690 个/(cm²)的严重缺陷[2].碳化物残留在硅片上,造成新的颗粒性的污染,破坏了器件的完整性.

1986 年已提出将 1M DRAM 用高纯水的 TOC 降至<20ppb[1].而制作 4M DRAM 用高纯水的 TOC 降至 5ppb[3],16Mbit 时 TOC 要求<2μg/L,若为 256Mbit 位电路则 TOC 要求<0.5μg/L[4].目前大规模集成电路已达 1G(1×10⁹)位,光刻线条宽为 0.13μm,对水质的要求越来越高.

有关水中 TOC 的去除机理工作不多,文献[5]提到以乙醇为例经过下列反应成为 CO_2

$$CH_3CH_2OH \longrightarrow CH_3\underset{\|}{C}H \longrightarrow CH_3\underset{\|}{C}OH \longrightarrow CO_2$$
$$\qquad\qquad\qquad\quad O \qquad\qquad O$$

至于其中的能量关系则未考虑.

本文从能量的角度分析了 185nm 紫外光去除水中 TOC 的机理,提出了一个能量传递光化学模型,计算了去除水中 TOC 所需紫外光的能量,并与实验对比,理论计算与实验符合得很好.

2. 185 纳米紫外线降低高纯水中总有机碳(TOC)的能量传递光化学模型

2.1 高纯水中常用 254nmUV 和 185nmUV 的比较

185nm 紫外线是一种波长较短,能量较高的紫外线,其能量相当于 6.7eV,而一般用于高纯水中的 254nm 紫外,其能量相当于 4.88eV.对于这两种紫外去除有机物,效果有所不同.

表 1 某些有机物化学键的键能及相应的波长

化学键	键能			化学键	键能		
	kcal/mol	eV	波长 nm		kcal/mol	eV	波长 nm
C—C	83	3.6	344	C=O	174	7.6	163
C=C	147	6.4	194	C—N	73	3.2	387
C—C	194	8.4	148	C=N	197	6.4	194
C—F	117	5.1	243	C=S	114	4.9	253
C—CL	78	3.4	364	N=O	142	6.2	200
CH	99	4.3	288	O—H	111	4.8	258
C—O	86	3.7	335	Si—O	111	4.8	258

表 1 列出某些有机物化学键的键能及相应的波长[6].

根据表 1 所列各种化学键,若用 185nm 紫外,除 C—C,C=O 键外,其余化学键的键能均小于 6.7eV,若用 254nm 紫外,其键能为 4.88eV,那么 C=C,C—C,C—F,C=O,C=N,C=S,N—O 键的键能均大于 4.88eV,都不能被破坏,于是仍然存在于水中.185nm

紫外的能量为6.7eV,可以将上表中绝大多数的化学键都打断,最终形成CO_2从水中分离出来,从而降低TOC.这就说明与254nm波长相比,185nm紫外更能有效地破坏有机物,降低水中的TOC.

2.2 185nm紫外光降低水中TOC的能量传递光化学模型

2.2.1 直接吸收

此模型用氧化理论解释185nm紫外光降低水中的TOC,认为水中有机物直接吸收185nmUV能量[5],将其化学键断开.这对纯的有机物或浓度很大的溶液是可能的.但是自反渗透进入185nmUV照射器的高纯水中TOC浓度往往只有0.02~0.05mg/L.TOC杂质吸收的光通量仅为入射光通量的$2.5×10^{-8}$(假设TOC杂质的俘获光子截面与水分子一样).用紫外光照射时,水中TOC与光子碰撞的几率极低,靠水中TOC杂质直接吸收185nmUV光子能量再分解并形成CO_2逸出是极困难的.因此在极低TOC浓度条件下,直接吸收模型解释TOC的降低是不适宜的.

2.2.2 依靠水中溶解氧的光化学模型

在用真空紫外光(波长小于200nm)降解水中有机物含量较多时用这模型来解释[7],即水分子吸收光子后成为:$H_2O+h\upsilon \rightarrow H^* +OH^*$,生成的$OH^*$基将有机物RH分解$OH^* +RH \longrightarrow H_2O+R^*$,$R^*$与溶解氧结合生成$ROO^*$,$R^* +O_2 \rightarrow ROO^*$.$ROO^*$再进一步与溶解氧反应,经过一系列反应最后形成$CO_2$与$H_2O$.

这一模型在水中有足够溶解氧时是适用的,但在大规模集成电路用高纯水的制备过程中,进入紫外光照射室水中的溶解氧已基本去除,剩下溶解氧仅约0.1mg/L量级.而185nm紫外光照射水产生的H^*会消耗这剩下的溶解氧$2H^* +1/2O_2 \rightarrow H_2O$,所以该模型不适用大规模集成电路用高纯水.

2.2.3 能量传递光化学模型

水受紫外光照射后吸收能量而离解为OH^-和H^+,OH^-再吸收光子能量而激化成为高能量的OH^{-*},四个高能量的OH^{-*}将能量传递给TOC,使碳的四个价键断开,生成的C^*进一步与OH^-反应生成CO_2.在这模型中,光子的能量是经过高能的OH^{-*}传递给TOC的.所以称为能量传递光化学模型.

水可以吸收紫外光的能量,物质吸收能量的特征参数是吸收系数α,且表达式为

$$\alpha = -(1/x)\ln(I/I_0) \tag{1}$$

其中:x为水层厚,I和I_0为出射和入射光的光强用185nm紫外照射水时,H_2O吸收光子后分解生成OH^-和H^+:

$$H_2O+h\upsilon \rightarrow OH^- +H^+ \tag{2}$$

考虑TOC从水中彻底去除,必需形成CO_2,所以将式(2)写为

$$4H_2O+4h\upsilon \longrightarrow 4OH^- +4H^+ \tag{3}$$

每个OH^-再进一步吸收一个185mm紫外光子的能量,形成激活的OH^{-*}

$$4OH^- +4h\upsilon \longrightarrow 4OH^{-*} \tag{4}$$

激活态的羟基OH^{-*}和TOC杂质反应,将能量传递给TOC分子,使碳的四个化学价

键全部破坏.首先考虑 C 原子以单价与四个基团或原子键合的情况,并以 $R\!-\!\underset{\underset{R}{|}}{\overset{\overset{R}{|}}{C}}\!-\!R$ 代表

一个 TOC 单元,其中四个 R 可以不相同,为了简明,仍用同一 R 代表.TOC 单元与激活态的羟基 OH^{-*} 发生下列反应:

$$R\!-\!\underset{\underset{R}{|}}{\overset{\overset{R}{|}}{C}}\!-\!R \;+\; 4OH^{-*} \longrightarrow 4R^* + C^* + 4OH^- \tag{5}$$

反应产物是游离的 C^* 和 R^*.其中 C^* 再与 OH^- 反应生成 CO_2 和 H_2O,即

$$C^* + 4OH^- \longrightarrow CO_2 + 2H_2O + 4e \tag{6}$$

$$4e + 4H^+ \longrightarrow 2H_2 \tag{7}$$

将式(3)+(4)+(5)+(6)+(7)得到总反应式

$$2H_2O + \underset{\underset{R}{|}}{\overset{\overset{R}{|}}{R\!-\!C\!-\!R}} + 8h\upsilon \longrightarrow 4R^* + CO_2 + 2H_2 \tag{8}$$

式(8)表示降解一个 TOC 单元要消耗 $8h\upsilon$ 的能量,第 3 节中将表明:本模型采用 OH^{-*} 为能量传递物,这样计算结果与实际相符.如果采用 $OH*$ 为能量传递物,则降解一个 TOC 单元只需要 $4h\upsilon$.计算结果与实验相差大,所以用式(2)~(8).

以 CH_3OH 为例,CH_3OH 只含有一个 TOC 单元,吸收 8 个 185mm 的光子后,生成 CO_2、H_2O 和 H_2,其反应为:

$$CH_3OH + 2H_2O + 8h\upsilon \longrightarrow 3H^* + OH^* + CO_2 + 2H_2 \tag{9}$$

反应生成的 H^* 和 OH^* 结合:

$$3H^* + OH^* \longrightarrow H_2 + H_2O \tag{10}$$

CO_2 逸出水面从而水中 TOC 得以降低.也可以用膜脱气法将 CO_2 去除从而有效降低 TOC.

有机物有可能含有双键,例如 $C\!=\!C$ 双键和 $C\!=\!N$ 双键,能量均为 6.4eV,二者皆可被 185mmUV 的能量破坏.这时只要有三个激活态的羟基 OH^{-*} 即可破坏一个

$R'\!=\!\underset{\underset{R}{|}}{\overset{\overset{R}{|}}{C}}\!-\!R$ TOC 分子,其代表反应为

$$R'\!=\!\underset{\underset{R}{|}}{\overset{\overset{R}{|}}{C}}\!-\!R + 3OH^{-*} \longrightarrow R^* + 2R^* + 3OH^- + C^* \tag{11}$$

但要将 C^* 转化为 CO_2,仍然需要四个羟基 OH^-.这样有下列几个反应:

$$4H_2O + 4h\upsilon \longrightarrow 4OH^- + 4H^+ \tag{12}$$

$$3OH^- + 3h\upsilon \longrightarrow 3OH^{-*} \tag{13}$$

$$C^* + 4OH^- \longrightarrow CO_2 + 2H_2O + 4e \tag{14}$$

$$4e + 4H^+ \longrightarrow 2H_2 \tag{15}$$

将式(3)+(13)+(11)+(14)+(15)得到总反应式

$$2H_2O + R'\!\!=\!\!\overset{\overset{\textstyle R}{\textstyle |}}{C}\!\!-\!\!R + 7h\nu \longrightarrow R'^* + R^* + CO_2 + 2H_2 \tag{16}$$

式(16)表示,含有一个双键的 TOC 单元需要七个 185nm 波长的光子照射,生成 CO_2 和 H_2O.

对于含有两个双键的 TOC 分子则可以得到下式:

$$2H_2O + R'\!\!=\!\!\!=\!\!C\!\!=\!\!\!=\!\!R \longrightarrow R'^* + R^* + CO_2 + 2H_2O + 2H_2 \tag{17}$$

式(17)表示,含有二个双键的 TOC 单元需要六个光子才能从水中消除.

有的有机物双键能量很高,例如 $C\!\!=\!\!O$ 键能为 7.6eV,则不能被 185mm 紫外破坏.

3. 模型验证——消除水中 TOC 所需 185nmUV 灯的功率的计算

根据式(8),(16)和(17),要消除水中 TOC 分子所需光子数与分子中所含双键数有关.如果分子中含双键数为 0,1,2,则所需光子数为 n 且 $n = 8, 7, 6$.

设水中 TOC 的分子分数为 A:

1 升水中含 N 个水分子,则水中 TOC 浓度为 AN/l;

设待处理水流量为 $F1/s$,则待处理的 TOC 流量为 AFN/s:

设每个光子的能量为 E eV(对 185nm 紫外光 $E = 6.7$ eV);

每处理一个 TOC 颗粒使之变为 CO_2 所需光子数量为 n($n = 8, 7$ 或 6),则每秒所需光子能量为 $nAEFN$ eV/s;

以瓦为单位,则需光功率为 $nAEFN \times (1.6 \times 10^{-19})$ W;

水吸收光能的百分数为 $1 - e^{-\alpha x}$;

如果不考虑光的反射折回,所需光功率为 $nAEFN \times (1.6 \times 10^{-19})/(1 - e^{-\alpha x})$ W;

设紫外灯发射 6.7eV 光子能量的效率为 n,则所需光功率 W:

$$W = nAEFN \times (1.6 \times 10^{-19})/(1 - e^{-\alpha x})\eta \text{ W} \tag{18}$$

实例

取 $n = 8$,

经过 RO 后水中 TOC 含量为 0.1ppm, $\Big\}$ $A = 10^{-7}$

即起始 TOC 分子分数

185nmUV 的能量为 $E = 6.7$ eV

设水流量为 1GPM = 0.22m^3/h 即 $F = 0.0611$ L/s

1 升水含 H_2O 分子数为 $N = 3.36 \times 10^{25}$ 个/L

纯水的吸收吸数 α 等于 $\alpha = 0.05$ cm^{-1}

水箱半径为 6.5cm $x = 6.5$ cm

紫外灯发射 6.7eV 的效率为 $\eta = 0.33$

代入式(18)得到 $w = 16.5$ Watt

即选用一根 16.5W 的 185nm 紫外灯即可处理 0.22m^3/h 的水中的 TOC.在上述计算中,我们未考虑光的反射,也未考虑紫外灯管的老化,前者可以提高紫外灯的吸收量,后者使紫外灯的输出下降.例如使用 4000 小时后,光强下降至 ~66%,这样又抵消了反射罩的好处,二者相互抵消.总之,我们计算值 16.5W 与实际值 17W 十分接近,证实了本模型的正确性.

4. 实际应用效果

4.1 用 185nm 紫外照射高纯水

用一根紫外灯管,通过大量实验,使兆位电路用水 TOC 下降到 <1μg/L,并在我国成功地用于 ULSI 生产、直径为 200mm 硅片生产和硬盘磁头生产中,效果很好.最近我们在 10T/h 的 ULSI 高纯水系统中,设计将 185nm 紫外放置在双级反渗透及电脱盐器后,使 TOC 浓度由 4200μg/L 下降到 0.7μg/L.表 2 列出在 185nn 紫外进、出口水中 TOC 的变化.实验条件:紫外灯能量为 17W,水流量为 0.2m³/h.

表 2　185nm 紫外进、出口水中 TOC 的变化(单位 μg/L)

测试时间	14:00	14:30	15:00	15:30	16:00	16:30
UV185nm 进口	8.1	8.2	8.1			
UV 185nm 出口				0.7	0.8	0.7

4.2 用 185nmUV 和膜接触器联用技术降低 TOC

由于 185nmUV 将有机物分解产生 CO_2,膜接触器除去可挥发的有机物及 CO_2,使原来经双级 RO、EDI、185nmUV 后的水中 TOC 由 0.7μg/L 再降至 0.3μg/L.又由于脱除了 CO_2,使精混延长了使用周期.水中 TOC 一直稳定在低水平,见图 1.

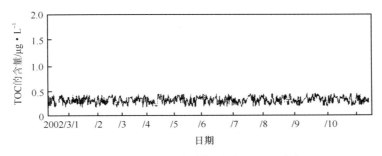

图 1　185nmUV 和膜接触器联用 TOC 浓度

4.3 高纯水制水工艺中各级产水的总有机碳浓度及电阻率

表 3　各级产水中总有机碳的浓度及电阻率

	总有机碳(μg/L)	电阻率(MΩ·cm)25℃
进水	600	0.500
RO 产水	134-170	0.5
EDI 产水	9.9-11.2	17.6
185nm 紫外后产水	0.7-<1	17.3
再经膜接触器脱 CO_2 后	0.7	17.5
双级 RO+EDI+185nnUV+膜接触器+混床	0.3	18.1

由表 3 明显看出在同样前处理情况下,185nm 紫外脱总有机碳效果最好.

实验证明 0.2m³/h 的高纯水中用一根 17W 的紫外灯管,能将高纯水中的 TOC 降至 0.3μg/L.

5. 结　　论

本文提出了用 185nm 紫外光去除水中微量 TOC 的能量传递光化学模型.185nm 紫外光首先被水分子吸收并分解为 OH^- 和 H^+,OH^- 进一步吸收光子能量成为激活态的 OH^{-*},后者能量传递给 TOC,碳的价键断裂,经一系列反应后,TOC 的碳以 CO_2 的形式逸出.理论计算得出的紫外灯功率与实验结果十分一致,说明模型的正确性.用 185nm 紫外灯照射并结合膜接触器除去 CO_2,使高纯水中 TOC 浓度降至 0.3μg/L,是目前高纯水中 TOC 浓度的最好结果,同时能延长混柱使用寿命 3~5 倍.我们还用在 10T/h 和 180T/h 高纯水设计中,效果都很好.

参考文献

[1] Ron Iscoff.The challenge for ultra-pure water[J].Semiconductor International,1986,(2):74-82.

[2] 闻瑞梅,陈胜利.控制超大规模集成电路用水中的溶解氧和总有机碳浓度的研究[J].电子学报,2001,29(8):1009—1012.

[3] 闻瑞梅,王在忠.高纯水的制备及检测技术[M].北京:科学出版社,1998.246-247.

[4] Y Motomura.Kufita water Industries Ltd.Ultrapure water quality target values for semiconductor manufacturing in Japan[J].Membrane Journal(Korea),1996,6(3):141—156.

[5] C C Anderson.A comparison of TOC mearnrements in high-purity water using commercially available equipment[J].Miero-contamination,1986,(4):39—45.

[6] W L Jolly.Modem Inorganic Chemistry[M].McGraw Hill New York,1984.Cpt.3.60—61.

[7] G Heit,AM Braun.VUV-Photolysis of aqueous systems,Spatial differentiation between volumes of primary and secondary reactions[J].Water Sci Teda,1997,35(4):25—30.

作者简介
　　闻瑞梅,女,1933 年 2 月生于湖北武汉,上海同济大学教授,博士生导师,1955 年毕业于武汉大学化学系,长期在第一线从事水化学基础、水处理及表征技术、环保治理及检测的研究,作为第一完成人的科研项目,先后获国家级、中科院、上海市和北京市各种科技奖十四次,专著 2 部、专利 17 项、已发表第一作者的中英文论文及国内外学术会议论文 120 多篇.

附　录

附录一

梁骏吾活动年表

1933 年 9 月	出生于湖北省武汉市
1939 年	进入汉口市立第七小学读书
1945 年	在武汉市立第一中学读书
1951 年 9 月	武汉大学化学系
1955 年 9 月	武汉大学毕业
1955 年	被中国科学院选派为留学生,赴苏联科学院冶金研究所,攻读半导体材料专业研究生
1960 年	获苏联科学院副博士学位
1960 年 10 月	从苏联回国,进入中国科学院半导体研究所工作
1960—1964 年	从事国家 12 年发展规划制定的"高纯区熔硅单晶研制"的任务,研制的"区熔硅单晶"纯度达到国际最好水平
1964 年	获国家科学技术委员会科技成果二等奖和新产品二等奖
1965—1969 年	研究了"硅外延及介质隔离硅片",为"156 工程"(计算机用集成电路)所需的集成电路提供了硅材料。研制成功了"砷化镓液相外延片",为我国第一支室温相干激光器的成功研制作出了贡献
1978—1982 年	研究大规模集成电路所用硅材料,生长了无位错、无漩涡、低微缺陷、低碳、可控氧量的优质硅单晶材料,为"4K 位、16K 位 MOS 动态随机存储器"所需材料作出了贡献
1979 年	"N 沟 MOS 4096 位动态随机存储器提高管芯成品率的研究"获中国科学院重大科技成果一等奖
1980 年	"16K 位 MOS 动态随机存贮器"获中国科学院重大科技成果一等奖
1980 年	"直拉硅单晶质量的研究"获中国科学院重大科技成果三等奖
1981 年	"硅中碳固溶度及单晶质点的研究"获中国科学院重大科技成果三等奖
1981 年	"直拉硅单晶碳沾污的研究"获中国科学院重大科技成果三等奖
1983 年	"掺氮硅单晶的制备"获中国科学院重大科技成果三等奖
1983 年	"硅中碳的研究"获中国科学院重大科技成果二等奖
1984 年	"硅单晶中微缺陷的研究"获中国科学院科技成果三等奖
1985 年	"硅中微缺陷的研究"项目得到中国科学院表彰
1988 年	"掺氮中子嬗变硅单晶"获中国科学院科技进步一等奖
20 世纪 90 年代	因"微机控制光加热外延炉的研制和硅外延技术的研究"以及从事"有机金属化合物气相外延生长 GaAs/AlGaAs 量子阱超晶格材料"

	的研制,为提高我国半导体量子阱激光器的质量和成品率作出了贡献,两次获得了中国科学院科技进步奖二等奖
20 世纪 90 年代	还从事了电子工业废气废水的治理工作
1990 年	获国家级有突出贡献中青年专家称号
1994 年	"MOCVD GaAlAs/GaAs 超晶格、量子阱材料的研制及应用"获得中国科学院科技进步二等奖
1996 年	研究的"环境中砷的治理及检测新方法、新设备"获得国家科技进步三等奖
1996 年	"减压薄层硅外延片的研制"获中国科学院科技进步三等奖
1996 年	"环境中砷的治理及检测新方法、新设备"获的国家级科技进步三等奖
1997 年	当选为中国工程院院士
2000 年	被聘为同济大学兼职教授,并带研究生
2001 年	研究了"电子工业废气、废水的综合治理及痕量磷的检测新方法",并获得上海科技进步二等奖(发明奖项)
2002 年	在深圳,作了题为"GaN 基材料和器件的发展"报告
2004 年	主要研究重点为"日盲型铝镓氮紫外探测器材料"以及"太阳电池用材料",特别是多晶硅的研究和生产
2004 年 4 月	"GaN HVPE 生长炉"的图纸已经交河北工业大学并委托沈阳仪器厂加工
2004 年	参加"军用先进材料战略研究",分工"信息材料"
2004 年 6 月	在沈阳"集成电路设备制造业国际论坛"上,作了题为"我国 IC 装备业的发展及东北老工业基地面临的机遇和对策"的报告
2004 年 9 月	在成都"中国电子材料行业半导体材料分会 2004 年年会"上,作了题为"硅基及化合物半导体材料的发展"的报告。
2004 年 12 月	在广州"第二届广东省科协学术活动周"上,作了题为"电子材料的进展"的报告
2005 年	"水过滤器的自动反洗新方法及去除水中气相杂质和有机物方法"获得上海市科技进步发明三等奖
2005 年 3 月	向中央提出了《关于再建设一至二个大型半导体级多晶硅工厂的建议》
2005 年	"多并联、大通量过滤器的自动反洗方法"获得上海市发明专利奖
2005 年 9 月	在乌鲁木齐"中国电子材料行业半导体材料分会 2005 年年会"上,作了题为"我国半导体材料创新发展之路"的报告
2005 年 10 月	在"常州市太阳能产业发展论坛"上,作了题为"中国太阳能电池发展的机遇与基地的建立"的报告
2005 年 11 月	在宁波 International Forum on Advanced Materials and Industrialization, Ningbo, China 会上,作了题为"全球多晶硅短缺引起的太阳能产业减速及应采取的对策"的学术报告。

2005 年 12 月	在海南博鳌"中国工程院会议"上,作了题为"中国半导体材料的创新发展之路"的学术报告
2006 年 4 月	在北京 273 次"香山会议"上,作了题为"中国太阳能电池材料发展战略"的学术报告
2006 年 4 月	在武汉大学,作了题为"光伏材料与器件——留住今日灿烂的阳光"的学术报告
2006 年 9 月	在昆明理工大学,作了题为"光伏电池用晶体硅材料"的学术报告
2006 年 11 月	在东莞"2006 广东平面显示产业投资论坛"上,作了题为"中国平面显示产业发展方向的思考"的学术报告
2007 年 10 月	在深圳"院士论坛"上,作了题为"将太阳能转为电能的途径和任务"的学术报告
2007 年 12 月	在厦门主持 Second International Workshop on Science and Technology of crystalline Silicon Solar Cells 会议
2008 年 6 月	在上海"第四届中国太阳能级硅及光伏发电研讨会"上,作了题为"世界能源危机中的光伏产业"学术报告
2008 年 11 月	在海口"中国电子材料行业半导体材料分会 2008 年年会"上,作了题为"太阳电池材料、结构与电池的转换效率"的学术报告
2009 年 3 月	在呼和浩特中环光伏公司,作了题为"晶硅太阳能电池材料"学术报告
2009 年 3 月	在北京"中国工程院第 83 场工程科技论坛",共主席
2009 年 5 月	在浙江"院士专家衢州行",作了题为"新能源和光伏产业的现状和发展前景"的学术报告
2010 年 7 月	在秦皇岛"河北省院士联谊会"上,作了题为"扩大光伏装机量和提高创新能力是河北建成世界一流光伏产业的关键"学术报告
2010 年 8 月	在呼和浩特中环光伏材料公司,作了题为"晶硅太阳电池材料和器件进展"的学术报告
2010 年 9 月	在贵阳"中国电子材料行业半导体材料分会 2010 年年会"上,作了题为"薄膜光伏电池用半导体材料"的学术报告
2010 年 11 月	在南宁"第十二届全国固体薄膜会议"上,作了题为 SOME ASPECTS OF MATERIALS FOR THIN-FILM SOLAR CELLS 的学术报告
2011 年 3 月	在西安,作了题为 Is thin-film solar cell technology promising? 的学术报告
2011 年	受聘哈尔滨工业大学合约教授,在此之前还兼任武汉大学、华中科技大学、河北工业大学和昆明理工大学教授
2011 年 5 月	在中国科学院苏州纳米研究所,作了题为"太阳电池材料和器件如何应对竞争"的学术报告
2011 年 6 月	在哈尔滨工业大学,作了题为 Solar Cells: Materials and Devices 的学术报告
2011 年 8 月	在宁波"中国电子材料行业半导体材料分会 2011 年年会"上,作了题

	为"太阳电池材料与器件"的学术报告
2011 年 9 月	在哈尔滨工业大学,作了题为"非传统工艺的半导体陶瓷"的学术报告
2011 年 12 月	在天津中环电子信息集团,作了题为"区熔硅单晶的生长条件、杂质及完整性"的学术报告
2011 年	兼任江苏中能硅业科技公司、江西赛维 LDK 公司和北京恩菲工程技术公司院士工作站进站院士
2012 年 4 月	在西安电子科技大学,作了题为"半导体 LED 由显示向照明领域的扩展"的学术报告
2012 年 5 月	在北京航空航天大学"新能源与材料高峰论坛",作了题为"低潮声中话光伏"的学术报告
2012 年 8 月	在烟台"第十三届全国固体薄膜会议"上,作了题为"白光 LED 何时在照明市场取得实质性扩展?"的大会学术报告
2012 年 9 月	在大连"中国电子材料行业 2012 年年会"上,作了题为"白光 LED 衬底材料的进展"的学术报告
2012 年 10 月	在武汉华中科技大学,作了题为"硅光伏电池的发展——辉煌,困境,光明"的学术报告

附录二

梁骏吾获奖情况

1. 1964 年"高纯区熔硅单晶"获国家科学技术委员会科技成果二等奖,负责并实施,排名第二

2. 1964 年"区熔硅单晶炉"获国家科学技术委员会新产品二等奖,负责并实施,排名第二

3. 1979 年"N 沟 MOS4096 位动态随机存贮器提高管芯成品率的研究"获中国科学院重大科技成果一等奖,负责并实施,材料方面排名第一

4. 1980 年"16K 位 MOS 动态随机存贮器"获中国科学院重大科技成果一等奖,负责并实施,材料方面排名第一

5. 1980 年"直拉硅单晶质量的研究"获中国科学院重大科技成果三等奖,排名第一

6. 1981 年"硅中碳固溶度及单晶质点的研究"获中国科学院重大科技成果三等奖,排名第一

7. 1981 年"直拉硅单晶碳沾污的研究"获中国科学院重大科技成果三等奖,排名第一

8. 1983 年"掺氮硅单晶的制备"获中国科学院重大科技成果三等奖,排名第一

9. 1983 年"硅中碳的研究"获中国科学院重大科技成果二等奖,排名第一

10. 1984 年"P 型(号 00)硅单晶中微缺陷的研究"获中国科学院科技成果三等奖,排名第一

11. 1984 年"区熔硅单晶中微缺陷的研究"获中国科学院科技成果三等奖,排名第一

12. 1985 年"硅中微缺陷的研究"中国科学院表彰项目,排名第二

13. 1988 年"掺氮中子嬗变硅单晶"获中国科学院科技进步一等奖,排名第一

14. 1992 年"微机控制光加热外延炉研制和硅外延技术研究"获中国科学院科技进步二等奖,排名第一

15. 1994 年"MOCVD GaAlAs/GaAs 超晶格、量子阱材料的研制及应用"获中国科学院科技进步二等奖,排名第二

16. 1994 年"环境中砷的治理及检测新方法、新设备"获中国科学院科技进步二等奖,排名第二

17. 1996 年"减压薄层硅外延片的研制"获中国科学院科技进步三等奖,排名第一

18. 1996 年"环境中砷的治理及检测新方法、新设备"获国家级科技进步三等奖。证书号:01-3-019-02。排名第二

19. 2001 年"电子工业废气、废水的综合治理及痕量磷的检测新方法"获上海市科技进步二等奖。证书号:012040。排名第二

20. "水过滤器的自动反洗新方法及去除水中气相杂质和有机物方法"2005 年获上海市科技进步三等奖。奖励证书号:2005170018-3-02。排名第二

21. "多并联、大通量过滤器的自动反洗方法"获 2005 年上海市发明专利奖。奖励证书

号:05131-2。排名第二。

先后获国家及省部级奖 21 次,其中二等奖以上有:国家科学技术委员会科技成果二等奖和新产品二等奖各 1 次,国家科技进步三等奖 1 次、中国科学院重大成果和科技进步一等奖 3 次、中国科学院二等奖 4 次,上海市二等奖 1 次

附录三

所获得的专利目录

1. 梁骏吾，邓礼生,杨辉.《一种半导体气相外延反应管》
   实用新型专利号:90203696.3,证书号：50241
2. 闻瑞梅，梁骏吾等.《处理含砷及其化合物的废气的方法》
   发明专利号:ZL 96104510.8,证书号:55334
3. 闻瑞梅，邓礼生,刘任重.梁骏吾.《粉尘清除器》
   实用新型专利号:ZL 96222517.7,证书号:280691
4. 闻瑞梅,戴自忠,梁骏吾等.《多晶硅氢还原炉的可变截面积进气口装置》
   发明专利号:ZL 02137784.7,证书号：270324
5. 闻瑞梅，戴自忠,梁骏吾等.《用三氯氢硅和四氯化硅混合源生产多晶硅的方法》
   发明专利号:ZL 02137592.5,证书号:231766
6. 闻瑞梅，戴自忠,梁骏吾等.《一种去除水或水溶液中气相杂质的方法》
   发明专利号:ZL 02136913.5,证书号：172897
7. 闻瑞梅,梁骏吾等.《多并联、大通量过滤器的自动反洗方法》
   发明专利号:ZL 02111128.6,证书号184351
   2005 年获上海市发明专利三等奖,证书号:051312-2
8. 闻瑞梅，邓守权,梁骏吾等.《一种去除高纯水中痕量氨的方法》
   发明专利号:ZL 200410053426.X,证书号:312658
9. 闻瑞梅,梁骏吾等.《水过滤器反洗自动切换系统》
   发明专利号:ZL 01113321.X,证书号:237166
10. 胡正飞,梁骏吾,吴坚等．一种提高氮化镓基材料外延层质量的衬底处理方法
    发明专利号:ZL200410066479.5,证书号:374192
11. 冯淦,杨辉,梁骏吾．一种氮化镓及其化合物半导体的横向外延生长方法
    发明专利号 ZL02145890,证书号:216133
12. 闻瑞梅,刘任重,邓礼生,梁骏吾．处理含砷及其化合物的废气的方法
    发明专利号:ZL96104510.8,证书号:55334
13. 梁骏吾,邓礼生,杨辉,郑红军．一种半导体气相外延反应管
    发明专利号:ZL90203896.3,证书号:50241

附录四

学术报告目录

1. 世界太阳能电池材料的形势与中国的对策（2003 年 6 月）
2. 关于再建设一至二个大型半导体级多晶硅工厂的建议
   （院士给中央的建议 2005 年 3 月）
3. 全球多晶硅短缺引起的太阳能产业减速及应采取的对策
   （2005 年 10 月宁波）
4. 中国太阳能电池材料发展战略（2006 年 4 月北京香山会议）
5. 留住今日灿烂的阳光——光伏电池用晶体硅材料
   （2006 年 9 月 17 日在全国半导体材料行业会上报告）
6. Development of Polysilicon Industry in ChinaOPPTUNITIES & CHALLENGES（2007 年 10 月 "the 2nd International Workshop on Science and Technology of Crystalline Silicon Solar Cells".）
7. 将太阳能转为电能的途径和任务（2007 年 10 月深圳）
8. 世界能源危机中的光伏产业（2008 年 6 月上海）
9. 太阳电池材料、结构与电池的转换效率（2008 年 11 月海南）
10. 晶硅太阳能电池材料（2009 年 3 月呼和浩特）
11. 金融危机下的太阳能产业（2009 年 3 月北京）
12. 新能源和光伏产业的现状和发展前景（2009 年 5 月衢州）
13. 扩大光伏装机量和提高创新能力是河北建成世界一流光伏产业的关键（2010 年 7 月秦皇岛）
14. 晶硅太阳电池材料和器件的进展（2010 年 8 月呼和浩特）
15. 半导体硅基材料新进展薄膜光伏电池用半导体材料（2010 年 9 月贵阳）
16. 太阳电池材料和器件如何应对竞争（ 2010 年苏州）
17. SOME ASPECTS OF MATERIALS FOR THIN-FILM SOLAR CELLS（2010 年 11 月南宁）
18. 薄膜光伏电池中的材料问题（2010 年 11 月南宁）
19. 薄膜光伏电池用半导体材料（2011 年 3 月西安）
20. 太阳电池材料和器件如何应对竞争（2011 年 5 月苏州）
21. 应对竞争的晶硅太阳电池材料（2011 年 8 月宁波）
22. 区熔硅单晶的生长条件、杂质及完整性（2011 年 12 月天津）
23. Solar Cells Materials and Devices（2011 年 6 月哈尔滨）
24. 非传统工艺的半导体陶瓷（2011 年 12 月哈尔滨）
25. IS THIN- FILM SOLAR CELL TECHNOLOGY PROMISING？（2011 年 6 月西安）
26. 急流险滩话光伏（2012 年 7 月北京）

27. 半导体 LED 由显示向照明领域的扩展(2012 年 4 月西安)

28. 低潮声中话光伏(2012 年 5 月北京)

29.白光 LED 何时在照明市场取得实质性扩展?（2012 年 7 月烟台）

30.白光 LED 衬底材料的进展（2012 年 9 月大连）

31.硅光伏电池的发展——辉煌,困境,光明(2012 年 10 月武汉)

附录五

领导批示： 内部刊物

工程院院士建议

第 6 期（总第 92 期）

中国工程院政策研究室编 2005 年 3 月 28 日

关于打破垄断、政府主导、多方融资建设多晶硅工厂的建议

梁骏吾 周 廉 阙端麟

半导体级多晶硅（以下简称多晶硅）是用于制造半导体硅集成电路和器件以及硅太阳能电池的重要基础材料，它对发展我国信息电子产业和太阳能电池产业极为重要。目前，硅集成电路和器件是世界年产值达万亿美元的信息产业的主干和核心。它是当代高技术的制高点，更是一个国家现代化水平的重要标志；太阳能是一种取之不尽的、十分重要的清洁能源，太阳能发电具有广阔的发展前景，而绝大部分太阳能电池是用硅材料制造的。目前，全世界多晶硅的四分之三用于硅集成电路和器件制造，其它用于太阳能电池的制造。

一、世界市场多晶硅紧缺，中国多晶硅供应严重困难

目前美国、日本、德国等世界信息电子产业大国都具有强大的多晶硅生产能力，其中美国 Hemlock 公司年生产能力为 7000 吨，日本 Tokuyama 公司年生产能力为 6000 吨。全球 2003 年多晶硅产量为 24,400 吨，市场为 23,162 吨，供需大体平衡，生产能力略有富余。在过去这种情况下，中国进口多晶硅并不困难。但是，由于近几年来硅集成电路和器件以及太阳能电池产业发展很快，国际上对多晶硅的需求上升，2004 年全球多晶硅的市场需求迅速上升 7.4%，达到 26,201 吨，而产能为 24,900 吨，需求超出供应能力，全球多晶硅出现了短缺。我国 2004 年生产的多晶硅产量只有 60 吨，仅能满足国内市场需求的 2.6%，其余全部依赖进口，但即使我们提高采购价也买不到足够的多晶硅！在可预见的未来，全球多晶硅供应紧张将不得缓解，中国进口多晶硅会变得更加困难。

中国多晶硅工业在上世纪五十年代末、六十年代初开始创业，与中国的半导体硅集成电路和器件同步发展，到七十年代多晶硅生产厂家已达到上百家。但由于技术落后、规模小、成本高、质量低，所以到八十年代纷纷停产。目前，能生产多晶硅的工厂只剩下峨眉半导体材料厂和洛阳单晶硅厂两家。国家计委 2000 年批准了峨眉半导体材料厂兴

建 1000 吨多晶硅生产线项目,得到国务院批准。按计划,该项目应在 2004 年底投产验收,然而由于地方主管部门(电力公司)领导的原因,项目进展缓慢,目前仅完成了厂房建设,厂区还看不到生产设备,离原定投产验收目标尚有很大距离。2004 年,全国多晶硅产量从 2003 年的 88.3 吨下降到 60 吨,而需求却上升了 27%,由 1790 吨增加到 2280 吨,缺额高达 2220 吨。(见下表):

我国多晶硅生产与需求

年份	2003	2004	2005
硅集成电路和器件产生需求(吨)	746	910	1092
太阳能电池产业需求(吨)	1044	1370	2691
多晶硅总需求(吨)	1790	2280	3783
多晶硅产量(吨)	88.3	60	120
多晶硅缺额(吨)	1701.7	2220	3363

2005 年,全国对多晶硅的需求将进一步提高到 3,800 吨左右,而最乐观的产量估计仅为 120 吨,多晶硅缺额将高达 3,633 吨,缺额只能依靠大量进口来填补。然而,随着全球多晶硅需求的扩大,全世界多晶硅供应求,美国、日本、德国将必然首先满足本国的需求。因此,中国进口多晶硅出现了问题:首先是进口多晶硅价格大幅度上涨;集成电路多晶硅已由前年的 37 美元/kg 上涨到目前 60 美元/kg,涨幅为 66.7%;太阳能级多晶硅则由 13 美元/kg 猛涨到 46 美元/kg,涨幅高达 250%!更有甚者,国外多晶硅企业已经开始对我国企业实行限购或者禁止采购!我国半导体硅单晶行业已经陷入等米下锅、受制于人的被动困境。

多晶硅生产能力严重不足已成为我国硅集成电路和器件以及太阳能电池产业持续发展的重大瓶颈,从长远发展来看,很可能成为制约我国未来信息电子产业发展的关键因素,并对国家经济安全和国家安全产生十分不利的影响。中国作为世界信息电子产业大国,应当拥有自己的强大的多晶硅产业。因此,我们应当从战略高度认识多晶硅在国家发展中的重要地位,加快发展我国自主独立的多晶硅产业,尽快再建设一至二个大型半导体级多晶硅工厂,扭转目前十分被动的局面,并使我国多晶硅年产量达到 4000~5000 吨,确保长期安全供应。

二、外国企业不愿向中国出口多晶硅生产技术,也不愿建合资企业

我国至今尚无年产量大于 1000 吨的大型半导体级多晶硅工厂,全国的多晶硅产量只相当一家国外大企业的百分之一。二十多年来,为了发展我国的多晶硅产业,我们多次向美国、日本、德国提出购买多晶硅生产线设备和技术,一律遭到拒绝,提出中外合资方案也不理睬,甚至提出参观其工厂的要求也被拒绝。俄罗斯、乌克兰愿意与我们合作,出卖技术。然而其技术水平较低,产品质量也未用于高档的超大规模集成电路芯片,不是理想的技术合作伙伴。

为什么出现这种现象?原因之一是多晶硅生产技术的特殊垄断性和保密性。第一,各国企业投入大量的人力和资金研究开发出自己的工艺技术和生产线,希望通过保密维持垄断,从而获取更大的超额利润;第二,多晶硅工厂表现出显著的规模经济特征,即规

模越大,经济效益越大,所以这一产业呈现明显的垄断性;第三,多晶硅生产线是一个特殊设计、专门加工形成的庞大的体系,没有光刻机、单晶炉之类的现成的通用商品设备。目前,一个年产 1000 吨的多晶硅厂投资为十多亿元,只有一条 8 英寸硅芯片工厂投资额的十分之一,然而硅芯片工厂生产线的全部设备和技术虽然价格高昂,却可以买来,而多晶硅工厂的生产设备和技术却买不到。

三、国家应组织国内科技力量,攻克半导体级多晶硅生产技术难关

从国外引进技术是必要的,今后也应该争取,但在目前世界七家主要多晶硅公司联合起来禁止多晶硅技术转移到中国的形势下,我们无法得到现成的设备和技术。为了充分保障我国信息电子产业发展和国家安全,彻底摆脱受制于人的困境,我们必须打破封锁,打破垄断,政府主导、多方融资走自力更生发展多晶硅技术和产业的道路,尽快建成我国具有世界先进水平和较大规模的多晶硅生产线。这是历史赋予我们的自主创新的重任。

据预测,今年国内多晶硅市场需求可达 3800 吨左右,2010 年将超过 5000 吨。如果包括已批准 1000 吨的多晶硅厂,再兴建一至二个大型多晶硅厂,每个厂具有年产超过 2000 吨多晶硅的生产能力,将使我国多晶硅年产量达到 5000 吨。这将不仅可以保障我国未来发展对多晶硅的需要,还可以打破发达国家在多晶硅这一高技术产品的国际市场上的垄断和对我国的封锁,并为迎接满足未来信息电子产业对多晶硅性能越来越高的要求提供坚实的技术保障。

为实现这一目标,保证工厂的先进装备和工艺技术水平,以及产品的高质量和低成本,国家有关部门应组织国内硅工业生产的科技力量,并吸收其它行业,如化工、材料、自动控制、设备制造等方面的力量,尽快对以下关键技术组织重点攻关:

①先进的三氯氢硅生产技术;
②多级精馏技术和设备;
③大型节能还原炉技术;
④生产过程废弃物的循环利用技术;
⑤贯穿生产线节能和清洁生产技术。

整个生产应实现闭环清洁生产。应达到降低电耗和硅、氢、氯等原料消耗,降低成本,使产品具有国际竞争能力,质量应符合目前和未来超大规模集成电路和太阳能电池的要求。

四、建   议

1. 在发改委领导下,组织国内各方面力量协作,对兴建大型多晶硅厂的关键技术行攻关。

2. 在国家发改委领导下,尽快启动再建一至二个多晶硅生产厂的工作。应当由政府主导、多方融资、面向全国招标投资建厂。洛阳单晶硅公司已有多晶硅生产的基础,已被国家发改委批准建设一条年产 300 吨多晶硅的生产线,可以在此基础上扩充为建设一条年产 2000 吨多晶硅生产线。在有廉价电力的地区(如宜昌市)建厂也可以考虑。

建议人：

    梁骏吾 中国工程院院士 半导体材料
          中国科学院半导体研究所

    周廉   中国工程院院士 超导及稀有金属材料
          西北有色金属研究院

    阙端麟 中国科学院院士 半导体材料
          浙江大学

报：中共中央、国务院有关领导，中共中央办公厅，国务院办公厅，全国人大，全国政协。
送：中共中央和国务院有关部委，各省、自治区、直辖市、计划单列市，中国科学院，中国社会科学院，国家自然科学基金委员会；工程院院士，工程院主席团顾问。

· 333 ·

后　记

　　金秋时节,迎来了中国工程院院士梁骏吾先生 80 华诞,中国科学院半导体研究所编辑出版《华年日拾——梁骏吾院士 80 华诞记怀》一书,简要梳理梁骏吾先生 53 年的科研历程,谨以此表达对梁骏吾先生的敬仰之情。

　　本书从各个方面、不同角度反映了梁骏吾先生半个多世纪以来在半导体科学技术领域里辛勤耕耘、不断开拓,所取得的一系列开创性成果的奋斗历程。本书的编写是一项复杂的工程,凝聚了许多人的共同心血。中国科学院半导体研究所所长、党委书记李树深院士,中国科学院苏州纳米技术与纳米仿生研究所所长杨辉,中国科学院半导体研究所副所长、党委副书记张春先等在百忙之中给予了大力支持,并提出了宝贵的意见和建议;梁骏吾先生与闻瑞梅教授也亲自审订了编写提纲和框架结构,并提供了大量图文资料;中国科学院半导体研究所光电研发中心、图书信息中心和离退休办公室等部门,以及苏州纳米技术与纳米仿生研究所相关人员都从不同方面提供了大量素材,为本书的出版做了大量工作。在此,向他们表示衷心的感谢。

　　书中的图片、论文、获奖情况、学术报告、专利目录均反映了梁骏吾先生几十年来的成果和贡献。每一幅历史图片,都讲述着梁骏吾先生的生活故事与人文情怀;每一篇学术论文,都凝结着梁骏吾先生的心血与汗水;每一次学术报告,都寄托着梁骏吾先生的希冀和嘱托,但是这些也仅仅是他众多成果中的一部分。

　　由于编辑时间仓促,资料的搜集还不够全面,书中也难免有疏漏及错误之处,敬请读者见谅。

中国科学院半导体研究所

2013 年 9 月